Hand Made in Britain

THE VISITORS GUIDE

*Craft Centres, Workshops and Galleries
in England, Scotland and Wales*

Hand Made in Britain

THE VISITORS GUIDE

*Craft Centres, Workshops and Galleries
in England, Scotland and Wales*

Victoria Pybus

Published by Vacation Work, 9 Park End Street, Oxford
www.vacationwork.co.uk

Hand Made in Britain
by Victoria Pybus

First edition 2002

Copyright © 2002

ISBN 1-85458-265-8

Cover and Design by Miller Craig & Cocking Limited

Maps by Andrea Pullen

Section illustrations by Ed Walwyn

Cover illustration by Heather Jansch, sculptor

Cover photograph by Adam Woolfitt

Printed by William Clowes Ltd., Beccles, Suffolk, England

Foreword

by Janet Barnes, Director of The Crafts Council

I am very pleased to be able to write a few words of support for *Hand Made in Britain*. The crafts are a very diverse and vibrant aspect of the creative industries and this listing of craft centres, workshops and galleries can only help in promoting the crafts sector to a greater number of people.

The Crafts Council has contact with many craftspeople through our various activities and services.

At our exhbition gallery in Islington, London, we organise five major exhibitions a year and a series of showcases that feature displays of new work, We have also collected contemporary craft over 30 years, building up what is now a collection of national importance. From the collection we lend objects to museums for display and for inclusion in exhibitions.

We help craftspeople directly through the Setting-Up Scheme which has launched over 800 successful businesses over the last three decades. We also promote craftspeople and their work through our visual database Photostore® and through *Crafts* magazine – the leading publication of the crafts sector.

We recognise that the Crafts Council is only part of the complex infrastructure that helps promote and support the many craftspeople working in the field. The crafts world is a very broad church ranging from the professional maker to the interested amateur practitioner, and the wide variety of organisations, societies and institutions reflect the richness of the crafts. Often however it is difficult to find the sources of craft work. *Hand Made in Britain* will help people to navigate around the often hidden centres of excellence where original work can be seen and purchased. It is an invaluable resource for anyone interested in finding and buying objects of quality and skill.

Janet Barnes
November 2001

Crafts Council
44a Pentonville Road
London N1 9BY

For details of the Crafts Council see the *London and the Home Counties* regional section

Preface

At some time we all yearn for something that is not mass-produced; something, different, original and lovingly made whether it be an earthenware casserole or an abstract sculpture, a willow basket or a classic rocking-horse.

If you know where to look there is as much skill and talent in the making of crafts as there has ever been. *Hand Made in Britain* is a guide arranged by region and type of craft to enable you to find a product or artefact whether for yourself, or as a gift. The book describes the particular skills and crafts of the makers and tells you how to visit them and buy their work. There are also sections for craft shops and craft centres; the latter are often perfect for family outings. There is also a special section showcasing some of the country's most interesting and innovative galleries. Additionally, the number and frequency of craft fairs is increasing all the time and these can also make an excellent day out.

This book has been long in the preparation, and it behoves the editor to offer her thanks to all those who have offered help and encouragement, including craft organisations and makers; and in particular I would like to thank, Mark Ellis-Jones and Andrew James for editorial assistance and The Craft Council for their interest and help in recruiting makers nationally.

Happy hunting!

Victoria Pybus
November 2001

PUBLISHER'S NOTE

This first edition of *Hand Made in Britain* was researched through one of the most difficult times ever encountered by many rural crafts and businesses. We would like to take the opportunity to thank the many hundreds of people who have filled in forms and answered telephone calls during this difficult time, and to express the hope that now the majority of the countryside is again open for tourism, this book will help to promote the rich diversity of our hand made heritage.

Hand Made in Britain will be revised and updated on a regular basis. Editor Victoria Pybus welcomes any comments on this first edition and will be pleased to hear from craft centres, shops, galleries and makers who wish to be considered for the next one. Contact her at Vacation Work Publications, 9 Park End Street Oxford OX1 1HJ; e-mail victoria@vacationwork.co.uk

Contents

Cornwall

and Scilly Isles

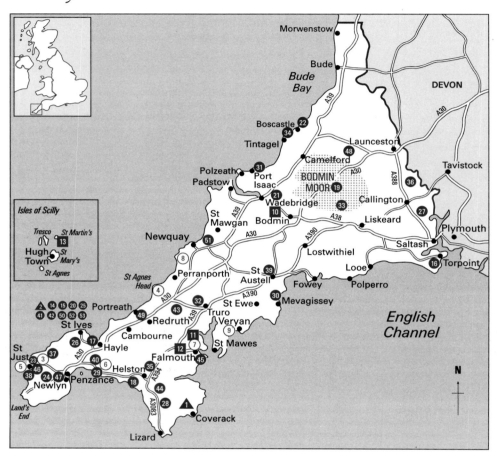

▲ Craft Centres   ■ Food and Drink

○ Shops and Galleries   ● Makers' Workshops

Bleak and beautiful Cornwall is redolent of Celtic mythology largely connected with the legend of King Arthur. A great deal of fascination is inspired by the Arthurian stories probably because of, rather than despite, the almost complete lack of historical evidence of his having existed. Like Devon, Cornwall had a tin-mining industry, but was also once infamous for its pirates and wreckers. The artistic proliferation which is so evident today, stems largely from the 1880s when artists as eminent as Rex Whistler took to painting there. Cornish towns famous for artists include Newlyn, St. Just and St. Ives. These days, St. Ives is probably the most overtly artistic town. The artists and sculptors who colonised it in the 1920s have been succeeded by a vast array of galleries and craft workshops.

Craft Centres

ROSKILLY'S BULLPEN GALLERY, Tregellast, Barton, St Keverne, Helston, Cornwall TR12 6NX

Tel: +44 (0)1326-280479
Fax: +44 (0)1326-280320
www.roskillys.co.uk
Est. several years
Parking available
Wheelchair access

The Roskilly family craft centre combines organic ice-cream and fudge etc. made on the premises, with Toby Roskilly's country ash, oak and elm furniture, plus textured glass by Bryn Roskilly. Some toys and pottery are also for sale. Commissions undertaken. Also on site is the Croust House Restaurant serving homemade food.

Directions: *Lizard road from Helston. Left at roundabout at the end of Culdrose; follow signs to St. Keverne. After 8 miles fork right to Coverack; follow signs to Roskillys.*
Opening hours: *Mon-Sun Apr-Oct. Weekends only in winter.*

SLOOP CRAFT CENTRE, Capel Court, St Ives, Cornwall TR26 IGS

Est. 1969
Tel: +44 (0)1736-796051
www.sloopcrafts.
moonfruit.com
Parking available
Wheelchair access
Credit cards (some makers)

The Centre comprises a small courtyard where twelve specialist craftspeople produce their work on the premises: silver and gold jewellery, woodcarving, artists, walking sticks, clocks, pottery, stained glass, silk painting and teddy bears. All the makers undertake commissions and welcome visitors wanting to view and talk about their work. Mail order available.

Directions: *50 yards from St Ives Harbour, behind the Sloop Inn and carpark.*
Opening hours: *Mon-Sun 10am-5pm summer; off season a little later.*

Craft Shops

CRAFTY CORNER, 2 Fore Street, St Just in Penwith, Penzance, Cornwall TR19 7LL

Est. 1992
Tel: +44 (0)1736-787784
Parking available
Wheelchair access
Credit cards

This shop is owned by Wendy Michelmore and sells traditional watercolour paintings and handspun and hand-felted hats. The hand-felted hats are made on the premises using fabrics including fine silks, and cashmere and other wools. Other items for sale include St Just pewter, silver, glass and pottery. Mail order available.

Directions: *close to centre of St Just on the Penzance Road.*

Opening hours: *10am-5pm. Closed Sunday.*

(3)

IMAGES OF CORNWALL & GAFFRON GALLERY, Peterville, St Agnes, Cornwall TR5 OQU

Est. 1986
Tel/fax: +44 (0)1872-553674
Parking available
Wheelchair access
(but difficult for gallery)
Credit cards

Images of Cornwall shop sells Celtic jewellery and gifts cast in local tin, copper and pewter, replicas of Cornwall's landmark stone crosses and model tin mines and framed prints representing the history and beauty of the area. Locally produced foods including biscuits, fudge and preserves. Reference books and maps. Gaffron Gallery (paintings) adjacent.

Directions: *in Peterville Square below the Saffron Gallery on the coast road.*

Opening hours: *Mon-Sat 9.30am-5.30pm.*

(4)

JUST CORNISH, 30 Fore Street, St Just, Near Penzance, Cornwall TR19 7LJ

Est. 1999 ,
Tel: +44 (0)1736-787877
Fax: +44 (0)1736-786742
www.justcornish.co.uk
Parking available
Wheelchair access
Credit cards

Milo Perrin and Holly Whitehead opened their shop to harvest the wealth of local creative talent by selling Cornish-made items including cards, candles, clocks, cupboards, cushions, boxes, baskets, pottery, clothes, foods, jewellery, healing and skincare products and books. Prices suit all pockets. They also hang prints and paintings. Mail order available.

Directions: *a short walk from St Just's Market Square down Fore Street.*

Opening hours: *10am-6pm, 7-day week in high season.*

(5)

P & T FRAMING GALLERY AND CRAFTS, Lukes Lane, St. Hilary, Penzance, Cornwall TR20 9DY

Est. 1997
Tel/fax: +44 (0)1736-762316
Parking available

Bespoke framing is done on the premises, and the craft shop and gallery sells locally made handicrafts including wrought ironwork, honey, candles, basketware, stained glass and sculpture. As bespoke framers we also have a gallery where you can purchase work by well-known artists. Cottage garden setting. Mail order available.

Directions: *A394 from Penzance. Left at roundabout (B3280) for one and a half miles. 1st right after sign for St. Hilary Churchtown (New Road).*

Opening hours: *Mon-Sat 10am-5pm.*

(6)

TALL SHIPS TRADING, 49 Church Street, Falmouth, Cornwall TR11 3DS

Est: 1995
Tel: +44 (0)1326-318888
www.Tallshipstrading.co.uk
Parking available
Wheelchair access
Credit cards

Tall Ships Trading is run by Cornishman John Spargo and has a distinctive marine and nautical theme, selling paintings, ceramics, painted furniture, model boats of all sizes (decorative, historical and for sailing on ponds) and ships in bottles all made by local crafts people. Gifts and prints also sold. Mail order available.

Directions: *centre of Falmouth on Main Street (Church Street) backing on to Church Street car park and the waterfront.*

Opening hours: *Summer every day 10am-6pm. Winter Mon-Sat 10am-5pm.*

(7)

Galleries

LORNA WILES, The Crantock Forge Gallery, Beach Road, Crantock, Cornwall TR8 5RE

Est. 1975, Gallery 1997
Tel: +44 (0)1637-830662
Fax: +44 (0)1209-820676
Parking available
Wheelchair access
Credit cards

Lorna Wiles has been producing unique printed and hand painted textiles for over twenty-five years. The gallery exhibits scarves, wall-hangings, ties, cushions, table linen and paintings. Crantock village is a picturesque location with thatched cottages, an ancient church, inspirational coastline and walks. Mail order available.

Directions: *on the right hand side of the road to the beach.*

Opening hours: *Sun-Fri 10.30am-4.30pm summer. Appointment necessary in winter.*

⑧

VERYAN GALLERIES, Veryan Green, Truro, Cornwall TR2 5QQ

Est. 1975
Tel/fax: +44 (0)1872-501469
Parking available
Credit cards

Veryan Galleries are situated in a delightful village on the beautiful Roseland Peninsula. The galleries are informal and relaxed and contain an ever-changing selection of original paintings, principally by Cornish artists. There is a selection of prints, photographs, ceramics, sculptures, pottery, silks, wood turning and cards. Mail order available.

Directions: *A3078 from Tregony to St Mawes. After 2 miles turn left to Veryan.*

Opening hours: *Tues-Sun 10am-6pm.*

⑨

Food & Drink

CAMEL VALLEY VINEYARD, Nanstallon, Bodmin, Cornwall PL30 5LG

Est. 1989
Tel/fax: +44 (0)1208-77959
www.camelvalley.com
Parking available.
Wheelchair assistance
Credit cards

Bob Lindo's vineyard produces multi award-winning red, white and rosé and sparkling wines from 8,000 vines growing on slopes above the river Camel in lovely Cornish countryside. Wines are for sale by the glass or bottle including Camel Valley Brut, Cornwall's first sparkling wine. Mail order available.

Directions: *signposted from the A389 Bodmin-Wadebridge Road.*

Opening hours: *Mon-Fri 2-5pm; vineyard tours at 2.30pm Easter to September.*

`10`

CORNISH CUISINE, The Smokehouse, Islington Wharf, Penryn, Cornwall TR10 8AT

Est. 1980
Tel: +44 (0)1326-376244
www.smokedsalmon-1td
Parking available
Wheelchair access

Award-winning smoker of speciality foods including salmon and other fish, shellfish, duck, chicken, pork, lamb, game, cheese etc. Gold medal for Great Taste - the 'oscar' of the food industry. All products are naturally smoked by hand in small 'kilns' using fruitwoods. Visitors welcome to buy at the smokehouse or via mail order.

Directions: *from Commercial Road, Penryn, take road signed Mylor by Riders Volvo Showroom. Islington Wharf 100 yards on right hand side*

Opening hours: *Mon-Fri 9am-5pm.*

`11`

CORNISH FARM HOUSE CHEESES, Menallack Farm, Penryn, Cornwall TR1 9PB

Est. 1988
Tel/fax: +44 (0)1326-340333
Parking available
Wheelchair access

Twelve types of cheese including goats' and ewes' milk ones, made on our farm in the beautiful Helford River area. View the maturing cheese in our long store barn. The farm shop has cheeses, which are also sold throughout Cornwall and in Fortnum and Mason, homemade chutneys, eggs etc. Mail order available.

Directions: *between Falmouth and Gweek, half a mile outside Trevera. Clearly signposted on left hand side going west.*

Opening hours: *Mon-Fri 9am-5pm; five days. Sat/Sun 9am-12.30pm.*

ST MARTIN'S VINEYARD, St. Martin's, Isles of Scilly, Cornwall TR21

Est. 2000
Tel: +44 (0)1752-862019
www.stmartinsvineyard.co.uk
Wheelchair access

The most southerly and westerly vineyard in the British Isles, St Martin's produces a range of medium dry, mostly white wines. The first vintage for owners Graham and Val Thomas, is 2000. The winery was started in 1996 when they diversified from traditional agriculture. Organised tours and wine tasting are available.

Directions: *from Higher Town Quay, St Martin's, across Pool Green then follow signs.*

Opening hours: *Mon-Sat 9am-4pm in summer period.*

General Gifts

CAROLINE KELLEY-FOREMAN, 5 Bowling Green, St. Ives, Cornwall TR26 1JH

Est. 1993
Tel: +44 (0)1736-794042
Parking available

Caroline makes a humorous, naive-style range of wooden items which are useful and/or decorative. A seaside theme dominates her mirrors, cupboards and quirky mermaids, fish and seagulls. Also available are large chunky letters and numbers and a range of silver jewellery also following a sea theme. Mail order available.

Directions: *given when appointment is made.*

Opening hours: *by appointment only.*

Glass

DEBORAH MARTIN STAINED GLASS, The Sloop Craft Market, St Ives, Cornwall TR18 4EB

Est. 1990
Tel: +44 1736-796051
Parking available
Wheelchair access

Deborah Martin Stained Glass has been producing **stained glass artefacts** in St Ives for over ten years. Her shop offers original glass designs to enhance the home, and also any number of other pieces, which would be suitable for gifts: lighting, jewellery, mirrors, clocks etc. Commissions undertaken. Mail order available.

Directions: *50 yards from St. Ives Harbour, behind the Sloop Inn and carpark.*

Opening hours: *Mon-Sun 10am-5pm. Telephone first in winter.*

WITCHCRAFT GLASS, Antony Road, Torpoint, Cornwall PL11 2JY

Est.1999
Tel: +44 (0)1752-816700
www.witchcraftglass.co.uk
Parking available
Wheelchair access
Credit cards

We specialise in making stained glass items in traditional and modern styles. Techniques include handstaining, fused glass and the copper foil method. Items include **windows, lampshades, wedding horseshoes, seahorses** and fairy mobiles and window hangings for children. Commission and restoration work undertaken including church and house windows. Mail order available.

Directions: *at the top of Torpoint town centre at the junction which turns into Trevor Road leading to H.M.S. Raleigh.*

Opening hours: *Mon-Sat 10.30am-5pm; closed Weds morning and early closing (3.30pm) Thurs.* **16**

Jewellery

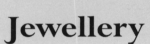

GEORGE NEED, Brookside Cottage, Lelant Downs, Near Hayle, Cornwall TR27 6LL

Est. 1962
Tel: +44 (0)1736-752655
Parking available
Wheelchair access
Credit cards

George Need has worked with precious metals for over thirty years and specialises in **individual jewellery inspired by Celtic themes** using silver, gold, platinum and precious stones. His workshop at the Sloop Centre is available for visits from potential customers. Silver items from £15; gold from £45. Commissions welcome. Mail order available.

Directions: *workshop at the Sloop Centre; 50 yards from St Ives harbour, directly behind the Sloop Inn and car park.*

Opening hours: *Mon-Fri 11am-4.30pm summer at the Sloop Centre. Otherwise phone for appointment at home.* **17**

TOMBODAMA, 5 Fore Street, Porthleven, Helston, Cornwall TR13 9HQ

Est. 1998
Tel: +44 (0)1336 560200
www.tombodama.com
Parking available
Wheelchairs: two steps up
Credit cards

Tombodama produces an extensive range of **jewellery for special occasions** by designer/maker Julia Schofield. All the jewellery is made on the premises using freshwater pearls, Austrian and Czech crystal, semi-precious stones and beautiful hand made and decorated beads made into necklaces, earrings, tiaras and 'Snow Maiden' headresses. Mail order brochure.

Directions: *on main street from Helston direction, we are on right just before the harbour.*

Opening hours: *Mon-Sat 11am-6pm; Sun midday-6pm.* **18**

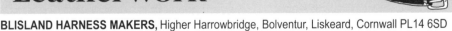

Leatherwork

BLISLAND HARNESS MAKERS, Higher Harrowbridge, Bolventur, Liskeard, Cornwall PL14 6SD

Est. 1980
Tel: +44 (0)1579-320593
Parking available
Wheelchair access
Credit cards

Master saddler Jane Talbot-Smith creates a range of **leather boxes and cases** to customers' own specifications. Also available are dog collars and leads, whistle lanyards, cartridge bags and belts, bellows and shooting-stools all kept in stock, alongside a full range of horse equipment. Mail order available.

Directions: *two and a half miles south of Bolventor on right; Bolventor is midway between Launceston and Bodmin on A30.*

Opening hours: *Mon-Sat 8.30am-5pm.* **19**

ST IVES LEATHERCRAFTS, 62a Fore Street, St. Ives, Cornwall TR26 1HW

Est. 1969
Tel: +44 (0)1736 793181
Parking available
Credit cards

John Grey started in 1969 as a wholesaler manufacturing belts. He moved in 1997 to present premises producing all types of **hand made leatherwork** from local cow hides. Hand-tooled, stitched and thonged leathergoods (shoulder bags, handbags, clutch bags and belts). Also high quality manufactured leatherwork. Mail order available.

Directions: *opposite Methodist Chapel at lower end of Fore Street.*
Opening hours: *seven days 10am-10pm. Out of season 10am-6pm.*

Pottery & Ceramics

ANDY TITCOMB, Lavender Cottage, Kelly Park, St Mabyn, Cornwall PL30 3BL

Est. 1979
Tel: +44 (0)1208-841340
www.andytitcomb
.cornwall.eu.org

Fun, functional teapots and salt and pepper shakers. I mostly work to order but have a limited stock for sale. Teapots: elephant, dodo, farm animals, chameleon, Adam and Eve, frog and rhinoceros, alien and UFOs. Commissions include a gamblers' salt, pepper and mustard set (cards, slot machine and coins). Mail order available.

Directions: *from St Mabyn pub carpark left down Station Road past first turning on left (no entry). Take second left (signed no through road). 3rd cottage on left.*
Opening hours: *by appointment.*

BOSCASTLE POTTERY, The Old Bakery, Boscastle, North Cornwall PL35 OHE

Est. 1962
Tel: +44 (0)1840-250291
Large carpark
Wheelchair access
Credit cards

Boscastle pottery is a studio workshop run by Roger Irving-Little and family, and is located in the picturesque Cornish fishing harbour of Boscastle. Roger is an expert in the art of **Mochaware**, having revived this ancient technique (whereby tree patterns appear on the pots as if by magic) some 45 years ago. Also, look out for the double-spouted tea-pot.

Directions: *opposite the only carpark in Boscastle.*
Opening hours: *360 days a year 10am-5.30pm.*

BOSCEAN POTTERY, St Just, Cornwall TR19 7QP.

Est. 1961
Tel: +44 (0)441736-787093
www.studiopottery.com
Parking available
Wheelchair access

Scott Marshall was master potter Bernard Leach's last apprentice, and came to Boscean with Richard Jenkins. They built a four-chambered climbing kiln with a capacity of 1,500 pots producing mainly **oven-to-table ware**. Scott now works alone on a smaller scale using mainly ash glazes. Some individual pots also made.

Directions: *from St Just Bank Square, take narrow road opposite the town clock for a mile.*
Opening hours: *7 days 10am-7.30pm throughout the year.*

DELAN COOKSON POTTERY, Lissadell, St Buryan, Penzance, Cornwall TR19 6HP

Est. 1988
Tel: +44 (0)1736-810347
Parking: limited
Wheelchair access

Delan Cookson works on his own, throwing **porcelain bowls, vases and bottles** in delicate, finely-turned shapes decorated with beautiful glazes including a particularly brilliant turquoise blue. The smooth whiteness of the porcelain brings out the brilliance of the coloured glazes. His work has featured in Cosmopolitan magazine. Mail order available.

Directions: *follow signs from Penzance to St. Buryan. Turn right to St. Just. Lissadell is 500 yards on the right.*
Opening hours: *by appointment advisable.* (24)

GINNIE BAMFORD, Sloop Craft Centre, Capel Court, St. Ives, Cornwall TR26 1LS

Est. 1984
Tel: +44 (0)1736-796051
Parking available
Wheelchair access

Ginnie Bamford produces **hand thrown earthenware** using terracotta clay coated with white slip and decorated with cobalt blue oxide. Some pieces are sponged, some hand painted. She makes a range of domestic ware including mugs, jugs, bowls etc. and also some one-off pieces that are slabbed and hand built. Mail order available

Directions: *50 yards from St Ives harbour, directly behind the Sloop Inn and car park.*

Opening hours: *11am-4pm daily.*

 25

JOHN & SYLVIA MIDDLEMISS, Wheal Vor, Lelant, St Ives, Cornwall TR26 3LF

Est. 1972
Tel: +44 (0)1736-754832
www.lelant.freeserve.co.uk
Parking: nearby, but not
on property

Individual ceramic vessels sculpture and functional ware intended for private and public collections. Different techniques and methods of forming, glazing and firing are used, but most are wheel thrown. The work is influenced by sacred architecture and geometry. A visit to the website is strongly advised before making a visit.

Directions: *the second cottage on the left past the war memorial in Lelant on B3074 towards St Ives.*

Opening hours: *strictly by appointment.*

26

MARY GOLDBERG, Stockwell Pottery, Stockwell Farmhouse, St Dominick, Saltash, Cornwall PL12 6TF

Est. 1987
Tel: +44 (0)1579-351035
Parking available
Wheelchair access

I make mainly brightly decorated, **white earthenware domestic hand thrown pots**. Several ranges available in different styles, mainly abstract, incorporating stripes, dots or a patchwork of colours. Variety of pieces available including toastracks and matching soap dishes and tiles for bathrooms. From very small gifts to large one-off pieces. Mail order available.

Directions: *In St. Dominick turn right at primary school. Turn right again (opposite Victory Hall) down small road and turn left at next crossroads down to end of track.* 27

MICHAEL HATFIELD, Kennack Pottery, Ruan Minor, Helston, Cornwall TR12 7LX

Est. 1969 originally;
1982 current location.
Tel: +44 (0)1326-290592
Parking available
Wheelchair access
Credit cards

Michael specialises in **porcelain and earthenware detailed models** of footwear (boots with leather laces wellies etc.) and miniature animals from mice on cheese to 14-inch elephants. Large DIY area for the public of all ages to try handthrowing pots or making models from moulds and painting them (£4.25). Tearoom. Mail order available.

Directions: *from Helston A3083 Lizard road. Left onto B3293. After Goonhilly Satellite Station right for Kennack Sands. In Kuggar turn left and Pottery is next to the inn.*

Opening hours: *9am-5.30pm most days. In winter please telephone first.* 28

PETER SWANSON, The Pottery, Prussia Cove Road, Rosudgeon, Penzance, Cornwall TR20 9AX

Est. 1976
Tel: +44 (0)1736-762167
www.southwestcrafts.co.uk
Parking available
Wheelchair access
Credit cards

Peter works from his small workshop/gallery producing a wide range of **functional domestic ware**. He also makes individual pieces. The glazes are made from specific wood ashes (i.e. beech, larch, oak etc.) mixed with local clays, various stone dusts and ground local granite producing subtle shades of greens, yellows and bluey greys.

Directions: *midway between Penzance and Helston on A394. Turning opposite the Falmouth Packet pub.*

Opening hours: *Mon-Fri 10am-5pm. Weekends by appointment.* 29

PHILIP GARDINER POTTERY, 8 Fore Street, Mevagissey, Near St. Austell, Cornwall PL26 6UQ

Est. 1983
Tel: +44 (0)1726-842042
Fax: +44 (0)1726-842266
Parking available
Credit cards

Philip Gardiner has been a potter since 1971 and he concentrates on **stoneware which is both decorative and strong** enough to withstand dishwasher and microwave use. All Philip's pots are hand thrown and dried for up to three weeks before being fired, decorated with coloured glazes and fired again.

Directions: *Mevagissey town centre opposite the Chemist.*

Opening hours: *Mon-Sat 9am-5pm; Sun 2-4pm Easter-end of October.*

 30

PORT ISAAC POTTERY, Roscarrock Hill, Port Isaac, Cornwall PL29 3RG

Est. 1979 in Stroud.
Tel: +44 (0)1208-880625
Parking available
Wheelchair access on request
Credit cards

We make and sell our own pottery from a converted Methodist chapel by the sea which we moved into in 1996. Our pots are all one-off pieces depicting **themes related to the sea and fishing**. Precious metal lustres and gold are used and work is fired three times. The showroom is open year round. Mail order available.

Directions: *centre of village, opposite the harbour.*

Opening hours: *10am-4pm 7 days.*

ROSEMARY SIMPSON, 15 The Crescent, Truro, Cornwall TR1 3ES

Est. 1989
Tel: +44 (0)1872-276780
Parking available
Wheelchair access

I make limited numbers of **stoneware and earthenware pots and figures** using local clays from a 500-year-old quarry. My work is hollow and very tactile and I enjoy playing with the tension between geometric and organic shapes. All my designs reflect my love of the countryside and coastline of Cornwall.

Directions: *from Sainsbury's descend hill and turn right immediately before the railway station and right into crescent.*

Opening hours: *by appointment.*

ST NEOT POTTERY, The Old Chapel, St Neot, Liskeard, Cornwall PL14 6NL

Est. 1985
Tel: +44 (0)1579-320216
Parking available
Wheelchair access can be assisted
Credit cards

A small studio pottery situated in a former Wesleyan chapel run by Penny and Jack Greenwood. Our pots are individually made on the premises from rich red earthenware clay and hand-decorated. There is always a good selection of **bowls, teapots, vases, jugs, bowls and dishes**. Mail order available.

Directions: *in St. Neot Village, fork right past the church 200 yards.*

Opening hours: *Mon-Sat 10am-5pm. Closed Sundays.*

TINTAGEL POTTERY, Tintagel, Cornwall PL34 0AY

Est. 1948
Tel: +44 (0)1840-770310
Parking available
Wheelchair access

The Tintagel Pottery makes a wide range of **earthenware pots thrown and decorated by hand.** Visitors are welcome to come and see a small pottery at work and look around our showroom which houses most of our product range. Our work is also sold by many local Cornish shops. Mail order available.

Directions: *At Bossiney on the Tintagel to Boscastle Road, approximately fifty miles east of Exeter.*

Opening hours: *Mon-Fri 10am-1pm/2pm-5.30pm.*

VISCAR POTTERY, Viscar Farm, Truro Lane, Helston, Cornwall TR13 OEJ

Est. 1992
Tel: +44 (0)1209-860348
Parking in farm lane

Small studio pottery making hand-thrown and brightly decorated very usable and **collectible domestic pottery**. Decorative themes are either the sea, boats and fishes or landcape and skies, flowers and some abstracts. I use a lightly grogged terracotta clay, decorated with coloured clays and finished with a bright, clear glaze. Mail order available.

Directions: *on A394 between Falmouth and Helston. Turn at junction in Retanna. Farm entrance 400 yards on left.*

Opening hours: *by appointment Mon-Thurs. 10am-4pm and weekends.*

Textiles

HERMIONE DUNN, Sunnyside, Crockett, Stoke Climsland, Callington, Cornwall PL17 8HG

Est. 1994
Tel: +44 (0)1579-370689
Very limited parking

Individually designed, **framed and wearable hand-painted silk**. Hermione Dunn is a painter, who, inspired by Cornwall best finds expression in vibrant colours and the sheen of silk. Fish are a favourite motif and her work can be found in many collections in the UK and abroad. Mail order possible.

Directions: *Launceston Road from Callington to Kelly Bray. Then turning to Stoke Climsland. Crockett turning on right after half a mile.*

Opening hours: *by appointment only.*   **36**

SETA, Chun Barn, Higher Bojewyan, Pendeen, Penzance, Cornwall TR19 7TR

Est. 1998
Tel: +44 (0)1736-788549
Parking available

Karen Knowlton is a member of the Guild of Silk Painters, specialising in **fine art on silk** producing high quality individual pieces: hand painted cards, scarves, framed paintings, wallhangings etc. Themes are inspired by the Cornish landscapes and organic forms and vibrant colours. Commissions taken. Mail order available.

Directions: *B3318 to Pendeen. Turn right (B3306) and half a mile from Pendeen driveway on the right before last speed limit sign.*

Opening hours: *by appointment only.*   **37**

SMART TART, Blackbird Barn, Bank Square, St Just, Penzance, Cornwall TR19 7HJ

Est. 1998
Tel/fax: +44 (0)1736-787091
www.smarttart.co.uk
Parking available
Wheelchair access
Credit cards

Having studied printmaking in Australia and Falmouth, Karen Arthur transferred her zest for colour and pattern to textiles. She produces humorous, **luxurious, yet wonderfully practical accessories** including vintage velvets for bags and soft furnishings to hand-rolled felt bags. Her work is exhibited in the UK and the USA. Mail order available.

Directions: *from A30 follow signs to St Just. Studio is opposite clocktower, behind newsagent in Bank Square.*

Opening hours: *most days long hours. Please ring for appointment.*   **38**

Toys & Games

CHECK MATE, 76 Hallane Road, Boscoppa, St. Austell, Cornwall PL25 3EL.

Est. 1999
Tel: +44 (0)1726-69327
Parking available
Wheelchair access

Alan Giles makes **handcast and handpainted metal chess sets.** All are themed and include US Civil War, Napoleonic, Crusades, King Arthur and Fantasy. Can be bought unpainted if wished. If painted, colours are historically authentic. All sets come boxed. Also does repairs and repaints on purchased sets. Mail order possible.

Directions: *A30 to St. Austell. Follow signs to St. Austell past the Eden Project. After a mile approx to Boscoppa turnoff, then 2nd right.*

Opening hours: *telephone for appointment.*   **39**

CHERI-ROSE, 27 Collygree Park, Goldsithney, Penzance, Cornwall TR20 9LY

Est. 1994
Tel: +44(0) 1736-719148
Street parking.

Members of the Made in Cornwall scheme, Chéri-Rose specialise in **Victorian-style dolls dressed in Cornish tartan** and crafted from wood, plus rocking horses, hobby horses, dolls' houses, dolls' four-poster and bunk beds, wooden chests and other wooden gifts. Commissions are welcome. Mail order available.

Directions: *given once appointment is arranged.*
Opening times: *only by appointment.*

40

FAIRYLAND BEARS, Units 19 & 20, The Sloop Craft Centre, St Ives, Cornwall

Est. 2000
Tel: +44 (0)1736-799901
Parking available
Wheelchair access
Credit cards

Fairyland bears are **limited edition collectors' bears.** Each is different in character and expression. Limit of three on each design; some are one-offs. They are made from mohair, fully jointed, with glass eyes, coloured sparkling noses and some have earrings. From four and a half inches in size. Mail order available.

Directions: *50 yards from St Ives harbour, directly behind the Sloop Inn and car park.*
Opening hours: *Mon-Fri 11am-4pm; weekends 12pm-4pm.*

41

Woodturning & Furniture

GUY SUTCLIFFE, 1A Studio, Sloop Craft Market, The Wharf, St Ives, Cornwall TR26 1LS

Est. 1986
Tel: +44 (0)1736-796051
Parking available
Wheelchair access
Credit cards

Guy began carving wood about twenty years ago under the tuition of Wharton Lang, a gifted sculptor. The tactile nature of Guy's **sculptures** comes from his wanting to display the beauty of the grain and the play of the wood, which encourages people to feel and stroke them. Mail order available.

Directions: *studio at the main entrance to the Sloop Craft Market. 50 yards from St Ives harbour, directly behind the Sloop Inn and car park.*
Opening hours: *Mon-Sat 9.30-4pm.*

 42

JIM BENSON, The Hollies, Chyvelah Road, Threemilestone, Truro, Cornwall TR3 6BY

Est. 1997
Tel: +44 (0)1872-271948
Parking available

In retirement, I embarked on a career in woodturning, which was my hobby from an early age. I make mostly **bowls using hardwoods** (ash, oak, beech, yew etc), also milking stools, chairs, light pulls and honey dippers; also furniture to commission. I am more interested in form than embellishment. Mail order available.

Directions: *behind The Victoria Inn, Threemilestone. Access to left of pub via curved driveway.*
Opening hours: *Mon-Sat 9am-5pm.*

43

PHILIP & JULIET BRIDEWELL, Roskellan House, Maenlay, Helston, Cornwall TR12 7QR

Est. 1988
Tel/fax: +44 (0)1326-572657
Parking available

Philip makes bespoke furniture to commission. Juliet designs and makes **carved wooden boxes with pull-out drawers.** Clients have come from Japan, United States of America, United Arab Emirates, Australia and Continental Europe as well as nearer home. Mail order available. Send stamped addressed envelope for a brochure.

Directions: *A3083 Helston to Lizard road, three miles from Helston towards the Lizard. At the end of RNAS Culdrose cross mini-roundabout and next left.*
Opening hours: *by arrangement.*

 44

SCOTT WOYKA, 1 Windsor Quarry, Falmouth, Cornwall TR11 3EX

Est. 1995
Tel: +44 (0)1326-221628
Parking available
Wheelchair access via a step

Scott designs and makes one-off pieces of **contemporary furniture using native hardwoods** including ash, sycamore, cherry, elm and oak. He produces thoroughly practical pieces e.g. wall-cupboards, chests, benches etc. 'with a tactile and often organic feel.' All work is done to commission. Personalised service working closely with customers to establish their preferences.

Directions: *from 'the Moor' in Falmouth up Killigrew Street; first left Trelawney Road; first right Windsor Terrace; left into Windsor Court; left again into Windsor Quarry.*
Opening hours: *Mon-Fri normally 9am-6pm. Please telephone first.*   45

Other Makers

ARTWAVES, The Old Sunday School, Cape Cornwall Street, St Just, Penzance, Cornwall TR19 7JZ

Est. 1998
Tel: +44 (0)1736-788444
www.artwaves.co.uk
Parking available
Wheelchair access
Credit cards

Artwaves at the Old Sunday School Studio shows Alison Englefield's unique creations including **jewellery made from ground and recycled materials** especially paper: flying cats, mermaids, elephants and fat fairies. Her pictures are of imaginative sea and landscapes painted with paper pulp and acrylics and water colours. Also driftwood sculptures. Mail order available.

Directions: *from the Square in St Just sharp left after the clock tower into Cape Cornwall Street. 200 yards on left near junction with West Place.*
Opening hours: *usually Tues-Sun 10am-5pm. Telephoning ahead recommended.*   46

CREATE, 19 New Road, Newlyn, Cornwall TR18 5PZ

Est. 2000
Tel/fax: +44 (0)1736-330324
www.create.ltd.uk
Parking available

Nik Strangelove and Sarah Goldbart produce high quality, **handpainted and handmade, contemporary room screens,** fire/mini screens and paintings. There is a selection of designs to choose from in our brochure and on our website. We also work to commission, adapting designs, colours and sizes to match specific interiors. Mail order available.

Directions: *opposite Newlyn Art Gallery in Newlyn.*
Opening hours: *by appointment only.*   47

JOHN NORTHEY, Kepleigh, St Clether, Launceston, Cornwall PL15 8PU

Est. 1995
Tel/fax: +44 (0)1566-86624
Parking available

John Northey sells **copies of Cornwall's oldest recorded horseshoe** which he found in 1993 on Bodmin Moor. The British Museum dated it to 1450AD. He now produces pewter replicas cast from the original and sold to horse lovers and others interested in equestrian history from around the world. Mail order available.

Directions: *two and a half miles from Altarnun Village on the Camelford Road.*
Opening hours: *seven days a week. Call for appointment.*   48

LITTLE FAT BOATS, Little Homecroft, Paynters Lane, Illogan, Redruth, Cornwall TR16 4DS

Est. 1999
Tel: +44 (0)1209-843822

I work most evenings making **very strong papier-mâché boats** based on traditional Cornish fishing boats. They are 30cm long and 20cm high with either front or back masts. A wide variety of colours (yellow, green, blue, red etc) is available and they can be personalised to customers' wishes for instance the name of the boat on the stern, or the registration number on the prow. They cost £25 plus £5 carriage. Mail order only. Alternatively ring for details of outlets in St. Ives, Cornwall.   49

NATALIE J. PEARCE, The Sloop Craft Centre, Capel Court, St Ives, Cornwall TR26 1LS

Est. 1999
Tel: +44 (0)1736-796051
Parking available
Wheelchair access

Since opening her gallery, Natalie's paintings and prints have become very popular, both through sales and commissions undertaken. She is self-taught and her images are imaginative, bright and fun in the naive style, combining beautiful scenery, characters, and particularly the amatory adventures of her cat. 'My pictures make people happy.'

Directions: *50 yards from St Ives harbour, directly behind the Sloop Inn and car park.*

Opening hours: *seven days a week flexible hours.*

OCEANBORN, The Gardens, Nanswhyden, St Columb, Cornwall TR8 4HT

Est. 1995
Tel: +44 (0)1637-889077

David Pegg is a small scale designer/maker producing **raw and elemental pieces using driftwood** harvested from the north coast of Cornwall. A range of work includes gift cards, mirrors, furniture and objets d'art all fashioned from the wood and debris thrown ashore by the seas. Mail order available.

Directions: *take A3059 from the A30 following Newquay signs. At traffic island, go straight on for under a mile. Turn left signed Tregoose. Continue on until Nanswhyden Farm.*

Opening hours: *Mon-Fri 10am-5pm.*

ROY HARRISON, The Sloop Craft Centre, Capel Court, St Ives, Cornwall TR26 1LS

Est. 1984
Tel: +44 (0)1736-796051
Parking available
Wheelchair access

Roy makes **walking sticks and brushes and carvings**. He designs and carves walking sticks in English hardwoods. Great care is taken to ensure that however intricate the design of the stick, it will be completely comfortable in the hand. A well-chosen walking stick becomes part of its owner's personality. Mail order available.

Directions: *50 yards from St Ives harbour, directly behind the Sloop Inn and car park.*

Opening hours: *Mon-Fri 11am-4pm.*

WINDSWEPT AND INTERESTING, Sloop Craft Centre, Capel Court, St Ives, Cornwall TR26 ILS

Est.1999
Tel: +44 (0)1736-787927
www.windsweptninteresting
.fsnet.co.uk
Large car park
Wheelchair access

We specialise in **clocks made from wood**, papier-mâché and where possible we try to recycle. All clocks are totally individual, and can be made to order to the customer's specifications. We incorporate funky, abstract and nautical themes with local scenes in our handpainted examples. Mail order available.

Directions: *50 yards from St Ives harbour, directly behind the Sloop Inn and car park.*

Opening hours: *Mon-Fri 11am-4pm.*

Devon

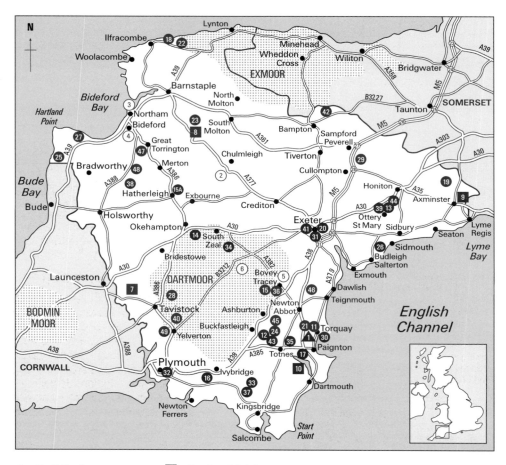

▲ Craft Centres   ■ Food and Drink

○ Shops and Galleries   ● Makers' Workshops

Devon has long been associated with rich and rolling farmland, pastel villages and seaside resorts. Dartmoor, Devon's vast national park was once the centre of a flourishing tin-mining industry. Historic cottage industries include lace-making (especially in Honiton) and pottery such as Devon slipware. The pottery tradition lives on through the many pottery makers who have taken up residence in Devon including a descendant and one apprentice of Bernard Leach. Cider is now produced on a factory scale, but there are also small, family-owned businesses which you can visit, and enjoy tastings. Devon has some major craft centres including the Devon Guild of Craftsmen in Bovey Tracey and the Dartington Press Centre near Totnes.

Craft Centres

COCKINGTON COURT CRAFT STUDIOS, Cockington, Torquay, Devon TQ2 7TE

Est. 1991
Tel +44 (0)1803-606035
Fax +44 (0)1803-690391
www.countryside-trust.org.uk
Wheelchair access
Parking available
Licensed café/restaurant
Credit cards

Set among 450 acres of beautiful parkland, the 16th century manor house of Cockington Court is home to some of the finest craftsmen and women in the southwest. Glassblowing - each piece is hand made using traditional techniques. Pottery - wheel thrown fine stoneware in the original Tudor kitchen. Patchwork quilts and contemporary textile art, including tuition and workshops. Calligrapher and artist - working in watercolour, gouache, gold leaf and ink - tuition. Jewellery - handmade designs in gold and silver. Aromatherapy - blending and distilling oils. Metal sculpture - copper sculptures and artworks by commission. Plasterwork - children may paint the plastercasts.

Directions: *follow the A380 into Torquay. Turn right along the seafront and follow the brown signs to Cockington.*

Open: *April-Sept 10am-4pm daily: phone for winter hours.*

Craft Shops

THE GALLERY AT EGGESFORD, Eggesford Gardens, Eggesford, Chulmleigh, Devon EX18 7QU

Est. 1998
Tel: +44 (0)1363-83410
Parking available
Wheelchair access
Credit cards

A co-operative craft shop run by local artists and craft workers. The beauty of Devonshire is reflected in the many original pieces. Items in wood, metal and basketry, textile, glass, china and fine art would make interesting and individual gifts. Prices from £1.50 (hand made cards) to over £1000. Mail order by arrangement.

Directions: *leave A377 at Eggesford Station. Cross over railway and river bridges. Follow road up hill and take first turning to left. Follow signs to Garden Centre.*
Opening hours: *Mon-Sun 10am-4.30pm in winter; 10am-5pm in summer.* ②

Galleries

APPLEDORE CRAFTS COMPANY, 5 Bude Street, Appledore, Bideford, Devon EX39 1PS

Est. 1991
Tel: +44 (0)1237-423547
Parking available
Credit cards

A co-operative gallery, which provides a showcase for North Devon's leading craftspeople. Members staff the gallery providing a uniquely knowledgeable and helpful commissioning service. There is an ever-changing display of the best contemporary art including metalwork, furniture, ceramics, mirrors, textiles, lighting, glass and woodwork. Mail order possible but not usual.

Directions: *on Appledore Quay. Left turn after the post office into Bude Street. Shop is 30 yards along on the right.*
Opening hours: *Mon-Sun 10am-6pm summer; Wed-Sun 10am-4pm winter.* ③

THE BURTON ART GALLERY & MUSEUM, Kingsley Road, Bideford, North Devon EX39 2QQ

Est. 1951
Tel +44 (0)1237-471455
Fax +44 (0)1237-473813
Est. www.burtonartgallery.co.uk
Parking easily available.
Wheelchair access.
Credit cards

The Burton Art Gallery and Museum has three exhibition areas and hosts an ever-changing programme of exhibitions and craftwork throughout the year. A permanent collection of oil and watercolour paintings, North Devon slipware, Napoleonic ship models, local historical artefacts are also part of the its attractions. Also a coffee shop, gift shop.

Directions: *take J27 off M5, continue on Link Road to Bideford, turn left at roundabout after Torridge Bridge; Gallery is on left in Victoria Park beside riverbank.*
Opening hours: *10am-4pm Tues-Sat, 2-4pm Sun.* ④

DEVON GUILD OF CRAFTSMEN, Riverside Mill, Bovey Tracey, Devon TQ13 9AF

Est. 1955 (Riverside Mill since 1986)
Tel: +44 (0)1626-832223
Fax: +44 (0)1626-834220
www.crafts.org.uk
Parking available
W/chair access (not gallery)
Credit cards

The South West's leading craft showrooms and gallery featuring work selected from over 240 makers and designers. Most exhibition work is for sale. Commissioning resource and ten months' interest free credit (Artcred) available. The Guild runs an education and outreach programme for artists and the public. Riverside café with courtyard seating.

Directions: *20 minutes from Exeter along A38 Plymouth Road. Turn off on to A382 to the centre of Bovey Tracey.*
Opening hours: *7 days 10am-5.30pm.* ⑤

FIELD OF MOOR DREAMS, North Bovey, Newton Abbott, Devon TQ13 8RG

Est. 1997
Tel: +44 (0)1647-432400
Fax: +44 (0)1647-433662
Parking available
Wheelchair access
Credit cards

Carol and Tony Hutchings run a stable yard gallery which features the West Country's finest craft talent and a range of shows to browse for unusual and original gifts. There is also a courtyard café where you can enjoy a glass of wine or a cream tea. Mail order available.

Directions: *adjacent the Miniature Pony Centre on the B3212, two miles west of Moretonhampstead towards Princetown.*

Opening hours: *Open from 10am every day Easter to November.*

Food & Drink

COUNTRYMAN CIDER, Felldownhead, Milton Abbot, Tavistock, Devon PL19 OQR

Est. 1858
Tel: +44 (0)1822-870226
Parking on site

Traditional cider making since 1858 by five generations of the same family (but current owners since 1997). All visitors are offered a free guided tour of orchards, apple mill and cider press and fermentations, with sampling afterwards. The farm shop sells cider in earthenware jars, English country wines and apple brandy.

Directions: *from Tavistock take the Launceston road (B3362) through Milton Abbot. After 1.75 miles turn right (signposted Kelly). The Cider farm is signed after half a mile.*

Opening hours: *Mon-Sat 9am-6.30pm.*

FISHLEIGH FARMHOUSE FOODS, Fishleigh Barton, Umberleigh, North Devon **EX37 9DZ**

Est. 2000
Tel/fax: +44 (0)1769-560242
www.fishleighfoods.co.uk
Parking available
Limited wheelchair access

From our 15th century farmhouse we bake award-winning pasties and cakes and prepare cream teas and light meals for our farm shop and tea-room. We also sell locally home-produced meats and hand made sausages and preserves, confectionery and drinks. Also a gallery with ceramics, wood and glass work etc.

Directions: *on the A377, 6 miles south of Barnstaple just after Chapelton (the scenic route from Barnstaple to Exeter).*

Opening hours: *Tues-Sat 8.30am-5.pm. Sun 10am-4pm.* **8**

LYME BAY CIDER COMPANY LTD, The Lyme Bay Winery, Shute, Axminster, Devon EX13 7PW

Est. 1994
Tel: +44 (0)1297-551355
Fax: +44 (0)1297-551366
Parking available
Wheelchair access
Credit cards

The Lyme Bay winery combines traditional cider-making skills with modern production techniques to produce a range of traditional and contemporary ciders from old fashioned cider apples including Kingston Black, Dabinett and Yarlington Mill. The on-site shop sells country wines, liqueurs, cider vinegar and cider brandy. Tastings and tours. Mail order available.

Directions: *two miles west of Axminster turn off A35 to Shute. The Lyme Bay Winery is signposted a mile after Shute.*

Opening hours: *Summer Mon-Fri 9am-5pm; Sat 10am-4pm; Sun 11am-4pm. Winter closed at weekends.* **9**

SHARPHAM VINEYARD & CHEESES, Sharpham Estate, Ashprington, Totnes, Devon TQ9 7UT

Est. 1983
Tel: +44 (0)1803-732203
Fax: +44 (0)1803-732122
www.sharpham.com
Parking available
W/chair access to shop & winery
Credit cards

This progressive vineyard is in a stunning location above Devon's meandering river Dart. Take an idyllic stroll followed by an informal tasting and explanation of winemaking in our new winery. Our world-class wines range from £5.50 to £29.95. Small adult admission fee. Cheeses from Jersey milk also made. Mail order available.

Directions: *From Totnes, follow A381 for Kingsbridge, turning off left for Ashprington. In Ashprington turn left at Durant Arms and follow lane, ignoring the 'no through road' signs.*

Opening hours: *Jun-Aug Mon-Sun 10.30am-5.30pm; closed Sun Sept-May.* **10**

Glass

OURGLASS, Studios 2 & 3, The Stableyard, Cockington Court Craft Centre, Torquay, Devon TQ2 6XA

Est. 1997
Tel: +44 (0)1803-606757
Fax: +44 (0)1803-607603
Parking available
Wheelchair access

Ourglass specialise in their own **contemporary studio glassware** (bowls, vases, candlesticks, paperweights, drinking glasses and glass fruits) with designs made using traditional blowing techniques in a range of vibrant colours in swirling patterns, or plain coloured. Each piece is unique. Demonstrations are given daily from 10am-3pm. Mail order available.

Directions: *stable yard behind Cockington Court Manor House, approx. 400 yards from Cockington village centre.*

Opening hours: *six days 10am-4pm plus Saturday mornings.*   **11**

ROBERTA AYLES STAINED GLASS, Old Torne, Rattery, South Brent, Devon TQ10 9LQ

Est 1976
Tel: +44 (0)1364-644116
Parking available

I started making **stained glass windows** in 1976 using traditional methods, and like to work closely with my clients from the design stage through to selecting the glass. I also make fused and slumped glass bowls, plates, mirrors and brooches. Stained glass lamps also made. Mail order available.

Directions: *leave A38 at Buckfastleigh and take A384. After a mile go right to Rattery then right after a mile at Rattery Sawmill.*

Opening hours: *visits by appointment only.*   **12**

Jewellery

JACQUI CAREY, Summercourt, Ridgeway, Ottery St Mary, Devon EX11 1DT

Est. 1988
Tel/Fax : +44 (0)1404-813486
www.careycompany.com
Parking available
Credit cards

Kumihimo (Japanese braidmaking). Although Jacqui's work stems from the traditional, she explores all the creative process's possibilities. Many of her original designs are produced in silk and semi-precious stones to form unique jewellery. Jacqui is the author of books on the subject and also supplies kumihimo equipment and materials. Mail order available.

Directions: *from Ottery St Mary take the Honiton Road past the Church. First right down Ridgeway, Summercourt is immediately on the right.*

Opening hours: *by appointment only.*   **13**

Pottery & Ceramics

BELSTONE POTTERY, Perrymans Farm, Belstone, Okehampton, Devon EX20 1RD.

Tel: +44 (0)1837-840206
Parking available
Wheelchair access

David Gundry makes a full range of **domestic, woodfired, stoneware** to cook in, store food in and eat from. He designs his pots to 'nourish all the senses' and feels that pots we see and use on a daily basis should be satisfying to handle and beautiful to look at.

Directions: *head for Belstone village on Dartmoor. Entering village take the first left (signed Skaigh). House and pottery 200 yards on right.*

Opening hours: *flexible. Please ring for appointment.*

14

DAVID LEACH, Lowerdown Pottery, Bovey Tracey, Devon TQ13 9LE

Est. 1930
Tel: +44 (0)1626-833408
Parking available
Wheelchair access

I am the oldest potting son of Bernard (one of England's most influential modernist potters) having started in 1930 at St Ives in Cornwall and moving to Bovey Tracey in 1956. I specialise in **hand thrown domestic stoneware and porcelain** ceramics and individual pieces made to commission. Mail order available.

Directions: *from Bovey Tracey take the Haytor Widecombe road to Lowerdown Cross (half a mile) and the pottery is on the left.*

Opening hours: *Mon-Fri 9am-6pm & Sat 9am-1pm but prior appointment necessary.*

15

HATHERLEIGH POTTERY, 20 Market Street, Hatherleigh, Devon EX20 3JP

Est. 1984
Tel: +44 (0)1837-810624
Fax: +44 (0)1837-810823
www.hatherleighpottery.co.uk
Parking available
Partial wheelchair access
Credit cards

In the heart of Hatherleigh, the Pottery **produces hand-thrown domestic ware** glazed with a woodash glaze which pools and flows during the firing. The very comprehensive range includes complete dinner services and oven to table ware along with garden pots, oil lamps and many other items. Mail order available.

Directions: *Hatherleigh is seven miles north of Okehampton on the A386.*
Opening hours: *10am-5pm Mon-Sat.*

MARION VALDER, Studio 10, Ermington Workshops, Ermington, Devon PL21 9NT

Est. 1996
Tel: +44 (0)1752-339664
Parking available
Wheelchair access

I make **decorative smoke-fired ceramics** including bird and animal sculptures. Pots are fired individually or in batches in a mixture of salt, copper carbonate, sawdust and various organic materials resulting in unique and dynamic surface patterns, colours and textures reminiscent of planets spinning in space, underwater worlds and volcanic eruptions.

Directions: *from A38 or A379 signed Ermington. The workshops complex is signed from the Church. Studio 10 is first in the lower car park.*
Opening hours: *by appointment.*

MICHAEL SKIPWITH, Aish Cross House, Aish, Stoke Gabriel, Totnes, Devon TQ9 6PT

Est. 1957
Tel: +44 (0)1803-782768
Parking available
Wheelchair access

Michael and Elizabeth Skipwith were potters at the Lotus Pottery for forty years. In 1984 Michael built a 22 cubic foot wood-fired kiln making **stoneware and porcelain**. In 1998 he moved to Aish House where he continues to make a limited amount of pottery despite the debilitating effects of Parkinson's disease.

Directions: *about a mile outside Stoke Gabriel.*
Opening hours: *appointment necessary.*

THE OLD CORN MILL AND POTTERY, Watermouth Road, Hele, Nr. Ilfracombe, N Devon EX34 9QY

Est. 1991 (1996 in Devon)
Tel: +44 (0)1271-863185
www.oldcornmillandpottery.co.uk
Parking available
Wheelchair access limited

Inexpensive **giftware, tableware and individual pieces**. Two showrooms of raku, dozens of individual different pots. Watch demonstrations or make your own pot and have it fired/glazed and mailed to you. The mill is 16th century, magnificently restored, with working machinery that produces flour and cereal for sale. Tea-room. Mail order available.

Directions: *on A399 Ilfracombe-Combe Martin Road. Bus stop at Hele 100 yards from centre. Approx. 20 minutes walk from Ilfracombe.*
Opening hours: *7 days Easter-end June 10am-5pm, July to end Aug. 10am-6pm. September-end Oct.*

THE OLD POUND POTTERY, Pound House, Membury, Axminster, Devon EX13 7AF.

Est. 1980
Tel: +44 (0)1404-881431
Parking available
Wheelchair access

Frances and Douglas Arkle make hand-thrown and modelled items **mugs, jugs, vases, goblets, bowls and candleholders**. The pottery is a 200-year-old building formerly used for cheese-making and a smithy workshop for making farm wagons. It has been a pottery since 1968.

Directions: *next to the church and school in Membury.*
Opening hours: *usually 7 days 9.30am-6pm.*

PAULINE ZELINSKI, 25 Exwick Hill, Exeter, Devon EX4 2AQ

Est. 1992
Tel: +44 (0)1392-252526
www.bott.freeserve.co.uk
Parking available
Credit cards

Pauline Zelinski designs and makes **domestic ceramics and tiles**. Her pieces include large platters, bowls, jugs, cups and vases, which she decorates with underglaze colours. Bold designs are hand painted in bright, tropical colours. She has recently started producing patterned tiles for interiors. Prices range from £10-120.

Directions: *from St David's railway station over railway line and river. Turn right at T-junction by church. Exwick Hill is on the left after the pub.*
Opening hours: *by appointment only.*

THE POTTERY COCKINGTON COURT, Cockington, Torquay, Devon TQ2 6XA.

Est. 1978
Tel/fax: +44 (0)1803-607773
Parking available
Wheelchair access
Credit Cards

Wheel-thrown **fine stoneware pottery**, extensive range from candlesticks and unique table lamps to a wide variety of items for the kitchen and table including distinctive bowls and dishes. Visitors can enjoy browsing in the atmosphere of a working studio located in the Court's original Tudor kitchen. Mail order available.

Directions: *follow signs for Cockington Village/Cockington Country Park. Pottery located on ground floor of Cockington Court set in 450 acres of parkland.*

Opening hours: *Mon-Sun 10am-4pm. Please telephone first.*

ROCK HAVEN POTTERY, Rockhaven House, Seaside Hill, Combe Martin, N. Devon EX34 0AW

Est. 2000
Tel: +44 (0) 1271-882302
Parking available
Wheelchair access

A family business owned by Leslie and Rosanne Higgins which **specialises in sculpture** and incorporates a workshop and a showroom. Visitors can watch the potter at work and for a small fee you can throw your own pot or make your own sculpture. Tea-room. Mail order available.

Directions: *from Barnstaple follow signs for Combe Martin. On the seafront overlooking the bay.*

Opening hours: *weekends and some weekdays 10am-6pm.*

ROGER COCKRAM CERAMICS, Chittlehampton Pottery, Chittlehampton, North Devon EX37 9PX

Est. 1976
Tel/fax: +44 (0)1769-540420
Parking available
Wheelchair access
Credit cards

Roger makes a practical **range of kitchen pots**. He also makes special individual pieces for which he has an international reputation. These are based on natural themes. Ros Cockram assists in the studio and makes her own range of decorative candlesticks and figures. She is also a painter (gouache). Mail order available.

Directions: *off the B3227, 5 miles west of South Molton. The pottery is at the western edge of Chittlehampton.*

Opening hours: *Mon-Fri 10am-1pm & 2pm-5.30. Weekends by appointment.*

TAMASINE HOLMAN, The Cottage, Bumpston Bridge, Nr. Buckfastleigh, Devon TQ19 0LB

Est. 1996
Tel: +44 (0)1803-762527
Parking available

I specialise in **ornamental ceramic vessels**. These are decorative items which are cut up when leather hard and then reassembled and pit-fired (in a hole outdoors) with various natural substances (seaweed, copper and other materials packed around the vessels etc) to impart surface swirls in natural, rusty colours. Mail order available.

Directions: *Staverton road from Totnes. First left after steam railway and another first left to large white house.*

Opening hours: *by appointment.*

WELCOMBE POTTERY, Welcome, Bideford, Devon EX39 6HG

Est. 1996
Tel: +44 (0)1288-331366
Parking available
Wheelchair access
Credit cards

Ben Lucas makes **functional handthrown and decorated earthenware** using the local Fremington clay. Ben specialises in wax relief and slip trailing to produce lively work, which is inspired in part by his love for the sea and its inhabitants: for instance blue glazed dishes with white line fish designs.

Directions: *take Welcombe turning off A39 between Bude and Hartland and follow signs to pottery.*

Opening hours: *Tues-Sat 9.30am-5.30pm Mar-Oct. Other months by appointment.*

Textiles

ANNE BULLEN, Otterton Mill, Nr. Budleigh Salterton, Otterton, Devon

Est. 1999
Tel: +44 (0)1395-274705
Parking available

Anne Bullen specialises in working with wool. She felts using wool to make **hats and bags** of all shapes and sizes. This interest developed during the time when she lived on a smallholding in North Wales. She also has a large floor loom on which she makes shawls, rugs etc.

Directions: *Otterton Mill in the village of Otterton, Nr. Budleigh Salterton.*
Opening hours: *Mon-Sat 10.30am-4.30pm.[maker 26]*

ANN JARVIS DESIGNS, Clovelly Silk, Lower Yard, Clovelly, Devon EX39 5TL

Est. 1995
Tel/fax: +44 (0)1237-431033
Parking available
Wheelchair access

Ann Jarvis was the head of studio at Liberty of London prints for ten years before she started Clovelly Silk. She designs and prints **silk and wool fabric/scarves, ties, cushions** and accessories. Designs are handprinted on to silks, velvets and fine wools. Day courses run. Mail order available.

Directions: *From A39 between Bideford and Bude follow signs to Clovelly.*
Opening hours: *7 days 10am-6pm summer, winter phone to confirm.*

BOBBIE COX, Higher Manor, Cudliptown, Peter Tavy, Tavistock, Devon PL19 9LZ

Est. 1975
Tel: +44 (0)1822-810305
www.bobbie.cox.net

Bobbie Cox is a designer/maker of **contemporary woven tapestries**. She works to commission for specific sites and does large pieces up to 8'x 6', or smaller domestic scale ones. Her designs feature specifically colour/texture. She dyes her own yarn and spins much of it for interesting textures.

Directions: *a mile from Peter Tavy. Ring for more details.*
Opening hours: *by appointment only.*

COLDHARBOUR MILL TRUST, Coldharbour Mill Working Wool Museum, Uffculme, Nr. Cullompton, Devon EX15 3EE

Est. 1982
Tel: +44 (0)1884-840960
Fax: +44 (0)1884-840858
www.coldharbourmill.org.uk
Parking available
W/chair access: ring ahead
Credit cards

Exclusive range of worsted knitting wool, worsted Devon and **Somerset tartan and woollen floor rugs**. The Mill, a working museum based around a Victorian Mill tells the story of the men, women and children who worked there. The Mill shop sells yarn and cloth made at the museum. Mail order available.

Directions: *just off junction 27 of the M5. Follow signs to Willand (B3181) and then Brown signs saying 'Working Wool Museum.'*
Opening hours: *10.30am-5pm, Apr-Oct Mon-Sun; Nov-Mar Mon-Fri.*

THE FABRIC GARDEN, Studio One, Cockington Court, Cockington, Torquay, Devon TQ2 6XA

Est. 1994
Tel/fax: +44 (0)1803-212965
Parking available
Wheelchair access
Credit cards

The Fabric Garden, owned by Alice Summers and located in the Cockington Craft Centre, produces **textile art, patchwork and bed quilts** hand and machine made. The studio displays quilts and stocks all products necessary for quilt work. Classes and tuition run from September to Easter every year. Mail order available.

Directions: *from Torquay follow signs to Cockington. Call at Cockington Court Visitor Centre and follow signs to Manor House.*
Opening hours: *10am-4pm Mon-Sat except Jan-Mar when by appointment only.*

HOOKED RUGS AND WALLHANGINGS, 10 New North Road, Exeter, Devon EX4 4HF

Est. 1995
Tel: +44 (0)1392-273465
Parking: at pay and display

Rebecca Holland studied fine art in Bath and makes **hooked rugs and wallhangings** using reclaimed materials. Her unique designs combine stunning arrangements of colour, shape and texture creating highly original work. She also teaches, lectures and runs workshops at her studio, as well as supplying tools and equipment by mail order.
Directions: *near the clock tower in central Exeter.*
Opening hours: *by appointment only.*

JANE WITHERIDGE, 55 Mariston Avenue, Keyham, Plymouth, Devon PL2 ILP.

Est. 1985
Tel: +44 (0)1752-561435
Parking available

Jane is established in the South West as a designer/maker of **batiks and silk paintings**, which are inspired from many sources: the beautiful Devon countryside, rich still life and drawings of the human figure. They are mainly sold framed. Commissions taken. Prices from £100. Mail order available.
Directions: *map provided after appointment confirmed.*
Opening hours: *by appointment only. Then map with directions provided.*

PEET LEATHER, Ham Farm, Loddiswell, Kingsbridge, South Devon TQ7 4RX

Est. 1995
Tel +44 (0)1548-550417
Fax +44 (0)1548-550861
Parking available
Wheelchair access
Credit cards

Playful, richly coloured and inventive **hats, coats, cushions and wallpieces felted from reclaimed materials** burst from my workshop in the run up to events and exhibitions throughout Britain. These have included OXO in London, the Chelsea Craft Fair, The Devon Guild of Craftsmen and the opening of the Museum of Hatting, Stockport. My work attracts female and male buyers with a twinkle in their eye, aged from nought to ninety-five! Prices range from: Children's hats £12-£22, adult hats £25-£85 (some hats are available here at sale price £10-£30), coats £350+, cushions £59, wall pieces £850+. Visitors always welcome.

Directions: *350 metres north of Loddiswell on South Brent road - signed just after Loddiswell Butts Industrial Estate on left.*

Opening hours: *any day but by prior appointment only.*

STOCK IN TRADE, 20 Market Street, Hatherleigh, Devon EX20 3JP

Est. 1995
Tel +44 (0)1837-810624
Fax +44 (0)1837-810823
www.stockintrade.co.uk
Parking available
Partial wheelchair access
Credit cards

Stock in Trade produces hand dyed and printed cotton fabrics suitable for the home. A colourful range of **cushions, tablecloths, lampshades etc.** and clothes are available in the showroom. This fabric may be purchased by the metre, Blinds, curtains, duvet covers etc. can be made to order. Mail order available.
Directions: *In the centre of Hatherleigh, which is situated on the A386 7 miles north of Okehampton.*
Opening hours: *10am-5pm, Mon-Sat.*

YULI SOMME, 8 Meldon Road, Chagford, Devon TQ13 8BG

Est. 1990
Tel: +44 (0)1647-433148
Parking available

I use local fleece to mould seamless one-off garments such as **coats inspired by Kurdish Kepeneks** (shepherds' coats). The felt is fine, warm, durable and wearable in addition to being truly unique pieces of art incorporating textural effects of other materials. Also wild animal portraits, rugs and wallhangings. Mail order available.
Directions: *given when making an appointment.*
Opening hours: *by appointment only.*

DAVID PLAGERSON, 28 Bridgetown, Totnes, Devon TQ9 5AD

Est. 1977
Tel: +44 (0)1803-866786
Parking fairly close.

For 24 years I have been making a range of **Noah's arks and animals** for children's play. They can be in natural wood or painted. If painted, customers can choose from over 100 pairs of animals and various Ark decorations. Commissions a speciality. Also farm, circus, nativity and chess sets. Mail order available.

Directions: *will be given once appointment is arranged.*
Opening hours: *by appointment only.*

Toys & Games

HOUSE OF MARBLES, The Old Pottery, Pottery Road, Bovey Tracey, Newton Abbot, Devon TQ13 9DS

Est. 1982
Tel: +44 (0)1626-835358
Fax: +44 (0)1626-835315
Parking available
Wheelchair access (partial)
Credit cards

A working **glass, toys and games** factory set in an historic pottery with listed kilns. You can watch glass-blowing when work is in progress. Three fascinating marble runs plus museums explaining history of Bovey potteries, glass board games and glass marbles. Café and restaurant. Factory seconds and gift shop. Mail order available.

Directions: *from A38 take road to Moretonhampstead signed at roundabout. Turn left at next small roundabout.*
Opening hours: *Mon-Sat 10am-5pm & Sun 10am-3pm Easter to end Sept.*

Woodturning & Furniture

CARL HAHN, Ham Farm, Loddiswell, Kingsbridge, Devon TQ7 4RX

Est. 1993
Tel +44 (0)1548-550861
Fax +44 (0)1548-550861
Parking available
Wheelchair access
Credit cards

I am a Crafts Council selected maker and member of the Devon Guild of Craftsmen, working mostly in wood on **furniture and sculpture inspired by nature**. Practical, decorative and built to last, new and signature pieces are exhibited and sold internationally. Visitors are welcome and will find prices for work on display here ranging from £90 to £11,000. Recent years include Chelsea Crafts Fair, 'Decadence' - views from the edge of the century (a millennial Crafts Council touring exhibition), three Sotheby's contemporary decorative arts selling exhibitions in London and New York and 'Fuzzy Logic' with Peet Leather at Oxo in London.

Directions: *signed 360 yards on right heading north on South Brent road from Loddiswell, past Reads Farm and before Reveton.*
Opening hours: *any time, any day but by prior appointment only.*

Dorset is famous for extensive quarrying of Purbeck marble, and Portland stone made fashionable by Christopher Wren. Cloth-covered button-making was a cottage industry in the second half of the nineteenth century in east Dorset, as a means of supplementing low agricultural wages.

Gloucestershire is famous for traditional cheeses. These days, there is a high number of makers of all sorts there producing quality hand-crafted work.

Willow weaving skills used today in the Somerset Levels go back to the Bronze Age.

Wiltshire was so wealthy from the wool trade that the wool merchants of Salisbury could afford the finest masons to build their Cathedral. Wicker hurdle-making for fencing is another, and a less durable, craft associated with the county, as are pottery and thatching.

Craft Centres

BARLEY WOOD WALLED GARDEN, Long Lane, Wrington, N Somerset BS40 5SA

Est. 1999
Tel: +44 (0)1934-863713
www.walledgarden.co.uk
Parking available
Wheelchair access
Credit cards

Barley Wood Walled Garden covers three acres and consists of a restored Victorian kitchen garden with tearoom, restaurant and craft shop. In another part of the garden is a converted barn housing six separate craft workshops whose products include copper fountains, garden ornaments and textiles. Opening times for workshops are by appointment.

Directions: *from Bristol on the A38 (Taunton direction) having passed Bristol Airport on right. Take next right to Wrington and Yatton. Walled Garden about 1 mile on left.*
Opening hours: *Mon-Sun 9.30am-5pm (shop, restaurant, tearoom and garden).*

BLACK SWAN ARTS, 2 Bridge Street, Frome, Somerset, BA11 1BB

Est. 1986
Tel: +44 (0)1373-473980
Fax: +44 (0)1373-451733
Parking available
Wheelchair access

A leading centre for promoting two and three-dimensional arts and crafts in a large exhibition gallery. There are also craftmakers' workshops on site where you can buy directly from the artist. Also a craft shop selling collectible pieces: decorative and functional ceramics, hand painted silks and limited edition prints. Wholefood café.

Directions: *follow the A36 into Frome, head for town centre. We are close to the library and adjacent to the main car park.*
Opening hours: *Mon-Sat 10am-5pm.* **2**

THE FOREST OF DEAN CRAFT WORKERS ASSOCIATION LTD, the Dean Heritage Centre, Soudley (Cinderford), Gloucestershire GL14 7UG

Est. 1989
Tel: +44 (0)1594-822170
Parking available
Wheelchair access
Credit cards

We are a cooperative of local craftworkers who offer our own locally made craftwork only. There are usually demonstrations of our various crafts. These include pyrography, jewellery, cross-stitch, pegloom weaving, painting, applied art and needlework. Situated in the Royal Forest of Dean, there is also a museum and café.

Directions: *follow the brown signs for the Dean Heritage centre from Blakeney, Cinderford or Littledean.*
Opening hours: *Nov-Mar 11am-4pm, Apr-Oct Mon-Sun 10am-6pm.*

HARTS BARN CRAFT CENTRE, Harts Barn, Monmouth Road, Longhope, **Gloucestershire GL17 0QD**

Est. 1996
Tel: +44 (0)1452-830954
www.fweb.org.uk/hartsbarn
Parking for 100 cars
Wheelchair access
Credit cards

Harts Barn is situated at the gateway to the Forest of Dean. The Norman hunting lodge, dated to 1068, and adjacent buildings form the site of the Centre, which offers hand made gifts, furniture, jewellery, picture framing, bridal wear, glassware and more. Coffee shop. Lake and picnic area. Mail order some makers.

Directions: *just off the A4136 between Longhope and Mitcheldean. Ross-on-Wye is 15 minutes; Cheltenham and Cirencester 20 minutes. Follow the brown signs.*

Opening hours: Tues-Sun 10am-5pm.

MILLHAMS STREET CRAFT STUDIOS AND SHOP, Millhams Street Craft Studio, Millhams Street,

Christchurch, Dorset
Est. 1970s
Tel/fax: +44 (0)1202-396788
Parking available

Arts and crafts centre for quality goods, housed in an 18th century coach house and hayloft. Founded as a platform for local artists and craftspeople to display and demonstrate their work, there are now some 40 craftworkers and artists (professional and hobbyists) who contribute to the show.

Directions: *turn off Christchurch High Street into Millhams Street. Immediately after the right-hand bend you will find the entrance to the shop and the Secret Gardens.*

Open: *Mon-Sat 10am-4.30pm in winter; Mon-Sat 10am-5pm in summer.*

STUDIO 21, Market Street, Nailsworth, Near Stroud, Gloucester GL6 OBX

Est. 2000
Tel: +44 (0)7961-914957
Parking available
Wheelchair access

Studio 21 is a workspace for three artists producing jewellery/metalwork, etchings and plasterwork, combined with a shop/gallery displaying their work alongside a variety of affordable work from other local artists. The Studio also has a database of artists should you not be able to find what you want on display.

Directions: *from Stroud on A46, over mini-roundabout, first turning right into Market Street. Studio on left. From Bath: A46 turn left at the Cross Pub.*

Opening hours: *Tues-Sat 10am-5.30pm; Sun 11am-4pm, Mon 2pm/5.30pm.*

Craft Shops

MADE IN STROUD SHOP, 16 Kendrick Street, Stroud, Gloucestershire GL5 1AA

Est. 2000
Tel: +44 (0)1453-758060
www.madeinstroud.org
Parking available

Stroud is very well-known for its artists and craftspeople and we stock as much of their work as possible. We have cards, books, CDs, soaps, toys, candles, pottery, woodturning, dolls' houses, felt, weaving, silks, cotton cloths and many more examples of the fine tradition of craft making in Stroud. Prices 50p-£300.

Directions: *we are in the centre of town next to the Subscription Rooms which house the tourist information centre.*

Opening hours: *Tues-Sat 10am-5pm.* ⑦

NATURE'S BOUNTY, 4 Church Walk, Trowbridge, Wiltshire BA14 8DX

Est. 1996
Tel: +44 (0)1225-719119
www.jacksonmakers.com
Parking available
Wheelchair access
Credit cards

Nature's Bounty is a maker-run shop and tapestry workshop housed in a Grade II listed townhouse. The tapestry workshop specialises in work inspired by, or incorporating natural materials. Textiles from the resident three makers are shown alongside contemporary work from guest artists and makers. Mail order not usual but possible by arrangement

Directions: *in the town centre, just off main shopping area of Fore Street, adjacent to St. James's church.*

Opening hours: *Tues-Sat 9am-5pm.* ⑧

Galleries

THE BLUESTONE GALLERY, 8 Old Stone Yard, Devizes, Wiltshire SN10 1AT

Est. 2000
Tel +44 (0)1380-729589
Fax +44 (0)1672-539202
www.avebury-arts.co.uk
Parking available nearby
Credit cards
W/chair access difficult (two steps) but not impossible.

The Bluestone Gallery aims to give expression to Britain's wonderful crafts; Work by over 100 makers is constantly on display and there are regular exhibitions. There is a superb collection of designer jewellery; ceramics range from classic salt-glaze through delicate porcelain to domestic ware; plus glass, wood and original paintings and prints.

Directions: *Follow signs to town centre. Central car park behind Tesco is next to Old Swan Yard; alternatively, we are two minutes walk from the marketplace.*

Opening hours: *10am-5pm Mon-Fri, 9.30-5.30 Sat.*

DANSEL GALLERY, Rodden Row, Abbotsbury, Weymouth, Dorset DT3 4JL

Est. 1979
Tel +44 (0)1305-871515
Fax +44 (0)1305-871518
www.danselgallery.co.uk
Good parking
Credit cards

Dansel Gallery displays the cream of contemporary craftwork in wood; more than 200 British woodworkers are represented, probably the largest concentration of its kind in the country. The impressive range runs from individually designed pieces of furniture through elegant jewellery boxes to toys, puzzles and three-dimensional jigsaws to one-off decorative pieces.

Directions: *entrance and car park on main road in Abbotsbury which is on the B3157 coast road between Weymouth and Bridport.*

Opening hours: *10am-5pm seven days a week; longer during the summer.*

FISHERTON MILL, 108 Fisherton Street, Salisbury, Wiltshire SP2 7QY

Est. 1995
Tel/fax +44 (0)1722-415121
www.fisherton.mill.com
Credit cards

The South's largest independent gallery, situated close to the heart of medieval Salisbury in a converted grain mill on three floors and showing all aspects of contemporary art and crafts design. The ground floor lifestyle shop offers an array of functional and decorative accessories. The first floor houses a selection of fine contemporary British furniture against a backdrop of painting and sculpture. The Beams and White Galleries on the first and second floors respectively are used for themed exhibitions which occur on a 6 to 8 week basis. The café serves a selection of lunches and light refreshments.

Directions: *please phone.*

Opening hours: *9.30am-5.30pm Tues-Sat.*

GLOUCESTERSHIRE GUILD OF CRAFTSMEN, Gloucestershire Guild Gallery, Painswick Centre, Bisley Street, Painswick, Gloucestershire GL6 6QQ

Est. 1933
Tel: +44 (0)1452-814745
Village carpark just off A46
Wheelchair access
Credit cards

The Gloucestershire Guild of Craftsman Gallery was opened in 2001 although the Guild itself goes back 68 years. The majority of members' work can be seen and bought in the gallery including: ceramics, woodturning, jewellery, printed, woven, knitted and felted textiles, printmaking, furniture, cards and more. Mail order possible.

Directions: *Painswick is 10 miles south of Cheltenham on the A46 (Bath road).*

Opening hours: *Tues-Sat, 10am-4pm.*

THE GUILD GALLERY, 68 Park Street, Bristol BS1 5JY

Est. 1984
Tel +44 (0)117-926 5548
Fax +44 (0)117-925 5659
Two multi-storey car parks nearby.
No wheelchair access
Credit cards: in shop only

Situated on the second floor of the prestigious Bristol Guild of Applied Art, the Guild Gallery was established in 1984 and is rented and stewarded by the exhibiting artists. There are monthly exhibitions by mainly, but not exclusively, West Country artists and craftspeople. 10% commission is charged on sales.

Directions: *5 minutes walk from the city centre; look for the University Tower.*
Opening hours: *9.30am-5pm Mon-Sat, except bank holidays.*

IMAGES GALLERY, 38 Market Street, Wells, Somerset BA5 2DS

Est. 1997
Tel +44 (0)1749-672959
Parking available nearby
Wheelchair access

Images Gallery was opened by Caroline Bagias to promote monochrome photography. Caroline's work, and sometimes that of other mono enthusiasts, is on permanent display. Prints can be viewed and purchased. A mail order service has recently been introduced whereby customers may select the image of choice from a high-class brochure (details on request).

Directions: *park in Tesco or Princes Road car park in Wells, enter Market Street from the latter. Courtyard on right hand side before reaching Queen Street.*
Opening hours: *11am-3pm Weds and Fri, Sat 11am-1pm.*

MAKERS, 6 Bath Place, Taunton, Somerset TA1 4ER

Est. 1984
Tel +44 (0)1823-251121
Easily accessible parking
Partial wheelchair access
Credit cards

Makers is a successful co-operative which has gained a reputation for exhibiting one of the West Country's finest selections of quality contemporary crafts. Work for sale includes furniture, woodturning, paintings and prints, pottery, hand-painted silks and velvets, knitwear, baskets and jewellery. Also regular exhibitions of the work of guest makers.

Directions: *standing in the High Street facing Boots the Chemist you will find Bath Place, a narrow covered walkway several yards to the right.*
Opening hours: *9am-5pm, Mon-Sat.*

WESSEX FINE ART AND CERAMICS, 13b North Street, Wareham, Dorset BH20 4AB

Est. 2000
Tel: +44 (0)1929-555331
Parking available
Limited wheelchair access
Credit cards

We specialise in ceramics from both new and established makers with an emphasis on Dorset potters. Prices range from £5 for mugs to £200 for some bowls. We sell paintings and prints which range in price from £20 to £500. We also display and sell glass, wood and jewellery. Mail order available.

Directions: *on entering Wareham from the north we are situated on the right of the Main Street.*
Opening hours: *Mon-Sat 9.30am-5.30pm.*

Baskets & Wickerwork

ROY YOUDALE BASKETMAKER, 6 Highbury Road, Horfield, Bristol, BS7 OBZ

Est. 1994
Tel: +44 (0)117-9511421
Parking available

Roy makes a wide range of **willow baskets and plant supports**. Most of his work is commissioned and he specialises in using natural willow bark colours and growing over thirty varieties of willow himself. For aspiring basketmakers, he runs day courses in the spring and autumn. Mail order available.

Directions: *just off Gloucester road, opposite Horfield Common. Please telephone for more detailed directions.*
Opening hours: *Mon, Tues, Fri. Appointment necessary.*

SALLY GOYMER BASKETMAKER, 37 Mendip Road, Cheltenham, Gloucestershire GL52 5EB

Est. 1979
Tel: +44 (0)1242-510724
www.sallygoymer.fsnet.co.uk
Street parking

Having initially trained in England, I am now the only basketmaker in the UK to have attended the Ecole de Vannerie, a school for professional basketmakers in France. My work is characterised by its neatness and attention to detail. I make **all types of baskets** and willingly undertake commissions. Mail order available.

Directions: *north side of Cheltenham, 1 mile from Racecourse. Detailed direction given when appointment made.*

Opening hours: *10am-5pm by appointment only.*

SOMERSET LEVELS BASKETS & CRAFT CENTRE LIMITED, Lying Road, Burrowbridge, near Bridgewater, Somerset TA7 0SG

Est. 1991
Tel/fax: +44 (0)1823-698688
www.somersetlevels.co.uk
Parking available
Wheelchair access
Credit cards

This is an exciting and unique countryside store offering a range of **basketware and willow withies** for gardeners. All baskets are made in the workshop with willow grown by the makers. Friendly service and good value for money, the centre also has a range of seconds. There is a saleroom on site.

Directions: *on the A361 between Taunton and Glastonbury, a quarter of a mile from Burrowbridge.*

Opening hours: *9am-5.30pm, not Tuesdays and Sundays.*

Food & Drink

AVALON VINEYARD, The Drove, East Pennard, Shepton Mallet, Somerset BA4 6HA

Est. 1984
Tel: +44 (0)1749-860393
www.pennardorganicwines.co.uk
Parking available
Wheelchair access

Small, family-run organic vineyard and fruit grower. Pick-your-own organic raspberries are ready in the autumn. These and other fruits are used to make fruit wines. Organic mead and traditional scrumpy cider also brewed. Farm shop and self-guided tour leaflet available - admission free. Sales from farm shop and by mail order.

Directions: *take A37. 5m south of Shepton Mallet, turn west at foot of steep hill opposite Queen's Arms at Wraxall. After 1.5m (before village), look for sign on right.*

Opening hours: *10am-6pm Easter to Christmas, by appointment at other times.*

BERROW BREWERY, Coast Road, Berrow, Burnham-on-Sea, Somerset TA8 2QU

Est. 1982
Tel: +44 (0)1278-751345
Parking available
Wheelchair access

Brewers of a range of real ales; from two to five different types depending on the time of year. There is an off-licence at the brewery which is in an outbuilding of a former farmhouse. The price of the ales ranges from £1 per pint to £1.25 per pint.

Directions: *on the coast road between Burnham-on-Sea and Brean. Quarter of a mile north of Berrow church.*

Opening hours: *9am-9pm seven days a week.*

21

HECKS FARMHOUSE CIDER, 9-11, Middle Leigh, Street, Somerset BA16 0LB

Est. 1897
Tel: +44 (0)1458-442367
www.regionalwebs.com/hecks
Parking available
Wheelchair access

The Hecks family have been making cider and apple juice for six generations since 1840. The cider is made from blending juice from apples grown in our own orchards. The cider is fermented in wooden barrels and sold draught from the wood in the traditional but increasingly disused way.

Directions: *follow the Cider Farm signs from the High Street.*

Opening hours: *Vary - telephone for exact times.*

22

MOORLYNCH VINEYARD, Moorlinch, Bridgewater, Somerset TA7 9DD

Est. 1991
Tel: +44 (0)1458-210393
Parking available
Wheelchair access
Credit cards

The vineyard, at a picturesque country site, has produced award winning wines for 15 years. Owner-winemaker Peter Farmer produces the popular blends Somerset (dry), Sedgemoor (medium dry) and Polden Hills (medium). Group wine tours, tastings and meals are available. There are also exhibitions and demonstrations of other crafts.

Directions: *the vineyard is signposted off the A39 between Glastonbury and Bridgewater and the A361 between Taunton and Glastonbury. Both are near junction 23 of the M5.*

Opening hours: *May-Sept Tues-Sat 10.30am-5pm and bank holidays. Appointment necessary outside of these times.*   `23`

OATLEY VINEYARD, Cannington, Bridgwater, Somerset TA5 2NL

Est. 1986
Tel/fax: +44 (0)1278-671340
www.oatleyvineyard.co.uk
Parking available

Iain and Jane Awty are the proprietors of the small (2.5 acre) Oatley Vineyard which makes award-winning white wines. Their wines regularly gain international and national awards. All have 'character' and are clean and unadulterated and suitable for vegans and vegetarians. Most are dry. Mail order available. Open days and visitors by appointment.

Directions: *one mile west of Cannington, three-quarters of a mile north from A39.*

Opening hours: *variable. Please telephone first.*   `24`

ST ANNE'S VINEYARD, Oxenhall, Newent, Gloucestershire GL18 IRL

Est. 1984
Tel: +44 (0)1989-720313
Fax: +44 (0)1242-227546
Parking available
Wheelchair access to shop

Small family-run vineyard in a beautiful setting. The vines were planted in 1979 and the first commercial vintage was 1984. Over 100 varieties of grape are grown; many experimentally. English wines and a distinctive range of country fruit wines (tayberry, orange/apricot etc) are all made at the vineyard. Shop. Mail order available.

Directions: *two miles north of Newent on the Kempley Road off the B4215.*

Opening hours: *mid Mar to mid Oct, Wed-Fri 2pm/6pm. Sat and bank holidays 11am/6pm. mid Oct to mid Mar Sat & Sun 11am/5pm.*   `25`

General Gifts

JENNIFER DAVIDSON, Workshop No.2, Barley Wood Walled Garden, Long Lane, Wrington, North Somerset

BS40 5SA
Est. 2000
Tel: +44 (0)1934-862366
www.artgardengallery.com
Parking available
Wheelchair access
Credit cards

Prints and cards reproduced from Jennifer's colourful landscape paintings - all on view in her studio workshop. She also makes hand-dyed and painted silk chiffon and velvet scarves and bead jewellery. An expert stencil artist, Jennifer is happy to accept commissions for anything from a cushion cover to whole rooms.

Directions: *from Bristol on the A38 (Taunton Direction) having passed Bristol Airport on right. Take next right to Wrington and Yatton. Walled Garden about 1 mile on left.*

Opening hours: *Tues-Thurs 11:30am-4:30pm, Most Sat-Sun 12pm-4:30pm. Prior appointment preferable esp. for other times.* **26**

Glass

BRISTOL BLUE GLASS LTD, 5 Three Queens Lane, Redcliffe, Bristol BS1 6LG

Est. 1990
Tel: +44 (0)117-9298900
Fax: +44 (0)117-9298995
www.bristol-glass.co.uk
Parking available
Wheelchair access
Credit cards

Bristol Blue Glass has been synonymous with Bristol for over 400 years. Today, our team of skilled glassmakers use the same authentic tools and techniques to produce the distinctive and highly original **freeblown lead crystal glass**. Colours are primarily Bristol Blue and ruby. Each piece bears the trademark insignia 'Bristol'.

Directions: *follow signs to St. Mary Redcliffe Church. Directly in front of the church take Redcliffe Street off the roundabout. Take the first right to 5 Three Queens Lane*

Opening hours: *Mon-Fri 9am-5pm.*

CHRISTCHURCH STAINED GLASS, 9 Donnington Drive, Christchurch, Dorset BH23 4SZ

Est. 1998
Tel: +44 (0)1425-275173
Parking available

Work is carried out by Martin Young at Millhams Craft Centre and displayed in the adjoining crafts shop. Martin is a stained glass artist specialising in **traditional kiln-fired painting on glass** and employing both period and contemporary design. Domestic and public commissions have been fulfilled for customers worldwide. Private tuition is available.

Directions: *halfway along the Christchurch High St, turn down Millhams Street. The Craft Centre is 200 yards on the right, opposite the church.*

Opening hours: *10am-4pm.*

EXMOOR GLASS LTD, Harbour Studios, Porlock Weir, Somerset TA24 8PD

Est. 1994
Tel: +44 (0)1643-863141
www.exmoorglass.co.uk
Parking available
Credit cards

Exmoor Glass produce **freeblown glassware** ranging from elegant tableware to stunning contemporary artwork. The glass studio is best known for its reproduction Cranberry work. The glassmakers can be seen at work doing a job virtually unchanged in style since Roman times. Also available are glass lamps and mirrors. Mail order available.

Directions: *follow the A39 from Minehead to Porlock village. Go through Porlock and follow the signs to Porlock Weir.*

Opening hours: *gallery 10am-5pm daily, workshop 8am-5.30pm Mon-Fri.*

MIKE ROWE DOT GLASS FUSING, Templar Road, Yate, Near Bristol BS37 5TF

Est. 2001
Tel/fax: +44 (0)1454-880892
Parking available
Wheelchair access

Producer of fused glass items: **tiles, bowls, tableware, vases, table tops, decorative giftware,** as well as fused glass for architectural purposes including door panels, shower screens and public art works. Most work is made to order. Also regular lessons for those interested in fusing glass as a hobby or business. Mail order available.

Directions: *will be given when appointment is made.*

Opening hours: *Mon-Fri 9am-5pm.*

OUT OF THE BLUE, 5 St Mary's Gardens, Hilperton, Trowbridge, Wiltshire BA14 7PG

Est. 1995
Tel: +44 (0)1225-760136
Parking available
Credit cards

Marie Curtis **paints windows, screens and a range of glass vessels** using vitrail enamel to catch light and reflect colour. Window art includes free standing triptychs and greetings cards. Commissions undertaken for individually designed windows. Also, glass and gemstone jewellery and wirework sculpture. Mail order available for jewellery and wirework only.

Directions: *on A361 Devizes to Trowbridge road. Follow signs for Bradford-on-Avon; turn left into Horse Road and right into St. Mary's Gardens.*

Opening hours: *by appointment only.*

PETER J BERRY ARCHITECTURAL STAINED GLASS, The Old Dairy, Swerves Farm, Ratford, Calne, Wiltshire SN11 9JX

Est. 1990
Tel: +44 (0)1249 817489,
+44 (0)7899 661022
www.bsmgp.org.uk
Parking available

Peter Berry established a studio after studying architectural stained glass at Swansea College of Art where he won a national competition for designing a window for Chichester Cathedral. Peter specialises in stained glass windows for homes and churches but produces **stained glass, panels, mirrors and lamps** to order.

Directions: *from the A4 leaving Calne and travelling towards Chippenham, take the right turn to Ratford and Bremhill. Swerves Farm half a mile on left.*

Opening hours: *9.30am-5.30pm. Prior appointment necessary.*

STARLIGHT STUDIO/ ROD FRIEND, Dove Cottage, 40 Summer Street, Stroud, Gloucestershire GL5 1NY

Est. 1972
Tel/fax: +44 (0)1453-750919
Some parking

Rod Friend is a well established British glass artist working near Stroud in Gloucestershire. Rod has a deep commitment to the making of traditional and contemporary **stained glass and glass paintings** for private and public buildings as well as therapeutic environments. Rod also runs regular hands-on practical courses.

Directions: *take A46 north from Stroud. Turn left onto A4173. Pass Edge Church on left. Bear right onto Sevenleaze Lane. Take first left track after the Holcombe sign.*

Opening hours: *appointment essential.*

STUDIO ART GLASS BY CHRIS ROUSE, Moorlynch Vineyard, Moorlinch, Bridgwater, Somerset TA7 9DD

Est 1993
Tel: +44 (0)1458-210546
Parking available
Credit cards

Chris Rouse produces freely blown and hand finished studio art glass, specialising in **perfume bottles, vases, plates, goblets and paperweights.** Each unique piece is designed to be both decorative and functional. Many of them incorporate precious metals. Commissions are welcome. Please telephone for details or visit to view this fascinating craft.

Directions: *in Moorlinch village, follow the Moorlynch Vineyard signs from the A39 or A361.*

Opening hours: Tues-Sat 10.30am-5pm. Sun 11am-4pm.

Jewellery

ALASTAIR GILL, 4 Christmas Steps, Bristol BS1 5BS

Est. 1988
Tel: +44 (0)117-9221204
www.FineRingsAndThings.co.uk
Parking available
Credit cards

Alistair Gill designs and makes **contemporary jewellery in silver, gold and platinum.** He also makes loveboxes, spoons and chopsticks. His background in architecture inevitably informs his designs which are an explanation of form, space and texture. Items are for sale and available for purchase by mail order. Commissions are also undertaken.

Directions: *from the city centre walk into the bottom of Christmas Steps. From Colston Street walk in at the top end. Moving workshop so e-mail alastair.gill@virgin.net, or check website first.*

Opening hours: *Fri and Sat 11am-6pm.*

CATHERINE TUTT, 88a Walcot Street (ground floor workshops), Old Orchard, Bath, Avon BA1 5BD

Est. 1998
Tel: +44 (0)775-4243629
Parking available

Designer and maker of all types of **jewellery in contemporary, personal style.** Most pieces are made from silver with gold details; gems and more expensive work are made to commission. Graduated in 1997 with a 2:1 BA(HONS) in design jewellery and metalwork. Can be seen working on pieces at workshop. Prices £20+.

Directions: *going south down the main London Road, turn left into Walcot St. No 88a is 200 yards along.*

Opening hours: *Tues, Thurs and Fri 9am-5pm. Prior appointment recommended.* 36

THE GREEN BUS GALLERY, Quest Cottage, Cathole Lane, Yawl, Lyme Regis, Dorset DT7 3XD

Est. 1995
Tel: +44 (0)1297-443048
Parking available
Credit cards

We make individually hand crafted **silver jewellery** using semi-precious stones including lapis, amethyst, turquoise, garnet and rose quartz. Drawing on nature for inspiration, designs are contemporary and ethnic, emphasising a simplicity of form. The gallery is housed in an old green bus next to the designer and maker's home.

Directions: *out of Lyme Regis drive through UpLyme. On reaching Yawl turn left into Cathole Lane. The Green Bus Gallery is on the right.*

Opening hours: *by appointment only.*

JADE WORKSHOP, New Road, Blakeney, Gloucestershire GL15 4DE

Est: 1999
Tel: +44 (0)1594 - 510519
    +44 (0)1594 - 510128
Own car park

JADE WORKSHOP

Jade Workshop was founded in 1999 by John and Dee Palin to produce original, **exclusive gold and silver jewellery** by Dee, and **oil paintings and prints** by John. Each piece is unique, and all the jewellery is hallmarked. Classes and courses are run in the daytime and evenings. Visitors, by appointment only, are welcome to watch John and Dee at work, and view the original art and craft work for sale. There is always time to enjoy a cup of coffee or tea with visitors! Postcards of their work are available and commissions are undertaken.

Directions: *off the A48 Gloucester/Chepstow road, signposted scenic route to Parkend.*

Opening hours: *visits by appointment only - no obligation to buy.*

LOUISE PARRY, Workshop 12, Brewery Arts, Brewery Court, Cirencester, GLoucestershire GL7 2RL

Est 1987
Tel: +44 (0)1285-657501
Fax: +44 (0)1285-657588
Parking available

Louise Parry has 15 years' experience of jewellery making. She designs and makes **contemporary silver, gold and base metal jewellery** on the premises with many pieces set with precious and semi-precious stones. Much of Louise's time is spent on private commissions. Unusual wedding and engagement rings are a speciality.

Directions: *Brewery Arts is in the centre of Cirencester.*

Opening hours: *Mon and Thurs, Fri, Sat 9am-5pm.*

THE SILVERWORKSHOP, Bow Street, Langport, Somerset TA10 9PQ

Est. 1976
Tel/fax: +44 (0)1458-251122
Parking available
Credit cards

We make **small silver and gold articles**; spoons boxes and jewellery. Pippa takes her inspiration from the fauna and flora of Somerset. Bernard produces *champlevé* and *cloisonné* enamelled jewellery, inspired by space form and colour. Commissions are regularly undertaken and buyers dicuss their precise requirements with the makers.

Directions: *Bow Street is the main street in Langport. We are on the left, facing towards Taunton on a lay-by.*

Opening hours: *Mon-Fri 9.30am-5pm, Sat 9.30am-4pm.*

TAMARA EMM, The Walled Garden, Long Lane, Wrington, N Somerset BS40 5SA

Est. 1996
Tel: +44 (0)1934-861000
Parking available
Wheelchair access
Credit cards

Tamara is a qualified jeweller working in the unusual mixture of silver and copper. Her designs are inspired by organic forms. Tamara's range of work varies from **toe-rings to tiaras,** which can be specially commissioned for weddings or other occasions to match or complement the design of your outfit. Mail order available.

Directions: *from Bristol A38, pass airport on right. The Walled Garden is signed shortly after to the right. Pass through Redhill until you see the imposing wall of the Walled Garden.*

Opening hours: *advisable to telephone in advance.* 41

Metalwork & Silversmithing

HARTS SILVERSMITHS, The Guild, Sheep Street, Chipping Campden, Gloucestershire GL55 6AG

Est.1908
Tel/fax: +44 (0)1386-841100
www.hartsilversmiths.co.uk
Parking available

We are a team of craftsmen specialising in the best traditions of **hand made silver.** This is the only surviving workshop of the C. R. Ashbee Guild of Handicraft which came to Campden in 1902. Most of our work is on a commission basis and primarily in silver. Visitors are always welcome to see us at work.

Directions: *we are just off the High Street.*
Opening hours: *Mon-Sat 9am-6pm.*

42

STRAWBERRY STEEL, Tickenham Forge, Clevedon, Somerset BS21 6SF

Est. 1994
Tel: +44 (0)1275-854004
www.strawberrysteel.com
Parking available
Wheelchair access

Colin Comrie's individual and distinctive style has earned him recognition all over England as well as the USA. His traditional **hand forged blacksmithing** techniques are used to produce uniquely designed beds, curtain poles, artistic railings, gates, sculptures and other *objets d'art.* Colin's work is displayed in galleries in Bristol and Salcombe.

Directions: *junction 20 off the M5 and then follow signs for Nailsea. Strawberry Steel is three miles along the B3130 next to the Rabbit Hutch centre.*
Opening hours: *Tues-Sat 10am-5.30pm.*

43

Musical Instruments

CHRISTOPHER BARLOW EARLY KEYBOARDS, 16 Landsdown Place, Frome, Somerset BA11 3HP

Est. 1978
Tel: +44 (0)1373-461430
www.barlowharps.demon.co.uk
Some parking available
Limited wheelchair access

Christopher is a **harpsichord and piano** maker. His instruments, renowned for their fine tone and appearance have featured in South Bank concerts and abroad. They include Viennese Fortepianos after Schantz (1795), Graf and others. The harpsichord range includes the late English models with full marquetry decoration. Commissions welcome.

Directions: *given when appointment is made.*
Opening hours: *please make an appointment.*

44

Pottery & Ceramics

BAYTREE GARDEN POTTERY, Baytree Cottage, 71 Brent Street, Brent Knoll, Somerset TA9 4DX

Est. 1990
Tel: +44 (0)1278-760768
Parking available
Wheelchair access difficult
Credit cards

Stuart and Anne Weichert make high quality, **handthrown, terracotta garden pots.** They use unique decoration techniques and offer a range of designs. They specialise in pots personalised for weddings, anniversaries, etc. A wide range of partially glazed, striped garden pots is also produced, adding a contemporary twist to this traditional craft.

Directions: *from junction 22 of M5 take A38 northbound. Then first left into Brent Street, Brent Knoll. About half a mile along Brent Street on the left is No. 71.*

Open: *10am-5pm in summer, 10am-4pm in winter (prior appointment advisable).*

BLACK DOG OF WELLS, Tor Street, Wells, Somerset BA5 2US

Est. 1984
Tel: +44 (0)1749-672548
www.blackdogofwells.com
Parking available
Credit cards

We design and make richly detailed **decorative relief tiles in natural terracotta.** The designs are often based on historical sources. We began our business making ceramic murals on a large scale and still accept commissions for these from public and private clients, Our work is frostproof and can go outside. Mail order available.

Directions: *we are on the east side and immediately behind Wells Cathedral.*

Opening hours: *most weekdays 9am-5pm, some evenings and some weekends.*

BREDON POTTERY, High Street, Bredon, Tewkesbury GL20 7LW

Est. 1994
Tel: +44 (0)1684-773417
Parking available
Wheelchair access
Credit cards

We make a range of **decorated earthenware pottery** for use in the house, kitchen, conservatory or garden. The kitchenware is in two styles; blue and white which has a fresh lively look, and traditional slipware in rich reds, browns, yellow and black. Wide range of planters also available. Mail order available.

Directions: *in the centre of Bredon follow the brown signs to the pottery. It is on the B2079 Tewkesbury to Evesham road next to the Royal Oak pub.*

Opening hours: *Tues-Sat 10am-6pm.*

CERAMIC CREATIONS, 7 Nursery View, Siddington, Cirencester, Gloucestershire

Est. 1997
Tel/fax: +44 (0)1285 651314
Parking available
Wheelchair access

Julie Sutton makes **ceramic wallhangings, birds and dishes.** The subjects range from buildings to pond and sea-shore life and are individually modelled in low relief, kiln fired and then painted with acrylic paints. Also commissions taken from customers who want a particular house made as a relief panel. Mail order available.

Directions: *from Cirencester follow signs to Siddington (2 miles). Take the last road on the right at the end of the village. Just past the Greyhound Pub.*

Opening hours: *Mon-Fri 10am-4pm. Prior appointment necessary.*

CETTA DI LIETO, Workshop 3, Brewery Arts, Brewery Court, Cirencester, Gloucestershire GL7 1JH

Est. 1999
Tel: +44 (0)1285-640403
Fax: +44 (0)1285-644060
Parking available
Wheelchair access
Credit cards

Cetta di Lieto makes **press moulded and slabbed forms** using light coloured clay which she then decorates using slips, *engobes* and stains applied in a painterly way. This spontaneous approach to decorative ceramics makes each piece individual. Mail order is available upon request. Please telephone for further details.

Directions: *the workshop is part of Brewery Arts at the centre of Cirencester.*

Opening hours: *usually Mon-Sat 10am-5pm. Telephone to check.*

CHRISTINE-ANN RICHARDS, Chapel House, High Street, Wanstrow, Shepton Mallet, Somerset BA4 4TE

Est. 1975
Tel/fax: +44 (0)1749-850208
www.christineannrichards.co.uk
Limited parking on street

Christine specialises in **thrown porcelain using crackle and monochrome glazes** in a Chinese/Japanese tradition. Also **large exterior works** using buff, terracotta and dark brown high-fired, vitrified earthenware clays, to produce large pots, planters, water features and sculptural ceramics. Exhibitor in prestigious exhibitions e.g.Sotheby's 'Contemporary Decorative Arts 1999' Made to commission. £50-£5,000.

Directions: *from Shepton Mallet A361, then right on to A359 at Nunnoc. Entering Wanstrow turn left at main crossroads. Studio behind Methodist chapel on right.*
Opening hours: *by appointment only.*   **50**

DB POTTERY, Church Street, Merriott, Somerset TA16 5PR

Est. 1986
Tel: +44 (0)1460-75655
Parking available
Wheelchair access

David Brown makes a range of **one-off, high fired pots** exploring subtle variations of colour and texture. David makes vases and bowls but is mainly interested in teapots, producing a wide range of both functional and sculptural versions. He mainly works in turquoise, blue and mauve. Prices range from £5-£350.

Directions: *the pottery is situated half way between church and Scott's nurseries opposite the King's Head pub in Merriott.*
Opening hours: *usually 9am until dusk but unpredictable closures may occur.*   **51**

HAND MADE POTS, 13 Keswick Road, Boscombe, Bournemouth, Dorset BHS 1LP

Est. 1998
Tel/fax: +44 (0)1202 396788
Parking difficult
Wheelchair access possible

Mainly **functional decorative stoneware pottery** thrown on the wheel. The work is decorated using various colours and several glazes for both patterned and pictorial designs. A wide range is available including; mugs, platters, casserole dishes, fruitbowls, large vases and animals and earthenware pumpkins. Tea sets and dinner services are available to order.

Directions: *east of Boscombe's main shoping area, off Christchruch Road, turn down Browning Avenue, then right into Keswick Road.*
Opening hours: *by arrangement.*   **52**

IAN SHEARMAN, Ivy Cottage, Hyde, Chalford, Stroud, Gloucestershire GL6 8NZ

Est. 1997
Tel : +44 (0)1453-882024
Parking available

Ian is a potter and an artist. He makes hand built and thrown **ceramics, raku and stoneware** fired in a wood-fired kiln. His work has a strong oriental influence and he produces one-off individual forms. As a painter he is concerned with grace and formal structure in landscape paintings. Mail order available.

Directions: *A419 Chalford road, up Hyde Hill, right into Knapp Lane. Cottage on right.*
Opening hours: *by appointment only.*   **53**

JONATHAN GARRATT, Hare Lane Pottery, Cranborne, Wimborne, Dorset BH21 5QT

Est. 1978
Tel: +44 (0)1725-517700
www.axisartists.org.uk/all/ref5810.htm
Parking available
Wheelchair access
Credit cards

Jonathan makes unusual **garden planters and tableware in woodfired terracotta** for the discerning gardener. Woodfiring produces a beautiful effect on his pots which take their inspiration from French prehistoric and traditional pots, West Africa and the Far East. Designs change frequently and many are unique to the pottery. Mail order is available.

Directions: *two miles east of Cranbourne towards Alderholt or two miles west of Alderholt near Fordingbridge.*
Opening hours: Mon-Sun 10am-5pm.   **54**

KAREN HARRISON POTTERY, Anstyrose Cottage, Wyke Road, Gillingham, Dorset SP8 4NH

Est. 1989
Tel: +44 (0)1747-825374
Parking available

Karen is a local domestic potter established 12 years; she works in a large garden studio and welcomes visitors. She makes **large dishes and bowls, jugs, mugs, vases** and handled planters. All are in soft misty blues and greens, purples, cream and peach; they are oven and dishwasher proof and quite affordable.

Directions: *take the B3081 out of Gillingham towards Wincanton. It is a detached house on the left at the edge of town near a pub and Talisman Antiques.*
Opening hours: *Mon-Sun 10am-5pm.*

LESLIE GIBBONS - THE OWL POTTERY, 108, High Street, Swanage, Dorset BH19 2NY

Est. 1965
Tel: +44 (0)1929-425850
Parking available
Wheelchair access (2 steps)

I produce highly decorated, hand made and hand-painted **earthenware pottery, hand decorated tiles, small animals** and paintings. Specialising in individual dishes with pictorial motifs and intricate designs in majolica and slip on thrown and moulded pieces. My work is found in private collections in 50 countries. Work sold direct only.

Directions: *from the square go up the High Street, past town hall and Methodist Church. We are on right at top of hill.*

Open: *resident so usually available; also evenings in summer. Closed Sun & Thurs pm.*

MELLORS GARDEN CERAMICS, Rosemead, Marshwood, near Bridport, Dorset DT6 5QB

Est. 1977
Tel/fax: +44 (0)1297-678217
Parking available
Wheelchair access
Credit cards

Kate Mellors makes a range of **ceramic stoneware for the garden and conservatory,** including planters, urns, birdbaths, sundials, water features and Japanese inspired lanterns. The ceramics are hand made using traditional methods and glazed to give a rugged stone-like texture which can range from stony blue to greenish brown.

Directions: *in the centre of the village 100 yards south of the shop on the B3165 Crewkerne to Lyme Regis Road.*

Opening hours: *appointment necessary.*

MICHELLE OHLSON, 7a Brewery Arts, Brewery Court, Cirencester, Gloucestershire GL7 1JH

Est 1978
Tel: +44 (0)1285-643332
Parking available

I produce a wide range of **ceramic clocks, mirrors and lamps.** The pieces are made in earthenware and decorated with landscapes and plant forms. They are richly coloured and highlighted with gold lustre. My work is elaborate whilst remaining functional. I also regularly work to commission. Please telephone for details.

Directions: *Brewery Arts is in the centre of Cirencester.*

Opening hours: *usually Mon-Sat 10am-5pm. Closed Weds and Sun. Phoning ahead advisable.*

MILL POTTERY, Wootton Courtenay, Minehead, Somerset TA2A 8RB

Est 1974
Tel: +44 (0)1643-841297
Parking on premises
Wheelchair access
Credit cards

For more than 25 years Michael Gaitskell has made **stoneware pottery for everyday use** as well as unique pieces with painted designs that have an established reputation. This beautiful site on Exmoor with a working waterwheel and accessible workshop ensures we have many regular buyers. Prices £10-£1000. Special request mail order.

Directions: *follow the brown tourist signs two miles west from Dunster on A396 or two miles west of Minehead on the A39 to Mill Pottery and Wootton Courtenay.*

Opening hours: *Mon-Fri 10am-1pm and 2-5.30pm; Sat 10am-1pm. Appointment necessary for Sunday and Jan-Mar.*

PAUL SULLIVAN, 9B Thorndale Mews, Clifton, Bristol BS8 2HX

Est. 1987
Tel: +44 (0)117-9706847
On-street parking

From his small studio, Paul produces a distinctive range of wheelthrown and handbuilt ceramics, concentrating mainly on **bottle, vase and bowl forms.** Emphasis placed on simplicity of line and subtle variation of colour. While feldspathic glazes are used to ensure functionality, many pieces are left unglazed using clay mixed with other materials.

Directions: *Thorndale Mews is accessed via Thorndale, off Alma Vale Road (BS8).*

Opening hours: *by appointment only.*

POTS FOR ALL SEASONS, Dean Heritage Centre, Campmill Soudley, Cinderford, Gloucestershire GL14 2UB

Est. 1984
Tel: +44 (0)1594-822170
Parking available
Wheelchair access
Credit cards

Victor Hugo runs this small pottery hand throwing almost everything on a potters' wheel. His range includes **frostproof terracotta flowerpots,** plain and decorative terracotta and glazed kitchenware including storage jars for bread, salt herbs and garlic, colourful earthen slipware for domestic use, frostproof bonsai pots, lampbases, housenames and numbers.

Directions: *from Blakeney on the A48. The Dean Heritage Centre is two miles along the BA277 at Soudley.*

Opening hours: *Apr-Oct Mon-Sun 10am/4.30pm, Nov-Mar 11am/3.30pm.*

POTTERS, Unit 19, Clifton Down Shopping Centre, Whiteladies Road, Bristol BS8 2NN

Est. 1996
Tel: +44 (0)117-9737380
www.pottersbristol.com
Parking available in centre
car park
Wheelchair access
Credit cards

We are a marketing cooperative of 50 professional potters producing an enormous range **decorative and functional ceramics** at very competitive prices. Products range from garden pots to sculpture to porcelain jewellery. Our members know and appreciate what they sell. Commissions are undertaken and mail order is available.

Directions: *follow signs for Clifton from the centre of Bristol. At the top of the hill follow the signs for Westbury-on-Trym. This is Whiteladies road which you follow for half a mile. Turn left on Alma Road for entrance to the car park.*

Opening hours: *Mon-Sat 10am-6pm, Nov/Dec Sun 11am-5pm.*   62

RIDGE POTTERY, The Pottery, High Street, Queen Camel, Yeovil, Somerset BA22 7NF

Est. 1977
Tel: +44 (0)1935-850753
www.mud2fire.com
Parking available

Douglas and Jennie Phillips make decorative and useful, thrown, woodfired stoneware with brush and glaze decoration. Pots are individually decorated with bold and rhythmic patterns and glazes are soft grey, sea-blue, warm brown/black and are made from local materials. From **egg-cups to large flower vases**. Also summer pottery courses.

Directions: *one mile south of A303 (Sparkford) on A359.*

Opening hours: *Mon-Sat 9am-6pm.*   63

RUARDEAN GARDEN POTTERY, West End, Ruardean, Forest of Dean, Gloucester GL17 9TP

Tel: +44 (0)1594-543577
Fax: +44 (0)1594-544536
Parking available
Wheelchair access
Credit cards

We make a range of **terracotta flowerpots** using traditional hand throwing and hand pressing techniques. Visit our extensive display including cats, dragons, lizards and large glazed high-fired pots. You will not see pots like these in any garden centre. All are frostproof and available by mail order.

Directions: *the pottery is at the centre of this small village and is signposted by brown signs.*

Opening hours: *Mon-Sat 9am/5.30pm, Apr-Sept Sun 1pm/5pm.*   64

SOMERSET COUNTRYWARE, Smocklands Farmhouse, Drayton, Langport, Somerset TA10 0JS

Est 1980
Tel: +44 (0)1458-251640
On-site parking

Somerset countryware is a range of **slip decorated oxidised stoneware** by Mary Kembery who has been potting in her native county for the last 20 years. Somerset is the inspiration for her designs from the willows and herons of the wetlands to the fruit from the cider orchards and strawberry fields. Prices range from £10 to £100.

Directions: *from the Drayton Arms in the village centre, proceed towards Curry Rivel. After two sharp bends, Smocklands is the first farmhouse on the right.*

Opening hours: *Mon-Fri 10am-4pm, Sat 10am-1pm and by appointment. Out of season please telephone first.*   65

SOPHIA HUGHES, 66 Kingscourt Lane, Rodborough, Stroud, Gloucestershire GL5 3PX

Est. 1990
Tel: +44 (0)1453-758565
www.sophiahughes.co.uk
Parking available

I make **thrown domestic stoneware** in a variety of blues and greens. Also handbuilt, one-off pots burnished, and often smoked before polishing to enhance their tactile quality. In addition, I make abstract, sculptural pieces, some incorporating chunks of glass or quartz. I have a well-stocked showroom. Mail order available.

Directions: *from Stroud A46 1 mile south, left at traffic lights, then first right. Court Way leads to Kingscourt Lane. Go quarter of a mile. Pottery on right.*

Opening hours: *10am-6pm daily (variable). Advise telephoning first.*   66

SUE MASTERS CERAMICS, Chasefield, 50 Portway, Wells, Somerset BA5 2BW

Est. 1996
Tel: +44 (0)1749-673547
Fax: +44 (0)1749-671596
Parking available

My most popular pieces are my **farm animals** such as cows, bulls, pigs and ponies and this year geese. In a contemporary and sometimes humorous style, hen and duck egg cups are available from £10. I have recently started work in a purpose-built studio to which visitors are welcome.

Directions: *taking Cheddar Road, Portway is on a hill out of Wells. Number 50 is on the brow of the hill on the right hand side at the bottom of a long drive.*

Opening hours: *available at most times.*   67

TOFF MILWAY - CONDERTON POTTERY, Conderton near Tewkesbury, Gloucestershire GL20 7PP

Est.1985
Tel: +44 (0)1386-725387
Parking available
Wheelchair access
Credit cards

I am a village potter living and working in the beautiful Cotswold village of Conderton. I specialise in **traditional saltglaze stoneware**; a technique that produces wonderful surface textures and glowing lustres which have an African influence. Almost everything made has a functional use associated with food for cooking storage or presentation.

Directions: *10 miles north of Cheltenham, the pottery is signposted off the A435-A46 Cheltenham to Evesham road, 5 miles from Tewkesbury near junction 9 of the M5.*

Opening hours: *Mon-Sat 9.30am-5.30pm.*

TRESTON HOLMES, Mill Lodge, Sea Lane, Kilve, Bridgwater, Somerset TA5 1EB

Est. 1991
Tel: +44 (0)1278-741314
Parking at carpark in village adjacent to A39

Treston Holmes specialises in **individual handthrown, burnished and smoked pieces**, some up to 450 mm in height and diameter. He also produces hand thrown stoneware and porcelain with matt and semi-matt glazes with carved or sculpted surfaces. His present studio gallery was set up at Kilve in 1991.

Directions: *Kilve is on the A39 approximately midway between Bridgwater and Minehead. At the Post Office turn onto Sea Lane; pottery on the right hand side.*

Opening hours: *prior appointment necessary.* 69

WINCHCOMBE POTTERY, Broadway Road, Winchcombe, Cheltenham, Gloucestershire GL54 5NU

Est. 1926
Tel: +44 (0)1242-602462
www.winchcombepottery.col.uk
Parking available
Credit cards

We make a wide range of pottery. The pottery produces **hand thrown stoneware pots** for domestic use fired in a down-draught wood-fired kiln. Stoneware pottery is hard, durable and entirely free from lead or any injurious chemicals. Visitors are welcome to look around the showroom and workshop. Mail order available.

Directions: *one mile north of Winchcombe on the B4632 Broadway Road.*

Opening hours: *Mon-Fri 8am-5pm, Sat 10am-4pm, Summer Sun 12pm-4pm.* 70

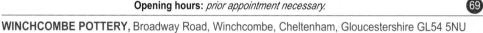

Textiles

COTSWOLD WOOLLEN WEAVERS, Filkins, Lechlade, Gloucestershire GL7 3JJ

Est. 1982
Tel: +44 (0)1367-860491
Fax: +44 (0)1367-860661
www.naturalbest.co.uk
Large carpark
Wheelchair access exellent
Credit cards

We make **woollen and cotton/silk cloths, garments and accessories**. The clack of our loom welcomes you to this 18th century mill. Watch fleece turned into fabric. Large shop selling pure wool cloth, garments and accessories. Other Cotswold crafts sold including iron-work and pottery. Museum/coffee shop/picnic area. Mail order possible.

Directions: *Cotswold Woollen Weavers is well sign-posted in the middle of the small village of Filkins, just off the A361 between Burford and Lechlade.*

Opening hours: *all year Mon-Sat 10am/6pm; Sun 2-6pm.*

DEAN NEEDLECRAFTS, 20 Albert Road, Cinderford, Gloucestershire GL14 2HS

Est. 1990
Tel: +44 (0)1594-826963

Local designer Elizabeth Hunt designs counted **cross-stitch embroidery kits** of the Forest of Dean, Ross, Monmouth and Chepstow. Her wide range of kit designs are suitable for beginners, intermediates and the advanced. Mail order available. She also makes completed embroidery items e.g. needlecases, paperweights and lavender bags with locally grown lavender.

Mail order only from the above address.

DOROTHY REGLAR 'COLOURS OF ASIA', Studio 6, Brewery Arts, Cirencester, Gloucestershire GL7 1JH

Est. 1980
Parking available
Credit cards

Dorothy is a designer/maker producing **orientally inspired one-off garments** in natural fibres. She is particularly concerned with the stitching details, texture, colours, simplicity and comfort. She is currently collaborating with small producer groups specialising in silk in north eastern Thailand and The People's Democratic Republic of Laos. Prices from £150.

Directions: *Brewery Arts is adjacent to Tesco in the town centre. Look for Brewery carpark (signposted). Studio 6 is off rear courtyard.*

Opening hours: *normally 10am-5pm. Closed Sun. Appointment advisable.*

LIZ LIPPIATT, The Textile Studio, Brewery Arts, Cirencester, Gloucester GL7 1JH

Est 1980
Tel/fax: +44 (0)1666-503517
www.liz-lippiatt.com
Parking available
Wheelchair access
Credit cards

Liz Lippiatt designs and hand prints textiles. Her textile design and **silk screen printed cloth** are for hand crafted fashion and furnishing accessories. Her range, made from silks, velvets and linens, includes scarves, bags, cushions and richly printed velvet bohemian coats. Liz supplies many small shops and galleries and John Lewis.

Directions: *in Brewery Arts in the centre of Cirencester.*

Opening hours: *Mon-Sat 10am-5pm.*

PATCHWORK BY JUDITH GAIT, St Mary's Cottage, Hemington, near Bath BA3 5XX

Est. 1987
Tel: +44 (0)1373-834033
Parking available

Bold, colourful and sometimes 'in your face'! **Patchwork quilts and wall hangings** bridge the gap between applied and fine art and provide enduring, positive focus for living spaces. will work on commission. Mail order available. Her work has been featured in magazines and is on display in the American Museum in Bath.

Directions: *from Radstock take A362 towards Frome. Take turning posted to Hemington after three and a half miles; then on the right just past the church.*

Opening hours: *by appointment.*

SARAH BEADSMOORE, Workshop 3, Brewery Arts, Brewery Court, Cirencester, Gloucestershire GL7 1JH

Est. 1984
Tel +44 (0)1285-640403
Fax +44 (0)1285-644060
Parking available
Wheelchair access
Credit cards

I trained in Textile Design at Derby College of Higher Education and became a resident craftworker at Brewery Arts in 1984. Most of my production is of **silk scarves for both women and men**, as silk is such a beautiful and versatile fibre and is easily dyed. I use a modern Swedish floor loom. My weaving techniques are simple, concentrating on colour and texture, sometimes combining cotton or linen with the silk. I also make throws and cushions, often to commission, and am working on a new line of household linens to include table mats, napkins and hand towels.

Directions: *Brewery Arts is in the centre of Cirencester close to the Brewery car park.*

Opening hours: *open most days Monday-Saturday; but ring first to check.*

THE TEXTILE STUDIO, Brewery Arts, Cirencester, Gloucestershire GL7 IJ4

Est. 1983
Tel/fax: +44 (0)1285-656263
Parking available
Wheelchair access
Credit cards

Hugh and Sophia Blackwell are designers, dyers, printers and makers of **dyed and printed devoré velvet silk**, satin and organza dip-dyed pashminas, shibori, chiffon scented pillows and nosegays, jewellery bags, coloured full sheepskin felt, velvet handbags, exotic feathery hairclips and ties, devoré window panels and panels, classic, reproductions, bolsters, pouffes and pillows.

Directions: *in the centre of Cirencester in Brewery Court downstairs and at the front of Brewery Arts.*

Opening hours: *Mon-Sat 10am-5pm.*

TULSI/PIE CHAMBERS TEXTILES, 16 Catherine Hill, Frome, Somerset BA11 1BZ

Est. 1972
Tel: +44 (0)1373-455690
Fax: +44 (0)1373-455992
Parking available
Credit cards

Pie Chambers is a weaver who makes **finished rugs, scarves and coats** in her workshop. In the shop, Tulsi, above you will find her own weaving and block printing, plus old rugs from Afghanistan and Iran, oriental textiles, carved furniture, boxes and tribal paintings and jewellery. Mail order available.

Directions: *Catherine Hill leads down through Stony Street to the Market Square.*
Opening hours: *Tues-Sat 10.30-4.40pm. Other times by appointment.*

Toys & Games

GROVELY JIGSAW PUZZLES LTD, Unit 5, BLDG C, Dinton Business Park, Catherine Ford Road, Dinton, Salisbury, Wiltshire SP3 5HZ

Est. 1999
Tel: +44 (0)1722-716000
Fax: +44 (0)1722-716070
www.grovely-jigsaws.co.uk
Parking available
Wheelchair access
Credit cards

We produce luxury cardboard 1000/500 piece **jigsaw puzzles** using wildlife artwork and giving a description of the fauna and flora on the base of the box. Wildlife photographers and film-makers bring a wide variety of animals and plants to our attention. Puzzles are designed mainly for adults. Mail order available.

Directions: *follow A30 from Salisbury to Barford. Turn right in Barford onto B3089 signposted Dinton/Chilmark. Go through Dinton and turn left at the crossroads.*
Opening hours: *Mon-Fri 9am-5pm but advance telephone call advised.*

Woodturning & Furniture

ALAN ROSS, 66 Providence Lane, Long Ashton, Bristol, North Somerset, BS41 9DN

Est. 1975
Tel: +44 (0)1275-392440
No parking

Furniture and stools made to order in a unique contemporary design. Small stools in English hardwood are in stock and all types of furniture in any type of wood are made on commission (cabinets, wardrobes, tables, chairs, etc.). Photographs and price list available. Delivery at cost. Mail order available.

Directions: *on Providence Lane which runs between the main Long Ashton Road and the Clevedon Road.*
Opening hours: *by appointment only.*

ARCADIAN FURNITURE, Lower Fields Farm, Hinton, Dyrham, Wiltshire SN14 8HJ

Est. 2000
Tel: +44 (0)117-9372320
Parking available
Wheelchair access

Arcadian furniture is a small company specialising in **cabinet making and furniture restoration.** The firm also make their own ranges of small occasional furniture. They choose to work in native hardwoods emphasising the character and charm of the grain. Commissions for any type of furniture or antique restoration are willingly accepted.

Directions: *from junction 18 on the M4 take the A46 towards Bath. Turn right to Hinton. The workshop is half a mile past Hinton on the right.*
Opening hours: *Mon-Fri 9am-5pm.*

ARNETT FURNITURE, 12 Old Yarn Mills, Westbury Road, Sherborne Dorset DT9 3RQ

Est. 1999
Tel: +44 (0)1935-812660
Fax: +44 (0)1935-812900
Parking available
Wheelchair access

Arnett Furniture specialises in **bespoke furniture and kitchens** using meticulous craftsmanship, traditional construction and the finest timbers. The designs are forward looking but do not lose sight of time-honoured principles. My portfolio of work can be viewed at my workshop in the historic abbey town of Sherborne.

Directions: *from the A30 turn into Horscastles Lane (leading to Ottery Lane). Yarn Mills is on the left at the end of Ottery Lane.*

Opening hours: *appointment necessary.*

BILL HADFIELD CHAIRMAKER, 2 South Place, Corsham, Wiltshire SN13 9HR

Est. 1979
Tel/fax +44 (0)1249-713006
www.handmadechairs.uk.com
Limited parking available nearby.

I have been hand-making chairs and only chairs for over 20 years, personally fashioning every part with care. Mine are genuinely handmade chairs. As proof of authenticity each chair has my initials carved into it. Hand made to order - my **chairs are "special, individual and personal"**. You'll find the traditional and something quite different - hand made chairs that display the beauty of wood and the skill of the craftsman. I am now concentrating on working with naturally weird and wonderful timber to create sculptural chairs. For these chairs I use the most amazing and rare timbers from my store.

Directions: *workshop just off the A4 two miles east of Corsham.*

Opening hours: *by arrangement.*

CHRIS EAGLES, The Willows, 44 Two Hedges Road, Bishops Cleeve, Cheltenham, Gloucestershire GS52 4AA

Est. 1995
Tel: +44 (0)1242-672334
Parking available
Wheelchair access

Chris Eagles offers a range of **freehand and artistic woodturning** products (fruit bowls, ashtrays, decorated containers, spinning tops, etc.) produced on a commercial basis. Chris is also an expert in the woodturning needed in the restoration of antique furniture (round table legs, chair legs, etc.). Mail order available.

Directions: *Bishops Cleeve is three miles NE of Cheltenham on the A435. Two Hedges Road is the main road through the village and No.44 is on the right.*

Opening hours: *10am-4pm. Prior appointment necessary.*

FURNITURE FROM THE WOOD, Yew Garden, Back Lane, Evershot, Dorset DT2 0DS

Tel/fax: +44 (0)1935-83580
Parking available
Wheelchair access with assistance

Working with the natural qualities of locally grown wood, Karen Hansen designs furniture with the aim of bringing together comfort and strength while allowing the living history of the material to shine. Her work includes public commissions for seating, gates etc and offers a **wide range of furniture for the home.**

Directions: *on the edge of the village, turn into Back Lane and follow it until the large Yew tree.*

Opening hours: *by appointment.*

I TRE FURNITURE, Chilcombe, Bridport, Dorset DT6 4PN

Est. 1991
Tel: +44 (0)1308-482666
Fax: +44 (0)1308-482433
www.itrefurniture.co.uk
Parking available
Wheelchair access after
20 metres over grass
Credit cards

Furniture in solid oak and English hardwoods which are often steambent into twists and arches and innovative designs inspired by Norwegian boat-building techniques. Work is made and often designed to commission. Previous commissions have been made for the National Gallery and the Barbican Art Gallery. Seven-foot conference table - £2,500.

Directions: *A35 W from Dorchester. After W'bourne Abbas 1st left off second stretch of dual carriageway. After a mile 1st left and park by sign. Track left of church track past cottage to workshop.*

Opening hours: *prior appointment necessary.* ⑧⑥

ROBERT PARKER, Woodcraft, Bishopwood, Chard, Somerset TA20 3RS

Est. 1997
Tel/fax: +44 (0)1460-234479

Robert lives and works in the Blackdown Hills. Predominantly making pieces from his large collection of English hardwoods, he makes **turned work as well as freeform carving.** His range includes large bowls, hand carved spoons and individual furniture. He is always willing to undertake commissions. Mail order is available.

Directions: *A303 west of Ilminster then half a mile past the Eagle Tavern. Turn to Bishopswood in the village past the pub on the right.*

Opening hours: *appointment necessary.*

TREVOR J COTTEL UNIQUE FURNITURE, Westcott, Burrow Wall, Burrowbridge, Bridgwater, Somerset TA7 0JQ

Est. 1981
Tel: +44 (0)1823-698127
Parking available
Wheelchair access

Trevor Cottel offers you freedom and conventionality with his **unique furniture** specialising in free-standing pieces and decorative items in a choice of woods. The range includes dining tables and chairs, rocking chairs, desks, stools, side tables, book shelves, bookstands, bookends, letter racks and unusual boxes. A visit is essential.

Directions: *On the A361 from Street to Taunton, we are halfway between Othery and Burrowbridge.*

Opening hours: *Fri/Sat only 9.30am-5pm.*

WOODWORKS, 45 Long Eights, Northway, Tewkesbury, Gloucestershire GL20 8QZ

Est 1998
Tel: +44 (0)7937-491060
Fax: +44 (0)1684-274853
www.mjksoftwood.co.uk
Parking available
Wheelchair access
Credit cards

After making wooden toys and gifts for family, friends and his own house, Mike Kilminster received requests to make special things for other people such as **banana trees and wheel barrows** for garden herbs and flowers, pencil holders etc. He now runs his own business making all items requested. Mail order available.

Directions: *on a small housing estate one mile from Ashchurch train station and junction 9 off the M5.*

Opening hours: *any time.*

Other Makers

ANNE WEARE BOOKBINDING, St Kevin's, Far Oakridge, Stroud, Gloucestershire GL6 7PM

Est. 1961
Tel: +44 (0)1285-760328
before 7pm
Parking available

I am the second generation of this family firm specialising in **conservation repair binding.** Prices start at around £45. I try to retain the original feel of your binding whilst making the construction sound. Carriage clock cases recovered. I also stock a range of books, cards, notelets, writing paper and pens. Mail order available.

Directions: *mid-way between Stroud and Cirencester. Phone for directions.*

Opening hours: *prior appointment necessary.*

90

AZURE, Swingletree, Stone Allerton, Aybridge, Somerset BS26 2NW

Est. 1997 (in the UK)
Tel: +44 (0)1934-713146
Parking available
Wheelchair access

Before producing her **hand made tiles** in Britain Deirdre Bethell had been working successfully in Portugal for years. She specialises in panels for kitchens, bathrooms, gardens etc. and in portraits of animals. All work is on commission and produced specifically to suit each customer's individual requirements. Prices from £15. Mail order available.

Directions: *in the village of Stone Allerton off the A38 and close to junction 22 of the M5.*

Opening hours: *9am-6pm daily. By appointment only.*

91

CIRENCESTER CRAFTSMAN'S MARKET, c/o The Old Forge, Hampton Street, Tetbury, Gloucestershire GL8 8LX

Est. 1975
Tel: +44 (0)1666-504838
Fax: +44 (0)1666-502389
www.cirencrafts.fsnet.co.uk
Parking available
Wheelchair access
Credit cards (some stallholders)

The Cirencester Craftsman's Market was formed to provide an opportunity for people to buy or commission **high quality hand made goods** direct from the craftsmen and women. About 40 craftspeople frequent the market. Many types of craft are represented ranging from stonework to footstools and from aromatherapy soap to baskets. Mail order available

Directions: *The Corn Hall Market Place, Cirencester. Situated in the centre of Cirencester.*

Opening hours: *1st and 2nd Sat each month. All year.*

CITRUS GLAZE TILES, The Walled Garden, Long Lane, Wrington, North Somerset BS40 55A

Est. 1998
Tel: +44 (0)1934 863938
www.citrusglaze.com
Parking available
Wheelchair access

Made to order tiles using a wide variety of decorating techniques. Orders may be made for any size of work from a single painted tile to large murals. Tiles can be used to decorate different areas, including swimming pools, garden walls, bathrooms, kitchen panels and religious buildings. Mail order available.

Directions: *off A38 towards Wrington. The Walled Garden is well signed*

Opening hours: *by appointment.*

COTSWOLD CRAFTSMEN, c/o The Secretary, DW Beck Esq, Barn House, Ripple, Tewkesbury, Gloucestershire GL20 6HA

Est. 1970
Tel/fax: +44 (0)1684-592191
www.cotswoldcraftsmen.org

Cotswold Craftsmen comprises **30 craft makers** who work largely from home. As individuals, their products include carved walking sticks, educational toys, baskets, glass, jewellery, and furniture. They offer demonstrations and sell as a group at shows. For an events and products brochure and list of members, contact the secretary. Demonstrations are given at shows.

ELEVENTH HOUR, 75 Redbreast Road, Bournemouth, Dorset BH9 3AN

Est. 1991
Tel: +44 (0)1202-241830
Fax: +44 (0)1202-241831
www.theeleventhhour.co.uk
Parking available
Credit cards

Sue Jeffrey makes **simple hammered silver jewellery** incorporating semi-precious stones and beach finds (pebbles and beach glass), wood and ceramic. She also does Kumihimo silk braid. Her husband Richard, at the same address, makes eclectic **clocks and mirrors** in native hardwoods, driftwood and inlaid ceramic faces. Mail order possible.

Directions: *will be given when appointment is made.*

Opening hours: *by appointment only.*

JOHN BURDEN, Collina Verde, 32 Astley Close, Pewsey, Wiltshire SN9 5BD

Est. 1977
Tel +44 (0)1672-563193
Parking available
Wheelchair access

I specialise in **collector's quality models in bottles**, which have been exhibited worldwide and also featured on television. My approach is to create an historically accurate model which will stand on its own as a piece of artwork while incorporating the 'cleverness' of old. Commission a model of your narrowboat/yacht/ship/vessel etc. in an appropriate scene (coastal/harbour/canal etc) or your house/cottage/pub etc. in a bottle, which can include a dedication. President of the European Association of Ships in Bottles 1984-1988: Waterways Craft Guild (with accreditation of) master: Guild of Waterways Artists. Leaflet available on request: mail order available.

Directions: *off the B3087 within Pewsey.*

Opening hours: *visitors by appointment only.*

LARK DESIGNS, 206 High Street, Batheaston, Bath BA1 7QZ

Est. 1990
Tel/fax: +44 (0)1225-852143
www.larkdesigns.fsnet.co.uk
Parking available

We produce **framed clocks and mirrors**. Using mouldings we make and finish in our workshop. We design and print all the faces for the clocks, which can be personalised. We also make stools, firescreens and trays, which can be ready made or customised for your own tapestries/needlework. Mail order available.

Directions: *from the A46/A4 junction on the outskirts of Bath, first exit on the roundabout signposted for Batheaston. Continue for approximately half a mile. We are on the right.*

Opening hours: *by appointment.*

MCCUBBINS, The Craft Shop, St. Briavels, Gloucestershire GL15 6TQ

Est/ 1979
Tel: +44 (0)1594-530297
www.appleonline.net/gillmcc/
Street parking
Wheelchair access
Credit cards

Gill McCubbin's wide range of **stoneware domestic pots** fit comfortably and efficiently in both kitchen and dining room. She also makes an expanding range of **contemporary silver jewellery**. 'I particularly enjoy making necklace and bracelets, which are highly individual in design but comfortable to wear.' Mail order available.

Directions: *take the B4228 from Coleford to Chepstow and turn into village towards castle/YHA. We are opposite the playing fields.*

Opening hours: *Thurs-Mon 10am-1pm and 2-5pm. Closed Tues and Wed. Variable hours Jan to Easter.*

MICHAEL CHAPMAN, The White Cottage, Burmetts Lane, Baltonsborough, Glastonbury, Somerset BA6 8RD

Est. 1997
Tel/fax: +44 (0)1458-851145
www.time-taken.com
Parking available
Wheelchair access

Michael Chapman has fairly recently returned from conservation to creative art. He makes **functional sculptures**, including clocks, garden benches, mirrors, planters and grottoes, some of which are installed in the ponds and woods of his garden. He also makes unusual prints of local beauty spots and old time film stars. Mail order available.

Directions: *from the Greyhound pub in the centre of the village, go up Ham Street. Burnetts Lane is first left and White Cottage is the first house on the left.*

Opening hours: *Mon-Sun 10am-3pm. Wise to ring first.*

PHILIP WOOD - DESIGNER MAKER, The Malthouse, High Street, Fordington, Dorchester, Dorset DT1 1J2

Est. 1994
Tel: +44 (0)1305-259200
Fax: +44 (0)1305-259201
www.philipwood.co.uk
Parking available
Credit cards

A **contemporary design and bespoke furniture makers** based in an 18th century malthouse. Philip is happy to discuss furniture commissions with clients and some hand made furniture is on sale. Interior products include lighting, linen, crockery, glasses, basketwear, candles, chairs, bins etc. many of which are sold mail order. Ask for catalogue.

Directions: *bottom of Dorchester High Street on the river. Look for old malthouse.*

Opening hours: *Mon-Sat 9am-5pm.*

SHEEP STREET GALLERY, The Guild, Sheep Street, Chipping Camden, Gloucestershire GL55 6DS

Tel: +44 (0)777-3081789
Parking available

I am a local artist living in Chipping Camden. My business was initially supported by the Prince's Trust which enabled me to produce **limited edition prints** from my originals which consist of Cotswold views featuring architectural details. I specialise in commissioned work based in the Cotswolds and display in my studio/ shop.

Directions: *on Sheep Street just off the High Street.*

Opening hours: *Mon-Sat 9am-5pm.* 101

SPIRIT OF THE ANCESTORS, 24 Northland Street, Glastonbury, Somerset BA6 9JJ

Est.1991
Tel: +44 (0)1458-833267
Parking available

'Spirit of the Ancestors' is a small studio producing **sculpture and photography** inspired by prehistoric and ice age neolithic, Bronze Age and Celtic artefacts and original works of art and sculpture. There is also a photo library of the neolithic sites of Britain and Ireland. Prices from £5-£5000. Mail order catalogue available.

Directions: *next to the exit to St John's car park in central Glastonbury.*

Opening hours: *any time by appointment.* 102

WATERSTONE FOUNTAINS, Unit 4, The Walled Garden, Long Lane, Wrington, Bristol BS40 55A

Est. 1996
Tel: +44 (0)1934-863864
www.waterstonefountains.com
Parking available
Credit cards

Hand-crafted **copper fountains and garden ornaments** can be viewed on the website. From £15 to £1200+. The copper ornaments depict various garden animals such as dragonflies, frogs and kingfishers. A selection can be seen at the Walled Garden and at the mobile showroom: all major flower shows are attended. Mail order available.

Directions: *from Bristol on the A38 (Taunton Direction) having passed Bristol Airport on right. Take next right to Wrington and Yatton. Walled Garden about 1 mile on left.*

Opening hours: *Mon-Fri 10am-4pm.*   (103)

THE SUSSEX GUILD'S SHOP, Bentley Wildfowl and Motor Museum, Halland, East Sussex BN8 5AF

Est. 1996
Tel: +44 (0)1825-840573
www.thesussexguild.co.uk
Parking available
Wheelchair access
Credit cards

A parkland setting provides a fitting backdrop for the work of twenty craftspeople who are members of the Sussex Guild. They produce a fascinating variety of work including ceramics, animal models, prints, etchings, batiks, embroidery, quilting, jewellery and handblown glass. Entry to the shop is free. Commissions taken. Events programme (+44 (0)1323-833239).

Directions: *signposted from the A22 and A26. 8 miles north of Lewes.*

Opening hours: *10.30am-4.30pm daily Mar-Oct 31.*

TSENA LTD, 6 Bond Street, Brighton BN1 1RD

Est. 1995
Tel: +44 (0)1273-328402
www.tsena.co.uk
Parking: ticketed carparks
Credit cards

Tsena offers an amazing range of original designer gifts. Whatever the occasion, we can help and inspire you to find the perfect present. Our collection incorporates a variety of glasswear, ceramics, jewellery, natural fabrics, pewter, stationery and hand made cards. Mail order available from our fully secure website.

Directions: *in North Laine area of Brighton city centre. From Churchill Square Shopping Centre, walk east down North Street. Bond Street is on the left.*

Opening hours: *10am-6pm Mon-Sat.*

VILLAGE CRAFTS, The Square, Forest Row, East Sussex RH18 5ES

Est. 1976
Tel: +44 (0)1342 823238
www.village-crafts.co.uk
Parking outside the door
Wheelchair access (narrow)
Credit cards

A craft shop that sells both finished hand made crafts and kits for hobbyists of all ages. Made crafts include jewellery, hand-painted glass goblets and vases, functional and decorative pottery, original watercolours and limited edition prints of Ashdown Forest and wood and pewter photograph frames. Mail order available.

Directions: *on A22 in village centre, next to The Chequers Hotel.*

Opening hours: *Mon-Fri 9.15am-5.30pm (Weds close at 1pm). Sat 9.30-5.30pm*

Galleries

ART AND CRAFT GALLERY, 48a George Street, Hastings Old Town, East Sussex TN34 3EA

Est. 1996
Tel: +44 (0)1424-201717
Seafront parking
Wheelchair access
Credit cards

The Gallery is run as a co-operative by local craftspeople who act as staff, as well as producing the range of goods which includes glassware, embroidery, textiles, jewellery, salt dough, traditional teddy bears, original paintings, woodturning, ceramics, knitwear, barge art, dolls' houses and silk painting. Some member demonstrations can be seen.

Directions: *George Street is pedestrianised and runs parallel to Hastings Old Town seafront.*

Opening hours: *Mon-Fri 10am-5pm.*   ⑧

CRAFTWORK GALLERY, 18 Sadlers Walk, East Street, Chichester, West Sussex P019 1HQ

Est. 1989
Tel: +44 (0)1234-532588
Parking available
Wheelchair access
Credit cards

Located in a modern shopping arcade conveniently opposite a café, the gallery sells pottery, stained glass, ceramic animals (cats a popular speciality), wall hangings (mixed textile with feather and wood), batik cards, etchings, prints and watercolours. These items are mostly locally made and include work by the Sussex Guild of Craftsmen.

Directions: *off lower end of East Street in Chichester city centre in Sadlers Walk shopping mall.*

Opening hours: *Mon-Sat 10am-5pm (closed Sundays and bank holidays).*

THE CRYPT GALLERY, Off Church Street, Seaford, East Sussex, BN25 1HE

Est. 1994
Tel +44 (0)1323-891461
Fax +44 (0)1273-484373
Public car park outside.
Wheelchair access.
Credit cards

Built around a beautifully restored medieval undercroft, the Crypt Gallery hosts a year-round programme of exhibitions and workshops, bringing together some of the finest contemporary artists and craftspeople in England. The programme ranges from screenprints and stone carving to ceramics, sculpture, photography, textiles and furniture as well as fine art.

Directions: *from Brighton pass Seaford station on the A259; right into Church Street at the mini roundabout; Gallery is behind Seaford Police Station via public car park.*
Opening hours: *10.30am-1.30 pm and 2.15-5pm Mon-Sat, 12-4pm Sun during exhibitions: closed Jan.* ⑩

THE GARDEN GALLERY, Rookery Lane, Broughton, Near Stockbridge, Hampshire SO20 8AZ

Est. 1994
Tel +44 (0)1794 301144
Fax +44 (0)1794-301761
Good local parking.
Wheelchair access.

The Garden Gallery exhibits sculpture, pots, furniture and mosaics for gardens and conservatories by some ninety contemporary artists, mostly displayed in a beautiful, tranquil garden during exhibitions, to illustrate the relationship between the works of art and the plants, trees, water and light, and how each can lend the other a new dimension. Payment can by instalments can usually be arranged.

Directions: *please ring.*
Opening hours: *vary - please telephone.* ⑪

HITCHCOCK'S, 11 East Street, Alresford, Hampshire SO24 9EQ

Est. 1976
Tel: +44 (0)1962-734762
www.hitch-hants.co.uk
Parking in car park
Wheelchair access (one step)
Credit cards

Joyce Hitchcock took over a minute craft shop in Winchester in 1976 and moved to Alresford in 1980 to enlarge the range of work, all from Britain. Hitchcock's specialises in textiles which are knitted, woven, painted etc. and also offers jewellery, ceramics, glass and toys. Sister gallery in Bath. Mail order.
Directions: *on the corner of East Street with George Yard, Nr. the Nat West Bank. East Street is at the Alton End of Alresford towards Alton.*
Opening hours: *Mon-Sat 9.30am-1pm, 2-5pm.* ⑫

PHOENIX ARTS ASSOCIATION, 10-14 Waterloo Place, Brighton BN2 2NB

Est. 1993
Tel: +44 (0)1273-603700
Fax: +44 (0)1273-603704
www.phoenixarts.org
Parking available
Wheelchair access

Phoenix is an independent arts group, a contemporary visual arts gallery and has a programme of classes and arts-related activities. It was set up by practising artists as a means of providing affordable studios. 100 artists and makers are currently based there. The gallery sells all manner of crafts from furniture to felt.
Directions: *opposite St. Peter's Church, Brighton.*
Opening hours: *Mon-Sat 11am-5.30pm; Sun 12-4pm. Phone for a list of gallery exhibitions.* ⑬

Baskets & Wickerwork

STEPHEN CAULFIELD, 58 Hayling Rise, High Salvington, Worthing, West Sussex BN13 3AQ

Est. 1992
Tel/fax: +44(0)1903-695958
Parking available

I make basketware, i.e. **bespoke baskets**, also hampers and storage, log, chairs, laundry, pet, toy, flower and shopping baskets. I have been making baskets full-time for fifteen years and had my own company for nine. Only finest Somerset willow is used. If not bespoke, baskets are made to standard sizes. Mail order available.
Directions: *located on the A27 between Worthing and Arundel, close to Worthing side.*
Opening hours: *by appointment only.*

THE SUSSEX JOURNEYMEN, 146 Brighton Road, South Lancing, West Sussex BN15 8LN

Est. 1958
Tel: +44 (0)1903-752164
Parking available
Credit cards

Small, family-run business specialising in **traditional English basketware.** Our products include baskets for shoppers, flowers, cycles, fishing, pets, logs, skips and laundry and duck nesting baskets, infact, we make anything in willow. Our most popular items are willow drawer baskets for kitchens and storage. Also old baskets copied. Mail order available.

Directions: *on the A259 coast road between Shoreham-by-Sea and South Lancing.*
Opening hours: *please make appointment.*

15

THE TRUGGERY, Coopers Croft, Herstmonceux, East Sussex BN27 1QL

Est. 1899
Tel/fax: +44 (0)1323-832314
Parking available
Credit cards

Sussex trugs have been made here for over a hundred years with traditional methods and tools using locally grown sweet chestnut and willow. There is a range of trugs to suit every purpose: for cucumbers, logs, a walking stick trug, garden trugs, flower trugs, even bowl and square trugs. Mail order available.

Directions: *from A22 at Hailsham Boship roundabout take A271 for four miles. The truggery is on the right at Stunts Green crossroads.*
Opening hours: *Tues-Fri 10am-5pm, Sat 10am-1pm.*

16

Food & Drink

BALLARD'S BREWERY LIMITED, The Old Sawmill, Nyewood, Petersfield, Hampshire GU31 5HA

Est. 1980
Tel: +44 (0)1730-821301
Fax: +44 (0)1730-821742
Parking available
Wheelchair access
Credit cards

Ballards Brewery, run by Carola Brown, is a small, craft brewery producing draught and bottle-conditioned real ales in a wide range of strengths and styles from mild to strong 'winter ales'. Visitors are welcome to purchase beers, T-shirts, tankards etc. Tours for a minimum of 12 people. Mail order available but expensive.

Directions: *from Rogate on A272, turn south by church, signed South Harting and Nyewood. Follow road for about 2 miles. Brewery on left 50 yards after Nyewood village sign.*
Opening hours: *Mon-Fri 8am-4pm. Weekends by appointment.*

17

BEARSTED VINEYARD, 24 Caring Lane, Bearsted, Maidstone, Kent ME14 4NJ.

Est. 1985
Tel/fax: +44 (0)1622-736974
www.bearstedwines.co.uk
Parking available
Wheelchair access
Credit cards

Four-acre vineyard with own winery producing white, rose and red award-winning wines. Specially noted for Bearsted Bacchus (a dry white) and Bearsted Brut (quality sparkling). Guided tour of the vineyard and winery for groups at £3 per head. Self-guided individual visitors free. Complimentary tastings offered to intending purchasers.

Directions: *Junction 8 (Leeds Castle turn off) off the M20. A20 towards Maidstone. Caring Lane is left turn after one mile; vineyard half a mile down lane.*
Opening hours: *Mon-Sat 10am-6pm; Sun by appointment.*

18

DAVENPORT VINEYARDS, Limney Farm, Castle Hill, Rotherfield, East Sussex TN6 3RR

Est. 1991
Tel: +44 (0)1892-852380
Fax: +44 (0)1892-852781
www.davenportvineyards.co.uk
Parking available
Credit cards (on-line)

Davenport Vineyards produce some of the UK's top quality wines, winning awards annually. The winery and vineyard at Rotherfield have been managed organically since 1999 and both are open for visitors to view. Wines can be bought at the vineyard from £5 per bottle. Mail order available on-line.

Directions: *follow Castle Hill, south of Rotherfield Village for two and a half miles.*
Opening hours: *please ring for details.*

19

DURLEIGHMARSH FARM SHOP, Drovers' Cottage, Durleighmarsh Farm, Petersfield, Hampshire GU31 5AX

Est. 1990
Tel: +44 (0)1730-821626
Parking available
Partially wheelchair accessible
Credit cards

A family-run farm shop and pick-your-own specialising in soft fruits: strawberries, raspberries, blueberries etc. and vegetables: asparagus, sweetcorn and pumpkins. The Shop stocks a wide range of local produce from high-quality small scale producers: cheeses, free range meats, smoked fish, preserves, bread, cakes and ciders. Special Christmas produce from 1 December.

Directions: *one and a half miles from from Petersfield on the A272 Midhurst road.*

Opening hours: *Mon-Sun 9.30am-5.30pm (closed 1pm Sun in winter). June, July & August 9am-7pm daily.*　　**20**

RIDGEVIEW ESTATE WINERY, Upper Furzefields, Fragbarrow Lane, Ditchling Common, East Sussex BN6 8TP

Est. 1995
Tel: +44 (0)1444-258039
Fax: +44 (0)1444-230757
www.ridgeview.co.uk
Parking available
Wheelchair access
Credit cards

Ridgeview Estate is dedicated solely to the production of highest quality sparkling wine from traditional champagne varieties and methods. Although only commercially selling wine since 1999, Ridgeview has won numerous international awards and extensive critical acclaim for their wines. Prices from about £14.95 per bottle. Mail order available.

Directions: *M25 south to A23 to B2112 through Ditchling, one mile left hand side Fragbarrow Lane/or A23 rom Brighton on to B2112.*

Opening hours: *bank holiday weekends 10.30am-4.30pm and Nov & Dec weekends. Other times by appointment.*　　**21**

SEDDLESCOMBE ORGANIC VINEYARD, Robertsbridge, East Sussex TN32 5SA

Est. 1979
Tel: +44 (0)1580-830715
Fax: +44 (0)1580-830122
www.EnglishOrganicWine.co.uk
Carpark on site
Wheelchair access
Credit cards

Meander at leisure through romantic vineyards and picnic in ancient woodlands. Learn about wine-making by a visit to the winery and taste the refreshing English wines or traditional Sussex ciders. Browse around the range of organic fruit juices, ciders, beers and various organic wines in the winery shop. Mail order available.

Directions: *8 miles north of Hastings, one and a half miles from the village of Sedlescombe on the B2244.*

Opening hours: *daily 10am-6pm.*　　**22**

WICKHAM VINEYARD, Botley Road, Shedfield, Southampton, Hampshire S032 2HL

Est. 1984
Tel: +44 (0)1329-834042
Fax: +44 (0)1329-834907
www.wickhamvineyard.co.uk
On-site parking
W/chair access (not vineyards)
Credit cards

Learn about grape growing and the making of award-winning wines from 18 acres of vines on a 40-acre estate owned by Gordon Channon and Angela Baart. An audio-tour guides you at a gentle walk through the vines and winery. Tastings and restaurant. Harvesting viewable in October. Mail order available direct or on website.

Directions: *the Vineyard is situated half way between Botley and Wickham on the A334. Take junction 7 off the M27.*

Opening hours: *Mon-Sat 10.30am-6pm (5pm winter), and 11.30am-5.30pm Sun.* **23**

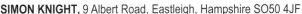

Glass

SIMON KNIGHT, 9 Albert Road, Eastleigh, Hampshire SO50 4JF

Est. 1988
Tel/fax: +44 (0)2380-613149
Parking available

Contemporary architectural stained glass on commission for public buildings such as churches and museums and for individual clients. Recent commissions include millennium windows for Godalming Museum and an 11th century church in Winchester and windows for a yoga room. Cost from £2,000; two to ten months work per commission.

Directions: *given as needed*

Opening hours: *visitors by arrangement.*

SIOBHAN JONES DESIGNER GLASS, Unit 19, Viables Craft Centre, Harrow Way, Basingstoke, Hampshire RG22 4BJ

Est. 1997
Tel: +44 (0)1256-472727
Fax: +44 (0)1256-358086
www.siobhanjones.com
Parking available
Wheelchair access
Credit cards

Inspired by light and pattern, Siobhan creates one-off objects of **kiln-formed glass.** Since graduation in 1996 and the start of her workshop her work has gained exposure in established galleries. In her own showroom you can view finished pieces and discuss your individual requirements with her. Mail order available.

Directions: *from junction 6 off the M3 follow signs to the A30 and Viables Craft Centre signs in the locality.*

Opening hours: *generally Mon-Fri 10am-5pm and weekends but advisable to telephone first.*

SUNRISE STAINED GLASS, 58-60 Middle Street, Southsea, Hampshire P05 4BP

Est. 1982
Tel: +44 (0)23-927 50512
www.stained-windows.co.uk
Parking available
Credit cards

Sunrise studio employs four full-time craftsmen producing high quality, **traditionally leaded stained glass panels.** Commissions include many prestigious new windows for churches, public buildings, restaurants, casinos, private houses etc. Also restoration projects. Over 3,000 stained glass windows made. Clients have included Chichester Cathedral. Shop stocking glass supplies and showroom of studio work.

Directions: *adjacent to Portsmouth University Art College near the city centre.*
Opening hours: *shop only, Mon-Fri 8.30am-5pm.*

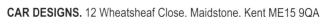

Jewellery

CAR DESIGNS, 12 Wheatsheaf Close, Maidstone, Kent ME15 9QA

Est. 2000
Tel/fax: +44 (0)1622-765989
Parking available
Wheelchair access

After graduating from the Kent Institute of Art and Design, Charlotte Rice began her own business as a goldsmith, silversmith and jeweller. She makes anything from **simple rings to intricate silverware** and large and small items of jewellery. Prices start at £5. Always a selection for sale and commissions welcome.

Directions: *A229 to Hastings. Past traffic lights at Wheatsheaf Pub. Wheatsheaf Close is 400 yards on left immediately before Maistone rail station.*
Opening hours: *by arrangement.*

INDEPENDENT JEWELLERY, Phoenix Studios, 10-14 Waterloo Place, Brighton BN2 2NB

Est. 1984
Tel: +44 (0)1273-298908
Fax: +44 (0)1273-603704
Parking available

Very individual jewellery **combining acrylic and silver with gold leaf and glazes** to create colourful pieces which can be to my own designs or commissioned privately including rings, bangles, brooches, earrings, necklaces, cufflinks etc. Sources for my own work vary from architecture to bazaars, circuses and natural stones. Mail order available.

Directions: *the east side of the Level, opposite St. Peter's Church.*
Opening hours: *most days but variable hours. Please make an appointment.*

Metalwork & Silversmithing

METALSMITHS, Unit 6, Sharlands Farm Workshop, Blackboys, Uckfield, East Sussex TN22 5HN

Est. 1992
Tel/fax: +44 (0)1435-865431
Parking available
Wheelchair access
Credit cards

Niki and Phil Marr make **contemporary metalwork and jewellery** in copper, brass and silver, specialising in clocks in copper and brass. Some clocks have a red oxidised copper finish. Jewellery is silver engraved pattern work: some plain, some with semi-precious stones. Also wedding tiaras to hire or buy.

Directions: *southbound on A22, past Uckfield to Halland roundabout. Turn left towards Blackboys. 4 miles. On left just past village.*

Opening hours: *Mon 10am-1pm; Tues-Sat 10am-5pm.*

Pottery & Ceramics

CHESSELL POTTERY, Chessell, Yarmouth, Isle of Wight P041 OUE

Est. 1978
Tel: +44 (0)1983-531248
Fax: +44 (0)1983-531210
www.chessellpottery.co.uk
Large car park
Wheelchair access award
Credit cards

Porcelain pottery designs based on the natural world: **indoor fountains, fantasy animal figurines** (including dragon collectables), fish, shells, vases etc. Situated in a converted barn comprising studio workshops, gallery and coffee shop. Factory shop also sells IOW crafts and food products. Children's play chalet and paint your own pottery. Mail order available.

Directions: *off B3399 road from Freshwater to Ventnor; 3 miles from Freshwater by right turning to Brook. B3401 Newport to Freshwater.*

Opening hours: *seven days 9am-5.30pm.*

J.C.J. POTTERY, Peelings Manor Barns, Hankham Road, Nr Stone Cross, Pevensey, East Sussex BN24 5AP

Est. 1974
Tel: +44 (0)1323-541985
Parking available
Wheelchair access
Credit cards

We make beautiful pots by hand for use in the home. We are one of the few potteries specialising in **brush decorated porcelain** domestic ware and reduction fired lustreware inspired by De Morgan and Hispano Moresque styles. Treated properly, they will give many years of service and pleasure.

Directions: *from Stonecross go North (B2104) towards Hailsham. 1st right after the flyover. Peelings Manor Barns are 400 yards on right.*

Opening hours: *10am-5.30pm.*

JILL PRYKE POTTERY, Unit 4, The Turner Dumbrell Workshops, North End, Ditchling Sussex BNG 8TG

Est. 1975
Tel: +44 (0)1273-845246
Parking available
Wheelchair access
Credit cards

I make hand thrown **earthenware pots for home and table**, with delicate line decoration based on natural forms and using soft blue, green or grey glazes and the 'sgraffito' (scratched glaze) technique or pierce work. Prices from £5 to £70. Commemorative mugs and plates made to each customer's requirements are a specialty.

Directions: *just north of centre of Ditchling on B2112 Haywards Heath to Brighton road (9 miles north of Brighton via A23/B2112).*

Opening hours: *Tues-Sat 10am-5pm. Closed Sun & Mon.*

MATTHEW BAYMAN POTTERY, Sharlands Farm, Craft Workshops, Blackboys, Uckfield, East Sussex
TN22 5HN

Est. 1986
Tel: +44 (0)1435-862652
Fax: +44 (0)1435-865431
Parking available
Wheelchair access

Matthew is a maker and teacher of pottery. He tends to work mostly in stoneware producing a wide range of **thrown, woodfired pots** for use, and individual pieces which blend elements of throwing and handbuilding. These express form and texture, though vessels are sculptural in spirit. Also sells other makers' work.

Directions: *take the Heathfield road at Halland from A22. Takes the Lewes road at Cross-in-Hand from A267.*

Opening hours: *Mon-Sat 10am-5pm. Other times by appointment.*

RYE POTTERY LTD, 77 Ferry Road, Rye, East Sussex TN31 7DJ

Est. 1869
Tel: +44 (0)1797-223038
Fax: +44 (0)1797-225802
Parking available
Wheelchair access:
one step to shop
Credit cards

Rye pottery has been collected for over 200 years and is still being made in the building specially designed as a pottery in 1869. Rye now produces **hand painted majolica figures, animals and limited amounts of studio pottery**. Prices from £10-£300. Mail order available. Also good stock of seconds (personal shoppers only).

Directions: *B2089 Rye-Battle Road. 200 yds west of Rye Station, right hand side beside river.*

Opening hours: *Mon-Fri 9am-5pm; Sat 9.30am-12.30pm & 1.30pm-4pm.*
Closed Sun. & bank hols.

SELBORNE POTTERY, The Plestor, Selborne, Nr. Alton, Hampshire GU34 3JQ

Est. 1985
Tel: +44 1(0)1420-511413
Fax: +44 1(0)1420-511413
Parking available
Wheelchair access
Credit cards

Hand thrown and turned stoneware. Although decorative, the pots are designed to be used. The firing process used results in colour variations especially the copper red glaze which can be bright red or pink. The gold lustre range adds a luxurious opulence not normally found on studio pottery. Mail order available.

Directions: *from Alton Selborne, Pottery is on left opposite Gilbert White Museum, behind Selborne Gallery, near church.*

Opening hours: *Mon-Fri 9.30am-6pm; Sat/Sun midday-5pm.*

THE WORKSHOP POTTERY, 94 Trafalgar Street, North Laine, Brighton, Sussex BN1 4ER

Est. 1979
Tel: +44 (0)1273-601641
www.workshop-pottery.co.uk
Pay carpark

Situated in Brighton's historic North Laine area, Peter Stocker's shop sells only pottery that he has made on the premises and most days it is possible to watch it being produced. He specialises in **colourful earthenware** pottery and he also makes silk screened hand made cards. Commissions welcome. Mail order available.

Directions: *Trafalgar Street runs between Brighton Station and St. Peter's Church on London Road.*

Opening hours: *Tues-Sat 10am-5.30pm.*

YOLANDE BEER, Almond Barn, Five Ashes, Mayfield, East Sussex TN20 6HX

Est. 1980
Tel: +44 (0)1825-830691
Parking available
Wheelchair access if
necessary

Handthrown, brush-decorated, figurative ceramics in stoneware and earthenware. Spent over two years in Japan at a tableware company on scholarship. Orders taken for sets and commemmorative pieces. 2000 received major order from Body Shop International. New ideas in progress include grafitto decorated slab-pots and relief work on tiles. Mail order possible.

Directions: *14 miles south of Tunbridge Wells on the A267, two miles south of Mayfield and the first building in Five Ashes on the left hand side.*

Open: *12 hours a day, six and a half days a week. Please telephone in advance.*

Textiles

CREATIVE GARMENTS, 19 Richmond Road, Bexhill, East Sussex TN39 3DN

Est. 1980
Tel: +44 1(0)1424-213818
http://creative garments.onza.net
Parking available

A member of the East Sussex Guild of Craftworkers, Shirley Cook has been a spinner and weaver for over twenty years, specialising in top quality **hand spun knitted or woven garments** made from pure wool and dog hair. Range includes hats, scarves, gloves, mittens, waistcoats, jerseys etc. Mail order available.
Directions: *from Collington rail station south down Richmond Road towards the sea. Last house on the left after a hundred yards.*
Opening hours: *10am-5pm. Appointment necessary.*

DESIGN BY HEATHMOOR, Denmor, Herschell Square, Deal, Kent CT14 7SH

Est. 1990
Tel: +44 (0)1304-363710
Fax: +44 (0)1304-366770
Parking available

We design and make our own **knitwear by hand or machine** ladies, men's or children's, made in a variety of yarns from acrylic to silk. Our styles appeal to all ages. Will make to customers' own specification if required. We also make sweatshirts and T-shirts decorated with appliqué or diamanté. Mail order available.
Directions: *A258 Dover Road, Past Q8 Garage, next left (by church), first right (Balfour Road) then first left (Herschell Square).*
Opening hours: *Mon-Sat 11am-4pm. Other times (eves) by appointment.*

DIANE ROGERS, Unit 8, The Turner Dumbrell Workshops, North End, Ditchling, East Sussex BN6 8TG

Est. 1997
Tel: +44 (0)1273-275105
Parking available

Diane Rogers produces commercial textile designs for the American and European markets. In addition Diane creates original designs using a variety of embroidery, hand printing and painting techniques on **scarves, cushions, silk pictures, mirrors** and greetings cards. These are for sale to the general public from her workshop.
Directions: *from Ditchling village go north on B2112 towards Haywards Heath and turn right on Dumbrells Court Road.*
Opening hours: *term time only Mon-Fri 10am-2pm.*

ELIZABETH SAUNDERS (TEXTILE DESIGN), 2 Stairs Hill, Empshott, Nr Liss, Hampshire GU33 6HP

Est. 1990
Tel: +44 (0)1420-538684
Parking available

Quilts and cushions. Besides full-size quilts made to commission, I make patchwork and quilted cushions in various designs and sizes, and also greetings cards. I use a variety of fabrics, including silks and velvets, and like to incorporate hand-dyed, painted and printed ones, also antique pieces. Mail order available.
Directions: *on main B3006 Alton to Liss road and about one and a half miles SE of Selborne on same road at the bottom of the hill.*
Opening hours: *by appointment only.*

JANICE BRITZ - FELTMAKER, Phoenix Arts Association, 10-14 Waterloo Place, Lewes Road, Brighton BN2 2NB

Est. 1997
Tel: +44 (0)1273-240919
www.janbritz.com
Parking available

Janice Britz makes individually crafted **hand-felted fashion accessories**. She welcomes visits to her studio to see her collection of hats, scarves, bags and slippers all made from natural wool in a gorgeous range of colours and visitors can see her at work and find out how felt is made.
Directions: *Phoenix Arts is a large office block housing a gallery and artists' studios opposite St. Peter's Church in Brighton. On foot: 5 mins from rail station.*
Opening hours: *all by arrangement.*   42

LOUISE BELL, 3 Peelings Manor Barns, Hankham Road, Stone Cross, East Sussex BN24 5AP

Est. 1982
Tel: +44 (0)1424-435216
Parking available
Wheelchair access

Visit the workshop to see a range of **patchwork and appliqué quilts, hangings, screens** and cushions in Liberty fabrics. Hangings are used like tapestries, or to replace bedboards. Screens are four-panelled, six feet high and can divide a room. I enjoy making to order and discussing designs and fabric choices.

Directions: *from Stone Cross B2104 (Hailsham Road); turn right after overpass. Peelings Manor Barns are 600 yards on right.*

Opening hours: *Tues-Sat 10am-6pm. Appointment advisable.*

SUSANNE WOLF CLOTHING, Sharlands Farm Workshops, Unit 4, Blackboys, East Sussex TN22 5HN

Est. 1997
Tel: +44 (0)1825-890921
Fax: +44 (0)1435-865431
Parking available
Wheelchair access

Hand made **clothing from hand-dyed linen and felted wool.** Can be made to order or off the rail. Wide range of plain colours from natural to bright rainbow ones. Made to mix and match, comfortable to wear, a pleasure to look at and suitable for every age. 'Clothes to live in.'

Directions: *southbound on A22, past Uckfield to Halland roundabout. Turn left towards Blackboys. 4 miles. On left just past village.*

Opening hours: *by appointment.*

WHITCHURCH SILK MILL, Whitchurch Silk Mill Trust, 28 Winchester Street, Whitchurch, Hampshire RG28 7AL

Est. 1990
Tel: +44 (0)1256-892065
www.whitchurch.silkmill.co.uk
Parking available
Partially wheelchair accessible
Credit cards

The Mill was built on the River Test 200 years ago and silk has been woven there since the 1820s. Watch the Victorian machinery and traditional noisy processes which turn silk yarn into **luxury fabrics for theatrical costumes, historic houses** etc. Wide range of silk gifts in the Mill shop. Textile exhibition. Tearoom.

Directions: *signposted from the A34. The Mill is in the centre of Whitchurch.*

Opening hours: *Tues-Sun 10.30am-5pm.*

Woodturning & Furniture

ALUN HESLOP CHAIR MAKING, Vigo Farmhouse Workshop, Hastingleigh, Nr. Ashford, Kent CT4 5AY

Est. 1996
Tel: +44 (0)1227-830301
www.chaircreative.com
Parking available
Wheelchair access

Dynamic and **innovative sculptural chair forms** created with an eye to the future and the roots of traditional chair-making. Hand made, beautifully styled and exceptionally comfortable, using sustainably-managed native English hardwoods. Large and small scale, interior and exterior seating projects. 'From the tree to the final form.' Mail order possible.

Directions: *situated in Hastingleigh signposted from the village of Wye. Vigo Farmhouse is the first building on the left on entering the village.*

Opening hours: *Mon-Fri 9am-5pm. Appointment necessary.*

A W WOODCRAFTS, Unit 1, Peelings Manor Barns, Hankham Road, Stones Cross, East Sussex BN24 5AP

Est. 1999
Tel: +44 (0)1323-725646
Fax: +44 (0)1323-764412
Parking available
Wheelchair access

Angus Wingfield is a designer and maker of **interior and exterior furniture**, specialising in English hardwood tables. Also garden furniture, pergolas, arbours, benches etc. and will do whole garden design including fencing. He works solely to commission and is always happy to discuss requirements. Also woodturning, french polishing and restoration work.

Directions: *from Stone Cross B2104 (Hailsham Road), turn right after overpass; Peelings Manor Barns are 600 yards on the right.*

Opening hours: *Mon-Sat 10am-6pm.*

BARRY M. MURPHY SUSSEX WINDSORS, Dormer's Farmhouse, Windmill Hill, Hailsham, East Sussex
BN27 4RY
Est. 1984
Tel/fax: **+44 (0)1323-832388**
www.thesussexguild.co.uk
Parking available

Barry M. Murphy is a highly skilled craftsman with 40 years' experience making bespoke furniture and commissioned acoustic musical instruments. Also **sets of chairs in Windsor styles**. He can offer: Lancashire broad-arm (ash and elm), best Gabbitas (yew and elm), Cabriole (cherry and elm), American fan back (ash and elm).
Directions: *on the A271 six miles east of Hailsham, at Windmill Hill.*
Opening hours: *Mon-Fri 10am-4pm. Appointment necessary.*

CEDAR WOODCRAFT, 133, London Road, Holybourne, Alton, Hampshire GU34 4EY
Est. 1991
Tel: **+44 1420-84922**
Parking available

Fred Clark makes all kinds of **small wooden items** including bowls, boxes for various uses, pot pourri pots, tea-light holders, coat hooks etc. All crafts are hand made from many species of timber from around the world. From £2 for a keyring to £60 for a jewellery box. Mail order available.
Directions: *exit A31 at Holybourne roundabout; 1st right into village. We are in the village centre close to the White Hart Hotel.*
Opening hours: *weekday afternoons by appointment only.*

CENTRIC, 7 Viables Craft Centre, Harrow Way, Basingstoke, Hampshire RG22 4BJ
Est. 1989
Tel: **+44 1256-811911**
Fax: **+44 1256-358086**

Brian Hannam is a woodturner registered with the Worshipful Company of Turners, specialising in **quality decorative work for home or office**. Many stock items available for visitors to purchase. Repairs and commissions welcomed. In addition, small furniture (or almost anything) made to order. Woodturning tuition by qualified tutor available one to one.
Directions: *leave M3 at junction 6; turn left (A30) at roundabout. Follow 'Viables' signs. At Golden Lion pub roundabout go straight on. Centre on left after 400 yards.*
Opening hours: *Mon-Fri 10am-4.30pm; Sat 2pm-5pm.*

GAZE BURVILL LTD, Newtonwood Workshop, Newton Valence, Alton, Hampshire GU34 3EW.
Est. 1992
Tel: **+44 1420-587467**
Fax: **+44 1420-587354**
www.gazeburvill.com
Parking available
Wheelchair access
Credit cards

The design is contemporary, the craftsmanship traditional. The final outcome is durable and graceful: **fine furniture, for the garden**, terrace, conservatory and poolside. The timber used is oak and ash from forests managed in a sustainable way. The furniture is versatile, stylish and extremely comfortable. Mail order available.
Directions: *phone for map when appointment made.*
Opening times: *office hours by appointment.*

HUW EDWARDS-JONES DESIGNER/CABINET MAKER, The Stable, Peelings Manor Barns, Hankham Road, Stone Cross, Nr Pevensey, E Sussex BN24 5NP
Est. 1979
Tel: **+44 (0)1323-732918**
Fax: **+44 (0)1323-732918**
www.finelot.com
Parking available
Wheelchair access

Huw Edwards-Jones is a top designer/cabinet maker; **Multi Guildmark award winner**, Liveryman for the Worshipful Company of Furniture Makers, Freeman of the City of London and Member of the Sussex Guild of Craftsmen. High profile clients include HRH Prince Edward. TV appearances include John Bly's 'Heirlooms' and with Carol Vorderman.
Directions: *from Stone Cross B2104 (Hailsham Road). Right immediately after overpass. Peelings Manor Barns are 600 yards on right.*
Opening hours: *Mon-Fri 10am-6pm.*

52

PETER ARCHER WOODWORK, 20 Turner Dumbrell Workshops, North End, Ditchling, East Sussex BN6 8TD
Est. 2000
Fax: **+44 (0)1273-556218**
www.turned-wood.co.uk
Parking available

Peter Archer produces **turned wooden bowls** in a range of hardwoods specialising in enhancing the grain through colour using stains and finishes. His work can be seen in Walford Mill Gallery, Wimborne Minster. He works from Turner Dumbrell Workshops in Ditchling and visitors are always welcome. Mail order available.
Directions: *from Brighton B2112 to Ditchling. Along High Street towards Haywards Heath, Turner Dumbrell Workshops on right at the edge of the village.*
Opening hours: *Mon-Fri 9am-4pm.*

WOOD DESIGNS WORKSHOPS, The Acre, Dappers Lane, Angmering, West Sussex BN16 4EN

Est. 1987
Tel/fax: +44 (0)1903 776010
www.brendandevitt-spooner.co.uk
Parking available
Wheelchair access

Brendan Devitt-Spooner specialises in designing and making fine **contemporary solid wood furniture** from the finest hardwoods. 'Simple designs, complimentary timbers and fine workmanship are all hallmarks of my work. A lot of my furniture uses local timber I have seasoned myself.' Clients can use their own trees if wished.

Directions: *from junction of A27 and A280 take A280 to Littlehampton. At 30mph signs for Angmering take right into Dappers Lane. 4th drive on right.*

Opening hours: *Mon-Fri 9am-5.30pm. Sat by appointment.*

WOODWORKS DESIGN, 3 The Oast Paddock, Staple Farm, Durlock Road, Staple, Kent CT3 1JX

Est. 1977
Tel/fax: +44 (0)1304-813223
Parking available
Wheelchair access

Woodworks Design is the **furniture design** workshop of Barry Feldman and his son Ben. Since graduating from the Royal College of Art, Barry has worked on a wide range of projects and his hands on approach enables him to accept commissions for domestic, leisure and contract sectors. Mail order available.

Directions: *from Sandwich take A256 towards Margate. Turn left (B2190) towards Manston. Turn left (B2049). First left towards Airfield. First Nissan hut on left.*

Opening hours: *Mon-Thurs 9am-6pm by appointment only.* 55

Other Makers

ACME ART SHOP, 40 Gloucester Road, Brighton, East Sussex BN1 4AQ

Est. 1995
Tel: +44 (0)1273-601639
www.acmeartshop.com
Parking available
Wheelchair access

Since 1995 Chris MacDonald has lived, worked and sold in the cosmopolitan North Laine of Brighton. He works with wood and old technology (cameras, gauges, propellors, pocket watches etc). He produces a variety of **sculpture** that can be haunting or humorous, but always unique and beautifully made. Mail order available.

Directions: *from rail station head towards the sea. Left at big tree into Gloucester Road. Shop is 100 yards on the right.*

Opening hours: *erratic. Best to phone first.* 56

CHARLES THOMSON, Almond Barn, Five Ashes, Mayfield, East Sussex TN20 6HX

Est. 1981
Tel: +44 (0)1825-830691
www.axisartists.org.uk
Parking on forecourt

Fine contemporary furniture especially cluster leg tables. My 'cluster' leg designs are well-developed; using local hardwood, English marble, ceramics, metalwork, plastics, leather etc as a unique concept for domestic and business interiors. Tabletops in timber, glass or stone. Examples are for sale and commissions taken. Also lamps, chairs, vases. Mail order possible.

Directions: *14 miles south of Tunbridge Wells on the A267, two miles south of Mayfield and the first building in Five Ashes on the left hand side.*

Open: *12 hours a day, six and a half days a week. Please telephone in advance.* 57

CUSTOM FRAMING LTD, Units 11 & 12, Viables Craft Centre, Harrow Way, Basingstoke, Hampshire

RG22 4BJ
Est. 1993
Tel: +44 (0)1256-479211
Parking available

Bespoke and commercial picture framers set within a Craft Centre in converted Victorian farm buildings. Custom Framing aptly describes the work we carry out. Photographs, prints and original paintings - everything we do is to the customer's personal choice and expert advice is on hand. Tea-room, restaurant and summer gallery.

Directions: *Junction 6 off M3, turn left at roundabout on to A30. Viables Craft Centre is signposted. At Golden Lion pub roundabout straight on; Centre is on left.*

Opening hours: *Mon-Fri 10am-5pm, Sat 10am-3pm; Lunch closed 12pm-1pm.* 58

FINE ENGLISH TOILETRIES, 15-17 Lansdowne Road, Shirley, Southampton, Hampshire SO15 4HD

Est. 1995
Tel: +44 (0)23-8077 7709
Fax: +44 (0)23-8077 5545
Parking available
Credit cards

George Bailey-Haigh's **cosmetic and skincare company** started with pure vegetable oil soap and formulations grew from there. All products are hand made using only the best raw materials and are lanolin free - over 50 products from aftershave balm to peppermint foot cream. All skin types particularly problem/sensitive. Mail order available.
Directions: *from M3 take M271 to Southampton. Left on Millbrook Road over flyover. Right at first set of traffic lights.*
Opening hours: *Mon-Fri 8.30am-6pm.*

JAN O'HIGHWAY, Studio 4, Art Space, 27 Brougham Road, Southsea, Hampshire PO5 4PA

Est. 1985
Tel: +44 (0)2392-581101
Fax: +44 (0)2392-874523
www.artspace.co.uk
Street parking
Wheelchair access

Jan is a mosaic and ceramic artist making **ceramic tiles, sculptures, mosaics and paintings** by combining glaze painting on tiles with mosaic. She experiments with resonant colours and tactile qualities of clay and glass. Vibrant and durable, these techniques are suitable for both domestic interiors and outdoor public places. Commissions welcome.
Directions: *east along Kings Road, Southsea, left into Green Road, 2nd left into Ring Street and follow one-way system round to Brougham Road. Studio 4 below Aspex Gallery.*
Opening hours: *three days a week by appointment.*

OLD BARN NURSERIES, A24, Dial Post, Horsham, West Sussex RH13 8NR

Est. 1992
Tel: +44 (0)1403-710000
Fax: +44 (0)1403-710010
Parking available
Wheelchair access
Credit cards

The Old Barn Nurseries is a large, independent garden centre which also sells a **range of collectables** including: Highland stoneware, Frith sculptures, and other pottery and glass from Moorcroft, Poole, Kellam, Cobridge and Dartington. There is plenty of space for browsing and also for refreshments in the 18th century barn restaurant.
Directions: *18 miles south of Horsham on the A24 on the left near Dial Post village.*
Opening hours: *Mon-Sat 9am-6pm. Sun 10.30am-4.30pm.*

RYE TILES LTD, Wishward, Rye, East Sussex TN31 7DH

Est. 1966
Tel +44 (0)1797-223038
Fax +44 90)1797-225802

We specialise in **hand-painted tiles featuring flowers, fruit, birds and boats** colour matched to fabrics etc. Each is painted by hand in an 18th century style of decoration on Rye White, Bristol White, Buttermilk or Sage Glazed tiles. Endless colour combinations and patterns can be achieved by using full pattern and corner decorated tiles in a variety of ways. Special murals can be made to order and a range of screenprinted wall tiles is produced. Seconds also available. The tiles are also available by mail order. Rye Tiles can be contacted by e-mail at sales@ryepottery.sagehost.co.uk.

Directions: *Wishward is a short road behind the Strand Quay almost at the bottom of Mermaid Street in Rye.*

Opening hours: *9am-5pm Mon-Fri, 10.15am-4.30pm Sat, closed Sun and bank holidays.*

London and the Home Counties

London, Berkshire, Buckinghamshire, Essex, Hertfordshire, Oxfordshire, Surrey

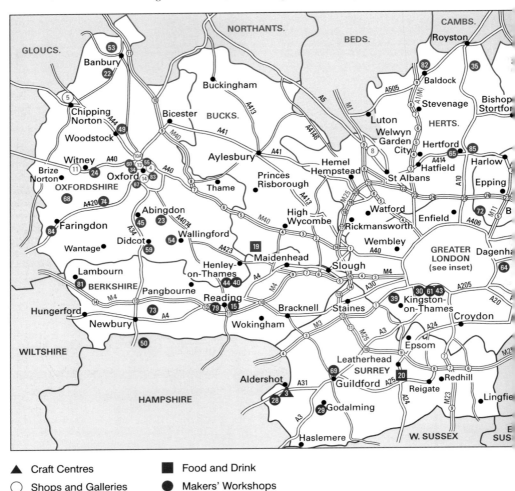

▲ Craft Centres
○ Shops and Galleries
■ Food and Drink
● Makers' Workshops

London's arts and crafts history goes back to mediaeval times. As you would expect, design-led craftspeople there, are working at the cutting edge of contemporary applied art.

You might think that DIY and building extensions are the nearest you will get to crafts in the Home Counties. However, Oxfordshire and Berkshire are known for their craft guilds and have thriving craft communities. Oxfordshire is strongly linked to the Arts and Crafts

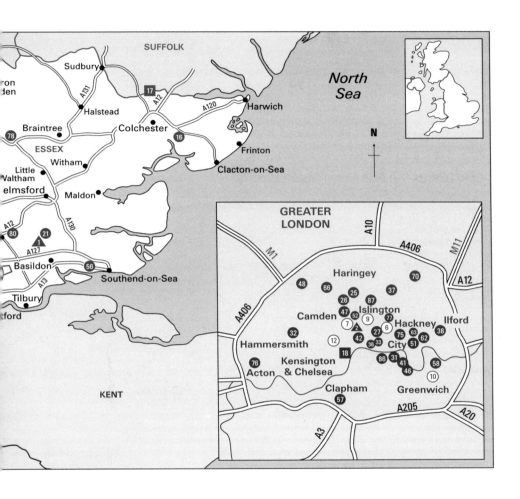

Movement founded by the Victorian architect, craftsman and interior designer William Morris, whose home, Kelmscott House is a museum of this style, especially furniture-making. South Buckinghamshire's economy once prospered from furniture hand made with Chilterns timber. In flat Essex, straw-plaiting for baskets and hats is an ancient craft and basketmaking continues there today.

Craft Centres

BARLEYLANDS FARM CRAFT CENTRE, Barleylands Road, Billericay, Essex

Est. 1991
Tel: +44 (0)1268-532253
Fax: +44 (0)1268-290222
Parking available
Wheelchair access
Credit cards (some units)

Comprises various craft shops including glassblowing studio, blacksmith, dolls' house shop and stained glass studio. Part of a large open farm attraction that includes a farm museum, animal centre, tearooms and restaurant. Many special events throughout the season including Essex Steam and Country Show with 150 craft stands. Mail order (some units).
Directions: *off A129 Southend road between Billericay and Wickford. Barleylands Farm is signposted off the A12 and A127.*
Open: *1 Mar-31st October daily; 10am-4pm; closed Mon (except bank holidays).*

CLERKENWELL GREEN ASSOCIATION, Cornwell House, 21 Clerkenwell Green, London EC1R ODP

Est. 1971
Tel: +44 (0)20-7251-0276
Fax: +44 (0)20-7251-0297
www.cga.org.uk
Parking available
Wheelchair access to ground floor only.

A charity which exists to maintain traditional skills associated with Clerkenwell for centuries, and which were in danger of being lost e.g. making jewellery, watches, musical instruments, textiles, ceramics and engraving etc. Through various initiatives including 80 on-site workshops, part-time workspaces and courses the Association has succeeded in preserving such skills.
Directions: *left out of Farringdon tube station, left again into Turnmill Street; the CGA building is at the end of Turnmill Street.*
Opening hours: *Mon-Fri 9am-5pm.*

FARNHAM MALTINGS, Bridge Square, Farnham, Surrey GU9 7QR

Tel: +44 (0)1252-726234
Fax: +44 (0)1252-718177
www.farnammaltings.com
Est. 1996
Parking available
Limited wheelchair access
Credit cards (some exhibitors)

Farnham Maltings is an arts and community centre which incorporates a selling exhibition of contemporary crafts, including ceramics, textiles, glass, metal, jewellery and wood. There is a potter and artist/sculptor in residence and courses are run in the above crafts. Also live demonstrations. Gallery and tearoom/restaurant.
Directions: *from the A31 follow signs to Town Centre and Farnham Maltings.*
Opening hours: *26/27 May-20/21 October 10am-5pm. Admission to exhibition £2.50; up to 15 years free.*

Craft Shops

BRIDGET WHEATLEY CONTEMPORARY JEWELLERY, 38 Cowley Road, Oxford, Oxfordshire OX4 1HZ

Est. 2000 at above address
Tel: +44 (0)1865-722184
Fax: +44 (0)1865-790858
www.bridgetwheatley.com
Parking available
Credit cards

The shop is a light and airy showroom for the work of many designer/makers, alongside Bridget's own ranges of unique jewellery. There is a welcoming atmosphere within a working environment. The jewellery is from an eclectic group of artists and is diverse in design and materials. A bespoke service is available.
Directions: *20 minutes walk from Oxford City Centre down the High Street and over Magdalen Bridge.*
Opening hours: *Tues-Sat 10am-5.30pm.*

OXFORDSHIRE CRAFT GUILD MARKETING CO-OPERATIVE (OCGMC), 7 Goddards Lane, Chipping Norton, Oxfordshire OX7 5NP

Est. 1994
Tel: +44 (0)1608-641525
www.ocgcraftshop.co.uk
Parking available
Credit cards

This co-operative venture is a small retail outlet for 20 members of the Oxfordshire Craft Guild and is staffed by craftspeople. Crafts include pottery, textiles, fine metals, wood, glass and jewellery. Most items are priced in the range of £10-£100 and several members are happy to accept commissions.

Directions: *the shop is located next to the daytime box office of the Chipping Norton Theatre in Chipping Norton town centre.*

PURE FAB EAST, 126 Columbia Road, London E2

Est. 1998
Tel: +44 (0)20-7328 2182
Street/meter parking.
Wheelchair access difficult

Annie Sherburne's shop Pure Fab East offers an eclectic range of contemporary applied art and crafts including jewellery made with mosaic, semi-precious stones or antique beads, etched or patinated (mixed metals). Also textiles including tufted rugs and wallhangings, felts and other work by British makers. Mail order available.

Directions: *tube to Liverpool Street/Old Street, then walk, taxi or bus to Shoreditch Church. Shop is half way along flower market opposite mosaic on school wall*

Opening hours: *only Sundays 9.30am-2.30pm.*

Galleries

BAGGY BOTTOM GALLERY, 4 Cornwell House, 21 Clerkenwell Green, London EC1R ODP

Est. 1999
Tel: +44 (0)20-7336 6837
Fax: +44 (0)20-7250 0297
www.hiddenart.co.uk
Parking available.
Wheelchair access
Credit cards (online only)

Rebecca Skeels's gallery exhibits and sells ceramics, textiles, glass, cards, bags, albums, paintings. Pieces are displayed individually and are made by local designers and makers. Work combines funky style with traditional methods. 'Experimentation with new materials and techniques, using dazzling combinations of form and texture creating wonderfully expressive pieces.' Mail order available.

Directions: *by tube/train: Circle, Hammersmith, Metropolitan or Thameslink to Farringdon tube station. Left from tube and left again into Turnmill Street, then right at end of street.*

Opening hours: *Tues-Fri 10am-6pm; Sat 10am-2pm. Other times by appointment.* (7)

COLLECTIONS OF HARPENDEN, The Leys, 38 High Street, Harpenden, Herts. AL5 2SX

Est. 1999
Tel +44 (0)1582-620015
Parking available.
Wheelchair access
Credit cards

Since opening in November 1999 in the centre of Harpenden Collections has received a very positive response to selling art and crafts in this part of Hertfordshire. The Gallery has a constantly changing display of ceramics, jewellery, glass, wood and textiles. Although many artists featured are well known, work by up-and-coming artists is also shown. As well as catering for the collector, Collections is the ideal place to find an unusual handmade gift for whatever the occasion. Gift wrapping is provided free of charge and prices range from under £15 to over £300. A Crafts Council recommended Gallery.

Directions: *located mid-way along the High Street, opposite WH Smith.*

Opening hours: *Tues-Sat 10am-5pm.*

(8)

CRAFTS COUNCIL GALLERY/SHOP, 44a Pentonville Road, Islington, London N1 9BY

Tel: +44 (0)20-7278 7700
Fax: +44 (0)20-7833 4479
www.craftscouncil.org.uk
No parking nearby
Wheelchair access
Credit cards

The Crafts Council gallery runs major exhibitions, a resource centre and a gallery shop. The Council aims to raise the profile of crafts and to strengthen and develop the crafts economy in support of craftspeople. The shop stocks a range of craftwork and handles sales for the gallery exhibitions. Mail order available.

Directions: *5 minutes walk from Angel tube station.*

Opening hours: *Tues-Sat 11am-5.45pm; Sun 2-5.45pm.*   ⑨

HARLEQUIN GALLERY, 68 Greenwich High Road, London SE10 8LF

Est. 1990
Tel: +44 (0)20-8692 7170
www.studio-pots.com
Meter parking
Wheelchair access
Credit cards

John Rastall's Harlequin Gallery exhibits both contemporary and classic (after Leach, Rie etc) studio pottery with about eight selling exhibitions a year. Recent exhibitions have included Mike Dodd, Jim Malone, Phil Rogers, Svend Bayer, Nic Collins, Ursula Mommens, Joanna Howells and Katerina Evangelidou. Also offered are paintings and sculpture. Mail order available.

Directions: *situated 150 yards west of Greenwich Docklands Light Railway station at the opposite end of the road.*

Open: *Thurs-Sun 11am-5.30pm (late Fri to 8pm). Other times by appointment.*   ⑩

INSPIRES ART GALLERY, 27 Little Clarendon Street, Oxford, Oxfordshire OX1 2HU

Est. 2000
Tel/fax: +44 (0)1865-556555
www.inspires.co.uk
Good local parking
Wheelchair access

The gallery specialises in the best of contemporary art and aims to show the widest possible range which can be viewed in relaxing surroundings. Bronze sculptures and figures, ceramics and glassware from an extensive range of sources are shown, plus original paintings by local and internationally known artists, framed etchings and lithographs.

Directions: *Little Clarendon Street is off the bottom of the Woodstock Road, 5 minutes walk north from central Oxford.*

Opening hours: *10am-6pm Mon-Fri, 9.30am-6pm Sat.*   ⑩a

PICTURE THIS ARTS AND CRAFTS GALLERY, 17 Corn Street, Witney, Oxfordshire OX28 6DB

Est. 2000
Tel: +44 (0)1993-708870
Parking available nearby

'Picture This' is a gallery and craft shop run by Janine Legard and Lily Stiffel, for local artists and craftspeople to show and sell their work. The range covers jewellery, hand-painting on silk/glass/china etc., mosaic work, wood, textiles, prints, original paintings. Prices from £1.50-£150. Mail order available.

Directions: *Corn Street is directly opposite the Buttercross, just past the market square, right off the High Street.*

Opening hours: *Mon-Sat 10am-5pm.*   ⑪

REBECCA HOSSACK GALLERY, 35 Windmill Street, London W1P 1HH

Est. 1988
Tel: +44 (0)20-7436 4889
Fax: +44 (0)20-7323 3182
www.r-h-g.co.uk
Parking available
Wheelchair access
Credit cards

The Rebecca Hossack Gallery has established itself as one of the leading champions in the British gallery scene. Exhibitions cover international and British makers and range from Pippa Small's jewellery and John Mackechnie's architectural screenprints to those featuring the products of African, Australian and Papua New Guinea artists and artisans.

Directions: *by tube to Goodge Street or Tottenham Court Road and 2 minutes direct walk.*

Opening hours: *Mon-Sat 10am-6pm.*   ⑫

STELLA CAMPION - COWLEY ROAD STUDIOS, The Workshop, rear of 100 Cowley Road,

Oxford, Oxon OX4 1JE

Est. 1987
Tel +44 (0)1865-790867
Parking at rear of Tesco

A newly opened gallery in east Oxford run by award-winning silversmith Stella Campion. Stella has produced silverware for many Oxford and Cambridge colleges and churches, including Christchurch Cathedral. In addition to silver Stella works with gold and platinum, both with and without stones; she produces jewellery, beakers and bowls. The gallery has a permanent exhibition of gold and silver jewellery and also holds regular exhibitions by artists and makers of many disciplines. Stella's work can also be seen at the 'Art in Action' Gallery at Waterperry in Oxfordshire and at prestigious galleries nationwide.. Products also available by mail order.

Directions: *5/10 minutes walk from the end of Oxford High Street: take the first right hand turn down the side of the Spice Tree Indian restaurant.*

Opening hours: *9am-5pm Mon-Sat.*

VERANDAH, 13 North Parade, Oxford, OX2 6LX

Est. 1998
Tel/fax: +44 (0)1865-310123
Parking available
Wheelchair access
Credit cards

Verandah is owned and run by five local designers, whose aim is to create a truly exciting shop in an unusual street. The gallery features the work of the owners and a rich mixture of other ceramics, jewellery, papier-mâché, prints, knitwear, painted silks, glass and metalwork - collected from makers throughout Britain.

Directions: *ten minutes walk from the centre of Oxford - off the Banbury Road.*

Opening hours: *Mon-Sat 10am-5.30pm.*

Baskets & Wickerwork

A. RICHARDS, 63 Tintern Crescent, Coley Park, Reading, Berkshire RG1 6HB

Est. 1901
Tel: +44 (0)118-9582320
Parking available
Wheelchair access

Basket-making has been in the Richards family for a hundred years. We make a large range of hand made baskets, including linen baskets, log and dog baskets, picnic hampers, flower display and fruit baskets. **English willow, rustic baskets a speciality**. We also re-cane chairs and do wicker repairs. Mail order available.

Directions: *off Berkeley Avenue close to Reading town centre.*

Opening hours: *by appointment.*

MALCOLM RUFFELL BASKET MAKER AND ORNAMENTAL WILLOW WORKER, Vine Cottage, Great

Bentley Road, Frating, Colchester, Essex C07 7HW

Est. 1997
Tel: +44 (0)1206-251704
Parking available

A self-taught basket maker, I make **traditional willow baskets** using willow grown on the Somerset Levels. Traditional baskets include shopping, picnic and dog baskets. More unusual commissions have included a basket for a mechanical ferret at Santa Land. I also make willow garden items. Mail order available.

Directions: *situated on the B1029 between Frating and Thorrington, 9 miles east of Colchester.*

Opening hours: *by appointment.*

Food & Drink

CARTER'S VINEYARD, Green Lane, Boxted, Colchester, Essex C04 5TS

Est. 1991
Tel: +44 (0)1206-271136
Fax: +44 (0)1206-273625
Parking available
Wheelchair access
Credit cards

Carter's vineyard sits in the beautiful Stour Valley and comprises seven acres of vines, a lake and a nature trail. It is a working vineyard producing English wines, and offers tours and tastings. Adults charged £2.50. Evening tours, tastings and candlit suppers for pre-arranged groups. Mail order available.

Directions: *from A134 at Great Horkesley, turn right into Boxted Church Road, then second right into Green Lane. Vineyard is a quarter of a mile further.*

Opening hours: *Easter to Oct, Tues-Sun 11am-5pm and bank holidays.*   `17`

CHATSWORTH FARM SHOP, 54/56 Elizabeth Street, London SW1W 9PB

Est. 2000 (main shop 1977)
Tel: +44 (0)20-7730 3033
Fax: +44 (0)20-7730 3188
www.gustum.com
Parking meters outside
Wheelchair access
Credit cards

The original Chatsworth Estate Farm Shop in Derbyshire was established as a direct outlet for the Estate's beef and lamb. The London shop offers one of the best ranges of speciality food and drink in Britain together with fresh baked foods from the Estate, and from the on-site kitchen. Mail order available.

Directions: *between Eaton Square and Victoria Coach Station in the heart of Belgravia. Nearest tube stations: Victoria and Sloane Square.*

Opening hours: *Mon-Fri 9am-7pm; Sat 9am-1pm.*   `18`

CHILTERN VALLEY, Old Luxters Winery and Brewery, Hambledon, Henley-on-Thames, Oxfordshire RG9 6OW

Est. 1984
Tel: +44 (0)1491-638330
Fax: +44 (0)1491-638645
www.luxters.co.uk
Parking available
Credit cards

David Ealand's first vineyard was planted in 1982 on the slopes of the Chiltern Hills, a well-known beauty area. Chiltern Valley wines are now served in some prestigious establishments. Tastings offered to the public. Additionally an independent brewery offering traditional farm-brewed 'real' ales. Liqueurs also sold. Mail order available.

Directions: *off the Henley-Marlow A4155 road, (junction 8/9 off M4). At the Mill End junction follow signs to Chiltern Valley Winery and Brewery. After Hambledon follow grape signs.*

Opening hours: *Mon-Fri 9am-5pm; Sat/Sun 11am-5pm.*   `19`

DENBIES WINE ESTATE, London Road, Dorking, Surrey RH5 6AA

Est. 1990
Tel: +44 (0)1306-876616
Fax: +44 (0)1306-888930
www.denbiesvineyard.co.uk
Own free parking
Wheelchair access
Credit cards

Located in the beautiful Mole Valley on the Surrey Downs, Denbies offers an orchestrated visitor experience: year round tours of the flint-clad winery by indoor/outdoor train, cellar tastings, a film about winemaking and browsing in the Wine and Gift Shop amongst diverse wines and related gifts. Mail order available. Entrance fee.

Directions: *on the A24, close to the M25 and A3 from London. By train: 15 minutes walk from Dorking station.*

Opening hours: *Jan-Mar Mon-Fri 11am-3pm, Sat 11am-4pm, Sun noon to 4pm. Apr-Dec open 1 hr later Mon-Fri.*   `20`

Glass

CUT'N'EDGE, Unit 10, Barleylands Farm Museum, Barleylands Road, Billericay, Essex CM11 2UD

Est. 1997
Tel/fax: +44 (0)1268-527900
Parking available

CUT'N'EDGE is a small stained glass workshop specialising in one-off **stained glass windows, doors and screens**. We are also able to execute restoration work, usually on-site; we have experience of Grade 1&II listed buildings. In addition, we can provide cast glass, sandblasting and laminating. All work is strictly unique.

Directions: *off A129 Southend road between Billericay and Wickford. Barleylands Farm is signposted off the A12 and A127. After entering the main gates, Cut'n'edge is above the blacksmith.*

Opening hours: *often out on installations so please phone first.*

JOLA GLASS, Willows End, Banbury Road, Bloxham, Oxfordshire OX15 4PD

Est. 1999
Parking available
Wheelchair access

Joan Kingston makes **bowls, glass panels, frames and jewellery**. She uses glass fusion to create layers of shape and colour, using high-quality glass. First she cuts shapes from a mixture of transparent and opaque mirrored glass then places one shape on another to create a three-dimensional effect. Mail order available.

Directions: *from Banbury take A361 towards Chipping Norton. Willows End is on the right hand side after the 30mph signs in Bloxham. About two miles from Banbury.*
Opening hours: *by appointment only.*

JULIA NEWBOLD, Woodlea, 6 Oxford Road, Dorchester-on-Thames, Oxfordshire OX10 7LX

Est. 1999
Tel: +44 (0)1865-340669
Fax: +44 (0)1865-340022
Parking available

Julia makes vibrant and **colourful, contemporary, kiln-formed glass**. She specialises in shallow vessels, screens, tiles and architectural glass for domestic and public applications. The work involves layers of glass with metal leaf and glass enamel inclusions creating an abstract image. Each piece is unique. Willing to discuss commissions.

Directions: *Oxford Road is at the northern end of Dorchester-on-Thames, past The Plough public house.*
Opening hours: *by appointment.*

JUNE KING, 18, Old Witney Road, Eynsham, Oxfordshire OX29 4PR

Est. 1996
Tel: +44 (0)1865-883830
Parking available

Creating **beautiful things from stained glass** became more than an absorbing hobby when friends started asking me to make unique personal items. A new design is always an exciting challenge: most of my panels, suncatchers, mirrors and mosaics are inspired by nature. Prices are from £10 to £300.

Directions: *located on the west side of the village approximately 100 yards past the furniture shop.*
Opening hours: *by appointment.*

REFIA SACKS, The Highbury Centre, 137 Grosvenor Avenue, London N5 2NH

Est. 1979
Tel: +44 (0)207-226 1815
Parking available

Commissions accepted for individual designs in stained glass. My work is sensitive and adaptable to your needs. I can produce **windows and decorative panels** made to my designs or yours, using painting, acid etching, sandblasting and leading. I also do all kinds of silverware to commission (e.g. boxes, bowls, picture frames etc).

Directions: *easy by public transport. Details given when appointment made.*
Opening hours: *very flexible but appointment necessary.*

STONEY PARSONS GLASS DESIGN, 231 Aberdeen House, 22-24 Highbury Grove, London N5 2EA

Est. 1994
Tel/fax: +44 (0)20-7226 4241
www.stoneyparsons.co.uk
Parking available
Wheelchair access
Credit cards

Architectural glass including **windows, doors and screens** made in high quality original stained glass. Everything is made to commission using traditional techniques such as painting and fining, acid etching and sand-blasting. Emphasis on sympathetic design, contemporary and traditional. Domestic, commercial and ecclesiastical. Stained glass classes also offered. Mail order available.

Directions: *in Aberdeen Centre, opposite Highbury Fields near Highbury and Islington tube (Victoria Line).*

Opening hours: *by appointment.*   (26)

Jewellery

BAGGY BOTTOM DESIGNS, 4 Cornwell House, 21 Clerkenwell Green, London EC1R 0DP

Est. 1994
Tel: +44 (0)20-7336 6837
www.hiddenart.co.uk
Parking available
Wheelchair access
Credit cards

Three dimensional contemporary silver jewellery made up of pod-like pieces with contrasts of colour, texture and form using mixed materials such as silver, textured rubber and foam. The necklaces, bracelets and pendants being the most dazzling pieces; double-sided with different colours and textures for different occasions. Mail order via internet.

Directions: *tube to Farringdon. Turn left out of tube; left again into Turnmill Street; right into Clerkenwell Road. Gallery on the opposite side.*

Open: *Tues-Fri 10am-6pm; Sat 10am-2pm. Other times by appointment.*   (27)

CLARE STREET, Little Orchard, Woodcut Road, Wrecclesham, Farnham, Surrey GU10 4QF

Est. 1968
Tel/fax +44 (0)1252-733232
Parking available for one car
No wheelchair access

Clare Street is a designer and jeweller whose work specialises in two areas. The first is hand engraving and includes her **award-winning seal engraved signet rings** for which a leaflet is available. Brooches and tie studs may be carved in positive relief, medal dies and line engraved silver plaques mounted on hardwood. Engraving to commission only, of heraldic or other design evolved after close consultation with her client, be they a private person or a corporation. Clare's second area of work is in gold and platinum jewellery, working mainly to commission though a limited collection is available including by mail order.

Directions: *will be given when an appointment is arranged.*

Opening hours: *by appointment only Mon-Sat.*   (28)

CORCYRA'S CREATION, The Old Firestation, Queen Street, Godalming, Surrey GU7 1BD

Tel: +44 (0)1483-239388
Fax: +44 (0)1483-414354
www.corcyra.co.uk
Parking available
Wheelchair access

Ann Nash of Corcyra Designer Jewellery produces a collection of **contemporary pieces in silver** with details of gold and semi-precious stones, inspired by gastropod shells, corals, sea urchins and other natural forms. Commissions welcomed. Mail order available. Customers include Hampton Court Palace, London and Sazabys in Tokyo.

Directions: *from Godalming High Street turn second left into Queen Street.*

Opening hours: *Tues-Fri 10am-6pm; Sat 10am-12pm.*   (29)

DANI C. CONTEMPORARY JEWELLERY DESIGNER, 6 High Cedar Drive, Wimbledon, London SW20 ONU

Tel: +44 (0)20-8947 4426
Fax: +44 (0)20-8947 3987
Parking available

Dani C creates modern jewellery in a range of materials, e.g. **precious metals, perspex and rubber**. Designs are bold, colourful and fun including Plastic Fantastic, a range of coloured perspex that glows under UV lighting and wedding accessories (rings, tiaras etc) to commission. Prices range from £8-£270. Mail order available.

Directions: *off Copse Hill, leading into Wimbledon village near the A3.*

Opening hours: *Mon-Tues by appointment.*

DAVID ASHTON, Shop 6, Gabriel's Wharf, 56 Upper Ground, London SE1 9PP

Est. 1980
Tel: +44 (0)20-7401 2405
Fax: +44 (0)20-7928 9762
www.davidashton.co.uk
Parking available
Credit cards

We work to commission in 18ct gold and platinum, diamond, sapphire and ruby to create **contemporary, individual, practical jewellery** including rings, bracelets and earrings. We are known for our unique two-tone stripe and dot rings. We use the finest stones and work to the highest standards. Mail order available. Ask for brochure.

Directions: *on South Bank half way between the Waterloo and Blackfriars bridges in Gabriel's Wharf, central London.*

Opening hours: *Tues-Fri 11am-5.30pm; Sat 11am-5pm.*

ISIS, 3 Portobello Green, 281, Portobello Road, London W10 5TY

Est. 1982
Tel: +44 (0)20-8968 5055
Meter parking.
Wheelchair access
Credit cards

Linda Atkinson is a graduate of the Royal College of Art, who has been designing and making jewellery for over 20 years. At her gallery/workshop customers can find **exclusive jewellery** which can only be bought there. Linda also offers a commission service for customers who want one-off pieces. Mail order available.

Directions: *entrance to Portobello Green is on Portobello Road. Isis is the first shop on the right. Nearest tube station: Ladbroke Grove.*

Opening hours: *9.30am-5.30pm.*

KATIE CLARKE, Studio W4, Cockpit Yard, Northington Street, London WC1N 2NP

Est. 1997
Tel/fax: +44 (0)20-7831 3441
www.katieclarke.co.uk
Meter parking.

Katie Clarke produces a collection of **contemporary jewellery and accessories** using feathers, elastic and precious metals. The range includes earrings, necklaces and large neckpieces, cuff-links, rings and drawstring evening bags (velvet and feather). She also does special commissions e.g. feather hair slides etc for weddings. Mail order available.

Directions: *nearest tubes: Russell Square, Holborn, Chancery Lane. Cockpit yard is off Northington Street and Great James Street off Theobald's and Grays Inn Roads.*

Open: *6 days a week by appointment only plus occasional open weekends.*

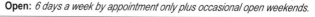

NICOLA HUNTER, 36 Chalfont Road, Oxford, Oxfordshire OX2 6TG

Est. 2001
Tel: +44 (0)1865 511578
Parking available
Wheelchair access

I make **bracelets, earrings and necklaces** of interesting and unusual materials including crystal beads, coloured pearls, and semi-precious stones. They are designed to be striking and individual as well as easy to wear. They make excellent presents as they suit most people and ages and are lightweight for posting.

Directions: *from city centre north up Woodstock Road. Turn left after about one mile down Polstead Road, then first right into Chalfont Road.*

Opening hours: *evenings Mon-Sat. Please telephone first for appointment.*

NICOLA HURST DESIGNER JEWELLERY, The Bath House,˙81 High Street, Barkway, Nr. Royston,

Hertfordshire SG8 8ED

Est. 1996
Tel: +44 (0)1763-848129
www.nicolahurst.co.uk
Street parking

Nicola designs, makes and exhibits **silver and 18ct gold jewellery** at her workshop in Hertfordshire. She also specialises in creating wedding accessories. New collections are created annually and can be viewed on her website. Commissions undertaken have included babies' christening bangles, initialled cuff-links and personalised napkin rings. Mail order available.

Directions: *given once appointment is made.*

Opening hours: *by appointment only.*

SARA HARTLEY DESIGNS, Studio E8, Cockpit Arts, Cockpit Yard, Northington Street, London WC1N 2NP

Est. 1998
Tel: +44 (0)20-7813 7904
Fax: +44 (0)20-7916 2455
www.sarahartley.co.uk
Parking available
Wheelchair access
Credit cards

An exciting range of designer, handmade 18ct **gold and diamond, and silver with gold jewellery** complementing an existing **silver collection of interlocking and connecting forms** displaying a full range of earrings, necklaces, rings, bracelets and cuff-links. Commissions always welcome to suit any request. Mail order for those familiar with the product.

Directions: *nearest tube Holborn. Go down Theobald's Road; left at Great James Street, follow road round to Northington Street; first on right. Building on left.*

Opening hours: *only by appointment (also two annual open days).*

ZYKOS JEWELLERY, Studio 4A, Leroy House, 436 Essex Road, London N1 3QP

Est. 1983
Tel/fax: +44 (0)207-359 9894
Parking in Dove Road

Esther Eyre undertakes **commissions in goldsmithing and jewellery** in traditional, modern and classic styles. Available from Fortnum and Mason in London, or arranged with individual clients. Commercial commissions include gold work and jewellery for films (including 'Orlando', 'Shakespeare in Love') and for London's Globe Theatre. Prices from £100-£50,000. Mail order available.

Directions: *situated at the intersection with Essex/Baels Pon Road, N1.*

Opening hours: *only by appointment.*

Leatherwork

DALLISONS LEATHER LINING, Unit 122, Stratford Workshops, Burford Road, Stratford, London E15 2SP

Est.1991
Tel: +44 (0)20-8519 0262
Fax: +44 (0)20-8503 0390
Parking available
Wheelchair access
Credit cards

Leather dressers for upholstery and furnishing. Our hand and pre-dyed hide and skivers are embossed blind or with gold. We do lining in our workshops and the products can be ordered loose to order or by post. We make **leather table tops and dummy book backs** or shelf-edging to order.

Directions: *on north side of River Thames, three miles east from City of London.*

Opening hours: *Mon-Fri 8am-5pm.*   (38)

DT LEATHERGOODS, The Coach House, Feltham Avenue, East Molesey, Hampton Court, Surrey KT8 9BJ

Est. 1993
Tel: +44 (0)20-8941 0820
Parking available
Wheelchair access

David Tendler designs and makes leathergoods, specialising in **handbags, wallets and fireside bellows**. Bellows are made from hide and hardwood. He welcomes commissions and enjoys working directly with clients. He also offers a comprehensive leathergoods repair service covering bags, cases, bellows, jewel boxes, leather clothes, footstools and other items.

Directions: *Enter Feltham Avenue off Riverbank, 200 yards from Hampton Court Bridge.*

Opening hours: *often Mon-Fri 9am-3pm; times vary appointment necessary.*   (39)

Metalwork & Silversmithing

BETHAN GRIFFITHS DESIGN, Hampstead Farm, Binfield Heath, Nr. Henley-on-Thames, Oxfordshire RG9 4LG

Est. 1999
Tel: +44 (0)118-9692969
www.bethan-griffiths.co.uk
Parking available
Wheelchair access

We specialise in the design and making of **wood and metal furniture and accessories**. Our furniture and other work combines the skills of blacksmithing and cabinet making to produce unusual and durable items ranging from candlesticks to staircases and railings. Small range of stock items; most work is to commission.

Directions: *farm access directly from A4155 between Shiplake and Playhatch. Do not go to Binfield Heath village. Please phone for further details.*

Opening hours: *variable 9am-5pm. Appointment necessary.* **40**

HOWARD FENN, 9 The Leathermarket, Weston Street, London SE1 3ER

Est. 1979
Tel: +44 (0)20-73789222
Fax: +44 (0)20-74036381
Parking available
Wheelchair access

Top designer silversmith specialising in **contemporary silver and metalwork**, often combined with glass, wood or slate. Wide range of items including tableware, trophies, cutlery, hairbrushes, candelabra, clocks etc. Prices £30-£10,000 suiting all kinds of clients. A variety of items can be viewed. Also teaches regular, fun one-day silversmithing workshops at the studio.

Directions: *close to London Bridge Railway and Underground. Studio/workshop is through the main gate to Leathermarket and to the back right of the complex.*

Opening hours: *Mon-Fri 9.30am-6pm; weekends by appointment.* **41**

JOCELYN BURTON LTD, 50c Red Lion Street, London WC1R 4PF

Est. 1969, Ltd. since 1991
Tel: +44 (0)20-7405 3042
Fax: +44 (0)20-7831 9324
www.jocelynburton.co.uk
Parking available
Wheelchair access

Jocelyn Burton is an admired creator of modern gold and silver work. She usually works by modelling her work in plaster, making the moulds in house, and sending them out for casting. She has worked with glass, crystal, precious stones etc. and her work ranges from enormous **table centrepieces to beautiful jewellery**.

Directions: *studio is down a small alley beside the Edoko Japanese Restaurant on Red Lion Street in Holborn.*

Opening hours: *10am-5pm. By appointment only.* **42**

KEITH REDFERN DESIGNS, 1 Akehurst Street, Roehampton, London SW15 5DR

Est. 1970
Tel/fax: +44 (0)20-8788 0398
Parking available

Highest quality design and craftsmanship in gold and silver. Individual designs for corporate and private clients made to commission. Specialisms: **table silver, fine jewellery**. Major commissions: Communion set for HM The Queen, water jugs for the Silver Trust. Major collections: The Goldsmiths Company, The Middle Temple. Prices from £100. Mail order possible.

Directions: *will be given when appointment made.*

Opening hours: *please make an appointment during normal working hours.* **43**

OLD HOUSE STORE, Hampstead Farm, Binfield Heath, Henley-on-Thames, Oxfordshire RG9 4LG

Est. 2000
Tel: +44 (0)118-9697711
Fax: +44 (0)118-9698822
Parking available
Wheelchair access

Offers a range of **traditional, hand-forged fixtures and fittings**. Their off-the-shelf range includes door and window furniture suitable for period houses both restored and newbuilt. Items include latches, hinges, curtain poles hooks, bolts etc. They also offer a bespoke designing service using traditional materials and methods where appropriate. Mail order available.

Directions: *located on the A4155 in the dip between Playhatch and Shiplake.*

Opening hours: *Mon-Fri 8am-5pm.* **44**

PHILIP WAKEHAM PEWTER AND BRONZE, 35 Stert Street, Abingdon, Oxfordshire OX14 3JF

Est. 2000
Tel: +44 (1235)525732
Parking available

Philp Wakeham makes a range of **sculptures, boxes, bowls, mirrors, candlesticks** etc. to his own original designs. He also works to commission and has completed a wide range of tableware, plaques, animals, urns, church fonts, chess sets, pewter worktops, trophies, candalabra etc. Work is to the highest quality. Prices are from £10-£3000.

Directions: *Stert Street is on the one-way system in town centre. Details given when arranging appointment.*

Opening hours: *by appointment only.[maker 45]*

 45

RICHARD FOX ASSOCIATES, 9A Peacock Yard, London SE17 3LH

Est. 1982
Tel: +44 (0)20-7701 5540
Fax: +44 (0)20-7708 0759
www.foxsilver.net
Parking available
Credit cards

Richard Fox's designs are based on strong flowing forms, the polished silver emphasising its geometry. Notable commissions by the Goldsmith's Company, The Archbishop of Canterbury, 10 Downing Street and Formula One Motor Racing. Work includes **tableware, trophies, awards, cutlery, candelabra** and gifts (wedding, anniversary, christening etc.). Mail order available UK and abroad.

Directions: *nearest undergrounds are Kennington or Elephant and Castle. Workshop is located between Newington Butts and Walworth Road in Southwark district.*

46

Pottery & Ceramics

ANDREA PETERS, Studio 3, Peabody Yard, Greenman Street, Islington, London N18

Est. 1996
Tel/fax: +44 (0)207-359 5646
Parking available

Andrea makes **contemporary, hand-built ceramics with reclaimed glass** (from wine, whisky, water and beer bottles) including hand-made sinks, tiles, mirrors, bowls, cups and saucers etc. Work ranges from tiny espresso cups to complete bathrooms. Exhibitions include The International Contemporary Furniture Fair in New York and the Canary Wharf Showcase.

Directions: *Peabody Yard in Greenman Street, is just off Essex Road within five minutes walk of Angel and Highbury and Islington underground stations.*

Opening hours: *by appointment or telephone for exhibition opening hours.*

 47

ANN STOKES, 20 Church Row, London NW3 6UP

Est. 1960
Tel: +44 (0)207-436 4899
(Hossack Gallery)
Parking difficult

Anne Stokes has been making pottery for over 40 years. Her work is instinctive and naturalistic, and is nearer to the Mediterranean tradition than the Northern one. She makes **pieces representing plants, animals and fish** as well as tableware, lamps, mirrors etc and she favours bright multicoloured effects.

Directions: *top of Fitzjohns Avenue.*

Opening hours: *by appointment.*

 48

AUDREY STOCKWIN, Glym Cottage, Glympton Road, Wootton, Woodstock, Oxfordshire OX20 1EL

Est. 1982
Tel: +44 (0)1993-811449
Parking available
Wheelchair access

I have worked and studied pottery in Australia and Japan over nearly 40 years. My **stoneware tableware** is functional and ovenproof and prices range from £10 for a mug to £45 for acasserole. I also make a range of decorative vases, bowls and bottles in porcelain priced from £12-£60. Mail order available.

Directions: *on the edge of Wootton on B4027, opposite Killingworth Castle pub.*

Opening hours: *flexible, please ring for an appointment.*

 49

GEOFFREY EASTOP CERAMICS, The Old Post Office, Ecchinswell, Nr. Newbury, Berkshire

Est. 1962
Tel/fax: +44 (0)1635-298220
www.bsgart.com
Parking available
Wheelchair access

Ceramics as sculpture in stoneware or porcelain and hand-built. My work is exhibited and is largely one-off and unique comprising 'hollow walls' in three basic shapes: rectangle with curved base, monolith and wave ('S' shaped from side view) and vary in height from nine to 35/40 inches. Can be indoor or outdoor pieces.

Directions: *from Newbury take A339 Basingstoke Road; right at roundabout signed Ecchinswell. Look for house with sheds, 200 yards past pond on right.*

Opening hours: *10am-6pm. Prior appointment necessary.*

GERALDINE MCGLOIN CERAMICS, Unit 232, Stratford Workshops, Burford Road, London E15 2SP

Est. 1999
Tel: +44 (0)20-8503 1030
Fax: +44 (0)20-8503 0390
www.geraldine.mcgloin.com
Parking available
Wheelchair access

I design and make **functional slip cast, semi-porcelain domestic ware.** My work contains a strong interactive element; pieces have individual functions, but also make bold group statements. Surface decoration is kept to a minimum, simple graphics with strong colours both retro and modish. Prices from £11. Mail order via the website.

Directions: *from Stratford centre, follow Stratford High Road west towards Bow/The City. Burford Road is the first left as you pass over the railway.*

Opening hours: *by appointment only.*

KIRSTON HAWKINS, Studio 3, Peabody Yard, Greenman Street, London N1 8SE

Est. 1999
Tel/fax:
 +44 (0)20-7359 5646
Parking available

Kirston studied ceramics as an apprentice in Bolivia. Her collection of **domestic tableware** consists of bowls, plates, mugs and beakers. Pieces are thrown individually in stoneware or fine, translucent porcelain and demonstrate fine craftsmanhip. Inspired by traditional forms, her work is given a contemporary look by the use of beautiful modern glazes.

Directions: *Peabody Yard in Greenman Street, is just off Essex Road within five minutes walk of Angel and Highbury and Islington underground stations.*

Opening hours: *please telephone for an appointment.*

KNR CERAMICS, The Old Dairy, Prescote Manor Farm, Cropredy, Banbury, Oxfordshire OX17 1PF

Est. 1999
Tel: +44 (0)1295-738125
Fax: +44 (0)1295-738129
www.info.shopart.uk.com
/Kirstie-Reynolds
Parking available

Kirstie Reynolds specialises in **porcelain and crank sculptural forms, vases and platters** using functional glazes (food-safe and water-tight) for the home and garden. Prices range from £10-£500. Studio open to the public during art weeks (May) and the Christmas period (Nov/Dec). Her ceramics are inspired by her extensive travels. Mail order available.

Directions: *J11 M40, A361 to Cropredy. Into Red Lion St after Spar Shop. End of road, turn right over bridge. Down track. Turn left for dairy unit.*

Opening hours: *By appointment.*

LUCIENNE DE MAUNY, The Pottery, Blenheim Farm, Nr. Wallingford, Oxfordshire OX10 6PR

Est. 1984
Tel/fax: +44 (0)1491-839707
www.luciennedemaunypottery.co.uk
Parking available

Lucienne de Mauny established the Pottery at Blenheim Farm after training in the English and French country potting traditions. She makes a wide range of fine, **handthrown, slip-decorated, high-fired earthenware** including distinctive 'Olive' tableware. Commemorative pottery and house names and numbers made to order. £3.50-£500. Mail order available.

Directions: *two miles east of Wallingford, quarter of a mile south off the A4130.*

Opening hours: *Tues-Fri 10am-5pm. Sat 10am-4pm.* 54

THE OXFORD PAINTING ROOM, 88 Old Road, Headington, Oxford, Oxfordshire OX3 7LP

Est. 1996
Tel: +44 (0)1865-768854
Fax +44 (0)1865-872473
Parking available

Carol Whetter is a highly skilled artist who for many years lived in the East where her love for **porcelain painting** began. Her designs reflect the character and tradition of a formal training and oriental discipline. A combination of design and careful pen work bring to life the humblest butterfly. Using fine Limoges porcelain each stage of decoration is completed entirely by hand and finely gilded with 24 carat gold. The lamps, bowls, plates and boxes can be viewed and discussed at the studio. Each item is exquisite; they are tomorrow's antiques. Every commission is unique.

Directions: *at the junction of Old Road and Windmill Road in Headington: number 88 is the house on the corner.*

Opening hours: *By appointment.*

RICHARD BAXTER, Old Leigh Studios, 61 High Street, Old Leigh, Leigh on Sea, Essex SS9 2EP

Est. 1981
Tel: +44 (0)1702-470490
www.richardbaxter.co.uk
Parking available
Wheelchair access
(two small steps)
Credit cards

Richard makes a **full range of pottery for the home and garden** in earthenware, plus one-off 'wave bowls' and porcelain. Domestic ware is sturdy and robust, while the one-off pieces are highly sophisticated with beautiful glaze colours and have been sold through Bonhams of Knightsbridge. Prices are from £5-100. Mail order available.

Directions: *A13 from London heading east past Hadleigh. Follow signs to Leigh Railway Station. After station fork right; fork right again into Old Leigh. Half way along on left.*

Opening hours: *Tues-Sun 11am-5pm.*

RUTH DUPRE, 18 Rectory Grove, London SW4 OEA

Est. 1980
Tel/fax: +44 (0)20-7720 6236
Parking available

Figurative ceramics and unusual glass sculpture. Ceramics include shoes (inspired by the V & A collection) and portrait busts (e.g. Tudor prince). Glass sculptures are complicated, abstract stand alone shapes with an outer layer of coloured (blue, lime green and aubergine), powdered glass giving opaque effect. Prices £100-£1,000. Commissions welcome. Mail order available.

Directions: *tube to Clapham Common and seven-minute walk. Buses: 88, 77, 77a, or drive via Clapham Common.*

Opening hours: *by appointment.*

SARAH PERRY, 55 Annandale Road, Greenwich, London SE10 ODE

Est. 1968
Tel/fax: +44 (0)20-8858 2663
Parking available
Credit cards

I make one-off **stoneware clay vessels and porcelain jewellery** using vibrant matt glazes of turquoise, blue, mauve and green and sometimes with metallic lustres. I was taught by Lucy Rie and Hans Coper at Camberwell School of Art. Pottery prices are £25-£250 and jewellery £10-£20. Mail order available.

Directions: *off Vanbrugh Hill, Greenwich or Woolwich Road.*

Opening hours: *flexible but telephone for appointment.*

SIDNEY HARDWICK, Cedarwood, Streatham Road, Upton, Didcot, Oxfordshire OX11 9JG

Tel/fax: +44 (0)1235-850263
Parking available
Wheelchair access

Sidney makes **stoneware that is both decorative and useful.** She is especially interested in washbasins with tiled surrounds, lamps, serving dishes, casseroles, bowls, pots for plants and sun dials. She uses coloured glazes in red, blue, greens, brown and off-white. Prices are from £15 to £150. Mail order available.

Directions: *between Oxford and Newbury on the A417. Take Station Road, second turn right, down Pound Lane, left at the bottom and then second house on right.*

Opening hours: *10am-5pm. Appointment necessary.*

TAM FRISHBERG CERAMICS, 10 Hayward Road, Oxford, Oxfordshire OX2 8LW

Est. 1998
Tel: +44 (0)1865-454274
Parking available
Wheelchair access

In my home studio I make **slipcast vases** as well as a range of hand thrown bowls and other functional pieces in stoneware: jugs, casseroles, pasta and salad bowls and other serving pieces which are nice to use, but are also works of art. Vases are hand-painted in brighter colours than slipware.

Directions: *Hayward Road is off Harbord Road, just north of the Banbury Road roundabout on the northern bypass around Oxford.*

Opening hours: *by appointment only.*

TONY GANT POTTERY, 53 Southdean Gardens, Southfields, London SW19 6NT

Est. 1961
Tel: +44 (0)20-8789 4518
Road parking

Tony and Janet Gant make **functional domestic stoneware** (bowls, dishes, plates, jugs, mugs and vases) reduction fired in a gas kiln. Shapes are simple, classic and austere (conical, cylindrical) and three basic pastel matt glazes are used: straw to creamy, harebell to bluebell blue and jade green. Mail order possible.

Directions: *near Southfields District Line station.*

Opening hours: *Mon-Sat 10am-5pm. Please telephone first.*

WORKSHOP, 77a Lauriston Road, Hackney, London E9 7HA

Est. 1975
Tel: 020-8986 9585
www.carollinebousfield.co.uk
Parking available
Wheelchair access
Credit cards

Formerly a coachhouse, the Workshop is a pottery studio and shop selling a large range of domestic stoneware made on the premises. **Thrown pots for all uses**; also candle-holders, vases etc. Mainly blue/white/green. Also for sale are greetings cards, small toys and terracotta flower pots. Mail order available.

Directions: *one mile east of City of London on the edge of Victoria Park. Nearest tube: Mile End or Bethnal Green. Buses: 277 or 26.*

Open: *Tues, Weds, Fri, Sat 10.30am-5.30pm and other times by appointment.*

Textiles

BARLEY MASSEY, Fabrications, 7 Broadway Market, Hackney, London E8 4PH

Est. 2000
Tel: +44 (0)20-7275 8043
www.fabrications1.co.uk
Parking available
Wheelchair access

I produce **contemporary and innovative textiles** suitable for all kinds of applications. I weave, stitch and 'treat' all kinds of materials including yarns, plastics and rubber, as well as incorporating recycled materials. My work is available in batch production, but I also work to commission and produce one-off pieces. Mail order available.

Directions: *visit the websites: www.fabrications1.co.uk or www.broadwaymarket.org.uk for a map and London transport options, or telephone.*

Opening hours: *Tues-Sat 12am-5pm by appointment.*

CECILIA FONTENELLE MILLINERY, 29 Mafeking Avenue, Newbury Park, Ilford, Essex IG2 7AW

Est. 2000
Tel: +44 (0)7946 090312
Parking available

Cecilia, a largely self-taught milliner, makes ladies' and children's **blocked and soft fabric hats**. Occasion one-off floral hats include blocked felts, silks and straws embellished with ribbons, dried and fabric flowers and feathers, suitable for weddings, Royal Ascot etc. Fleeces for children are decorated with ribbons, tassels and pom-poms. Commissions undertaken.

Directions: *five-minute drive (ten minutes walk) from A12 at Newbury Park tube station.*

Opening hours: *by appointment only.*

CRIMSON DRAGON DESIGNS, 24 Fordwich Hill Hertford, Hertfordshire SG14 2BQ

Est. 2001
Tel: +44 (0)1992-553461
www.crimsondragondesigns.co.uk
Credit cards

Crimson Dragon Designs - 'celebrating fun and fantasy.' We produce **designer clothing for both men and women.** Each garment is a work of art and as such is a unique creation. Currently we produce: jackets, casual trousers, jerkins, silk T-shirts, ties, scarves and shawls. Mostly to commission. Some ready-made items available.

Directions: *given when appointment is made.*
Opening hours: *by appointment only.*

HILLU LIEBELT, 15 Shepherd's Hill, London N6 5QJ

Est. 1993
Tel/fax: 020-8340 7785
Parking available

Hillu makes contemporary-style figurative or design-based **handwoven tapestries following the classic Gobelin technique.** The use of rigid or flexible wires creates new possibilities: the flat woven pieces can be moulded, gaining some three-dimensionality. In a further development wire frameworks are used to devise abstract textiles structures on different planes.

Directions: *by Northern Line tube to Highgate station. Less than five minutes walk from the station.*
Opening hours: *every day, but appointment necessary.*

JANE OLDCORN, FELTMAKER, 49 Randolph Street, Oxford, Oxfordshire OX4 1YA

Est. 1995
Tel: +44 (0)1865-725758
www.ark-t.org/Artist's Fellowship
Parking available

The **sculptured textile hangings** I make are inspired by colours, forms and textures found in nature: my current work is a response to trees. I hand-dye and form my felt using unique methods, which I have developed through experimentation. I also make shawls and jumpers and am happy to undertake commissions.

Directions: *will be given when appointment is made.*
Opening hours: *visits to studio space by appointment only.*

LIBBY CALVERT, Marsh Cottage, Back Lane, Aston, Bampton, Oxfordshire OX18 2DQ

Est. 1965
Tel: +44 (0)1993-850658
Parking available
Wheelchair access

Libby Calvert has been making **patchwork bedspreads** for over thirty years having been inspired by her mother. She also makes cushions, wallhangings, cotspreads, tablecloths for chess, backgammon or bridge using only pretty cotton fabrics. She will match any desired colour combination or size. Each finished piece is unique. Commissions taken.

Directions: *A40 Oxford to Cheltenham Road, take the Abingdon and Witney (A415) turning. Half a mile, turn right to Aston for three miles. First turn on right; first house on right.*
Opening hours: *please make an appointment.*

NICKI WILLIAMS - TEXTILE ARTIST, Ground Floor, 201 Worplesdon Road, Guildford, Surrey GU2 9XJ

Est. 1990
Tel: +44 (0)1483 236211
Parking available

My pieces are very **theatrical and highly decorative textiles** in their shape, colour and texture. I use a wide range of media to produce a variety of 2D and 3D pieces: stitched textiles, incorporating papers, silks, organzas and taffetas; sculptural papier-mâché bowls, mirrors and jewellery which are embedded with my embroidery.

Directions: *given when appointment is made.*
Opening hours: *by appointment only.*

PAT BLOOR TAPESTRIES, 49 St John's Road, Walthamstow, London E17 4JG

Tel: +44 (0)20-8523 4688
www.patbloor.com
Parking available

Pat produces woven tapestry with **figurative imagery using Gobelin tapestry technique.** She favours domestic pieces for specific environments. A training in fine art is behind her colourful narrative tapestries. Pat has recently worked on a piece for Portcullis House, Westminster. Visitors are welcome to view her portfolio and discuss their requirements.

Directions: *Wood Street area of Walthamstow accessible by bus and rail. Full directions when appointment made.*
Opening hours: *Mon-Wed and Fri; appointment necessary.*

SILKWOOD ANGORAS, 23 Cedar Road, Sutton, Surrey SM2 5DG

Est. 1976
Tel: +44 (0)20-8643 6140
Fax: +44 (0)20-8661 6577

Handspun and handpainted wool, silk, mohair for creative stitching and knitting. Colours are vegetable based or craft dyed and can be commissioned to match a project. Also medieval-style knitting frames for scarves and larger items, hand drop spindles and pure angora yarn from our own angoras. Mail order catalogue and samples available

Directions: *ring for detail of our countrywide show venues.*

Opening hours: *not applicable.*

Toys & Games

DOLLMAKERS STUDIO LTD, 17 Station Road, North Chingford, London E4 7BJ

Est. 1995
Tel: +44 (0)20-8523 9293
Fax: +44 (0)20-8524 8130
www.dollmakers.demon.co.uk
Plenty of parking
Wheelchair access
Credit cards

High quality **porcelain dolls** handmade on the premises. Limited editions made to your own requirements by qualified dollmakers. Choice of 400 moulds, ranging from modern to reproduction antique. We hold weekly dollmaking courses from beginners to advanced. Also weekend speciality seminars. All supplies for dollmaking. Worldwide mail order.

Directions: *by main line train: Liverpool St to Chingford (20 minutes). Exiting from Chingford Station turn left; 8 minutes walk. By road: 6 minutes from the M25 (exit Junction 26), and Chingford is en route to Woodford.*

Opening hours: *10am-4.30pm Weds, Fri, Sat; 10am-8.30pm Tues & Thurs.*

JOHN FIRTH HAND MADE TOYS AND GAMES, Dornecliffe, Burden's Heath, Upper Bucklebury, Near Reading, Berkshire RG7 6SX.

Est. 1994
Tel: +44 (0)1635-861326
Parking available
Credit cards

John makes **games and puzzles from many countries** using reclaimed, recycled timbers, stoneware tiles and porcelain/stoneware counters. His designs allow variation in shapes/sizes/materials/colours, making each piece unique: hence no catalogue. Prices from £5-£100. He sells at market twice monthly (first and third Saturday) in the Corn Hall Cirencester.

Directions: *for home workshop: from A4 (Thatcham) follow signs to Upper Bucklebury. Once in village, first left, left again, seventh house on left.*

Open: *prefers customers to visit him at market; other times by appointment.*

ROBERT LONGSTAFF WORKSHOPS, Appleton Road, Longworth, Oxfordshire OX13 5EF

Est. 1977
Tel: +44 (0)1865-820206
Fax: +44 (0)1865-821089
www.longstaff.co.uk
Own car park
Limited wheelchair access.
Credit cards

Robert Longstaff makes **jigsaws and puzzles in wood**: children's puzzles, advanced puzzles, historic puzzles and personalised puzzles (e.g. your pets or faces). Also laserbuild castles and farms and dolls' houses, miniature furniture, kits and components in one twelfth and one twenty-fourth scale for collectors and DIY. Mail order available.

Directions: *A415 Witney road from the A420. Follow the signs to Longworth. On entering village (30mph sign), we are 300 yards on the left.*

Opening hours: *Mon-Thurs 9am/5pm; Fri 9am/3pm.*

SARA REUBEN, 112A Amhurst Road, Hackney, London E8 2AG

Est. 1980
Tel: +44 (0)20-7249 5405
Fax: +44 (0)20-7690 7952
www.memorialbears.com
Parking available
(Sunday market only)
Wheelchair access

Sara Reuben makes **teddy bears** from a favourite article of clothing from some event that you never want to forget including wedding, children's first garments, and also for those who want to remember a loved one following a bereavement. Possible to use any item of clothing. Mail order available.

Directions: *Jubilee Market Hall, Covent Garden, London.*

Open: *Saturday & Sunday 10am-6pm in Jubilee Market. Other times by appointment.*

Woodturning & Furniture

CHRISTOPHER HUGHES FURNITURE, 3rd Floor, 231 The Vale, Acton, London W3 7QS

Est. 1994
Tel: +44 (0)20-8743 8182
Parking available
Wheelchair access

Christopher makes **contemporary one-off furniture commissions.** After training as an architectural/interior designer, he went to Parnham College to concentrate on furniture and now makes and designs the highest quality pieces in hardwoods, mostly for private clients in and around London. His work is bold, modern and exquisitely made.

Directions: *opposite Acton Park on the Vale, turn into Eastman Road and look for Bombay Duck (who share the building).*

Opening hours: *9am-6pm. Appointment necessary.*   **76**

MAX E. OTT LTD, 1A Southcote Road, Tufnell Park, London N19 5BJ

Est. 1954
Tel: +44 (0)20-7607 1384
Fax: +44 (0)20-7607 3506
Parking difficult
Wheelchair access

One-off designer cabinet work to order, ranging from modern and traditional furniture and built-in joinery, to antique repairs. We will also make copies of antiques. Larger commissions include a reception desk for the Cardinal Vaughan school in West London and a meditation annexe. For bathrooms and kitchens we ally with other trades.

Directions: *workshop is down alleyway at the rear of Tufnell Park and Brecknock Roads.*

Opening hours: *Mon-Fri 6.15am-7.30pm. Appointment advisable.*   **77**

NICK & KATHLEEN ABBOTT, Crouches, The Broadway (B1057), Great Dunmow, Essex, CM6 3BQ

Est. 1993
Tel/fax: +44 (0)1371-872705
Parking available
Wheelchair access

We specialise in handmade, beautiful and comfortable **Windsor and ladderback chairs, especially armchairs,** made from locally grown hardwoods, some from our own woodland. Other work includes settees, stools and inscribed breadboards. Commissions are accepted and visitors are welcome to try out our sample chairs to find the perfect fit for their seat.

Directions: *from Church End, Dunmow follow B1057 for 200 metres beyond speed restriction sign. We are the second house on the right.*

Opening hours: *by appointment.*   **78**

Other Makers

ANNE FINNERTY, 61 Winser Drive, Reading, Berkshire RG30 3EG

Est. 1975
Tel: +44 (0)118-958 8274
www.anniesbeading.com
Parking available
Wheelchair access

Anne has an extensive range of glass/gemstone/pearl **necklaces and beadwork jewellery** and beadwork lampshades for sale. She also restores antique beadwork, tapestries and supplies of clasps, pearls, stone beads etc. Professional restringing service to the trade or individuals, in person or by mail order. Commissions undertaken and deadlines met.

Directions: *from junction 12 of M4, A4 towards Reading. Two miles to right turn at roundabout, right again into Southcote Lane, then immediately left into Kenilworth Avenue and left into Winser Drive.*

Opening hours: *Mon-Fri 9am-5pm. Other times by appointment.*
Prior appointment advisable.   **79**

COUNTRY AT HEART, 31 The Redinge, Billericay, Essex CM11 2QH

Est. 1997
Tel: +44 (0)1277-631639
Fax: +44 (0)1277-632282

I make **American-style folk art and primitive country craft**. The vast majority of things I produce are from wood and wire. These include wall plaques, free-standing pine objects, folk art and cloth dolls, angels, ornamented wreathes, cushions, scented pillows, dried scented garlands, embroideries and more. Mail order available.

Directions: *on confirmation of appointment.*

Opening hours: *Mon-Sat 9am-6pm. Appointment necessary.*

HILARY REEM, Highbury, East Garston, Hungerford, Berkshire RG17 7HW

Est. approx 1960
Tel +44 (0)1488-648887
Some parking available
Partial wheelchair access
to workshop

I have always found shapes of wood interesting. I started carving olivewood in Florence, now I use local woods like yew, box, walnut and cherry for my **wood sculptures**. Human forms are helped by my yoga, with my pony and goat models for carving and inspiration for the drawings on my pottery. This **stoneware, teapots, bowls, jugs** etc, is handthrown and fired in my own kilns. The combination of wood ash glazes used produces an effect individual to each piece. Wood sculptures cost from £500-£2,999, stoneware pottery from £2 for an egg cup to £50 for an inscribed commemorative piece.

Directions: *situated 3 miles north of M4 junction 14; turn right to East Garston off Great Shefford/Lambourn road. Confirm directions when phoning for an appointment.*

Opening hours: *by appointment only.*

MARIANNE FORREST, 3 and 8 Coach House Cloisters, Hitchin Street, Baldock, Hertfordshire SG7 6AE

Est. 1983
Tel: +44 (0)1462-491992
www.marianne-forest.com

Clocks and watches; wristwatches from £46 up to half a million pounds for a public piece. Range of materials e.g. silver, gold, concrete, glass, plastic etc, depending on the piece. Contemporary customised wristwatch in silver inlaid with coloured golds from £1,000. Larger pieces e.g. wall-mounted clocks in any material. Mail order available.

Directions: *given when appointment is made.*

Opening hours: *by appointment only.*

OXFORD CRAFT STUDIO, 443 Banbury Road, Oxford, Oxfordshire OX2 8ED

Est. 1991
Tel: +44 (0)1865-552073
Fax: +44 (0)1865-310848
www.oxfordcraftstudios.co.uk
Parking available
Wheelchair access
Credit cards

Jennie and Colin Holmes run the Oxford Craft Company specialising in the production of high quality **ceramics** (plain and/or hand painted with animals, birds and florals) and three-dimensional **découpage** pictures, hand made cards and original paintings. All items are hand made on the premises. Commissions taken. Mail order available.

Directions: *from Oxford city centre follow Banbury Road north through Summertown. Approx. one mile from Summertown over roundabout. Craft Studio on left by Five Mile Drive.*

Opening hours: *Wed-Sun 10am-5pm. Closed Mon/Tues.*

PAT ELMORE RBA, Nutsford Lodge, Longcot, Near Faringdon, Oxfordshire SNF 7TW

Est. 1980
Tel: +44 (0)1793-782258
Parking for 20 cars
Exellent wheelchair access

Pat is a **stone and wood carver; also ceramist** making one-off planters, gargoyles, fountains, half size resin sheep and other smaller and larger animals. Also portrait busts carved or cast in bronze from clay models. Has a one and a half acre sculpture garden. Takes commissions and runs workshops. Mail order available.

Directions: *next to The King and Queen Pub in Longcot off the A420 Oxford to Swindon road.*

Opening times: *belongs to National Garden Scheme - open to public two weeks per year. Other times, please telephone for an appointment.*

ROBERT SMITH PEUGEOT PEPPERMILLS, 1 Homeleigh Cottages, Whempstead, Near Ware, Hertfordshire SG12 OPL

Est. 1980
Tel/fax +44 (0)1920-830478
www.rpturners.co.uk
Parking available
Wheelchair access
Credit cards

We are a small company with limited production dedicated to producing the very **finest pepper and salt mills**. Each one is individually turned and finished by hand and then fitted with the Peugeot mechanism which has been produced for over 100 years and has its own enviable reputation. Peppermills can be made in any size, any colour, to match any decor. Timber is carefully selected to produce a product which will last for generations. Prices range from £20-£100 each. Robert is on the Register of Professional Turners, supported by the Worshipful Company of Turners in London. Mail order available.

Directions: *situated midway between Ware and Stevenage off the A602 (the Whempstead-Benington Walkern road).*

Opening hours: *10am-4pm Mon-Sun but please phone first.*

STUDIO FUSION, Unit 1:06, Oxo Tower Wharf, Bargehouse Street, London SE1 9PH

Est. 1996
Tel/fax: +44 (0)20-7928 3600
www.oxotower.co.uk
Pay parking
Wheelchair access
Credit cards

Specialises in **contemporary glass and enamel on metal** in the applied arts. The members are established, award-winning designer enamellists, who make jewellery and silverware in precious metals, and larger works on copper and steel. The gallery also features special exhibitions by leading British and international enamellists and glass artists. Commissions welcomed.

Directions: *the Oxo Tower is situated on the South Bank of the River Thames between Waterloo and Blackfriars bridges.*

Opening hours: *Tues-Sun 11am-6pm.*

SUE D HALL, Peabody Yard, Greenman Street, Islington, London N18.

Est. 1998
Tel: +44 (0)207-286 9282
Fax: +44 (0)207-266 0025
Parking available
Wheelchair access

My **ceramic sculptures'** origins lie in the traditions of ceramics as applied art, although my work is neither domestic or functional. I aim to express ideas and a narrative through sculptured form, including the human head, using clay or other materials. Work is available for sale in my studio. £20-£300.

Directions: *Peabody Yard in Greenman Street, is just off Essex Road within five minutes walk of Angel and Highbury and Islington underground stations.*

Opening hours: *by appointment.* **87**

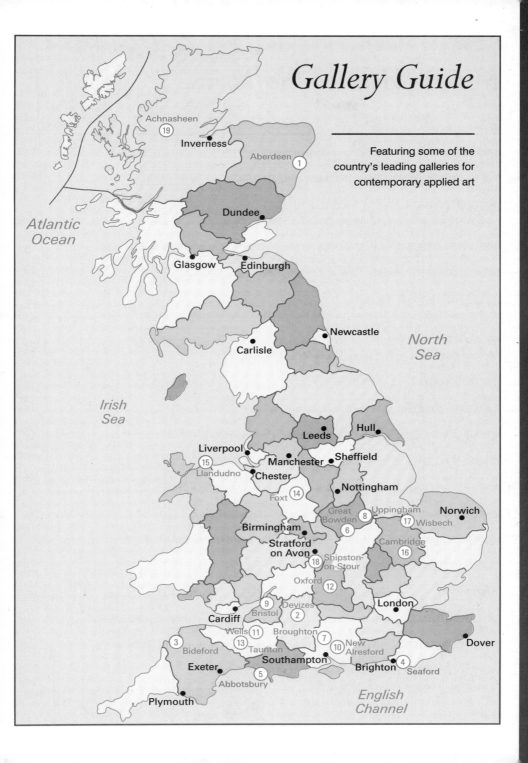

Gallery Guide

Featuring some of the country's leading galleries for contemporary applied art

Atlantic Ocean

Achnasheen
⑲
Inverness •

Aberdeen
①

Dundee •

Glasgow •   • Edinburgh

Carlisle •

Newcastle •

North Sea

Irish Sea

Leeds •   Hull •

Liverpool •   • Sheffield
⑮   Manchester •
Llandudno   Chester •

Nottingham •

Foxt ⑭

Great Bowden ⑧   Uppingham
⑥   ⑰   Wisbech   Norwich •

Birmingham •   Cambridge
Stratford   ⑯
on Avon •   Shipston-
        ⑱ on-Stour
        Oxford
            ⑫

③   Bideford

⑨   Devizes
Bristol   ②

Wells ⑪   Broughton
⑬   ⑦
Taunton   ⑩ New Alresford

London •

Dover •

Cardiff •

Exeter •
Abbotsbury   ⑤

Southampton
Brighton •   ④
    Seaford

Plymouth •

English Channel

Key to Map of Galleries

ABERDEEN ART GALLERY
Schoolhill, Aberdeen AB10 1FQ
Tel +44 (0)1224-523700
Fax +44 (0)1224-632133
E-mail info@aagm.co.uk
www.aberdeencity.gov.uk
Opening hours: 10am-5pm Mon-Sat, 2-5pm Sun
Car parks nearby at Denburn and Harriet Street.
Wheelchair access with assistance from staff.

The North of Scotland's premier local authority-funded art gallery with a long-established reputation for promoting crafts, particularly from Scotland. Collections include work by Bernard Leach, Michael Cardew, textiles by Tadek Beutlich and Peter Collingwood and jewellery from Susanna Heron. More recent acquisitions range from Lucie Rie to Wendy Ramshaw and Malcolm Appleby, with an emphasis on Scottish metalwork and jewellery. Visitors are advised to check first if they wish to view work by a particular artist. A wide range of ceramics, glass, jewellery and other crafts is available from the Gallery Shop. The gallery was opened in 1885.

(1)

THE BURTON ART GALLERY & MUSEUM
Kingsley Road, Bideford, North Devon EX39 2QQ
Tel +44 (0)1237-471455
Fax +44 (0)1237-473813
www.burtonartgallery.co.uk
Opening hours: 10am-4pm Tues-Sat, 2-4pm Sun
Parking easily available. Wheelchair access.

The Burton Art Gallery and Museum was built in 1951 by Thomas Burton in memory of his daughter Mary. Refurbished in 1994, it now has three exhibition areas and hosts an ever-changing programme of exhibitions and craftwork throughout the year. A permanent collection of oil and watercolour paintings, North Devon slipware, Napoleonic ship models, historical artefacts relating to Bideford are also part of the Gallery's attractions. The coffee shop, gift shop and craft gallery overlooking the adjacent Victoria Park and Riverside Walk make the Gallery Bideford's greatest asset. Admission is free. All areas are wheelchair accessible including toilets and lift to first floor.

(3)

THE BLUESTONE GALLERY
8 Old Stone Yard, Devizes, Wiltshire SN10 1AT
Tel +44 (0)1380-729589   Fax +44 (0)1672-539202
E-mail guy@avebury-arts.co.uk
www.avebury-arts.co.uk
Opening hours: 10am-5pm Mon-Fri, 9.30-5.30 Sat
Parking available nearby.
Wheelchair access difficult (two steps) but not impossible.

The Bluestones were brought by early man from the Preseli mountains in Wales to form the inner circle of stones at Stonehenge, an amazing feat of skill, vision and conviction. **The Bluestone Gallery** is in Devizes, a market town with a rich architectural heritage and the longest flight of canal locks in Britain, near both Stonehenge and the Avebury Stone Circle.

The aim of the Gallery is to give expression to Britain's wonderful crafts. It was opened in May 2000 by Guy and Janice Perkins. Guy has been a full time professional potter since 1977 and has exhibited widely in Britain and abroad. Guy and Janice travel widely to hand-pick work from many sources.

Work by over 100 makers is contantly on display in the Gallery and there are regular exhibitions. There is a superb collection of designer jewellery (including work by Jane Adam, Anne Farag and Fi Mehra). Ceramics range from classic salt-glaze (Phil Rogers) through delicate porcelain (Bridget Drakeford) to domestic ware (Roger Cockram). There is glass (Siddy Langley), wood (Dave Regester) and original paintings and prints. With two floors of fine work, friendly staff and a very comfy sofa, the Gallery is an oasis of peace and beauty!

THE CRYPT GALLERY

Off Church Street, Seaford,
East Sussex, BN25 1HE
Tel +44 (0)1323-891461
Fax +44 (0)1273-484373
E-mail carole.buchan@lewes.gov.uk
Opening hours: 10.30am-1.30 pm and
2.15-5pm Mon-Sat
Public car park outside. Wheelchair access.

The Crypt is an intriguing gallery built around a beautifully restored medieval undercroft, known locally as The Crypt, and is only a few minutes' walk from one of the most photographed clifftops in England. The Gallery hosts a year-round programme of exhibitions and workshops, bringing together some of the finest contemporary artists and craftspeople in England.

The programme ranges from screenprints by Patrick Caulfield to stone carving from Zimbabwe. The Gallery also features ceramics, sculpture, photography, textiles and furniture as well as fine art. The opening hours above apply during exhibitions.

The Gallery is usually closed in January.

DANSEL GALLERY

Rodden Row, Abbotsbury, Weymouth DT3 4JL
Tel +44 (0)1305-871515
Fax +44 (0)1305-871518
E-mail dansel@wdi.co.uk
www.danselgallery.co.uk
Opening hours: 10am-5pm seven days a week; longer during the summer. Open all year round.
Good parking. No wheelchair access.

Set in a delightful thatched converted stable block near the centre of Abbotsbury, **Dansel Gallery** opened in 1979 and is Britain's leading showcase for the cream of contemporary craftwork in wood. It houses a superb selection of high quality hand-made items, all carefully selected for good design and quality of finish. More than 200 British woodworkers are represented, probably the largest concentration of its kind in the country. The impressive range runs from individually designed pieces of furniture through elegant jewellery boxes to toys, puzzles and three-dimensional jigsaws to one-off decorative pieces that highlight the inventiveness and versatility of the woodworker.

⑤

THE FRANK HAYNES GALLERY
50 Station Road, Great Bowden,
Market Harborough, Leicestershire LE16 7HN
Tel +44 (0)1858-464862
 www.marketharborough.com/gallery
Opening hours: 10am-5pm, Thurs-Sun;
sometimes closed for holidays.
Parking available on-site.
Wheelchair access to both the Art Gallery
and Pottery Shop.

The Frank Haynes Gallery was set up in 1987 to provide an outlet for semi-professional painters and pottery makers. To an extent this continues, but more and more professionals are now showing their work. The Gallery exhibits and sells paintings from the region; each month sees a completely new mixed-subject show, whilst in April 'the human figure in art' is the theme. The Pottery Shop offers ceramics from more than forty makers from the Midlands and other parts of Great Britain, with blue/red stoneware domestic ware and unique 'figure bowls' by resident potter and proprietor Frank Haynes.

THE GARDEN GALLERY
Rookery Lane, Broughton, Near Stockbridge,
Hampshire SO20 8AZ
Tel +44 (0)1794 301144
Fax +44 (0)1794-301761
E-mail gardengallery@compuserve.com
Opening hours: vary - please telephone
Good parking. Wheelchair access.

The Garden Gallery exhibits sculpture, pots, furniture and mosaics by some ninety contemporary artists, both well-established and new to their careers, for gardens and conservatories. Most of the work is displayed in a beautiful, tranquil garden during exhibitions, enabling customers to understand the relationship between the works of art and their setting - plants, trees, water and light - and how each can lend the other a new dimension. Visits by arrangement on non-open days are welcome. A portfolio of photographs of artists' work can be viewed; special commissions can be arranged. The Gallery regrets that no facilities are available.

⑦

8

THE GUILD GALLERY
68 Park Street, Bristol BS1 5JY
Tel +44 (0)117-926 5548
Fax 0117-925 5659
E-mail bristolguild@70parkst.freeserve.co.uk
Opening hours: 9.30am-5pm Mon-Fri,
except bank holidays.
Two multi-storey car parks nearby.
No wheelchair access.

First established in 1984, **The Guild Gallery** on the second floor of the prestigious Guild of Applied Art (itself linked to the original Art and Craft Movement) provides an excellent display area for two and three dimensional work. In 1984 there was a severe shortage of galleries in Bristol. There is now a Bristol Association of Galleries, producing a quarterly brochure distributed throughout the South West. **The Guild Gallery** is rented by mainly, but not exclusively, West Country artists and craftspeople. Exhibitions last for three weeks and the venue is felt to be ideal both for established artists and newly graduated students.

(9)

IMAGES GALLERY
38 Market Street, Wells, Somerset BA5 2DS
Tel +44 (0)1749-672959
Opening hours: 11am-3pm Weds and Fri,
Sat 11am-1pm
Parking available nearby. Wheelchair access.

Images Gallery was opened in 1997 by Caroline Bagias to promote monochrome photography. Caroline's work, and sometimes that of other mono enthusiasts, is on permanent display. Prints can be viewed and purchased. A mail order service has recently been introduced whereby customers may select the image of choice from a high-class brochure (details on request).

All prints are produced on quality paper to archival standards. These prints and many more can be seen and purchased from the Gallery. Specialist commissions which include portraiture and photojournalism may also be undertaken. Prices from £75. Appointments by special arrangement.

(11)

HITCHCOCKS'

HITCHCOCKS'
11 East Street, New Alresford,
Hampshire SO24 9EQ
Tel/fax +44 (0)1962-734762
E-mail joyce@hitch-hants.co.uk
www.hitch-hants.co.uk
Opening hours: 9.30am-1pm and 2-5pm Mon-Sat.
Parking at 3 minutes' walk.
Accessible by wheelchair.

Hitchcocks' opened in Winchester in 1976 and is now located in New Alresford. It is a Craft Council listed gallery and a member of the Independent Craft Galleries Association. Specialises in textiles as clothing; knitted, woven, painted, in silk, cotton and wool. Includes work from Janet Gough, Maggie White, Sarah Burnett, Carol Waller, Terry Macey and many designers from Ireland and Scotland including Orkney. We also have a continuous display of jewellery, toys and automata; domestic decorative ceramics; glass and wood; plus changing small 'showcase' exhibitions.

Hitchcocks' has a sister gallery also called **Hitchcocks'** at 10 Chapel Row, Bath. BA1 1HN. 01225 330646. Its oddly shaped Georgian Building is devoted entirely to the promotion of 3D work: this includes mechanical toys, folk toys, automata, and has recently been joined by children's wooden toys. The only place of its kind, **Hitchcocks'** also runs an exhibition programme, which includes themed shows and solo exhibitions from individual makers. Work is largely British and German, but some comes from the United States and France. **Hitchcocks'** is open Tuesdays to Saturdays during each exhibition season. Please ring 01225 330646 for details, or visit our website www.hitchcocks-bath.co.uk

INSPIRES ART GALLERY
27 Little Clarendon Street, Oxford OX1 2HU
Tel/Fax: +44 (0)1865-556555
E-mail: artgallery@inspires.co.uk
Website: www.inspires.co.uk
Opening hours: 10am-6pm Mon-Fri, 9.30am-6pm Sat.
Good local parking.
Wheelchair access.

Inspires is a contemporary art gallery started in 2000 by business partners Danielle Walker and Emily Ashley, both of whom grew up in families involved in the art world. Danielle ran an art gallery in Cape Town for five years and her parents still run one there, and **Inspires** retains strong links with South African art as the two galleries exchange works.

The gallery specialises in the best of contemporary art and aims to show the widest possible range which can be viewed in relaxing surroundings. Bronze sculptures and figures, ceramics and glassware from an extensive range of sources are shown, in addition to original paintings by local as well as internationally known artists, framed etchings and lithographs. The gallery also offers a framing service.

Amongst recent exhibits have been a selection of glass by Will Shakespeare, ceramics by Majolandile Dyalvani and Hennie Meyer, birds made from American Cedar by Mike Lythgoe and bronze sculptures by Stanley Dove. A regular programme of exhibitions shows the very latest works. The Website www.inspires.co.uk lists a fuller selection of the artists whose work is displayed, but the Gallery is able to source many more. ⑫

MAKERS
6 Bath Place, Taunton, Somerset TA1 4ER
Tel +44 (0)1823-251121
Opening hours: 9am-5pm, Mon-Sat.
Easily accessible parking.
Partial wheelchair access.

Makers is a successful co-operative established in 1984. Over the years it has gained a reputation for exhibiting one of the West Country's finest selections of quality contemporary crafts.

Makers is owned and run by the makers themselves and displays an exciting and ever-changing collection of their work. There is always a maker on duty in the shop to assist you and discuss commissions.

Work for sale includes furniture, woodturning, paintings and prints, pottery, hand-painted silks and velvets, knitwear, baskets and jewellery. Regular exhibitions of the work of guest makers are held in the first floor gallery. ⑬

THE STUDIO JEWELLERY WORKSHOP GALLERY AND CAFE
Achnasheen, Wester Ross IV22 2EE
Tel/Fax +44 (0)1445-720 227
E-mail info@studiojewellery.com
www.studiojewellery.com
Opening times: 9.30am-6pm, 7 days a week.
Parking easily available. Wheelchair access.

The Studio Jewellery Workshop has been established for twenty two years and has built up a reputation for the quality of jewellery and silverware produced. The jewellery is made by Susan Plowman who graduated from the Glasgow School of Art with B.A. (Hons) and specialises in fine enamel work. She is a member of the British Society of Enamellers and the Society of Contemporary Jewellers and works mainly to commission. Also on show is the largest selection of contemporary jewellery in the Highlands, fine art prints, glass, designer clothing and ceramics. There is also a fabulous wholefood café. ⑲

NEWFIELDS GALLERY
Foxt, Near Froghall, Staffordshire Moorlands ST10 2HS
Tel +44 (0)1538-266334
www.peakdistrictproducts.co.uk/newfields
Opening hours: 9am-5pm most days; please telephone to check
Parking available.
Visitors with special needs please telephone first.

Newfields Gallery sells only the work of Roger Sutton and Gail Keep, artists in ceramics and wood. They started working together in the early 1970s, challenging traditional methods of making, and developing special clays to produce their finely sculptured models. In 1977 their own business Ceramico Designs was established. Being surrounded by hedgerow, woodland, meadow and stream, it is not surprising that their keen observation of wildlife influenced their detailed relief designs which took the form of jewellery, boxes and miniature wall plaques.

Roger carves English oak, specialising in plant form and the magic of foliage. His intricately carved panels are achieved by the use of many chisels he also makes himself. The photographs illustrate a small selection of their work. An oak spray carved from oak, ceramic jewellery and ceramic pieces mounted into carved oak and turned beech frames.

Newfields is a small 16th century south-facing hill-farm in the Staffordshire Moorlands on the southern fringe of the Peak District. The gallery displays and sells this unique work; ceramics range from £10-£100: the woodcarvings start at £250. Admission to the Gallery is free and well worth a visit for anyone who recognises something different.

ORIEL MOSTYN GALLERY
12 Vaughan Street, Llandudno, LL30 1AB
Tel +44 (0)1492-879201
Fax +44 (0)1492-878869
E-mail post@mostyn.org
www.mostyn.org
Opening hours: 11am-6pm Mon-Sat
Parking available nearby.
Wheelchair access

Oriel Mostyn Gallery is the leading gallery for contemporary art in Wales, and was described in the Guardian newspaper as 'one of the most adventurous contemporary art venues in the country'. Naturally-lit from above and superbly proportioned, the exhibition galleries are among the most beautiful in Britain.

The Gallery shows seven exhibitions each year. Covering painting, sculpture, photography, video and new media, they are often innovative and challenging. It has a strong profile nationally and internationally, attracting artists of the highest standard, including over the next two years artists from Japan, Ghana, Canada, Nigeria and elsewhere. **Oriel Mostyn** also has a particular objective of showing artists and exhibitions of interest to Wales, acting as a showcase for the best emerging and established artists, and a focus for the artistic community in North Wales.

Ranging from the quirky to the classic, the individual handmade crafts in the Craft Shop are the most distinctive to be found in the region. They include pottery, glass, textiles and wood, and a particularly notable collection of contemporary jewellery. The Shop is Crafts Council registered, reflecting the high standard of work in it by makers from around the United Kingdom.

PRIMAVERA
10 King's Parade, Cambridge CB2 1SJ
Tel +44 (0)1223-357708
Fax +44 (0)1223-576920
www.primaverauk.com
Opening hours: Mon-Sat 9.30am-5.30pm, Sun 11am-5pm
Car park nearby. No wheelchair access downstairs.

Situated opposite the entrance to King's College in the heart of Cambridge, **Primavera** brings together a well-researched exploration into some of the finest arts and crafts to be found in Britain today. **Primavera** was founded by Henry Rothschild and first opened its doors at 140 Sloane Street, London in 1946. In 1967 **Primavera** moved to 17 Walton Street, remaining there until its closure in 1970. In 1960 **Primavera** (Cambridge) opened at its present site at 10 King's Parade. It is the oldest contemporary art and crafts gallery in the country.

Today **Primavera** has over 400 of the best contemporary artists in Britain. Exhibitions in the downstairs gallery run alongside ever-changing displays of wonderful and unique jewellery (ranging from £15-£15,000), paintings (£100-£75,000), innovative modern furniture, ceramics, sculpture, glassware, clocks, watches, automata, woodwork, silverware, wrought iron, textiles and hand-made card and paper.

www.primavera.com reveals many of the works we have on display in the gallery, lists all the artists we represent at **Primavera** and gives information on forthcoming exhibitions. The gallery owner, Jeremy Waller, was an undergraduate at Cambridge University. Whilst living and working in London, Beirut, Paris and Nairobi and now in Cambridge again he continues to help many artists with finance, marketing and design concepts.

SKYLARK STUDIOS
Hannath Road, Tydd Gote, Wisbech, Cambridgeshire PE13 5ND
Tel +44 (0)1945-420403
www.skylark.studios.dial.pipex.com
Opening hours 10am-5pm Tues-Fri, 11am-5pm Sat
Car park at front.
Wheelchair access.

Skylark Studios is a contemporary gallery and art studio housed in a beautifully restored Grade II Listed Building set in the quiet East Anglian countryside. It was set up in 1993 by artist/printmaker Louise Williams.

Skylark Studios is a unique privately owned gallery with a professional and friendly service. Specialising in a balanced range of accessible innovative work across a variety of media including ceramics, cards, jewellery, etchings, linocuts, screenprints and original paintings, representing a good selection of work of artists from all over the UK.

The gallery is committed to showing good quality original work at affordable prices, where browsers or serious collectors can both find work by local and national artists and makers.

The gallery also offers a framing service with expert advice on choosing individual frames to suit the work whether it is two or three dimensional. Part of **Skylark Studios** also houses Louise's printmaking studio with large etching press and screenprinting vacuum bed. She runs art classes here for 'adults and children with small friendly groups in a relaxing atmosphere.

Look on the website www.skylark.studios.dial.pipex.com for a list of changing exhibitions and courses available and to view a selection of original prints by Louise Williams.

(17)

THE STOUR GALLERY
10 High Street, Shipston on Stour, Warwickshire CV36 4AJ
Tel +44 (0)1608-664411
Fax +44 (0)1608-664433
E-mail stourgallery@dial.pipex.com
Opening times: 10am-5.30pm, Monday-Saturday
Parking easily available.
Wheelchair access: one shallow step but help always available.

Behind a small shopfront on the main street of the lovely old town of Shipston-on-Stour, **The Stour Gallery** should be high on any art-lover's list of places to visit. The gallery emerged from owner Sarah Stoten's pleasure and interest in contemporary art and has an important collection of works for sale - paintings, prints and ceramics by modern artists. Cornwall has always been a particular source of inspiration to painters, printmakers and potters and there is a particular emphasis on Cornish and West Country work which reflects the owner's fascination with that tradition.

The work of artists with growing national reputations is displayed alongside paintings and pieces by established artists of international renown: painters like Sandra Blow R.A., Terry Frost R.A., Breon O'Casey, Bruce McLean and Ceri Richards; potters like David Leach, Peter Beard, John Ward, Mary Rich, John Maltby, Chris Carter and Jane Perryman.

The work on display changes regularly, with special exhibitions throughout the year, so there will be something new and exciting on every visit. Future exhibitions will include work from all over the country while continuing to reflect the gallery's style and enthusiasm: those visiting the gallery should find it both welcoming and inspiring.

Wales

▲ Craft Centres   ■ Food and Drink

○ Shops and Galleries   ● Makers' Workshops

Wales has legends, witchcraft, castles, poets and singers, and its inhabitants speak a language with few vowels. The powerful Celtic revival in the last few decades has ensured that Wales has retained a distinctive culture frequently reflected in its crafts.

Eric Gill the stone-carver and calligrapher lived on a farm in the Black Mountains in the 1920s. Before the industrialisation of south-east and south Wales, the hillsides and valleys were full of skilled craft makers, especially weavers. Swansea was famous for straw hat production in the 18th century, and also produced fine Swansea porcelain. The Solva Valley in Pembrokeshire is renowned for tweeds and flannel, still made there today. Indeed, talented textile makers are attracted to Wales generally. In Ceredigion at Cenarth, you can see coracles, skin-covered, wicker-framed boats, hand made since prehistoric times.

Craft Centres

ABBEY MILL WYE VALLEY CENTRE, Abbey Mill Wye Valley Centre, Tintern, near Chepstow, Monmouthshire NP16 6SE
Est 1989
Tel: +44 (0)1291-689228
Fax: +44 (0)1291-689220
Parking available
Wheelchair access
Credit cards

Set amidst breathtaking scenery and situated on the banks of the River Wye, Abbey Mill offers a relaxed setting for you to enjoy. The centre houses a collection of several interesting shops selling arts, crafts and quality gifts. Street entertainers perform regularly. Mail order is available upon request.

Directions: *A466 Chepstow to Monmouth road, 400m north of Tintern Abbey in Tintern village. Centre on right travelling north.*

Opening hours: *Mon-Sun 10.30am-5.30pm, Winter closes 5pm.*

AFONWEN CRAFT AND ANTIQUE CENTRE, Afonwen, near Caerwys, Mold, Flintshire PH75 5UB
Est 1967
Tel: +44 (0)1352-720965
Fax: +44 (0)1352-720346
Parking available
Wheelchairs to groundfloor
Credit cards

The largest craft and antique centre in North Wales and the Borders, we have thousands of fabulous items for all. The range of products available include crafts, pictures, prints, cards, antiques, collectables and unusual curios. We also have a magnificent restaurant for light bites or a special treat. Mail order available.

Directions: *follow tourist signs off the A55, or off the A541 to the Craft and Antique Centre.*

Opening hours: *Tues-Sun 9.30am-5.30pm.*

CORRIS CRAFT CENTRE, Corris, Machynlleth, Powys SY20 9RF
Est 1983
Tel: +44 (0)1654-761584
Fax: +44 (0)1654-761575
Parking available
Wheelchair access
Credit cards

We house six craft workshops where visitors are invited to view at first hand the skills of the craftworkers and buy from the displays of woodcraft, toy making, pottery, jewellery, leather work and hand made candles. Crwyby Restaurant provides refreshments throughout the day. There are picnic and play areas. Mail order available.

Directions: *on the A487 between Machynlleth and Dolgellan.*

Opening hours: *Mon-Sun Summer 10am-6pm, winter 10am-4pm.*

GLYN-COCH STUDIOS, Glyn-Coch Farm, Ffynnongain Lane, Pwll-Trap, St. Clears, Carmarthenshire SA33 4AR

Est. 1980
(present owners 2000)
Tel: +44 (0)1994-231867
Fax: +44 (0)1994-231863
www.glyn-coch.com
Own car park
Credit cards

Glyn-Coch studios offer crafts from over 30 local makers from porcelain to woodturning and Celtic jewellery to painted glass. Commissions can be undertaken. Visitors can also see a pottery and artists' studios, enjoy a woodland walk, see rare breed Norfolk sheep and be refreshed at the tearooms. Mail order available.

Directions: *follow brown tourist signs half a mile west of St Clears on the A40. Two minutes from the main road.*

Opening hours: *Tues-Sat 10.30am-5.30pm; Sun 12.30-5.30pm all year.*

GOWER HERITAGE CENTRE, Parkmill, Gower, Swansea SA3 2EH

Est 1990
Tel: +44 (0)1792-371206
Fax: +44 (0)1792-371471
www.gowerheritagecentre.
sagehost.co.uk
Parking available
Wheelchair access
Credit cards

The centre is based around a 12th century working water powered cornmill, together with craft workshops, tea-rooms, puppet theatre, resident potter, wheelwright's workshop, blacksmith, farming museum, fishpond, play area and countryside walks. Ideal for coach parties and groups who can pre-book a guided tour of the centre.

Directions: *8 miles west of Swansea on the A4118 main route to Gower. Follow the brown tourist signs to the centre.*

Opening hours: *Mon-Sun winter 10am-5pm, summer 10am-5.30pm.*

STEPASIDE CRAFT VILLAGE & ART GALLERY, Pleasant Valley, Stepaside, Kilgetty, Pembrokeshire SA67 8LN

Est 1989
Tel: +44 (0)1834-811686
Fax: +44 (0)1834-811104
www.saundersfoot.co.
uk/craftvillage
Parking available
Wheelchair access
Credit cards

Situated in the picturesque surroundings of Stepaside near Saundersfoot, we offer a choice of artistic styles in the gallery. Craftspeople can be viewed at work in their individual units making a wide range of crafts. Prices range from £2 to £500. Picnic area and tea-room adjacent. Mail order available.

Directions: *off A477 dual carriageway to the east of Kilgetty, follow the brown signs to Stepaside village. Turn right into car park off Pleasant Valley Road.*

Opening hours: *Easter to October Mon-Fri 10am-5pm, Sun 11am-5pm.*

TAN LAN CRAFT CENTRE, Bethel, Anglesey LL62 5NW

Est 1997
Tel/fax: +44 (0)1407-840237
Parking available
Wheelchair access

Set in an 18th century farm building where visitors can browse amongst craft items, some of which are made locally. We also run one day workshops in various craft skills. Our needlecraft centre specialises in needlepoint, kits, accessories, books, patchwork and quilting fabrics.

Directions: *on the B4422 near Bethel.*

Opening hours: *Tues-Sat 10am-5.30pm.*

Craft Shops

BEACONS CRAFTS, Bethel Square, Brecon, Powys LD3 7JP

Est 1996
Tel: +44 (0)1874-625706
Parking available
Wheelchair access
Credit cards

We are a cooperative of craftspeople selling quality work made by hand in Wales and the Welsh Borders. Staffed by members we offer the opportunity to meet with a maker whilst viewing the work of our 50 producers. Being a cooperative of considerable size, we offer a very wide range.

Directions: *adjacent to supermarket car parks and tourist information centre in the centre of Brecon.*

Opening hours: *Mon-Sat 10am-5pm.*

THE CRAFT CABIN, Inside Treasure 29-31 Newton Road, Mumbles, Swansea SA3 4AS

Est 1996
Tel: +44 (0)1792-410717
Parking available
Wheelchair access
Credit cards

This cooperative was set up to provide an outlet for local craftspeople to display their wares. The shop is always staffed by a member of our group. Crafts on offer include metalwork, stained glass, tiles, turned wood, watercolours, pottery, jewellery, painted wood, teddy bears and much, much more. Mail order available.

Directions: *to Mumbles along Mumbles Road from Swansea; right at mini-roundabout onto Newton Road; shop 20 yards on the left.*

Opening hours: *Mon-Sat 10am-5.30pm, Sun in summer and school holidays.*

DRAGONS CELTIC CRAFTS, Dragons, Market Street, Llanrhaeadr-ym-Mochnant, Near Oswestry, Powys SY10 OJN

Est. 2000
Tel: +44 (0)1691-780049
Fax: +44 (0)1691-780445
Parking available
Accessible to wheelchairs
after two small steps
Credit cards

Issard-Davies' gallery is near one of the seven wonders of Wales, the Llanhaeadr waterfall, and sells Welsh and Border arts and crafts. Around 50 paintings are displayed in the new gallery (exhibitions every 4-6 weeks). Pottery, ceramics, slate, glass, felt and other objets d'art are shown in the craft shop. Mail order available.

Directions: *take B4396 from A5 north fo Shrewsbury. The shop is in the middle of Llanhaeadr, on the corner of the road to the waterfall.*

Opening hours: *Thurs-Tues 10.30am-6.00pm.*

HILL TOP STUDIO, 56 High Street, Old Town Llantrisant, Mid-Glamorgan CF7 8BR

Est. 1984
Tel: +44 (0)1443-229015
Parking available
Credit cards

On the High Street in Llantrisant, you will find this attractive Victorian shop bearing its original appearance and displaying flowers, scented candles, paintings, pottery and unusual country crafts. A shop full of colour with a welcoming atmosphere. New lines regularly added like the current range of blue and white pottery.

Directions: *junction 34 off M4, follow brown signs to Craft and Design Centre. In centre of old town on the approach to the Bull Ring in Llantrisant.*

Opening hours: *Wed-Sun 10am-5pm.*

THE OLD BAKEHOUSE POTTERY STUDIO, 7a Swan Street, Llantrisant, Mid-Glamorgan CF72 8ED

Est. 1994
Tel: +44 (0)1443-225899
Fax: +44 (0)1443-222882
Parking available
Wheelchair access
Credit cards

The Old Bakehouse Pottery Studio shows ceramics by owner Christine Gittins, as well as selected quality art and craft from Britain and South Africa handpicked by Christine. The quaint, restored seventeenth century cottage forms a suitable backdrop for a display of one-off pieces that have been chosen for their distinction.

Directions: *exit 34 off the M4 and follow signs for Llantrisant, and then brown signs for Craft Centre. Opposite the Model House.*

Opening hours: *when potter is at work (usually Mon-Sat). Please telephone first to avoid disappointment.*

PENNAN CRAFT AND COFFEE SHOP, Bow Street, near Aberystwyth, Ceredigion SY24 5AA

Est 1983
Tel: +44 (0)1970-820050
Parking available
Wheelchair access
Credit cards

A craft and coffee shop situated in renovated farm buildings. The craft shop stocks Welsh crafts, jewellery, knitwear, leather goods and many more crafts and gifts. The coffee shop prides itself on traditional Welsh home-cooking, serving lunch and snacks, sweets and cakes all day.

Directions: *Bow Street village is four miles north of Aberystwyth on the A487.*

Opening hours: *Jun-Sept Mon-Sun, otherwise closed Mon, 10am-5.30pm.*

PRESANT, 23 Frogmore Street, Abergavenny, Monmouthshire NP7 5AH

Est 2000
Tel: +44 (0)1873-855177
Fax: +44 (0)1982-552020
Parking available
Wheelchair access
Credit cards

We have scoured the Principality to bring together a range of crafts that represent the best that our country has to offer in contemporary gifts from a modern Wales. Visit us if you are looking for things Welsh or for well designed and beautiful items. We also have a shop in Builth Wells. Mail order available.

Directions: *a few shops down from Tesco Metro.*

Opening hours: *Mon-Fri 10am-5.30pm, Sat 9.30am-5.30pm.*

WYE VALLEY CRAFTS ASSOCIATION SHOP, Abbey Mill Centre, near Chepstow, Monmouthshire NP16 6SE

Est 1994
Tel: +44 (0)1291-689228
Parking available
Wheelchair access

The work of over 20 craftspeople is on sale in the the WVCA's shop within the Abbey Mill Centre. Crafts include woodwork, jewellery, barge-painting, glassware, ceramics, painting and photography etc. On-site tearoom and four other gift shops, post office and trout pond. Regular craft demonstrations. Mail order available from individual members.

Directions: *A466 Chepstow to Monmouth road, 400m north of Tintern Abbey in Tintern village. Centre on right travelling north.*

Opening hours: *Mon-Sun 10.30am-5pm.*   ⑮

Galleries

BUTCHERS ARMS GALLERY AND COFFEE SHOP, Common Road, Llantrisant, Mid Glamorgan CF72 8DA

Est 1995
Tel: +44 (0)1443-229285
Parking available
Credit cards

A gallery where Gill and Noel Garnham display and sell a wide range of arts, crafts and gifts. The range of products available includes paintings, fine furniture, wrought iron, pottery and gifts. Visitors are always welcome to browse or join the proprietors for coffee in the coffee shop.

Directions: *M4 junction 34; follow brown signs to craft and design centre in centre of town at top of hill.*

Opening hours: *Wed-Sun 10am-5pm.*   ⑯

MODEL HOUSE CRAFT AND DESIGN CENTRE, Bull Ring, Llantrisant, Rhondda Cynon Taff CF72 8EB

Est 1989
Tel: +44 (0)1443-237758
Fax: +44 (0)1443-224718
Parking available
Wheelchair access
Credit cards

This Crafts Council selected gallery is dedicated to the promotion of quality, contemporary craft and displays the work of over 60 makers including a dazzling selection of 21 jewellery designers. Exhibitions all year culminating in the Christmas 'Top Dressing,' showcasing the work of 80 jewellery and textile designer/makers. Also, courses and workshops.

Directions: *junction 34 off the M4 and follow signs north to Llantrisant.*

Opening hours: *Tues-Sun 10am-5pm.*   ⑰

MOUNTAIN SKY STUDIO, Llain Tyddyn, Cilrhedyn, Llanfrynach, Pembrokeshire SA35 0AE

Est 1998
Tel/fax: +44 (0)1239-698337
Parking available
Wheelchair access

The studio is based around the work of Valerie James. It is situated close to the Preseli Mountains of Pembrokeshire. Inspiration for a wide range of products including paintings, sculpture, silk scarves, wall hangings and wooden items, is drawn from the natural world; trees, rivers, stones and weather, together with mythology and the history of the land. Mail order available. Commissions undertaken.

Directions: *Telephone for directions*

Opening hours: *Prior appointment necessary.*   ⑱

ORIEL LLANGOLLEN, 5 Oak Mews, Oak Street, Llangollen, Denbighshire LL20 8NR

Est 2000
Tel: +44 (0)1978-869444
Parking available
Wheelchair access
Credit cards

We are a contemporary gallery and coffee shop with ongoing selling exhibitions of contemporary arts, crafts and design by established and emerging artists. Browse in our gallery before enjoying a coffee in our shop. Mail order available upon request and a good sample of the work we display is available on our website.

Directions: *off Castle Street in the heart of Llangollen.*

Opening hours: *Tues-Sat 10am-5pm, Sun 11am-4pm.*   ⑲

ORIEL MOSTYN GALLERY, 12 Vaughan Street, Llandudno, Conwy LL30 1AB

Est. 1978
Tel +44 (0)1492-879201
Fax +44 (0)1492-878869
Parking available
Wheelchair access
Credit cards

The Oriel Mostyn Gallery is the leading gallery for contemporary art in Wales with exhibition galleries that are among the most beautiful in Britain and a strong profile nationally and internationally. The Gallery shows seven exhibitions each year; covering painting, sculpture, photography, video and new media, they are often innovative and challenging.

Directions: *500 yards from Llandudno Station and 500 yards from bus station; next door to main Post Office.*

Opening hours: *11am-6pm Mon-Sat.*

ORIEL SANGLIER, Pentre Road, St Clears, Carmarthenshire SA33 4AA

Est 1978
Tel: +44 (0)1994-231085
Fax: +44 (0)1994-230318
Parking available
Wheelchair access

We specialise in selling and taking orders and commissions for ironwork designed and made by David, Aaron, Toby and Gideon Peterson at their Forge Studio a few minutes from the gallery. We also sell local crafts, greeting cards, wooden items and furniture made from local woodland timber. Mail order available for some items.

Directions: *centre of main street in St Clears near the river bridge. St Clears is off the A40, 8 miles from Carmarthenshire.*

Opening hours: *Mon-Sat 9am-4pm, Wed/Sat 9am-1pm.*

Food & Drink

ANGLESEY SEA SALT CO LTD, Brynsiencyn, Llanfairpwll, Anglesey LL61 6TQ

Est 1997
Tel: +44 (0)1248-430871
Fax: +44 (0)1248-430213
www.seasalt.co.uk
Parking available
Wheelchair access
Credit cards

Halen Mon is hand produced, Soil Association certified sea salt. Visit our premises to see how sea salt is harvested and buy a range of beautifully crafted salt cellars in slate, oak, Bristol blue glass, Bath Aqua Glass and earthenware. We share our site with the Anglesey Sea Zoo. Mail order available.

Directions: *from A5 Britannia Bridge onto Anglesey. Take first road left to Brynsiencyn and follow tourist signs for Sea Zoo.*

Opening hours: *Mar-Oct Mon-Sun 10am-5pm.*

CAWS CELTICA, Capel Gwynda, Rhydlewis, Llandysul, Ceredigion SA44 5RN

Est. 1999
Tel: +44 (0)1239-851419
Parking available

Winner of 'Best Welsh Cheese' and gold medals at World/British Cheese Awards 2000. Caws Celtica is a range of handcrafted ewes milk cheeses made by Sue and Roger Hilditch from milk produced by their Friesland milking sheep flock that graze the chemical free pasture at Capel Gwnda Farm. Mail order available.

Directions: *given when appointment made.*

Opening hours: *by arrangement. Please telephone.*

CAWS CENARTH, Fferm Glynelthinos, Lancych, Boncath, Dyfed SA37 DLH

Est 1987
Tel/fax: +44 (0)1239-710432
www.cawscenarth.co.uk
Parking available
Wheelchair access

Individuals and families are welcome to watch the making of award winning traditional farmhouse cheese in several varieties suitable for vegetarians, GMO free and organic since May 2001. We also have an animal farm on site. Our shop has free cheese samples for visitors to try. Mail order is available upon request.

Directions: *take the leisure centre road from Newcastle Emlyn for four miles from Carmarthen to Cardigan and follow signs.*

Opening hours: *most days from early until late.*

CWM DERI VINEYARD, Martletwy, Near Narberth, Pembrokeshire SA67 8AP

Est. 1994
Tel/fax +44 (0)1834-891274
www.cwm-deri.co.uk
Car park for 50+ cars
Wheelchair access
Credit cards

A boutique Welsh vineyard where 'John the Grape' has created a wonderful range of wines, liqueurs, schnapps and mead, all bottled at the vineyard; the bottling can be seen through a viewing window. 'Buy and try' a tray of tasters and have fun choosing favourites, with something to suit most palates. Wine and refreshments in the wine shop or on the patio overlooking the vineyard ensure that there is a warm welcome whatever the weather. The show team is on the road around the year, (details on the Website) to restock your wine racks. Prices from £5.50. Mail order available.

Directions: *M4 from Cardiff/Swansea then A40 (Haverfordwest/St Clears), take A4075 at Canaston Bridge (signposted Pembroke); after 2 miles take turning for Martletwy and follow brown tourist signs.*

Opening hours: *11am-5pm daily in summer; in winter open weekends 12-4.30pm.*

`25`

GRAIG FARM ORGANICS, Dolau, Llandrindod Wells, Powys LD1 5TL

Est. 1998
Tel: +44 (0)1597-851655
Fax: +44 (0)1597-851991
www.graigfarm.co.uk
Credit cards

Craig Farm organics is run by Bob and Carolyn Kennard who started it as an outlet for their organic produce. The shop has won awards every year since 1998. Wares include meat, fish, pies, bread, fruit, vegetables, alcoholic beverages, woollens and skin care products. Mail order can be done on the award-winning website.

Directions: *situated on A488 east of Dolau, between Penybont and Knighton.*
Opening hours: *Mon-Sat 9am-5.30pm.*

`26`

LLANGLOFFAN CHEESE CENTRE, Llangloffan Farmhouse Cheese, Castle Morris, Haverfordwest,

Pembrokeshire SA62 5ET
Est. 1978
Tel: +44 (0)1348-891241
Fax: +44 (0)870-0561043
www.welshcheese.com
Parking available
Wheelchair access
Credit cards

Created by Leon and Joan Downey, award-winning Llangloffan Farmhouse Cheese is renowned around the world and can be bought on site, or from exclusive shops. Cheesemaking starts 6am; public can watch the process from 10am (last admission 11.45am) to 12.45pm. Shop selling cheese, bread, jams, chutney, honey etc. Museum/tearoom. Mail order available.

Directions: *follow brown tourist signs on A40 at Scleddau, two miles before Fishguard.*
Opening hours: *Mon-Sat 9am-6pm. Closed Sun. Open bank holidays.*

`27`

NEW QUAY HONEY FARM, Cross Inn, Llandysul, Ceredigion SA44 6NN

Est 1995
Tel: +44 (0)1545-560822
Fax: +44 (0)1545-560045
www.thehoneyfarm.co.uk
Parking available
Wheelchair access
Credit cards

A working honey farm with a shop, meadery, tea-room and exhibition showing live bees in their natural habitats. Our shop sells honey, mead, honey beer, beeswax polish and candles and beekeeping equipment. Visitors are welcome to taste our different varieties of honey. Mail order is available upon request.

Directions: *follow brown signs from Synod Inn junction on the A487 Aberystwyth to Cardigan road.*
Open: *summer Mon-Sun 10am-5.30pm, winter Tues-Sat 11am-5pm.*

 `28`

General Gifts

JAN FRY, Mill Cottage, Derwydd, Ammanford, Carmarthenshire SA18 3LQ

Est 2000
Tel: +44 (0)1269-851044
www.Janfry.co.uk
Parking available

Mill Cottage is an open studio where you can meet the artist specialising in watercolour and pastel landscape paintings, prints, silk scarves and ceramics. Prices from £4 to £300. Day courses are available through the summer. Also contact Jan Fry for information on ancient yew trees in Wales.

Directions: *Llandeilo turning at Cross Hands roundabout between Swansea and Carmarthen. After 6 miles and big crossroads take first right off road and past mansion.*

Opening hours: *Jul/Aug Suns plus August bank holiday weekend.*

MICHAEL POWELL PRINTS, 6 Vere Street, Roath, Cardiff CF24 3DS

Est 1997
Tel/fax: +44 (0)2920-496000
www.michaelpowellprints.co.uk
Parking available
Wheelchair access
Credit cards

Michael opened his own gallery last year. His unique collection of colourful and vibrant ink and watercolour limited edition prints, greeting cards and cross stitch kits are displayed, as are the original paintings. Cards cost from £1 to £25, prints from £8.50 and cross stitch from £17.95. Mail order available.

Directions: *from Newport Road turn into city road. Take the second on the right (opposite Maplins) into Vere Street to the yellow building on the right.*

Opening hours: *Mon-Fri 10am-5pm, Sat 10am-12pm. Appointment preferred.*

PINENEEDLES, Gower Heritage Centre, Parkmill, Gower, Swansea SA3 2EM

Est 1989
Tel: +44 (0)1792-371231
Parking available
Wheelchair access
Credit cards

Our workshop is within the only working watermill on Gower. We make small high quality wooden items, clocks, mirrors, letter racks, bookends etc. We specialise in gifts for children such as money boxes, mobiles, jigsaws, name jigsaws and name plaques which are made while you wait. Mail order available.

Directions: *8 miles west of Swansea on the A4118 near Three Cliffs Bay.*

Opening hours: *winter Mon-Sun 10am-4pm, summer 10am-5.30pm. Phone first.*

Glass

A1 STAINED GLASS STUDIO, Unit 6 Tan Lane, Bethel, Bodorgan, Ynys Mon LL62 5NW

Est 2001
Tel: +44 (0)1407-840893
Parking available
Wheelchair access

Martin Farrant makes items in stained glass using original leaded light style and costing from £10. His range of work includes **lamp shades, boxes, clocks, terrariums and chess boards.** Commissions for customised items taken. All your ideas can be realised. Mail order is available upon request.

Directions: *take Rhrostrewfa turn-off A55 and follow signs for Rhrostrewfa, Gwalchmai A5, then take left (B4427) Aberffraw. We are two and a half miles on the left.*

Opening hours: *Mon-Sat 10am-7pm.*

THE GLASSBLOBBERY, Glanyrafon, near Corwen, Denbighshire LL21 0HA

Est 1986
Tel: +44 (0)1490-460440
Fax: +44 (0)1490-460247
www.glassblobbery.com
Parking available
Wheelchair access
Credit cards

We are a craft workshop and gallery exhibiting our own work. Using a technique called lamp work or bench glass blowing we sculpt a range of **glass designs** such as birds, dragons and dolphins. Metal oxides are applied to the glass surface to give a range of varying hues. Mail order available.

Directions: *from Corwen on the A5, turn left at the second set of traffic lights onto the A494 for Bala. We are one and a quarter miles on the right.*

Opening hours: *Easter-Oct 10.30am-5pm closed Tues.*

GLASSCRAFT, 16 Pentre-Poeth Road, Bassaleg, Newport, Gwent NP10 8LL

Est 1985
Tel/fax: +44 (0)1633-895786
Parking available
Credit cards

Our hand **engraver** can engrave or sandblast almost any subject on glassware, a gift to mark a special occasion to club trophies. We can offer a while-you-wait service with prices ranging from £2 to £65. A one pint tankard with a subject of your choice and lettering is £7. Mail order available.

Directions: *given when appointment is made.*

Opening hours: *seven days a week but appointment necessary.*

LLEWELYN WILLIAMS, Clyro, Glanymor Road, Goodwick, Pembrokeshire SA64 0EP

Est 1980
Tel: +44 (0)1348-873083
Parking available

I keep a range of glassware and **engrave my own designs** which are mostly of flora and fauna. I also design and engrave corporate and private commemorative presents on the premises and can create the appropriate decoration of your choice. Large range of prices mostly from £10-£100. Mail order is available.

Directions: *from roundabout by Fishguard ferry harbour, take road to Goodwich village then up hill for Strumble. First left on hill and then right after 500 yards.*

Opening hours: *Mon-Sun 9am-5pm. Appointment necessary.*

MIRAGE GLASS, Llangedwyn Mill, Llangedwyn, Oswestry, Powys SY10 9LD

Est. 1978
Tel/fax: +44 (0)1691-780618
Parking available for coaches and cars
Wheelchair access
Credit cards

Mirage has over twenty years experience in the design and creation of architectural and **decorative stained glass** using traditional and innovative techniques. Also for sale are panels, lamps, mirrors, jewellery and gifts. Tools and materials for hobbyists are available. Glass staining courses are regularly run (SAE for details).

Directions: *follow brown craft signs. Turn off the A483 at Llnclys onto the B4396. In Llangedwyn turn left at the school. Llangedwyn Mill faces you 200 yards down the road.*

Opening hours: *Mon-Fri 10am-5pm.*

MORIATH GLASS, Nant, Cwmpengraig, Drefach, Felindre, Llandysul, Carmarthenshire, Wales SA44 5HY

Est 1991
Tel: +44 (0)1559-371585
Parking available
Wheelchair access
Credit cards

I have been **painting glass** for ten years, attracted by the vibrant colours that catch the light and eye. My work is predominantly Celtic in origin, also drawing on organic forms, and includes goblets, vases, candlesticks, bowls and hangings. Children can feed my ducks and chickens while parents browse. Mail order available.

Directions: *Carmarthen road from Newcastle Emlyn; right at Pentrecagal. In Drefach Felindre proceed over the bridge and up the valley. Gallery signposted half mile beyond Cwmpengraig.*

Opening hours: *flexible but advisable to telephone.*

Jewellery

ABBEY JEWELLERY, Gorse Cottage, St Arvans, Chepstow, Monmouthshire NP16 6EZ

Est 1979
Tel: +44 (0)1291-626083
Limited parking

I learned the art of jewellery-making from an elderly relative, then developed my own styles and designs. Using the solderless wirework technique to make jewellery in **rolled gold and sterling silver,** I incorporate semi-precious stones, crystal, fossils etc. About 30 types of gem including jade, garnet and moonstone are used. Mail order is available.

Directions: *from A466 Chepstow to Monmouth Road, find St Arvans village. Turn left on the Devanden Road for one mile. Cottage on the right.*

Opening hours: *by appointment or at Abbey Mill, Tintern every day; please telephone for details.*

FURIOUS FISH CONTEMPORARY JEWELLERY, 14 Market Square, Narberth, Pembrokeshire SA67 7AU

Est 1995
Tel/fax: +44 (0)1834-861722
www.jewellerywales.com
Parking available

Furious Fish is where Sarah Lloyd-Morris can be seen making her own individual style of **jewellery featuring interesting coloured patterning,** combined with precious and semi-precious stones. She derives much of her inspiration from the shoreline and produces collections from her travels. Mail order is available upon request.

Directions: *south side of High Street opposite the war memorial, next to Step Studios Digital Video Gallery.*

Opening hours: *Tues-Sat 10am-5pm.*

GARETH C. LEAVES, Gower Heritage Centre, Parkmill, Gower, Swansea SA3 2EH

Est 1994
Tel: +44 (0)1792-371206
Fax: +44 (0)1792-371471
www.gowerheritagecentre
.sagehost.co.uk
Parking available
Wheelchair access
Credit cards

Gareth is a jobbing gold and silversmith jeweller with over 25 years experience. He specialises in working in the old traditions of handmade **gold and silver jewellery** and repairs. Customers can, by appointment, watch their own gold and silver being made into an item of their choice. Mail order available.

Directions: *telephone for directions.*

Opening hours: *advisable to telephone first.*

JOHN AND VICTORIA JEWELLERY, Yolanddegwm, Llechryd, Cardigan, Pembrokeshire SA43 2PP

Est 1976
Tel: +44 (0)1239-682653
Fax: +44 (0)1239-682653
www.johnandvictoria.co.uk
Parking available
Wheelchair access
Credit cards

Visitors to the workshop can see John and Victoria and their daughter Bryony designing and hand making **silver and gold jewellery**. Their lively and individual work is on sale in the showroom. The range includes rings, earrings, bracelets, brooches and necklaces. Prices from £3 to £500. Mail order available.

Directions: *from Cardigan take A484 to Llechryd. At bottom of hill, turn right and cross river; continue for one and a half miles and we are on the left.*

Opening hours: *May-Sept Mon-Thurs 10am-5.30pm.*

RHIANNON WELSH GOLD CENTRE, Main Square, Tregaron, Ceredigion, Wales SY25 6JL

Est 1971
Tel: +44 (0)1974-298415
Fax: +44 (0)1974-298690
www.rhiannon.co.uk
Parking available
Wheelchair access
Credit cards

Rhiannon designs and makes very **special Celtic jewellery**. Every design is original and every piece is hand made in Wales. The jewellery is inspired by old Celtic legends, the beautiful Welsh countryside and wildlife. Visitors are always welcome and a free mail order catalogue is available upon request.

Directions: *Main Square in Tregaron, on A45 from Carmathen (34 miles) to Aberystwyth (18 miles).*

Opening hours: *Mon-Sun 9.30am-5.30pm, closed Suns Oct-May.*

SHARPE DESIGNS, Dolafon Road, Newtown, Powys SY16 2AP

Est 1999
Tel: +44 (0)1686-623433
www.sharpe-designs.com
Parking available
Credit cards online

Our current range is the 'Curious Celtic Collection', a collection of **inspired jewellery and small pots** including 'Y Doraig Geltaidd': the Celtic dragon box. Produced in polished bronze and copper with garnets and etched slate. Designs are partly based on the Sutton Hoo treasure and Saxon linch-pins and torques. Mail order available.

Directions: *A483 to Newtown. Across Cambrian Bridge at Pool Road, at other end of bridge.*

Opening hours: *prior appointment necessary.*

 43

Leatherwork

HIDEAWAY, 24 Clwyd Street, Ruthin, Denbighshire LL15 1HW

Est 1986
Tel: +44 (0)1824-704889
Parking available

Goods are made entirely by hand, ranging from **key fobs to handcrafted handbags** and leather sandals; made to measure if customers require. The shop occupies a 17th century oak beamed property in the heart of medieval Ruthin in the beautiful Vale of Clwyd. Mail order is available upon request.

Directions: *up Clwyd Street towards St Peter's Square; shop is on the left, where the street splits.*

Opening hours: *Tues-Sat 9.30am-5.30pm.*

44

SIMPLY LEATHER, Unit 5, Corris Craft Centre, Machynlleth, Powys SY20 9RF

Est 1983
Tel/fax: +44 (0)1654-761618
www.simplyleather.co.uk
Parking available
Wheelchair access
Credit cards

We are one of six craft makers in a fully manufacturing craft centre. We mainly produce **ornamental leatherwork** which includes a range of clocks and barometers of many sizes and designs. In addition we also make belts, bags, dishes, spectacle cases and holsters to name just a few. Mail order available.

Directions: *on A487 at Corris, midway between Dolgellau and Machynlleth.*

Opening hours: *Apr-Nov Mon-Sun 10am-5pm.*

 45

Metalwork & Silversmithing

SAM RHODRI LONGHURST - ARTIST BLACKSMITH, The Old Custom House, Pilot House Wharf, West Pier, Swansea Marina, Swansea, Wales SA1 1HN

Est 2000
Tel: +44 (0)1792-642121
Parking available
Wheelchair access

A working blacksmith's shop located in a 19th century customs watch house rejuvenating Swansea's heritage in metalworking whilst producing unique hand forged **ornamental and practical ironwork**. Any requests are welcome as well as visitors. Prices range according to size and detail. There are a number of local galleries and museums nearby.

Directions: *Marina Road off Oystermouth Road and follow until end where parking is available, then follow West Pier past trawlers to forge at end of pier.*

Opening hours: *Mon-Sat 9am-5pm.*

 46

WELSH SLATE MUSEUM LLANBERIS, Padarn Country Park, Llanberis, Gwynedd LL55 4TY

Est 1972
Tel: +44 (0)1286-870630
Fax: +44 (0)1286-871906
www.nmgw.ac.uk
Parking available
Wheelchair access
Credit cards

Quality hand crafted iron work produced in the museum's smithy by blacksmith Dylan Parry. The range includes pokers, **ornamental flowers** including daffodils, lilies and roses. We also produce the Welsh Dragon in various iron forms. We also cast names in brass in the museum foundry. Commissions undertaken and mail order available.

Directions: *A55 along north west coast; take Llanberis exit near Bangor; follow signposts to Llanberis. Museum is located in the country park.*

Opening hours: *Easter-Oct Mon-Fri 10am-5pm, Nov-Easter Sun-Fri 10am-4pm.*

Musical Instruments

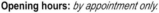

BAMBOOZLE, The Bowery, Old Post Office Lane, Rhosneigr, Anglesey LI64 5JA

Est 1979
Tel/fax: +44 (0)1407-810431
www.bamboozle.co.uk
Parking available
Wheelchair access
Credit cards

We have been making **flutes and digeridoos** since the 1970s. The flutes are all transverse, accurately tuned and can be made in any key. Six-holed 'D' flutes are popular with folk musicians. The digeridoos come in all sizes and keys. All our instruments are beautifully hand decorated. Mail order available.

Directions: *given when appointment is made.*

Opening hours: *by appointment only.*

Pottery & Ceramics

ANVIL POTTERY, The Smithy, Llanrhaeadr, Denbigh LL16 4NL

Est. 1981
Tel: +44 (0)1745-890532
www.anvilpottery.co.uk
Parking available
Wheelchair access

Traditional pottery workshop situated in 200-year-old smithy in picturesque village. Chat with potters and watch all stages of making. A full range of **domestic ware** is produced, with emphasis on use rather than ornament. Inspiration for design and decoration comes from natural shapes and things Celtic, paying homage to the Welsh connection.

Directions: *in the centre of the village opposite pub, next to church.*

Opening hours: *Mon-Sat 9am-5pm; Sun 10am-5pm; closed 31 Dec-Easter.*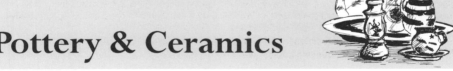

CWM POTTERY, Trefor, Caernarfon, Gwynedd LL54 5NB

Est 1977
Tel: +44 (0)1286-660545
Parking available
Wheelchair access
Credit cards

The pottery was set up in an old restored watermill and produces a wide variety of fired stoneware. Traditional shapes and natural colours; blues and greens through to rust and black are dipped or brushed on. **Large bowls, dishes with handles, goblets, teapots** and large, one-off vases.

Directions: *A499 to Llanaelhaearn; turn onto B4471 for Nefyn. Take first right in Llanaellhaearn along narrow lane for one and a half miles.*

Opening hours: *Easter-Oct Mon-Sun 10am-6pm.*

EARTHWORKS POTTERY, Lower Street, St Asaph, Denbighshire, North Wales LL17 0SG

Est 1987
Tel: +44 (0)1745-582412
Parking available
Credit cards

I make decorative and **domestic ware** which is colourful with bold decoration and a tropical feel, featuring flowers and animals etc from the natural world. As well as decorative, I also make **carved and pierced slipware**, earthenware and pottery. Telephone for details of galleries featuring my work. Mail order is available.

Directions: *St Asaph is just off the A55. Pottery between River Bridge and bottom of the High Street; on the left just past the pub.*

Opening hours: *Most times but telephone first.*

EWENNY POTTERY, Ewenny, Bridgend, South Wales CF35 5AP

Est 1800
Tel: +44 (0)1656-653020
www.ewennypottery.com
Parking available
Wheelchair access
Credit cards

Ewenny Pottery has been continually owned by the Jenkins family, the present potters being the sixth and seventh generations. They make a range of **glazed earthenware** pottery for ornamental and domestic use. Visitors are welcome to watch the pots being made and to view the finished ware in the showroom.

Directions: *one mile from Bridgend on the B4265 Llantwit major road.*

Opening hours: *variable so telephone first.*

GWILI POTTERY, Pontorsais, Carmarthen, Carmarthenshire SA44 5ET

Est 1979
Tel: +44 (0)1267-253449
Parking available
Credit cards

We have specialised in producing high quality **slip decorated white earthenware** for the past 20 years. The work is of a domestic, yet artistic nature, appealing to all ages and tastes. The workshop is open to allow visitors to view the production of the pottery. Mail order is available upon request.

Directions: *A485 Carmarthen to Lampeter road, sign on road on left after 4 miles.*

Opening hours: *Mon-Sat 9am-5pm, Sun 11am-3pm.*

ISLAND POTTERY, Llanrhuddlad, Holyhead, Anglesey LL65 4HT

Est 1979
Tel: +44 (0)1407-730705
www.islandpottery.co.uk
Parking available
Wheelchair access
Credit cards

Based on the island of Anglesey, we make high quality hand made stoneware pottery. Our speciality is in **ceramic figures and animals**. We make everything from aardvarks to giraffes and from elephants to cows. Our pottery is on display in both Llandudno and Machynlleth. Telephone for details. Mail order available.

Directions: *on A5025 in Llanrhuddlad on north west coast of Anglesey.*

Opening hours: *Summer Mon-Sun 10am-5pm. Winter telephone first.*

LITTLE HAVEN POTTERY, Berry Cottage, Little Haven, Haverfordwest, Pembrokeshire SA62 3UG

Est 1989
Tel: +44 (0)1437-781015
Parking available
Wheelchair access
Credit cards

The pottery opened in 1989 and produces a range of originally designed and decorated **stoneware pottery** in blue, green and white. All the products are hand thrown, functional and are oven and microwave proof. The range includes colanders, lamps, storage jars, cutlery and drainers. Prices range from £4 to £25.

Directions: *follow B4341 through Broad Haven to Little Haven. Pottery and craft shop is at the bottom of the hill on the left.*

Opening hours: *Easter-Oct 10.30am-5.30pm. Closed for lunch.*

PORTH LLWYD POTTERY, Cevnant, Tal-y-Bont, Conwy LL32 8SL

Est. 1978
Tel: +44 (0)1492-660772
www.claywales.co.uk
Parking available

Vicky Buxton and Philip Owen's workshop and showroom is open to the public and produces gas-fired reduction stoneware and porcelain. Wide range of individually-made items from **mugs, bowls, breadcrocks etc to more sculptural and garden wares**. Also made on the premises are high quality copper enamel boxes and other enamelwork.

Directions: *take B5106 heading south from Conwy for six miles. Look out for signs on the right after Dolgarrog School.*

Opening hours: *Mon-Sat 9.30am-5.30pm variable. Advisable to phone first.*

THE POTTERY STUDIO, 91 Conway Road, Colwyn Bay, Conwy LL29 7LW

Est. 2000
Tel: +44 (0)1492-534010
Parking available
Credit cards

Eccentric Bill Owen makes ceramic **humorous models, sculptures, toby jugs, animals, Punch and Judy figures** etc. He also works to commission including caricature models of people from photographs. Can also do copies of Martinware (17th century grotesque birds). His wife Karen is a potter and painter in pastels and oils. Mail order available.

Directions: *on the main road at the west end of Colwyn Bay.*
Opening hours: *Mon-Sun 9am-5pm.*

R.J. WILLIAMS, Lakeside View, Bwlch-y-Garreg, Pontdolgoch, Caersws, Powys SY17 5NE

Est 1999
Tel: +44 (0)1686-688263

We are makers of 1:12 **scale porcelain dolls' house miniatures**. Our Staffordshire style pieces are realistic in finish to larger originals. Other items include tea pots, floral pastel burners, Staffordshire spaniel pairs in five sizes, cats and dogs. Much more is available. Please telephone for a full price list. Commissions welcome.
Mail order only and limited retail outlets - ring for details.

RUTH AND ALAN BARRETT-DANES, The Laurels, 83 Chapel Road, Abergavenny, Monmouthshire ND7 7DR

Est 1960s
Tel: +44 (0)1873-854329
Parking available

We have been producing an original and **varied range of ceramic work** for over 30 years. Our work ranges from individual pieces in porcelain to the present range of decorated tableware. We have work represented in major museums in the UK and overseas. Prices range from £15 to £200.

Directions: *A40 Abergavenny to Brecon road and take first right after Station Pub into Chapel Road. Laurels is halfway up Chapel Road.*
Opening hours: *any time by appointment.*

SHEILA HICKEY, Venn Farm, Waterston Road, Milford Haven SA73 1DN

Est 1995
Tel: +44 (0)1646-690190
Parking available
Wheelchair access

I produce **finely made pottery, artistically decorated** with flora and fauna designs. Each piece is made on the potter's wheel, individually handpainted with vibrant images of irises poppies, daffodils, brambles, puffins and other sea birds. All work is produced on a limited scale making every pot unique and collectable.

Directions: *halfway between Waterston village and Milford Haven on the B4325. We are signposted as Venn Farm at the top of the lane.*
Opening hours: *Mon-Sun 10am-6pm, closed Wednesdays.*

STILES, 19 Langland Road, Mumbles, Swansea SA3 4ND

Est 1987
Tel: +44 (0)1792-360551
Fax: +44 (0)1792-361108
Parking available

I produce designs on **ceramic tiles** for kitchens, bathrooms etc. Designs include farm animals, flowers, cats and sea creatures. Commissions are welcomed and fabrics and furnishings can be matched. I can work onto any plain glazed tile. Gift items include mirrors with the surrounds, pot stands and coasters. Mail order available.

Directions: *up Newton Road from Swansea Bay and turn left onto Langland Road. We are 20 yards along on the left.*
Opening hours: *prior appointment necessary.*

Textiles

BLUEBERRY ANGORAS, Ffynnon Watty, Moylegrove, near Cardigan, Pembrokeshire SA43 3BU

Est 1995
Tel: +44 (0)1239-881668
Parking available

Luxurious yarns and handknitted garments in fine quality hand-dyed mohair and natural handspun wools. We also produce woven goods including rugs, throws and cushions, beautiful angora goat skin rugs, delicate cobweb scarves and comfortable socks. We also sell spinning and weaving equipment and provide spinning tuition. Mail order available.

Directions: *from the centre of the village, take the narrow turning by the chapel to Ceibur. The studio is signposted on the left.*

Opening hours: *Sun-Fri 10am-5.30pm, Sat 2pm-5.30pm.*

CURLEW WEAVERS WOOLLEN MILL, Rhydlewis, near Newcastle Emlyn, Ceredigion SA44 5RL

Est 1961
Tel/fax: +44 (0)1239-851357
www.westwales.co.uk/curlew.htm
Parking available
Wheelchair access
Credit cards

Curlew Weavers is a small firm with many years' experience and specialise in producing a wide range of woollen products including fabrics, **travel rugs, throws, blankets, bedspreads, shawls, curtains**, upholstery and garments. Also specialists in making bespoke garments for people with disabilities. Mail order, exporters and wholesalers welcome. Free admission.

Directions: *from Newcastle Emlyn take B4571 for 3.7 miles miles; turn left, then first right then first left.*

Opening hours: *Mon-Fri 9am-5pm.*

DE MONT AND WRIGHT STUDIO, Lower View, Sarn, Newtown, Mont, Powys SY16 4HH

Est. 1977
Tel: +44 (0)1686-670793
Parking available
Wheelchair access possible

Steve Attwood-Wright teaches part-time at Middlesex University and in his workshop, researching unusual weave structures, effects and finishes producing textiles especially **gallery and art pieces**. Many of these explore Welsh mythology with printed images and words. Other textiles (blankets, throws, rugs etc) made to order. Mail order available.

Directions: *take lane opposite Sarn Inn, left at 'Y' fork, right at telephone box, twist through hamlet, steep drive on left.*

Opening hours: *five days a week; not Wed or Sat in summer. Please telephone for an appointment.*

DESIGNER WEAVING COMPANY, Lower Penlan, Whitton, Knighton, Powys, Wales LD7 1NL

Est 1999
Tel: +44 (0)1547-560332
www.designerweavingco.co.uk
Parking available
Wheelchair access

From our studio located in the stunning borders of the Welsh countryside, traditional looms produce **contemporary fabrics** using the finest natural yarns which are then sold by the metre or tailored into ladies' jackets and suits. Visitors are always welcome to come and discover the age old craft of weaving. Mail order.

Directions: *entering Whitton, take the B4357 towards Knighton. Take the next right and we are 1 mile at the end of the lane.*

Opening hours: *variable so advisable to telephone first.* 65

MADY GERRARD, Grove Cottage, St Arvans, Monmouthshire NP16 6EU

Est. 1957
Tel +44 (0)1291-625764
Fax +44 (0)1291-621890
Parking available
Wheelchair access difficult
Credit cards

Mady Gerrard has been designing and making exclusive fashion items all her life. Trained in her native Hungary, Mady has worked first in Cardiff, later in New York. Presently, she is **painting silk and velvet** in beautiful colour combinations, which are made into ladies' tunics, jackets, evening tops and skirts. Another speciality is hand-painting silk waistcoats for men with matching bow or regular tie. The latest project is velvet cushions, which are backed with 100% silk and are hand painted. We can match any colour and everything is strictly one of its kind. Big selection in stock. Special orders welcome!

Directions: *to Chepstow via M4 and M48, then proceed on road towards Devaundon and Trellec: second left turning after 3 blocks of cottages.*

Opening hours: *visits at any time by appointment only.*

MELIN TREGWYNT, Tregwynt Mill, Castle Morris, Haverfordwest, Pembrokeshire SA62 5UX

Est. 1912
Tel: +44 (0)1348-891225
Fax: +44 (0)1348-891694
www.melintregwynt.co.uk
Parking available
Wheelchair access
Credit cards

Traditional mill famous for **contemporary designs in blankets, throws, cushions and bedspreads** in heavy felted wool, lightweight lambswool, luxurious angora blends, fine ribs and textured weaves. Exports to designer shops and hotels in USA, Europe and Japan. Watch the weaving (weekdays only) and browse in showroom. Coffee shop. Mail order available.

Directions: *off A487. Four miles from Fishguard and ten miles from St. David's.*

Opening hours: *Mon-Sun 10am-5pm.*

OPAL KNITWEAR, St Pierre Farm, Portskewett, Caldicot, Monmouthshire NP26 5TT

Est. 1989
Tel: +44 (0)1291-420519
Parking available
Credit cards

My **fully-lined mohair jackets with applique** (£75-£96) are made totally by myself so I can make to order any combination of size or colour. I also make sweaters and cardigans (£50+). I work only in mohair and have been doing so for the last 12 years. Ask for mail order catalogue.

Directions: *phone for details.*

Opening hours: *by appointment.*

PATSY BESWICK, Guidfa House, Crossgates, Llandrindod Wells, Powys LD1 6RF

Est 1985
Tel: +44 (0)1597-851241
Fax: +44 (0)1597-851875
Parking available

We are spinners and weavers producing textured yarns to create a range of **sweaters, jackets and rugs** in a unique and exciting combination of natural colours as well as canvaswork cushions and rugs using dyed wools. We also supply wool by the kilogram for hand knitting. Residential courses are run regularly.

Directions: *two and a half miles on the A483 north from Llandrindod Wells at Crossgates roundabout.*

Opening hours: *prior appointment necessary.*

PRESELI MOHAIR CENTRE, Dolav Isaf Farm, Mynachlog-Ddu, Clynderwen, Pembrokeshire SA66 7SB

Est 1992
Tel/fax: +44 (0)1994-419327
Parking available

Our **exclusive garments and quality mohair knitting yarns** are spun from the fleece produced by the flock of angora goats farmed here. We have a small showroom where we stock a range of socks, hats, locally woven travel rugs, hand-crocheted baby wear and angora goat skins. Mail order available.

Directions: *A478 to Glandy Cross then road signposted Mynachlog-Ddu for two and a half miles then first right at the bungalow for half mile; first farm on left.*

Opening hours: *May-Sept Tues-Fri 11am-5pm.*

RIITTA SINKKONEN-DAVIES HANDWEAVING, Mathom House, Moorland Road, Freystrop,
Pembrokeshire SA62 4LE

Est 1998
Tel: +44 (0)1437-890712
www.rasdavies.co.uk
Parking available
Wheelchair access

This is a small interesting workshop specialising in **linen weaving.** There is always a variety of work in progress on different looms including a rare damask loom. A wide variety of products is available for sale including rugs, cushions, colourful table linen, pictures, hangings and greeting cards. Commissions welcomed. Mail order available.
Directions: *Burton/Llangwm road from Haverfordwest. In Freystrop turn right and immediately right again onto Moorland Road. Third house on left.*
Opening hours: *Easter-October Tues-Thurs 10am-6pm.*
Other times by appointment.

ROCK-MILL, Capel-Dewi, Llandysul, Ceredigion SA44 4PH

Est 1890
Tel: +44 (0)1559-362356
Parking available
Wheelchairs some areas
Credit cards

Positioned in the heart of the Teifi Valley, Rock-Mill survives as a working legacy to the woollen industry. Built in 1890 by the greatgrandfather of the present owner and housing the last of the working waterwheels, our range includes **tapestries, bedspreads, blankets, throws, rugs and scarves.** Mail order available.
Directions: *on the B4459 at Capel-Dewi off the A475 Lampeter to Newcastle Emlyn road.*
Opening hours: *Mon-Fri 10am-5pm, Sat 10am-1pm.*

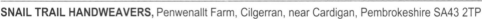

SNAIL TRAIL HANDWEAVERS, Penwenallt Farm, Cilgerran, near Cardigan, Pembrokeshire SA43 2TP

Est 1976
Tel/fax: +44 (0)1239-841228
www.snail-trail.co.uk
Parking available

Makers of colourful 'one-off' **floor rugs, hangings, cushions, scarves and fabrics.** Our custom service means we can match or complement your own colour schemes. We offer weekly residential and non-residential courses in weaving, spinning and dyeing from Easter to September according to demand. Commissions welcomed. Mail order available.
Directions: *off A478 Cardigan to Tenby road. Turn at Rhoshill towards Cilgerran. After half a mile turn right and keep left. Follow Snail Trail signs along half mile farm road.*
Open: *Easter-Sept Mon-Fri 10am-5pm. Phone first out of season or if travelling far.*

SOLVA WOOLLEN MILL, Middle Mill, Solva, Haverfordwest, Pembrokeshire SA62 6XD.

Est. 1907
Tel: +44 (0)1437-721112
Fax: +44 (0)
www.solvawoollenmill.co.uk
Parking available
Wheelchair access
Credit cards

One of the original woollen mills of Pembrokeshire, it now specialises in the manufacture of quality woven **carpets and floor rugs** in contemporary and traditional Welsh designs. Commissions taken for carpets. The Mill shop also has a wide range of woollen products for sale apart from rugs and carpets. Mail order available.
Directions: *signposted from the A487 between Solva and St Davids, the A487 between Fighguard and St Davids or walk/drive one mile up the valley from Lower Solva.*
Opening hours: *Mon-Fri 9.30am-5.30pm; Sat 9.30am-5.30pm and Sun 2pm-5.30pm Easter-Sept.*

SUE HILEY SILKS, The Mill, Tregoyd Mill, Three Cocks, Brecon, Powys, Wales LD3 0SW

Est 1985
Tel/fax: +44 (0)1497-847421
www.suehileysilks.co.uk
Parking available
Credit cards

Sue Hiley Harris, **textile artist and supplier of silk,** creates 3D woven sculpture, handwoven silk scarves and hand-pleated natural-dyed silk scarves. Her work shows a clear continuity in simplicity of shape, design and weave structure and attention to detail. The silk room houses Sue's silk fibre supply. Mail order available.
Directions: *Please telephone or fax for directions.*
Opening hours: *last Friday of month, 10am-4pm.*

TREFRIW WOOLLEN MILLS LTD, Trefriw, North Wales LL27 0NQ

Est. 1859
Tel: +44 (0)1492-640462
Fax: +44 (0)1492-641821
www.t-w-m.co.uk
Parking available
Wheelchair access (shop and tearoom)
Credit cards

Run by the same family for over 140 years, Trefriw Woollen Mills produces traditional Welsh **'tapestry' bedspreads, tweeds, travelling rugs and knitting wools** from the raw wool. Visitors can see the weaving and hydro-electric turbines which generate our electricity. Hand-spinning demonstrations and 'try weaving yourself' in summer. Tearoom. Mail order available.
Directions: *centre of Trefriw on the B5106, five miles north of Betws-y-Coed.*
Opening hours: *Mon-Fr 9.30am-5pm all year. Handspinning demonstration: June-end Sept, Mon-Fri 10am-5pm.*

TY HEN ANGORAS, Ty Hen, Penbryn, Sarnan, Llandysul SA44 6RD

Est 1990
Tel: +44 (0)1239-811323
Parking available

We sell a range including **hand knitted jumpers, cardigans, Christening shawls and shawls.** All are entirely local products. The mohair is from our own flock of goats. Only our finest 'kid' mohair is sent to Natural Fibre Co. to be spun and hand dyed. Our skilled knitters all live locally.

Directions: *turn off Aberystwyth to Cardigan road at Tan-y-Groes 'Car Dismantler' sign. Cross over at the next road junction. Ty Hen is on the left.*

Opening hours: *usually open all day. Phone first.*

Toys & Games

A.P.E.S. Rocking Horses, Ty Gwyn, Llannefydd, Denbigh, Conwy LL16 5HB

Est. 1978
Tel: +44 (0)1745-540365
Limited parking

Pam and Stuart MacPherson are graduates in sculpture and painting (Liverpool Art College) and award-winning members of the British Toymakers' Guild. They make lifelike horses - **arabs and unicorns** in limited editions of rideable and model versions plus traditional carved **English-style rockers.** Restoration work also undertaken - free estimate with photo. Mail order available.

Directions: *a map and details to find the farmhouse workshop will be provided on request.*

Opening hours: *any time arranged by appointment.*

OLD BARN HOBBIES, Shop 17 and 18, Aberaeron Craft Centre, Clos Pengarreg, Aberaeron, Ceredigion

SA46 0EN
Est 1999
Tel/fax: +44 (0)1545-571634
Parking available
Wheelchair access
Credit cards

Our craft shop **caters for all modellers,** selling a wide range of railways, dolls' houses, dolls' house furniture, boats and aircraft items and kits. We also sell modelling tools and materials. We also have a small 'G' scale model railway for which there is a small admission charge. Mail order available.

Directions: *follow brown tourist signs for the craft centre from the A487 or A482 in Aberaeron.*

Opening hours: *Mon-Sat 10am-5pm, Sun 2-5pm.*

TRADITIONAL TOYS, 6 Bull Ring, Llantrisant, Mid Glamorgan CF72 8EB

Est. 1986 approx.
Tel: +44 (0)1443-222693
Parking available
Credit cards

Noel Garnham's shop sells hand made **wooden toys including superb rocking horses** and dolls' houses, castles, trains, garages, dominoes, animal sets, garages, spinning tops, children's bedroom furniture and desks, chairs and toy boxes. Other toys include teddy bears, gollies and marbles. Opposite the Butchers' Arms Gallery and coffee shop.

Directions: *take junction 34 off M4 follow brown signs to Craft and Design Centre. We are in centre of old town at the top of hill.*

Opening hours: *Wed-Sun 10am-5pm. Closed Mon and Tues.* (80)

Woodturning & Furniture

BRYNLEY EDWARDS, 26 John Street, Rhos-y-Waun, Chirk, Wrexham LL14 5HY

Est 1995
Tel: +44 (0)1691-773309
Parking available

A former school teacher, Brynley Edwards has been wood turning small items for six years. He makes a wide range of useful **everyday objects out of different woods:** wedges, bowls, keyboards kitchen knives, games, sewing boxes, wine bottle stoppers, mirrors, clocks, barometers, lamps and fruits. Mail order available.

Directions: *on entering Chirk, turn by the hospital and the workshop is on the left.*

Opening hours: *prior appointment necessary.*

CREATIVE WOODWORKING, Llangedwyn Mill, Llangedwyn, Oswestry, Powys, SY10 9LD

Est. 1996.
Tel: +44 (0)1691-780181
Fax: +44 (0)1691-780601
Parking available
Wheelchair access
Credit cards

Range of quality **kitchenware, gifts, lovespoons, traditional games** and toys, all made from a wide range of beautiful native timbers. Traditional and historic games include Tower of Hanoi, Nine Men's Morris and The Boat Puzzle (American). Also available, turning and carving blanks for customers' own carving. Commissions welcome. Mail order available.

Directions: *ten miles west of Oswestry on the B4396 at Llangedwyn.*

Opening hours: *Mon-Sat 10am-4.30pm; Sun 10am-4pm.*

JIM HARRIES WOODTURNERS, Siop Fach, Mathry, Haverfordwest, Pembrokeshire SA62 5HD

Est. 1972
Tel: +44 (0)1348-831379
www.harrieswoodturner.co.uk

A family business offering high quality furniture including **Welsh dressers, dining-room tables and chairs and coffee tables**; also produces many smaller items including salad and fruit bowls, platters, breadboards etc., which make ideal gifts. You can watch skilled craftsmen working in the adjacent workshop. Other local crafts sold. Mail order available.

Directions: *situated in the centre of Mathry village, just off the B487, between St. David's and Fishguard.*

Opening hours: *from Easter to 1st September Mon-Fri 9.30am/5.30pm; Sat 10am/4pm; Sun: 11am/5pm. Other times by appointment.*

JIM HEATH: SCULPTURE, 2 Hand Terrace, Holyhead Road, Chirk, Wrexham LL14 5EU

Est 1992
Tel: +44 (0)1691-772710
www.woodmart.co.uk
Parking available

Jim Heath is a creator of **large scale wooden sculptures** which are usually made on a commission basis. Prices start from £25 for 'tree spirits.' Private, public and corporate commissions are all undertaken. His work is on display at a number of centres throughout Britain. Mail order is available upon request.

Directions: *the workshop backs onto the main car park in Chirk.*

Opening hours: *variable. Advisable to telephone first.*

MAKEPEACE CABINET MAKING, Derw Mill, Pentrecwrt, Llandysul, Carmarthenshire SA44 5DB

Est. 1968
Tel/fax: +44 (0)1559-362322
www.makepeace-furniture.com
Parking available

Our furniture is of the best possible standard. Style varies from **contemporary smooth maple to traditional oak** cabinets. The quality of our work speaks for itself. Our unbeatable service will help guide you through the design process, whether you need a table, dresser or a complete kitchen or bedroom.

Directions: *just off the A486 near Llandysul, in Pentrecwrt village. Follow sign in village.*

Opening hours: *Mon-Fri 9am-5.30pm. Sat 10am-2pm.*

MARK HANCOCK, The Forge, The Estate Yard, Glanusk Park, Crickhowell, Powys NP8 1LP

Est 1989
Tel: +44 (0)7747-195404
www.markhancock.co.uk
Parking available
Wheelchair access

Mark has now been wood turning for over ten years, developing his own distinctive style. He specialises in **decorative hollow forms** which he cuts and carves after turning. His high quality decorative and functional bowls cost from £40 and the sculptural hollow forms cost from £100. Mail order available.

Please telephone for directions and appointments.

NATURAL EDGE WOODTURNING, 15 Cambrian Terrace, Llanfyllin, Powys SY22 5BD

Est 1990
Tel: +44 (0)1691-648396
Parking available
Wheelchair access

I make a variety of turned items, many embellished with carving and colour and on display in several galleries. I only use locally grown hardwoods from reclaimed or sustainable sources. The range includes **turned bowls, lamps and hollow forms.** Commissions and furniture repairs are also undertaken. Mail order is available upon request.

Directions: *opposite the Llanfyllin High School Entrance on the A490, 15 miles from Shrewsbury.*

Opening hours: *variable. Advisable to telephone first.*

TREE TO THEE, Frondeg, Fron, Caernrfon, Gwynedd LL54 7BS

Est. 1995
Tel +44 (0)1286-880179
Parking available
Wheelchair access

Designer/maker Peter Boyd **works with wood and stone to create highly distinctive, functional works of art.** Mirrors, cabinets, bowls, house signs and memorials, tables and chairs are made; commissions are welcome. He uses quality hardwoods such as walnut, oak, cherry, elm and lime gleaned from tree surgeons, storm damage and driftwood. Each piece is a unique fusion of his woodcarving skills and artistry and the character of the tree. He holds woodcarving courses in his workshop, 1,000 feet high in the Snowdonia mountains: a fully serviced residential caravan with panoramic views is available for participants and their families. Mail order available.

E-mail peter@frondeg.freeserve.co.uk.

Directions: *4 miles south of Caernarfon on the A487, turn left up the mountain at Groeslon to the end of the road in Fron.*

Opening hours: *visits by arrangement only.*

Other Makers

ASCENT, The Old Sewing Room, Prya Centre, Hospital Road, Talgarth, near Hay-on-Wye, Powys LD3 0DS

Est. 1997
Tel/fax: +44 (0)1497-847788
Parking available
Wheelchair access
Credit cards

Ascent is a small natural artisan **perfumery blending essential oils and absolutes** from natural origins. The scents are inspired, blended, compounded, filtered three times and bottled by hand. We also keep a range of 19th century recipes including Hovenia, Rondeletia and Napoleon Farina cologne. Mail order available.

Directions: *take Abergavenny Road to Brecon from Hay-on-Wye. Take the first left over the bridge and then reach the Prya Centre sign.*

Opening hours: *variable, advisable to ring first.*

CAERWEN ARTS STUDIO, Glandwr, Hebron, Whitland, Pembrokeshire SA34 0UA

Est. 1982
Tel: +44 (0)1994-419537
Parking available
Wheelchair access

Ceramic sculptures are all one-offs and include candleburners, interior and exterior **waterfalls, garden sculptures, totem poles and porcelain landscapes.** Paintings of local land and seascapes, flowers and abstracts and small selection of local artists' work are also available. Garden water features and totem pole commissions, all designed and made by Lindy Dennis.

Directions: *Turn off A478 towards Glandwr between Penbluin and Cardigan. Three-quarters mile down hill, take first right along track. Second property on left.*
Opening hours: *Weds-Fri and Sun 10am-5pm; telephone for other times.*   **89**

CELTIC GARDEN, Bron Meillion, Tregeiriog, Llangollen, Wrexham LL20 7HT

Est 1999
Tel: +44 (0)1691-600259
www.CelticGarden.co.uk
Parking available
Credit cards

Celtic Garden is an original concept. Artists and design makers Sylvia and Trefor Jones, inspired by Celtic themes, have created a contemporary Celtic style for the home and garden. Makers of **furniture, lighting and garden artefacts** using local, sustainably managed hardwoods. Prices from £2 to £2,000. Commissions accepted. Mail order available.

Directions: *follow brown Geirog Valley signs from A5 at Cyirk. 10 miles on valley road to second house on right after pony trekking in Pandy.*
Opening hours: *10am-5pm. Closed Mon/Tues.*   **90**

GRAIG FACH STUDIO, Graig Fach, Llangennech, Llanelli, Carmarthenshire. SA14 8PX.

Tel: +44 (0)01554-759944
Parking available
Wheelchair access

Place; an organic smallholding in a wood above the river Morlais. My artwork; **images and sculptures from hand made paper, paint, print, drawings, montage.** Workshops; one hour to all day or week-end. All ages and abilities; painting, drawing, printmaking, paper making, paper and junk crafts, fabric printing, weaving, macramé - for sculptures, wall hangings, jewellery, bowls, and furniture. Recycling. Or visit and walk: camping and B&B available.

Directions: *From J48 off M4. A4138 towards Llanelli. Right at first roundabout. Mile and a half up country lane, right at 'Y' junction, on for a quarter of a mile.*

Opening hours: *by arrangement any time.*

91

DAVID BEATTIE ETCHINGS, Paisley Villa, Llandygwydd, Cardigan SA43 2QT

Est. 1980
Tel: +44 (0)1239-682649
www.original-etchings.co.uk
Parking available
Credit cards

David is an artist printmaker producing finely detailed and limited edition **landscape, livestock and people etchings** using traditional hand methods unchanged in over 400 years. David exquisitely captures the character of his local west Wales region. His work can be viewed on his website. Mail order is available upon request.

Directions: *the gallery is situated in the village of Llandygwydd off the A484 Cardigan to Newcastle Emlyn road. The gallery is opposite the village phone box.*
Opening hours: *Easter-October 10am-4pm Mon-Fri; closed Weds.*   **92**

DRAGONSILK, Tycandl, Cemaes Head, Poppit, Cardigan SA43 3LP

Est 1997
Tel/fax: +44 (0)1239-612034
www.thesilkstudio.co.uk
Parking available
Credit cards

Innovative works of **art on silk and paper** are inspired by the natural world. Everthing is created in our studio set on a cliff halfway between the sea and the sky. Our range includes framed paintings, wallhangings, abstract landscapes, botanicals, hand painted silk scarves and cards. Commissions welcomed.

Directions: *St Dogmaels Road from Cardigan; right for Poppit Sands; past lifeboat station on beach; lane labelled no through road; two miles and over cattle grid to low house.*
Opening hours: *prior appointment necessary.*   **93**

ELIZABETH LEWIS, 14 Kyveilog Street, Cardiff CF11 9JA

Est. 1970
Tel: +44 (0)29-2023 3251
www.musart.demon.co.uk
Parking available
Wheelchair access

Elizabeth works with metals and resins making **jewellery, boxes, mirror frames, free-hanging wall sculptures.** Special corporate pieces are made with a company's own products (e.g. engine parts). Wide range of designs including wildlife, abstract, symbols from ancient ethnic art forms, e.g. Celtic, pre-Columbian, Viking. Prices start at £20 (jewellery).

Directions: *from city centre Kyveilog Street is off Cathedral Road, on the right. Ferriers Hotel is on the corner.*

Opening hours: *flexible; by appointment only.*

FIRE AND FIBRE, Units 3 and 5, Vyrnwy Craft Centre, Lake Vyrnwy, Llanwddyn, Nr. Oswestry, Powys SY10 0LZ

Est 1991
Tel: +44 (0)1691-870386
Fax: +44 (0)1691-870399
www.villworks.demon.co.uk
Parking available
Wheelchair access
Credit cards

We are situated in the Vyrnwy Craft Centre and offer a variety of **craft materials and equipment** for sale. Our range includes woolly rugs, hand spun wool and corn dollies. All are produced on the premises. Demonstrations are given most afternoons upstairs in Unit 5. Mail order available.

Directions: *Lake Vyrnwy is well signposted from Oswestry, Shrewsbury and Welshpool.*

Opening hours: *Mon-Sun 10am-5pm.*

HILARY BRYANSTON, Craig-y-Betting Gwrhyd Road, Pen Rhiwfawr, Upper Swansea Valley, Southwest Wales SA9 2SA

Est. 1984
Tel: +44 (0)1639-831309
www.fortunecity.co.uk
/southbank/craft/837/stonecarving
Parking at Gwrhyd Chapel
advised.

Hilary 'the visionary artist' **works directly on stone** using hand tools for carving. She also creates **assemblages from ceramics and wood.** Additionally, she is a versatile painter, working with abstract imagery or imaginative and realistic subject matter. She does portraits from life, and landscapes inspired by her surroundings. Mail order available.

Directions: *M4, junction 45 to Pontardawe. Then A474 (direction Ammanford) for 2 miles. Right at Travellers Well (direction Cwmllynfell) to Gwrhyd Common. Parking at Gwyrhud Chapel and down track to right.*

Opening hours: *by appointment only.*

J.S. HOMECRAFT, 18 Heol Broch, Birch Grove, Swansea SA7 9PG

Est. 1997
Tel: +44 (0)1792-816653
Parking available
Wheelchair access

John Bevan makes many types of **clocks in solid woods** with various types of finish. He also makes pen and clock sets, bowls, table lamps, children's clocks with individual designs and Disney characters. John is a member of the Welsh Craft Council. Prices start from £5. Mail order available.

Directions: *junction 44 off the M4 to Birchgrove; up hill to traffic lights. Straight across lights, up hill for 150 yards and turn into Heol Broch*

Opening hours: *prior appointment necessary.*

MOSAIC, Units 5 and 6, Lighthouse Business Park, Bastion Road, Prestatyn, Denbighshire LL19 7ND

Est. 1992
Tel: +44 (0)1745-888911
Parking available
Wheelchair access

Mosaic makes a wide range of vibrant handmade papier-mâché mirrors, clocks, boxes, decorations and personalised mirrors. All are ideal bright and fun gifts for adults and children alike. All our products are hand made in partnership with adults with learning disabilities. Prices range from £3 to £30. Mail order available.

Directions: *at traffic lights on the coast road in Prestatyn turn down towards the beach. We are on the right 400 yards from the beach.*

Opening hours: *Mon-Thurs 9am-5pm. Fri 9am-4pm.*

ODYN COPR, Padarn Country Park, Llanberis, Gwynedd LL55 4TY

Est. 1984
Tel/fax: +44 (0)1286-871366
Parking available
Wheelchair access
Credit cards

Specialist in **enamelled jewellery, boxes and dishes.** Watch daily demonstrations of enamelling. Rich colours melt and swirl together in the kilns. We also gather flowers from Snowdon and make framed, pressed flower pictures; also pyrography designs on bed and cheese boards, pen holders etc.

All items are made in our workshop.

Directions: *follow signs to Llanberis Lake Railway. Our workshop is in the car park.*

Opening hours: *Mar-Nov 10.30am-5pm daily.*

PEMBROKESHIRE CANDLE CENTRE, Trefelin, Cilgwyn, Newport, Pembrokeshire SA42 0QN

Est. 1976
Tel: +44 (0)1239-820470
Fax: +44 (0)1239-821245
Parking available
Wheelchair access (mostly)
Credit cards

Pembrokeshire Candle Centre is the only place in Wales where you can see **hand-dipped candles** made just as they were centuries ago without any mechanical aids. The candles are created with unique graded colours and exotic scents including specially blended essential oils. Mail order is available upon request.

Directions: *located at Cilgwyn Bridge about 2 miles from Newport. Follow the signs from the A487 at the end of Newpal or from the B4329 at Tafarn-y-Bwlch.*

Open: *April-Oct 11am-5pm. Nov-Dec 12am-4pm. Other times please phone first.*

PEMBROKESHIRE CRAFTSMENS CIRCLE, St. Mary's Hall, Cathedral Grounds, St David's, Pembrokeshire SA62.

Est. 1972
Tel: +44 (0)1646-690190
Parking available
Credit cards

Craft Circle producing a range of high quality crafts including jewellery, hand weaving, etchings, ceramics, wood, dried flower pictures, enamel work and pewter work and only exhibiting at St David's. Holds five selling exhibitions per year in the Cathedral Hall situated in the grounds of St David's Cathedral. Mail order (some members).

Directions: *signposted in the grounds of St. David's Cathedral, Pembrokeshire.*

Opening hours: *Apr-Oct (not Aug) 10am-5pm. 7-16 days per exhibition. Phone for dates.*

THE SLATE WORKSHOP, Pont Hywel Mill, Llangolman, Clunderwen, Pembrokeshire SA66 7XJ

Est. 1985
Tel/fax: +44 (0)1994-419543
www.slate-workshop.co.uk
Parking available
Wheelchair access
Credit cards

From our renovated 18th century cornmill we design and make high quality items in Welsh slate. **Specialising in fine lettering,** we make nameplates, numbers, sundials, plaques and memorials, planters and vases, bookends, clocks, barometers and cheeseboards. Richard Boultbee creates slate sculpture. Commissions are very welcome. Mail order available.

Directions: *from Efailwen, on the A478 Cardigan to Tenby Road, turn towards Llangolman. We are beside the river at the bottom of the valley.*

Opening hours: *Mon-Sat 9am-5.30pm, Sun 10.30am-4pm. Telephone ahead in winter.*

Central England West

Cheshire, Herefordshire, Shropshire, Staffordshire, Warwickshire, Worcestershire

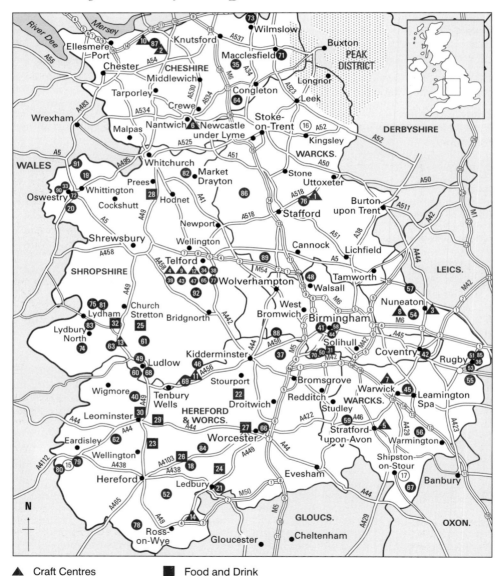

▲ Craft Centres   ■ Food and Drink

◯ Shops and Galleries   ● Makers' Workshops

Cheshire cheese, The Birmingham Jewellery Quarter, The Staffordshire Potteries, Herefordshire cider and Worcester gloves are all traditional craft industries (though Worcester glovemaking is now the stuff of museums).

Historically, Stoke-on-Trent in Staffordshire is Britain's biggest pottery and china-producing centre, where famous names like Spode, Royal Doulton, Wedgwood, Aynsley etc are still producing their wares.

Worcester has been home to the production of beautiful Royal Worcester porcelain for centuries. Cottage industries included fish-hook making, and sewing needles from the Redditch area. In the northern part of the county hand made nails were a speciality until machines finally outpaced hands.

The agricultural county of Herefordshire is chiefly famous for the literary and second-hand book centre of Hay-on-Wye which also boasts a thriving artistic and craft community.

Craft Centres

AMERTON FARM, Stowe by Chartley, Stafford, ST18 OLA

Est. 1986
Tel/fax: +44 (0)1889-270294
300 car spaces
Wheelchair access
Credit cards

Amerton is a busy craft complex with lots to do and see. In addition to crafts from puppets to wrought iron there is a Wildlife Rescue Centre, farmyard shop, bakery, steam train and new play area. Plants, fabric and home made ice-cream also sold. *See also: Food, Pottery, Metalwork, Toys and Other Makers.*

Directions: *on the A518 Stafford to Uttoxeter Road, a mile east of Weston.*
Opening hours: *Mon-Sun 9am-5.30pm.*

BLAKEMERE CRAFT CENTRE, Chester Road, Sandiway, Northwich, Cheshire CW8 2EB

Tel: +44 (0)1606-883261
Fax: +44 (0)1606-301495
www.blakemerecrafts.co.uk
Own car parks
Credit cards
Wheelchair access mostly

Blakemere is a craft centre comprising over a dozen craft workshops including teddy bears, ironwork, pottery etc. plus another 17 craft shops, the latter selling unusual crafted items from Britain and around the world. Also at the centre: large garden centre, aquatic and falconry centre, children's playbarn and a restaurant and coffee shop.

Directions: *on the junction of the A556 and A49 at Sandiway, approximately five miles from Northwich heading towards Chester.*
Opening hours: *Tues-Fri 10am-5pm; Sat, Sun and bank hols 10am-5.30pm.*

CHILVERS COTON CRAFT CENTRE, Avenue Road, Nuneaton, Warwickshire CV11 4LU

Est. 1990
Tel: +44 (0)24 7637 6490
Parking available
Wheelchair access

Chilvers Coton Craft Centre is a purpose-built craft centre of 21 units and is operated by the Borough Council. Crafts range from jeweller-goldsmith to radio-control model airplanes. There is also a café. See also: *Craft Shops, Food and Drink, General Gifts, Glass, Jewellery, Pottery, Toys and Games and Other Makers.*

Directions: *from M6, junction 3, then A444 into Nuneaton and right at railway arches into Avenue Road. Craft Centre is on the left. If coming from the North M69 and then the A5.*
Opening times: *Tues-Sat 10am-4pm.*

COALPORT CHINA MUSEUM, Ironbridge Gorge Museum Trust, High Street, Coalport, Shropshire TF8 7H2

Est. 1976
Tel: +44 (0)1952-580650
Fax: +44 (0)1952-580627
Parking available
Wheelchair access (mostly)
Credit cards

Coalport is a working museum, combining demonstrations of ceramic processes, displays of its extensive national ceramic collections, a gallery focussing on the life of Coalport workers, an interactive children's gallery and regular temporary exhibitions. The gift shop sells a range of ceramic ware produced by potters on site. Mail order available.

Directions: *off M54, junction 4. Follow brown signs for Ironbridge Gorge Museums, then local signs to Coalport China Museum.*

Opening hours: *daily 10am-5pm.*

COX'S YARD, Bridgefoot, Stratford-upon-Avon, Warwickshire CV37 6YY

Est. 1998
Tel: +44 (0)1789-404600
Fax: +44 (0)1789-404633
Parking available nearby
Wheelchair access
Credit cards

Cox's Yard was created from a restored timber mill overlooking the River Avon and comprises tea-rooms, gift shop, art gallery, restaurant and pub. The Gallery exhibits a wide range of art forms, mostly by local artists, using a variety of media and all work is for sale. Visit also the micro-brewery.

Directions: *Stratford is off M40 (junction 15), approx. 50 minutes from Oxford, 30 minutes from Birmingham and 20 minutes from Warwick. Centre is adjacent to Bancroft Gardens and Clapton Bridge.*

Opening hours: *Mon-Sun 9am-5pm (gallery only).*

DAGFIELDS CRAFTS AND ANTIQUES CENTRE, Dagfields Farm, Crewe Road, Walgherton, Nantwich, Cheshire CW5 7LG

Est. 1988
Tel: +44 (0)1270-841336
Fax: +44 (0)1270 842604
Parking available
Wheelchair access
Credit cards (some traders)

The Dagfields Crafts Centre is home to leather, dried flower and candle workshops. There are also displays of timber toys, tapestries, hand crafted and rustic garden furniture, stained glass, teddy bears and dolls, fine arts and mirrors. In addition there is a large antiques complex with 150 dealers.

Directions: *off the A51 on the B5071 between Bridgemere and Stapeley.*

Opening hours: *10am-5pm 7 days a week.* 6

HATTON COUNTRY WORLD, Dark Lane, Hatton, Near Warwick, Warwickshire CU35 8XA

Est. 1982
Tel: +44 (0)1926-843411
Fax: +44 (0)1926-842023
www.hattonworld.com
Parking available
Wheelchair access
Credit cards

Hatton shopping village at Hatton Country World is based around 19th century farm buildings and is home to one of England's largest craft centres with 25 craft workshops/ shops including makers of stained glass, jewellery, ironwork, wooden toys and much more; also fashions, china, kitchenware, books and a cafe. Mail order some units.

Directions: *five minutes from junction 15 of the M40. Take the A46 towards Coventry and leave at the first exit turning left onto A4177, then follow the signs.*

Opening hours: *Mon-Sun 10am-5pm.*

HOAR PARK CRAFT VILLAGE, Ansley B4114, Near Nuneaton, Warwickshire CV10 0QU

Est. 1993
Tel/fax: +44 (0)2476-394433
Parking available
Wheelchair access
Credit cards

Quality hand made crafts are for sale or can be commissioned in a courtyard complex of 18th century restored farm buildings set in a working farm of 143 acres. Hoar Park also includes: Antique Centre, Garden Centre, restaurant, Children's Farm, saddlery and horse feed, and offers country walks, picnics and fishing.

Directions: *on B4114 between Ansley and Over Whitacre, near Coleshill. 15 minutes by car from Birmingham National Exhibition Centre and the Belfry Hotel.*

Opening hours: *Tues-Sun 10am-5pm. Closed Mon. Open bank holidays.*

IRONBRIDGE GORGE MUSEUMS, 3/4 Wharfage, Ironbridge, Telford, Shropshire TF8 7AW

Est. 1969. World Heritage Site 1986
Tel: +44 (0)1952-433522
Fax: +44 (0)1952-432204
www.ironbridge.org.uk
Parking available
Wheelchair access
Credit cards

Blists Hill is a Victorian town which brings to life old crafts and customs. In this working museum you can see traditional iron forging in the foundry. There is also a tin smith, candlemaker and decorative plasterers. Products from these and other crafts are on sale on site. Mail order available.

Directions: *from M54 Blists Hill Victorian Town is well signposted.*

Opening hours: *Mon-Sun 10am-5pm.*

LADY HEYES CRAFT AND ANTIQUE RESTORATION CENTRE, Kingsley Road, Frodsham, Near Warrington, Cheshire WA6 6SU

Est. 1999
Tel: +44 (0)1928-787919
Fax: +44 (0)1928-787015
www.ladyheyescraftandantiquecentre.co.uk
Ample parking
Wheelchair accessible
Credit cards

This award-winning Centre comprises seven buildings and over 55 workshops and offers a very varied selection of arts, crafts, gifts and antique collectables. Crafts include ceramics, bronzes, lace-making, sculptures, painted furniture, dolls and furniture, wedding dresses and accessories, art gallery, paper crafts, candle-making etc. Also hand made chocolates and a tearoom/restaurant.

Directions: *junction 12 off M56 to Frodsham. At the main Frodsham lights (The Bear's Paw), turn left (B5152) for Kingsley. Centre is two and a half miles on left.*

Opening hours: *Mon-Sat 10am-5pm; Sat 11am-5pm.*

MAMBLE CRAFT CENTRE, Church Lane, Mamble, Near Bewdley, Worcestershire DY14 9JY

Est. 1995
Tel: +44 (0)1299-832834
Fax: +44 (0)1299-832132
www.mamblecraftcentre.co.uk
Parking available
Wheelchair access
Credit cards

Housed in 17th century barns with stunning views to the Clee Hills, the Centre houses a range of traditional and contemporary arts. There are four workshops, a tea room, craft gallery, craft exhibition room and gift shop. The Gallery shows glass and pottery, clocks, barometers, silver etc. Mail order available.

Directions: *half way between Bewdley and Tenbury Wells off the A456.*

Opening hours: *Tues-Sun 10.30am-5pm.*

MAWS CRAFT CENTRE (JACKFIELD LTD), Unit B2, Maws Craft Centre, Jackfield, Telford, Shropshire TF8 7LS

Est. 1988
Tel: +44 (0)1952-883030
Fax: +44 (0)1952-883285
Credit cards: some makers

Over twenty individual workshops housing wide variety of art, craft and design businesses including ironwork, stained glass, mosaics, pottery and bespoke furniture. Situated in the Victorian Factory of Maws and Co, once the world's largest tile manufacturer. Licensed tea-rooms. Near Severn Valley Way long distance path. Mail order available from some makers.

Directions: *south side of the New Bridge over the river Severn between Ironbridge and Brosely. Turn left along river through Jackfield following signs for Maws Craft Centre.*

Open: *variable for individual workshops. Centre is open 10am-late afternoon.*

SECRET HILLS, SHROPSHIRE DISCOVERY CENTRE, School Road, Craven Arms, Shropshire SY7 9RS

Est. 2001
Tel: +44 (0)44 1588-676000
Fax: +44 (0)44 1588-676030
Parking available
Wheelchair access

The Secret Hills Gallery is part of a recently opened attraction and features local arts and craftspeople's work including glass, ceramics, wood, jewellery and more: some is on exhibition only, but much is for sale. The Centre has a café, information centre, shop, meadows and trails and education and activities rooms.

Directions: *on the A49 in Craven Arms, 20 miles south of Shrewsbury, 7 miles north of Ludlow. 500 yards from Stokesay Castle.*

Opening hours: *open every day at 10am.* 🔟③

WOBAGE MAKERS GALLERY, Wobage Farm Craft Workshops, Upton Bishop, Ross-on-Wye, Herefordshire HR9 7QP

Est. 1977
Tel: +44 (0)1989-780495
Fax: +44 (0)1989-780495
Credit cards

Wobage Farm is the home and workshop of potters Mick and Sheila Casson. The workshops also accommodate a group of ten makers (seven potters, two woodworkers and a jeweller). The Gallery offers customers a chance to see a variety of works and to meet the craftspeople. *See also Pottery and Woodturning.*

Directions: *on the B4224 between the A449 and A40, two and a half miles from Junction 3 on the M50.*

Open: *Thurs-Sun 10am-5pm (Apr-Oct). Otherwise 10am-5pm Sat & Sun.* 🔟④

Craft Shops

ANTIQUES & COLLECTABLES SHOP, Units 6 & 8, Chilvers Coton Craft Centre, Avenue Road, Nuneaton, Warwickshire CV11 4LU

Est. 1994
Tel: +44 (0)7778-065164
Parking available
Wheelchair access
Credit cards

Stella Olliver's two shops sell a wide range of hand crafted goods including walking sticks, greetings cards for all occasions, tapestries, antique furniture large and small, porcelain by various makers and collectable items and bygones. All items are sold at affordable prices. The Centre also has a café.

Directions: *M6 junction 3, then A444 towards Nuneaton. At large traffic island (before Nuneaton Centre) follow signposts to Craft Centre which is 100 yards from the 'Coton Arches' railway bridge.*

Opening hours: *Tues-Sat 10am-4pm.*

Galleries

THE HAY MAKERS GALLERY, St. John's Place, Hay-on-Wye, Herefordshire HR3 5BN

Est. 1990
Tel: +44 (0)1497-820556
www.haymakers.co.uk
Parking available
Wheelchair access small step
Credit cards

The Hay Makers is a cooperative of ten professional designer/makers. Their quality work includes pottery, painted silk, glass, sculpture, furniture, wood carving and turning, mirrors and embroidery. Prices range from a few pounds to a few hundred pounds. There is also a programme of visiting exhibitors from Easter to Christmas.

Directions: *the Gallery is round the corner from the Butter Market in the town centre (off Lion Street).*

Opening hours: *Mon-Sun 10.30am-5pm. Closed 1.30-2pm.*

NEWFIELDS GALLERY, Foxt, Near Froghall, Staffordshire Moorlands ST10 2HS

Est. 1990
Tel +44 (0)1538-266334
www.peakdistrictproducts.co.uk
/newfields
Parking available.
Visitors with special needs
please telephone first.

The Newfields Gallery sells only the work of Roger Sutton and Gail Keep, artists in ceramics and wood. Their work is a celebration of the countryside around them. Finely detailed relief ceramics, jewellery, boxes and plaques also intricate woodcarvings in English oak. Ideal for gifts, collections and very special occasions.

Directions: *on A52 at Froghall (Stoke-on-Trent 14 miles, Ashbourne 10) turn to Foxt. Once through Foxt village turn right at cross-roads; Gallery is 400 yards on right.*

Opening hours: *9am-5pm most days; please telephone to check.*

THE STOUR GALLERY, 10 High Street, Shipston on Stour, Warwickshire CV36 4AJ

Est. 1997
Tel +44 (0)1608-664411
Fax +44 (0)1608-664433
Parking easily available.
Wheelchair access: one
shallow step but help
always available.

The Stour Gallery emerged from owner Sarah Stoten's pleasure and interest in contemporary art and has an important collection of works for sale - paintings, prints and ceramics by modern artists. The work of artists with growing national reputations is displayed alongside paintings and pieces by established artists of international renown.

Directions: *on Shipston-on-Stour's main street.*

Opening times: *10am-5.30pm, Monday-Saturday.*

Baskets & Wickerwork

JENNY PEARCE BASKETMAKER, Canon Frome Court, near Ledbury, Herefordshire HR8 2TD

Est. 1998
Tel: +44 (0)1531-670574
http://welcome.to/willowbaskets
Parking available

I base the design of my **traditional hand made willow baskets** on regional Celtic and English basket-making. I also produce a range of contemporary basketry. I make a wide range of shoppers, carriers and linen baskets. Commissions are undertaken and courses in basic basket-making are available. Customers can also purchase by mail order.

Directions: *off A417 between Ashperton and Stretton. Turning to Canon Frome by small UK garage.*

Opening hours: *by appointment only.*

TED BRUCE - BASKETMAKER, The Mallards, Perthy, Ellesmere, Shropshire SY12 9HX

Est. 1998
Tel: +44 (0)1691-622915
Roadside parking

A small country workshop where Ted Bruce combines traditional methods with contemporary design to craft **functional willow baskets** in a variety of beautiful natural colours. The product range includes shopping baskets, garden trugs, umbrellas, Ali Babas, bottle carriers, picnic and storage baskets and bowls. Prices start from £16. Mail order available.

Directions: *take turning for Perthy on A495 between Ellesmere and Whittington. After half a mile, fork right. 50 yards on left.*

Opening hours: *prior appointment essential.*

WERN COPPICE CRAFTS, The Wern, Turners Lane, Llynclys, Oswestry, Shropshire SY10 8LL

Est. 1999
Tel: +44 (0)1691-831070
Parking available

A coppice-worker based near to Offa's Dyke, Allan Houseman sells high quality products including **wattle hurdles, rakes and barbecue charcoal**. Through his work, Allan is keen to promote the positive management of native woodland. Most work is on a commission basis. Courses are run for the general public.

Directions: *Turners Lane is quarter of a mile west of the A483/B4936 junction, 4 miles south of Oswestry.*

Opening hours: *appointment essential.* 20

WILLOW WORKS, The Coach House, Skipp Alley, Ledbury, Herefordshire HK8 1BN

Est. 2001
Tel/fax: +44 (0)1531-636660
Parking available at Bye Street car park
Wheelchair access
Credit cards

Willow Works specialise in willow products for the garden; including **fencing, trellis and living willow.** A popular product is the 'twigwam' for children. Kits are available and workshops are run. Prices range from £1 to £250. Willow Works appear at large garden shows and mail order is also available.

Directions: *Skipp Alley is next to the National Westminister Bank in Ledbury.*

Opening hours: *Mon-Sat 10am-5.30pm.*

Food & Drink

AMERTON BAKERY, Amerton Working Farm, Stowe-by-Chartley, Staffordshire ST18 0LA

Est. 1986
Tel: +44 (0)1889-271442
Parking available
Wheelchair access

The Barker family's busy Amerton Bakery is housed in a converted cow-shed in the Amerton Farm craft centre. It produces bread, cakes, pies (various fillings of fruit and meat), pasties, vegetarian dishes and diabetic cakes all made on site by hand from fresh ingredients and free of additives. Open to public.

Directions: *the Farm is on the A518 between Stafford and Uttoxeter, half a mile from its junction with the A51.*

Opening hours: *seven days a week 9am-5.30pm (5pm winter).*

ASTLEY VINEYARDS, Astley, Stourport-on-Severn, Worcestershire DY13 0RU

Est. 1984
Tel/fax: +44 (0)1299-822907
Parking available
Wheelchair access (to shop)
Credit cards

Run by Jonty Daniels and Janet Baldwin, Astley is a five-acre valley vineyard planted in 1975, which specialises in small production runs of high quality international, award-winning white wines (including sparkling). The vineyard shop is open to customers for tasting and buying. Small group tours by appointment. Mail order available.

Directions: *on B4196 between Shrawley and Stourport-on-Severn. Look for brown heritage sign pointing down Crunders Lane. 300 yards down this on right.*

Opening hours: *Mon and Thurs-Sat 10am-5pm. Sun noon-5pm. Tues, Wed and other times by appointment.* `22`

BODENHAM ENGLISH WINES, Broadfield Court, Bodenham, Herefordshire HR1 3LG

Est. 1972
Tel: +44 (0)1568-797483
Fax: +44 (0)1568-797859
www.bodenham-englishwines.co.uk
Parking available
Wheelchair access
Credit cards

Broadfield Court dates back to 1086, though vines have been grown since Roman times. We produce six white still and sparkling wines which are all ready for tasting. Pre-booked wine-tasting parties can also be catered for. There are five acres of glorious English gardens, teas and coffees. Mail order available.

Directions: *follow the A417, at Bodenham turn opposite the Murco Garage and follow brown signs.*

Opening hours: *9am-5pm Mon-Fri, 10am-5pm Sat/Sun.* `23`

CODDINGTON VINEYARD, Near Ledbury, Herefordshire HR8 1JJ

Est. 1990
Tel/fax: +44 (0)1531-640668
Parking available
Limited wheelchair access

Dennis and Ann Savage's Vineyard lies to the west of the Malvern Hills. Four varieties of grape are grown: Bacchus, Orgega, Kerner and Pinot Gris. The wines are well-balanced, aromatic and fruity and are produced in the vineyard winery. Tastings are offered to customers in the vineyard shop. Mail order available.

Directions: *from the Ledbury to Malvern road (A449) take the turning to Colwall (B4218) and follow brown signs to the vineyard.*

Open: *Thurs-Mon 2-5pm. Otherwise by appointment. Closed Jan and Feb.* `24`

CORVEDALE BREWERY, The Sun Inn, Corfton, Craven Arms, Shropshire SY7 9DF

Est. 1999 (Brewery)
Tel: +44 (0)1584-861239
www.thesuninn.netfirms.com
Parking available
Wheelchair access
Credit cards

Norman Pearce brews The Sun Inn's very own ales including 'Norman's Pride' in the on-site boutique brewery which he built at the back of the pub. He is happy to show visitors the beer being made before they buy it at the bar, or to drink at home. Bottles and barrels available.

Directions: *leave M54 at junction 4 (signed Ironbridge Gorge Museum) into Much Wenlock. Follow signs for Craven Arms (B4368) at 5-road junction and at next junction. Inn is 4 miles after the second junction.*

Open: *Mon-Sat 11am-2.30pm and 6-11pm. Sun 12-3pm and 7-10.30pm.* 25

FROME VALLEY VINEYARD, Paunton Court, Bishops Frome, Herefordshire WR6 5BJ

Est. 1997
Tel: +44 (0)1885-490735
Fax: +44 (0)1885-490736
www.fromewine.co.uk
Parking available
Wheelchair access
Credit cards

David and Clare Longman's vineyard in Paunton hamlet, by the river Frome, comprises 4,000 vines in about four acres producing quality white and rose wines. 'Model vineyard' where demonstrations of growing, pruning and trellising wines are given. Walk around the vineyards and have a tasting. Groups by arrangment. Mail order available.

Directions: *from Worcester off M5 at junction 7; from Hereford (A4103). Follow brown signs to vineyard passing through Bishops Frome.*

Open: *Wed-Sun 11am-5pm and bank holiday Mons. Groups need to book ahead.* 26

LIGHTWOOD CHEESE, Lower Lightwood Farm, Lightwood Lane, Cotheridge, Worcestershire WR6 5LT

Est. 1989
Tel/fax: +44 (0)1905-333468
www.farmhouse-cheese.com

Makers of traditional farmhouse cheese, using only the milk from our own premier Friesian dairy herd to make medal and award-winning cheeses. 'Let your taste buds loose with Elgar Mature, Severn Sisters or Olde Gloucester (Double Gloucester coloured with carrot juice) and savour our Lightwood Smoked.' On-site shop and mail order.

Directions: *take A44 Bromyard/Leominster road to the west of Worcester, past Laylocks nurseries, next road on right, 500 yards on left.*

Opening hours: *Thurs-Sat 9am-6pm. Appt necessary for groups of ten or more.* 27

MAYNARDS FARM BACON LTD, Hough Farm, Weston under Redcastle, Shrewsbury, Shropshire SY4 5LR

Est. 1985
Tel +44 (0)1948-840252
Fax +44 (0)1948-841204
www.maynardsfarm.co.uk
Parking available
Wheelchair access
Credit cards

Maynards Farm has been producing traditional home cured bacon and hams for the last 15 years; over 20 regional varieties including several smoked flavours, **various ham recipes and preservative-free sausages**. We use only top quality unrefined sugars and syrups imported specially from Mauritius, mixed with herbs and salts and combined with unique processes that embellish the flavour of our farm assured pork. Visit our farm shop where you will be guaranteed a warm welcome and good old fashioned service. We have a range of traditional local fayre as well as our speciality bacon and hams. Mail order available.

Directions: *located near Weston under Redcastle on the A49, 11 miles north of Shrewsbury.*

Opening hours: *9am-6pm Weds-Sun and bank holidays.* 28

MONKLAND CHEESE DAIRY, The Pleck, Monkland, Leominster, Herefordshire HR6 9DB

Est. 1996
Tel: +44 (0)1568-720307
www.mousetrapcheese.co.uk
Parking available
Wheelchair access
Credit cards

Monkland's product is based on the Little Hereford cheese made by Ellen Yeld at the turn of the last century. It is hand made all year round and the flavour subtly alters with the seasons. Visitors can see and appreciate the various stages of cheese-making. Café and cheese shop. Mail order available.

Directions: *on the A44 two miles west of Leominster in Monkland village.*

Opening hours: *Tues-Sat café and farm shop 10am-5.30pm (closed Sun and Mon and Nov-Easter). Cheese-making demonstration Mon, Wed, Fri 10am-2pm).* 29

ORCHARD, HIVE AND VINE, 6 the Buttercross, Leominster, Herefordshire HR6 8BN

Est. 1997
Tel/fax: +44 (0)1568-611232
www.ordhard-hive-and-vine.co.uk
Parking available
Wheelchair access
Credit cards

We are a specialist off-licence selling only local products from small-scale producers including ciders, apple juice (20 different flavours), beers, local wines, blackcurrant, damson and raspberry gins and Beowulf Mead. Winner - Flavours of Herefordshire Specialist Retailer of the Year Award 2000. Many products are award-winning specialities. Mail order available.

Directions: *off A49, follow Town Centre signs to central car park. In arcade between the library and Barclays Bank.*

Opening hours: *Mon-Sat 9am-5.30pm.*   30

ORGANIC ROOTS, Dark Lane, Kings Norton, Birmingham B38 0BS

Est. 1992
Tel: +44 (0)1564-822294
Fax: +44 (0)1564-829212
www.organicroots.co.uk
Parking available
Good wheelchair access
Credit cards

Organic roots is the only certificated organic shop in the West Midlands. We stock 500 lines of organic food including fruit, vegetables, wholefoods, all sorts of organic meat, rod caught fish, potted goods, jams, pickles etc. Large-scale suppliers of organic seedlings. Home delivery service locally or nationwide. Mail order available.

Directions: *A435 to Maypole. Take Alcester Road towards south, turn right into Dark Lane after three-quarters of a mile. Farm shop is a mile up lane.*

Opening hours: *Thurs, Fri, Sat 10am-4pm.*   31

SPECIALITY CAKES BY JANICE HILL, Unit 15, Chilvers Coton Craft Centre, Avenue Road, Nuneaton, Warwickshire CV11 4LU

Est. 1994
Tel: +44 (0)7855-618247
Ample parking
Wheelchair access

Janice Hill designs and makes cakes for any occasion, for example: weddings, new baby, christenings, anniversaries, birthdays, retirement, graduation, confirmation/first Communion. She works with the customer's ideas and own designs when required. She also makes chocolate wedding cakes which can also be made to the client's own design.

Directions: *M6 junction 3, then A444 towards Nuneaton. At large traffic island (before Nuneaton Centre) follow signposts to Craft Centre which is 100 yards from the 'Coton Arches' railway bridge.*

Opening hours: *Wed-Sat 1-4pm.*   ▲3

THE WOOD BREWERY LTD, Wistanstow, Craven Arms, Shropshire SY7 8DG

Est. 1980
Tel: +44 (0)1588-672523
Fax: +44 (0)1588-673939
www.woodbrewery.co.uk
Parking available
W/chair access to Plough Inn
Credit cards (at Plough Inn)

Wood's brewery is in a converted stables next to the Plough Inn. In twenty years it has doubled in size to cater for demand, and to create a new set of brews for Sam Powell beers - recipes rescued from a defunct Welsh brewery. Fine, cask-conditioned and bottled beers. Mail order available.

Directions: *A489 from A49 one mile north of Craven Arms. First or second right will bring you to Wistantow and The Plough Inn.*

Opening hours: *Plough Inn noon-3pm and 7-11pm.*   32

General Gifts

CREOSOWALLT CRAFTS, Powis Hall Market, Bailey Head, Oswestry, Shropshire SY11 1PZ

Est. 1996
Tel: +44 (0)1961 652423
Parking available
Wheelchair access

A small marketing group for craftworkers specialising in local themes and crafts. Strict standards ensure all products are of the highest quality. The range of goods for sale include jewellery, pottery, wildlife paintings, watercolours and woodturning. Members occasionally demonstrate and commissions are taken. Prices are very reasonable. Mail order available (some items).

Directions: *Market Hall is at the top of Bailey Street at the centre of the outdoor market.*

Open: *Wed & Sat 9.30am-3.30pm. Also at Farmer's Market last Fri every month (outside).*   33

GINGHAM CHICKEN, Unit C 21B, Maws Craft Centre, Jackfield, Near Ironbridge, Telford, Shropshire TF8 7LS

Est. 1999
Tel: +44 (0)1952-881138
Fax: +44 (0)1952-883923
Parking available
Wheelchair access
Credit cards

I started making and designing at home before expanding into a business at the Maws Craft Centre. I specialise in nostalgia, simple and practical things, made from bright colourful cotton prints. Items include: children's aprons, tie-on tea cosys, peg bags, appliquéd pictures, patchwork and dolls' pram bedding etc. Mail order available.

Directions: *south side of the New Bridge over the river Severn between Ironbridge and Brosely. Turn left along river through Jackfield following signs for Maws Craft Centre.*

Opening hours: *usually Mon-Fri 10.30am-5.30pm. Sat/Sun 11am-5pm.*

SUSIE P, Unit 7, Chilvers Coton Craft Centre, Avenue Road, Nuneaton, Warwickshire CV11 4LU

Est. 1994
Parking available
Wheelchair access
Tel: +44 (0)770-3791437
Fax: +44 (0)1827-717110
Credit cards

I specialise in original high quality teddy bear vacuum covers. They are made of curly fur and are dressed as maids in black and white with frilly pinafore and mob-caps (other colours available). Doorstop mice, traditional rag dolls, gollies and draught excluders are also available and all made in house. Mail order available.

Directions: *M6 junc 3, then A444 towards Nuneaton. At large traffic island (before Nuneaton Centre) follow signs to Craft Centre which is 100 yds from the 'Coton Arches' railway bridge.*

Opening hours: *Tues-Sat 10am-4pm.*

WELLTROUGH DRIED FLOWERS, Welltrough Hall Farm, Lower Withington, nr Macclesfield, Cheshire SK11 9EF

Est. 1991
Tel/fax: +44 (0)1477-571616
Parking available
Wheelchair access
Credit cards

Converted farm buildings house a vast selection of silk and dried flowers, ceramics, candles, gifts and flower arrangements. Demonstration days with a national demonstrator take place throughout the year. We pride ourselves on our customer service with flower arrangements designed to suit individual requirements. Mail order available but well worth a visit!

Directions: *Junction 18 off M6 or from Chelford: follow A535 and turn onto Holmes Chapel Road, following the brown tourist board signs.*

Opening hours: *Mon-Fri 9am-5pm, Sat/Sun 10am-5pm.*

Glass

CLASSIC GLASS STAINED GLASS STUDIO, Studio 3, Churchside Arcade, Little Church Street, Rugby, Warwickshire CV21 3AW

Est. 1988
Tel: +44 (0)1788-537161
Parking nearby

Christopher and Jeanette Bates design, **make and restore stained glass windows/ leaded lights** (either single glazed or encapsulated in double-glazed units). They also have a large selection of Tiffany-style lamps. Other items include mirrors, glassware, wall-lights, fan-lamps, trinket boxes. Also suppliers of stained glass materials and providers of courses for hobbyists.

Directions: *Little Church Street is situated in the centre of Rugby to the rear of Macdonalds and Marks and Spencer.*

Opening hours: *Mon-Sat 9.30am-5pm.*

GLAZAM, Ruskin Glass Centre, Wollaston Road, Amblecote, Stourbridge, West Midlands DY8 4HF

Est. 1997
Tel: +44 (0)1384-399468
www.glazam.co.uk
Large car park
Wheelchair access

Glazam stained glass studio is owned and run by glass designer and maker Shirley How and painter Tim Seaward. They offer traditional or contemporary leaded, stained, kiln-fired, painted, restored **windows, panels, mirrors, sculptures** etc suitable for the home or office. Corporate and private commissions are welcome.

Directions: *from Stourbridge ring road follow the signs for the 'Glass Quarter', which takes you on to High Street, Amblecote A491. Left at 2nd traffic lights into Wollaston Road.*

Opening hours: *by appointment only.*

JONATHAN HARRIS STUDIO GLASS LTD, Coalport, Nr. Ironbridge, Shropshire TF8 7HZ

Est. 1999
Tel: +44 (0)1952-246381
Fax: +44 (0)1952-248555
www.jhstudioglass.com
Parking available
Wheelchair access
Credit Cards

In a studio located at the Coalport China Museum, Jonathan and his team of craftsmen specialise in producing beautifully coloured studio glass **perfume bottles, vases, paperweights, chalices, jewellery** etc. Highly skilled techniques employed include: Graal (multi layers of glass and enamel) and Cameo (engraving and carving through multi layers). Mail order available.

Directions: *M54 from B'ham towards Telford. Leave motorway at junc 4. Follow signs to Ironbridge Gorge Museum continue downhill until you can fork left signed Coalport Museum.*
Opening hours: *shop Mon-Sat 10am-5pm Apr-Oct. Glass making Mon-Fri 10am-4pm. Phone ahead for times out of season.*   **(38)**

STAINED GLASS ART, Unit C15, Maws Craft Workshops, Jackfield, Telford, Shropshire TF8 7LS

Est. 1982
Tel/fax: +44 (0)1952-884240
Parking available

David Green of Stained Glass Art is a well-established maker, specialising in traditional and contemporary design, **manufacture and repair of stained glass windows.** Prices range from £20, and there is no upper limit. Also, he teaches two-day courses for beginners to learn the basics of this fascinating art.

Directions: *south side of the New Bridge over the river Severn between Ironbridge and Brosely. Turn left along river through Jackfield following signs for Maws Craft Centre.*
Opening hours: *Mon-Sat 10am-3pm.*   **(39)**

STAINED GLASS AND CERAMIC DESIGN, Unit 11, Chilvers Coton Craft Centre, Avenue Road, Nuneaton,
Warwickshire CV11 4LU

Est. 2000
Tel: +44 (0)0794-0131314
www.yourpagespace.co.uk
Large carpark
Two steps for wheelchairs.

Giovanna Nicklin is a stained glass **artist/teacher creating individual designs** as well as more traditional stained glass work such as lamp covers. Her inspirations come mainly from organic forms, nature and her love of the rugged coastline found in and around Somerset and Devon. Commissions and restoration undertaken.

Directions: *M6 junc3, then A444 towards Nuneaton. At large traffic island (before Nuneaton Centre) follow signs to Craft Centre which is 100 yds from the 'Coton Arches' railway bridge.*
Open: *usually Tues-Fri 9am-3pm. Sat 10am-5pm. Closed Sun/Mon.*   **(3)**

Jewellery

BLAKE AND JANETTE MACKINNON, Waterloo Lane, Orleton Common, near Ludlow, Shropshire SY8 4JG

Est. 1994
Tel/fax: +44 (0)1584 831445
www.jmackinnon.freeserve.co.uk
Parking available
Wheelchair access

Designers of ceramic jewellery, we make **a wide range of porcelain beads.** The majority are extruded, then reworked by cutting, turning or pressing. Decorations are made with glazes and lustre, making colour very important. From these beads we make a diverse range of colourful jewellery. Prices range from £10 to £300.

Directions: *go north on A49 from Leominster. At B4362 turn left. Go straight across junc with B4361, towards Goggin which is signed. Take second on the left to Waterloo for 300 yds.*
Opening hours: *Mon-Sat 10am-5pm. Phone in advance.*   **(40)**

DESIGN FROM MEMORY, The Jewellery Quarter, Hockley, Birmingham.

Est. 1997
Tel: +44 (0)7702-910469
Fax: +44 (0)1527-879239
Parking available

Memory Stather is passionate about gems and is a gemstone artist, jeweller and enameller producing **mostly earrings and necklaces made from carved gemstones** and gem objects including penholders and perfume bottles. She also makes objects including bowls using *plique-à-jour* enamel with vibrant colours and play of light. Mail order not usual.

Directions: *workshop is in the Jewellery Quarter of Birmingham which is well-signposted from all main approaches to the City Centre. Full directions given with appointment.*
Open: *usually 9am-5pm Mon-Sat. Closed Sun. Appointment essential.*   **(41)**

THE EARRING CAFE, 53b Mount Street, Chapelfields, Coventry, Warwickshire CN5 8DE

Est. 1994
Tel/fax: +44 (0)24-76714501
www.glass-beadmakers.
freeserve.co.uk/gallery

One of only 50 glass beadmakers in the UK, Amanda specialises in funky, **glass bead designs** which can be bought loose, or combined with sterling silver in wearable jewellery designs. She makes wire and bead tiaras to order and also offers mail order (catalogue available). Tea and coffee provided.

Directions: *Take junction 7 off the Coventry ring road. Turn left at the Texaco garage into Mount Street.*

Opening hours: *by appointment.*

JOHN NICHOLAS, Unit 16, Chilvers Coton Craft Centre, Avenue Road, Nuneaton, Warwickshire CV11 4LU

Est. 1992
Tel: +44 (0)2476-354092
Fax: +44 (0)2476-737460
Parking available
Wheelchair access
Credit cards

John Nicholas is a jeweller/goldsmith making **jewellery in precious metals** using precious and semi-precious stones. Also a popular goldsmithing service where clients supply their own gold from old, broken, unwanted jewellery and it is melted down and remade into jewellery to customers' specification. Mail order available.

Directions: *M6 junc 3, then A444 towards Nuneaton. At large traffic island (before Nuneaton Centre) follow signs to Craft Centre which is 100 yds from the 'Coton Arches' railway bridge.*

Opening hours: *Tues-Fri 9.30am-5pm. Sat 10am-5pm. Closed Mon/Sun.*

KATE CADMAN, Coalport China Museum, Ironbridge, Telford, Shropshire TF8 7HZ

Est. 1999
Tel: +44 (0)1952-580650 day
Fax: +44 (0)1952-418634
Parking available
Wheelchair access

Following twelve years' of demonstrating traditional porcelain techniques at Coalport China Museum, I decided to start my own business hand making **bone china jewellery and giftware.** I also accept commissions for hand painted bone china commemorative pieces. Prices from £2.50 for jewellery; £20 for a small birth plate. Mail order available.

Directions: *off M54, junction 4. Follow brown signs for Ironbridge Gorge Museums, then local signs to Coalport China Museum.*

Open: *Weds, Thurs, Sat, Sun 10am-5pm. Appointment necessary.*

MAGNI PRETII JEWELLERY, 94 Vyse Street, Hockley, Birmingham B18 6JZ

Est. 1994
Tel/fax: +44 (0)121-5549057
www.magni-pretii.co.uk
Parking available
Credit cards

Magni Pretii are independent jewellers specialising in the design and crafting of **contemporary pieces** which are made and sold on the premises. One-off rings in gold and platinum are very popular, particularly as wedding rings. Their pendants, again in one-off designs, are also highly sought after. Commission work is regularly undertaken.

Directions: *directly opposite the Jewellery Quarter train station in Hockley.*

Opening hours: *All day Tues-Sat.*

PETER TRIGGS, 5 Clarendon Square, Royal Leamington Spa, Warwickshire CV32 5QJ

Est. 1984
Tel: +44 (0)1926 425157
Parking available

An experienced designer goldsmith, jeweller and valuer, Peter Triggs creates **individual jewels** from a wide selection of gold, silver and jewels in a studio workshop which adjoins Napoleon III's home during exile. Repairs and remodelling are also carried out. Prices for modern and antique jewels range from £10 to £4000.

Directions: *up hill at top end of town. Turn left at the end of the parade and 300 yards along Clarendon Avenue to Clarendon Square.*

Opening hours: *Tues-Sat 10am-5pm.*

45

ROCK OF AGES - FOSSILS AND STONES, Unit 4, Mamble Craft Centre, Church Lane, Mamble, Shropshire DY14 9JY

Est. 1999
Tel: +44 (0)1299-832601
www.gorockofages.co.uk
Parking available
Wheelchair access

We make jewellery from hand-polished **Whitby jet, amber, blue john** and other gemstones and sell more than 100 different healing crystals. We have a good selection of British and American fossils and dinosaur bones, mineral samples for collectors, paperweights, quartz dusters, amethyst cathedrals, pyramids, spheres and wands. Mail order available.

Directions: *off the A456 Bewdley to Tenbury Wells Rd. It is part of the Mamble Craft Centre.*

Opening hours: *Tues-Sun 10.30am-5pm.*

46

SUE ROBERTS PAPIER-MÂCHÉ JEWELLERY, 46 Lincoln Hill, Ironbridge, Telford, Shropshire TF87QA

Est. 1996
Tel: +44 (0)1952-432031

Sue's **papier-mâché earrings and brooches** are unusual, unique and quirky. They are decorated with a combination of iridescent lightproof inks, metal leaf, silver and gold wire spirals, crystals and finished with several layers of lacquer. The jewellery is light-weight, suitable for sensitive skins, easy to wear and reasonably-priced. Mail order available.

Directions: *300 yards up Lincoln Hill on the right. Lincoln Hill is opposite the Museum site in Ironbridge on the wharfage.*

Opening hours: *weekends. Other times by appointment.*

Leatherwork

WALSALL LEATHER MUSEUM, Littleton Street, West Walsall, West Midlands WS2 8EQ

Est. 1988
Tel: +44 (0)1922-721153
Fax: +44 (0)1922-725827
Parking available at pay and display opposite
Wheelchair access
Credit cards

A living and working museum (free admission), housed in a Victorian factory, tracing Walsall's fascinating history as the centre of the UK's leathergoods and saddlery trades. Visitors can watch skilled leatherworkers in the process of hand crafting **unique designer leathergoods**. There are also free guided tours and a large factory shop.

Directions: *on the north side of Walsall town centre, adjacent to the ring road (A 4148) and approximately 10 minutes from M6 junctions six and seven.*

Opening hours: *Tues-Sat 10am-5pm, Sun 12am-5pm (closes 4pm Nov/Dec).*

Metalwork & Silversmithing

AMERTON FORGE, Amerton Farm, Stowe by Chartley, Staffordshire ST18 OLA

Est. 1997
Tel: +44 (0)7970-259679
Ample parking
Wheelchair access

Nick Leech at Amerton Forge specialises in one-off commissions made to customers' requirements. He makes all types of **wrought ironwork including gates, fireside baskets, bracket** etc. Styles can be contemporary, medieval or copies of antique items. Visitors can watch Nick at work in his forge. All work is handcrafted to a high standard.

Directions: *from Stafford take the A518 Uttoxeter Road. Amerton Farm is on left about 7 miles from Stafford.*

Opening hours: *Tues-Sun 10am-5pm.*

IN THE HEAT OF THE MOMENT, Wood Yard Forge, Wood Yard off Corve Street, Ludlow, Shropshire SY8 1HA

Est. 1999
Tel: +44 (0)1584-874877
Parking available
Wheelchairs: limited space

John Herbertson is a designer blacksmith working with traditional forging techniques in **contemporary wrought iron work** from jewellery and small domestic work to furniture and sculptural garden pieces. Visitors are welcome to watch work in progress, examine pieces in stock and discuss commissions. The forge is small and essentially unmechanised.

Directions: *opposite The Compasses in Corve Street and behind The Feathers. Access also from Somerfield carpark and Attorney's Walk.*

Opening hours: *Tues-Sat 9am-5pm.*

MARTYN PUGH, 8 Winyates Craft Centre, Winyates, Redditch, Worcestershire B98 ONR

Est 1977
Tel/fax +44 (0)1527-502513
Parking available
Wheelchair access
Credit cards

An MA silversmith graduate in 1976, Martyn works from his oak-beamed workshop in Worcestershire designing and making his unique **award-winning collections of silverware and jewellery**. A freeman of the Worshipful Company of Goldsmiths, he was a founder member of the Association of British Designer Silversmiths. Combining silver with crystal and wood, his style is of simple elegance and clean lines. His jewellery combines precious metals with unusual shaped previous and semi-precious stones. Choose from claret jugs, decanters, candlesticks, bowls, spoons, glasses, tea or coffee sets, rings, earrings, chokers or brooches. Private commissions are welcomed. Prices start from around £80.

Directions: *will be given when appointment is made.*
Opening hours: *visits by appointment only.*

Pottery & Ceramics

AMERTON POTTERY, Amerton Working Farm, Near Weston, Staffordshire ST18 OLA

Est. 1994
Tel: +44 (0)1889-270821
www.amertonpottery.co.uk
Parking available
Wheelchair access

James Gauge's small studio pottery and shop is located in the busy Amerton Craft Centre with tearooms. He produces a wide range of hand thrown **domestic stoneware, lamps, water features** and gifts, plus a small range of terracotta wall pots. He also stocks frostproof patio pots. Mail order available.

Directions: *from Stafford take the A518 Uttoxeter Road. Amerton Farm is on left about 7 miles from Stafford.*
Opening hours: *7 days a week; 9am-5pm.*

BRIDGET ALDRIDGE, 14 Morson Crescent, Abbots Farm, Rugby, Warwickshire CV21 4AL

Est. 1989
Tel: +44 (0)1788-575629
Parking available

Bridget has created a niche in experimental **sculptural and thrown ceramics** as well as agateware and reduction fired mixed clays. Her thrown porcelain forms have spiral streaks of colour or other types of clay. Also available are saggar fired porcelains and glazings which mimic weathered rocks, mud and bark.

Directions: *follow the Hillmorton Road for a mile out of Rugby; left at Loverock Crescent at beginning of dual carriageway; first right to 14 Morson Crescent.*
Opening hours: *prior appointment essential.*

BRIDGET DRAKEFORD, Upper Buckenhill Farmhouse, Fownhope, Herefordshire HR1 4PU

Est. 1976
Tel/fax: +44 (0)1432-860411
Parking available
Credit cards

Bridget's work takes inspiration from classical forms, drawing on both European and Oriental influences. Her **vases, bowls, teapots, jugs and lamps** are both elegant and functional. Her designs are particularly sought after and are featured in collections across the globe. Prices range from £40 to £400 and mail order is possible.

Directions: *situated on the B4224 on the Ross-on-Wye side of the village of Fownhope*
Opening hours: *visitors welcome by appointment.*

CAROL WHEELER POTS 'N' PAINTINGS, 74 Norton Leys, Rugby, Warwickshire CV22 5RT

Est. 1993
Tel: +44 (0)44 1788-813279
www.carolwheeler.org.uk
Parking available

I make **studio ceramics and paintings** and greetings cards. My work reflects my interest in surface pattern. My ceramics include textured coiled pots and planters, raku bowls and plates, impressed and lino-printed ware and patchwork platters and dishes. Rocks and the sea form the main theme of my paintings. Mail order available.

Directions: *A45 to Dunchurch then towards Rugby. Left at roundabout, straight over roundabout by Sainsbury's, then first right, right again; I'm on next corner on right.*

Opening hours: *by appointment.*

CITRUS TREE COURT, Hoar Park Craft Village, nr Ansley, Nuneaton, Warwickshire CV10 0QU

Est. 1998
Tel: +44 (0)24-76395421
Parking available

We combine our talents for surface decoration in **handthrown pottery and appliquéd table linens**, with everything from tablecloths to tureens. Also available are a wide range of gifts and gardenware. All our products can be viewed at our studio and showroom where we can be seen making and decorating. Mail order available.

Directions: *the studio showroom is on the B4114 between Coleshill and Nuneaton.*

Opening hours: *Tues-Sun 10am-5pm.*

DOT CROWE, 4 Cleves Cottages, Daventry Road, Barby, nr Rugby, Warwickshire CV23 8TF

Est. 2000
Tel: +44 (0)1788-891465
Fax: +44 (0)432-860864
Parking available

Working mainly in clay, Dot is based in a studio-cum-workshop within an organic garden from which she draws inspiration and materials which are incorporated into her **organic pottery**. Her works are slab or coil formed and reflect the local seasonal landscape. Dot welcomes visitors from around the world.

Directions: *on the A45 to Dunchurch follow signs for Barby. Cleves Cottages are one mile beyond Barby village past the water tower.*

Opening hours: *prior appointment essential.*

JAN BUNYAN, 4 Bridge Road, Butlers Marston, Warwick CV35 0NE

Est. 1980
Tel: +44 (0)1926 641560
Parking available
Limited wheelchair access

I am a studio potter making quality **contemporary tableware** which is thrown and decorated by hand in clear colours with original designs. I regularly undertake commissions. A good selection of my work can be seen and purchased from the studio. Prices range from £11 for a mug to £150 for special pieces.

Directions: *from junction 12 on the M40 follow signs to Gaydon, then Kineton, then Butlers Marston. The pottery is on the left 100 yards after entering the village.*

Opening hours: *Mon-Fri 10am-5pm; other times by appointment.*

56

JEREMY STEWARD, Wobage Farm Craft Workshops, Crow Hill, Upton Bishop, Ross-on-Wye, Herefordshire HR9 7QP

Est. 1996
Tel: +44 (0)1989-780448
Parking available

Jeremy makes wood-fired pottery and soda glazed domestic stoneware. His **kitchen, table and ovenware** is hand thrown on a momentum wheel, simply decorated, fired and exquisitely glazed. The pearly iridescence of the wood-fired surface extends through a colour range of pinks, creams, oranges and greens. Prices from £9 to £96.

Directions: *on the B4224 between the A449 and A40, two and a half miles from Junction 3 on the M50.*

Opening hours: *10am-5pm Apr-Sept Thurs-Sun; Oct-Mar Sat/Sun.*

14

J.G.S. DESIGN, Unit 2, Chilvers Coton Craft Centre, Avenue Road, Nuneaton, Warwickshire CV11 4LU

Est. 1994
Tel/fax: +44 (0)24 76387123
Parking available
Wheelchair access
Credit cards

Jacqueline and Justin Shelley are specialists in hand thrown **terracotta planters, urns, jugs and jars**. Colours vary from soft creamy peach to vibrant red. Also 'Cretan' urns up to a metre in height. Also reproduction Medieval and period artefacts including griffins, wall plaques and water features. Also stoneware cookware. Prices £3-£300.

Directions: *M6 junc 3, then A444 towards Nuneaton. At large traffic island (before Nuneaton Centre) follow signs to Craft Centre which is 100 yds from the 'Coton Arches' railway bridge.*

Opening hours: *Tues-Sat 10am-4pm.*

3

JO CONNELL, Witherley Lodge, 12 Watling Street, Witherley, Atherstone, Warwickshire CV9 1RD

Est. 1986
Tel +44 (0)1827-712128
Fax:+44 (0)1827-712947
www.gallery1.co.uk
On-site parking
Limited wheelchair access

Joanna makes highly individual ceramics using coloured clays and slips. Her range includes functional and sculptural pieces as well as **tables, birdbaths and garden water features.** Cost from £15-400. With 30 years' experience of potting and teaching, Jo also runs courses and holds mixed exhibitions at her workshop. Mail order available.

Directions: *situated on the A5 (Watling Street), one mile east of Atherstone, half way between the two turnings into Witherley Village. Near the Bull Inn.*

Opening hours: *visitors welcome by appointment.*

KERRY O'CONNOR, Unit D, 59 Caroline Street, Jewellery Quarter, Hockley, Birmingham B3 1UF

Est. 2000
Tel/fax +44 (0)121-236 5601
Parking available

As a contemporary designer and maker of ceramic and silver tableware I specialise in high quality hand-made slipcast items including **salt and pepper pots, nibble dishes, plates** and containers of various sizes, all of which have been inspired by forms of nature and have stylistic, sophisticated qualities. Customers wishing to place larger orders have the opportunity to choose their own colour range. **Silverware** such as spoons, vessels, cruet sets and an award-winning parmesan cheese dish can all be seen at the workshop and is available by commission only. Mail order available. The workshop is located near Birmingham's famous jewellery quarter.

Directions: *a two minute walk from the jewellery quarter's clock tower.*

Opening hours: *10am-5pm, Monday-Friday.*

LOUISE DARBY, Clay Barn, Redhill, Alcester, Withseason, Warwickshire B49 6NQ

Est. 1984
Tel: +44 (0)1789-765214
Parking available
Wheelchair access

Louise makes **fine thrown stoneware and porcelain pots** using her own satin-finish glazes with freehand incised designs, simple wax-resist banding or brush decoration. Visit her beautiful studio/home and garden with well stocked showroom. Prices from £6.50. See work in progress. Studio exhibitions twice a year.

Directions: *4 miles between Stratford-upon-Avon and Alcester, just off the A46 behind the Stag Pub on top of Redhill.*

Opening hours: *prior appointment necessary.*

THE MARCHES POTTERY, 45 Mill Street, Ludlow, Shropshire SY8 1BB

Est. 1982
Tel: +44 (0)1584-878413
Parking available
Wheelchair access

We produce a wide selection of finely made **hand thrown table ware**, individual pieces and garden pots decorated in a range of Chinese glazes. All work is either highly fired stoneware or porcelain. Visitors are welcome to watch us work in our studio pottery in the heart of this historic market town.

Directions: *about 100 yards from the Market Square and castle.*

Opening hours: *Mon-Sat (not Thurs) 10am-5pm.*

MARK GRIFFITHS, The Pottery, Culmington, Ludlow, Shropshire SY8 2DF

Est 1975
Tel: +44 (0)1584-861212
Parking available
Wheelchair access to most areas

Mark makes a large range of hand thrown **terracotta garden pots**. He also works to commission for large individual architectural pieces. A good range of wood fired, salt glazed stoneware pottery can be viewed. His thriving business relies on his skill and the local clays known for their warm colour and durability.

Directions: *situated on the B4365 5 miles north of Ludlow.*

Opening hours: *Mon-Fri 9am-6pm; weekends by appointment only.*

MARY KENNY, The Pottery, Back Lane, Weobley, Herefordshire HR4 8SG

Est. 1993
Tel: +44 (0)1544-318557
www.marykenny.hayspace.co.uk
Parking available
Limited for wheelchairs

The showroom stocks decorative and domestic pottery in high fired stoneware and porcelain with uniquely delicate and subtle glazes (pale green/yellow, turquoise, pewter-black etc). The wide range of work includes **teapots, bowls, lamp bases and porcelain light holders, and water features.** Commissions taken e.g. large bowls for wedding presents.

Directions: *Weobley is just off the A4112 Leominster to Brecon Road. Pottery is four minutes walk from Centre shops.*

Opening hours: *five days a week 11am-4pm. Closed Wed & Sun.*

MICHAEL AND SHEILA CASSON, Wobage Farm Craft Workshops, Crow Hill, Upton Bishop, Ross-on-Wye, Herefordshire HR9 7QP

Est. 1977
Tel: +44 (0)1989-780233
Fax: +44 (0)1989-780495
Parking available
Wheelchairs: with helper
Credit cards

The Cassons have been potters for over 50 years. They specialise in making **saltglazed, mainly functional stoneware** including jugs, bowls, teapots and various vessels and pots. The glazes range from blue to different shades of brown. Prices e.g. £18 (small jug), £65 (largest teapot), smoked, handbuilt vessels £50-£100 and much in between.

Directions: *on B4224 between A449 and A40, two and a half miles from Junc 3 on M50.*

Opening hours: *Sat & Sun 10am-5pm all year plus 1 April to 30 Sept Thurs and Fri. Appointment needed for other times.*

THE OLD SCHOOL POTTERY. Edgton, Craven Arms, Shropshire SY7 8HN

Est.1984
Tel +44 (0)1588-680208
www.ukpotters.co.uk
Parking available
Wheelchair access

Pierre Brayford's pottery is located in what was Edgton's tiny school and is part workshop, part showroom. Visitors are welcome to look around without pressure. The pots are **mostly wheel thrown** and are fired in an oil-fueled kiln and made in batches of related forms, rather than large numbers of the same item.

Directions: *in the centre of the village.*

Opening hours: *Mon-Sun 10am-6pm.*

PATIA DAVIS, Wobage Farm Craft Workshops, Crow Hill, Upton Bishop, Ross-on-Wye HR9 7QP

Est. 1992
Tel/fax: +44 (0)1989-780495
Parking available
Credit cards

Patia makes **domestic stoneware thrown on a Saviac kick wheel.** Utility items include bowls of all sizes, teapots, vases, mugs, mixing bowls. All her work is characterised by porcelain slip decoration in a range of colours including tans, oranges and rich and earthy peats through all the greens. Commissions considered.

Directions: *on the B4224 between the A449 and A40, two and a half miles from junction 3 of the M50.*

Opening hours: *Apr-Sept Thurs-Sun; Oct-Mar Sat & Sun 10am-5pm. Appointment needed for other times.*

PETRA REYNOLDS, Wobage Farm Craft Workshops, Upton Bishop, Ross-on-Wye, Herefordshire HR9 7QP

Est. 1995
Tel/fax: +44 (0)1989-780495
Parking available
credit cards

A wide range of domestic pottery, constructed from clay slabs, cutting around paper templates and then joining the clay slab into the desired shape. The pots are all soda-glazed and wood-fired to a stoneware temperature. Items include, **dishes, plates, butterdishes, vases, colanders, beakers** and jugs. Price range from £7-£120.

Directions: *on the B4224 between the A449 and A40, two and a half miles from junction 3 of the M50.*

Open: *Apr-Sept Thurs-Sun 10am-5pm; Oct-Mar Sat & Sun 10am-5pm.*

THE POTTERS BARN, Roughwood Lane, Hassal Green, Sandbach, Cheshire CW11 4XX

Est.1979
Tel: +44 (0)1270-884080
Fax: +44 (0)1270-884593
www.thepottersbarn.co.uk
Parking available
Credit cards

A traditional pottery producing gifts for the home and garden, also exhibiting other potters and artists work. We specialise in handthrown, reduction fired **domestic stoneware and terracotta gardenware.** Pottery classes are held for adults and children every week. Group visits can be arranged. Commissions are regularly undertaken. Mail order available.

Directions: *from Sandbach, follow the A533 Newcastle Road over the M6. Take the first right at the New Inn and then the first right again at Hassal Green.*

Opening hours: *Mon-Sat 9.30am-5.30pm; Sun 1pm-5pm.*

RALPH JANDRELL POTTERY, Coalport China Museum, Nr. Ironbridge, Shropshire TF8 7HT

Est. 1977
Tel: +44 (0)1952-580650
Fax: +44 (0)1952-580627
www.ralphjandrell.co.uk
Credit cards

Based in the heart of Shropshire in the picturesque Ironbridge Gorge, Ralph Jandrell makes a unique range of functional and decorative pottery. His pots are **hand-thrown and decorated with stunning oak leaf designs** using a variety of techniques including sponging, glazing, dipping and detailed brushwork. Request leaflet for mail order.

Directions: *M54 from B'ham towards Telford. Leave m/way at junc 4. Follow signs to Ironbridge Gorge Museum continue past it down hill until you can fork left signed Coalport Museum.*

Opening hours: *the Museum shop open 10am-5pm, seven days a week, sells Ralph's work. Appointment needed to see him personally.*

65

ROYAL WORCESTER, Severn Street, Worcester. Worcestershire WR1 2NE

Est. 1751
Tel: +44 (0)1905-23221
Fax: +44 (0)1905-617807
www.royal-worcester.co.uk
Parking available
Wheelchair access
Credit cards

Founded in 1751, the Victorian buildings of the world-famous Royal Worcester's Visitor Centre line Severn Street. Royal Worcester's factory shops carry an extensive range of quality **bone china tableware**, porcelain oven-to-tableware, giftware, figurines and much more. Worldwide mail order is available. Visitors can take guided tours of the factory.

Directions: *from junction 7 of the M5, follow signs to Worcester city centre. Turn left into Edgar Street and bear left. At T junction bear right to Royal Worcester.*

Opening hours: *Mon-Sat 9am-5.30pm, Sun 11am-5pm.*

66

WHICHFORD POTTERY, Whichford, near Shipston-on-Stour, Warwickshire CV36 5PG

Est. 1976
Tel +44 (0)1608-684416
Fax +44 (0)1608-684833
www.whichfordpottery.com
Parking available
Wheelchair access but
limited in workshop
Credit cards

Jim Keeling and his highly-skilled team of potters have been making flowerpots for 25 years. They produce a mouth-watering range of **handmade flowerpots in traditional and contemporary styles**, all of which carry a ten year frostproof guarantee. The pottery is a fascinating place to visit and you will always receive a warm welcome. You can choose from a wide range of flowerpots with prices starting at under £5. You can see the potters at work, relax in the lovely courtyard garden and visit the gallery of ceramics, paintings and jewellery. The pots are also available by mail order.

Directions: *Whichford village is situated off the A3400 between Shipston-on-Sour and Long Compton.*

Open: *9am-5pm Mon-Fri, 10am-4pm Sat & bank holidays.*

67

Textiles

ALISON MORTON, The Old Coach House, Linney Gate, Ludlow, Shropshire SY8 1EF

Est. 1976
Tel: +44 (0)1584 873800
www.alisonmorton.co.uk

Alison has created a range of **contemporary handwoven textiles** for the home. She makes handtowels, bathtowels, table napkins, table runners, table mats and sacks. All are loom woven and in natural linen with colourful details such as hanging loops on the towels. Viewing by website and mail order is possible.

Directions: *the Old Coach house is in the centre of Ludlow adjacent to St. Laurence's Church.*

Opening hours: *prior appointment essential.*

68

BETH HOLLAND TEXTILES, Workshop 3, Mamble Craft Centre, Church Lane, Mamble, Worcestershire DY14 9JY

Est. 1999
Tel: +44 (0)790-874879
Parking available
Wheelchair access
Credit cards

After graduating with a degree in Textile Design I set up my own workshop with funding from The Prince's Trust. I make **screen-printed scarves, cushions, wall hangings** etc.; also pictures, hand made cards and printed feathers. Designs include images of leaves, ferns and feathers on velvet, satin, silk and metallic fabrics.

Directions: *via M5,leave at junction 3 signed West Midlands Safari Park. A456 through Kidderminster on to Clos Top junction and then follow signs for Mamble.*

Opening hours: *Tues-Sun 10.30am-5pm. Closed Mon.*   **69**

FIONA M. BANFORD, 42 Hawkesley Mill Lane, Northfield, Birmingham B31 2RL

Est. 1985
Tel: +44 (0)121-624 9924
Parking available

Fiona is a textile artist specialising in woven textiles, particularly **hangings and small framed pieces** made from a variety of media. She also produces hand made cards and gift wrapping. Fiona's details are on the Register and she is an Associate Member of the Royal Birmingham Society of Artists. Mail order available.

Directions: *from the Longbridge roundabout take the A38 (Bristol road) towards Northfield. After half a mile, turn right by Kalamazoo into Hawksley Mill Lane.*

Opening hours: *by appointment only.*   **70**

MACCLESFIELD MUSEUMS, Roe Street, Macclesfield, Cheshire SK11 6UT

Est. 1984
Tel: +44 (0)1625-613210
Fax: +44 (0)1625-617880
www.silk-macclesfield.org
Parking available
Wheelchair access
Credit cards

The silk museum tells the story of silk, linking Macclesfield with the Far East. Paradise Mill is nearby and is the location for 26 hand Jacquard looms. There is a demonstration weaver in residence. The Silk Shop has an exciting range of **Macclesfield silk scarves, ties and textiles**. Mail order available.

Directions: *follow the brown signs from the centre of Macclesfield.*

Opening hours: *Silk Museum Mon-Sat 11am-5pm, Sun 1pm-5pm; Paradise Mill Tues-Sun 1pm-6pm.*   **71**

PATCHWORKS, Unit 10, Radford's Field, Maesbury Road, Oswestry, Shropshire SY10 8HA

Est. 1993
Tel: +44 (0)1691-671923
Parking available
Wheelchair access

Workshop for people with learning difficulties, **patchworks throws, duvet covers and cushions** ready made or to order in their shop on site. The colours and prints for each of our patchwork covers are chosen individually and crafted from top quality material in flowers, checks, stripes and plain colours. Mail order available.

Directions: *turning to Oswestry at the A5 Mile End roundabout. Turn left at the Highwayman Pub, take the first right and then left at the bottom.*

Opening hours: *Mon-Fri 9am-3.30pm.*   **72**

QUARRY BANK MILL, Styal, Cheshire SK9 4LA

Est. 1978
Tel: +44 (0)1625-527468
Fax: +44 (0)1625-539267
www.quarrybankmill.org.uk
Parking available
Wheelchair access
Credit cards

Dating from 1784, with our own waterwheel, steam engine and village, we are probably the only water powered cotton mill in the world. We demonstrate all the processes of making **cotton clothing**. The finished products are available from our shop: calico, printed fabric, made-up aprons, shirts and curtains. Mail order available.

Directions: *we are signposted from the M56 between Manchester Airport/ Heald Green and Wilmslow.*

Open: *winter Tues-Sun 11am-5pm, summer Mon-Sun 11am-6pm.*   **73**

THOMAS CLOUGH UPHOLSTERY, Unit 1, Bicton Enterprise Centre, Bicton Clun, Shropshire SY7 8NF

Est. 1986
Tel/fax: +44(0)1588-640921
www.sofasonthenet.co.uk
Parking available
Wheelchair access

We **upholster traditional furniture** and have developed a range of top quality traditionally upholstered sofas, chairs, stools etc. Examples can be seen in our brochure and on our website. With Clun Valley Real Furniture and Crafts Group, we demonstrate at the Three Tuns Pub In Bishop's Castle every third weekend in September.

Directions: *take the A488 north from Clun. Follow signs to Bicton (three quarters of a mile). Pass between two cottages and we are on the left hand side in converted stables.*

Opening hours: *Mon-Sat 9am-5pm but best to phone first.*   **74**

Toys & Games

AMERTON FARM DOLLS' HOUSE SHOP, Amerton Farm, Stowe-by-Chartley, Nr Weston, Staffordshire ST18 OLA

Est. 1986
Tel: +44 (0)1889-271300
Parking available
Wheelchair access
Credit cards

Patricia Tripp and Jean Alden's shop sells hand-crafted **one-twelfth scale metal work for dolls' houses**. Items include railings, street lamps and associated metalwork, coach lamps, balconies etc. Also, dolls' house kits or ready built. 'You state your requirements and we will provide with pleasure.' Houses from £70 to £800. Mail order available.

Directions: *Amerton Farm Craft Complex is on the A518 between Stafford and Uttoxeter, Nr. Weston. Amerton Farm is well-signposted.*

Opening hours: *Tues-Sun 10am-5pm. Closed Mon.* **①**

CHILDHOOD DREAMS, Unit 10, Chilvers Coton Craft Centre, Avenue Road, Nuneaton, Warwickshire CV11 4LU

Est. 1999
Tel: +44 (0)7977-820307
Parking available
Wheelchair access

Patricia Moore produces **dolls' houses painted and decorated to order**. Customers can choose from a variety of styles including Georgian, Victorian, Tudor etc. and have the outside and interior decorating done as per their exact wishes. Most clients are adults. Also for sale are kits, mouldings, windows etc and furniture and miniatures.

Directions: *M6 junction 3, then A444 towards Nuneaton. At large traffic island (before Nuneaton Centre) follow signposts to Craft Centre which is 100 yards from the 'Coton Arches' railway bridge.*

Opening hours: *Tues-Sat 10am-4pm.* **③**

HOLLYBANK WORKSHOPS, Hemford, Minsterley, Shrewsbury, Shropshire SY5 OHN

Est. 1992
Tel/fax: +44 (0)1743-891481
www.grahamradley.co.uk
/dollshouses
Parking available
Wheelchair access

We produce **dolls' houses** suitable, in basic form for children and with added detail for collectors. Types of houses range from a country cottage to a Georgian town house. Commissions are undertaken for house copies, replica antique and odd houses. Houses are available in made, but unfinished, part or fully finished.

Directions: *on the A488 between Minsterley and Bishop's Castle by the Shelve/Hemford crossroads.*

Opening hours: *Mon-Fri 9am-5pm; Sat 9am-noon.* **75**

IDIGBO PUPPETS, The Puppet Shop, Amerton Farms, Stowe by Chartley, Stafford, Staffordshire ST18 OLA

Est. 1998
Tel +44 (0)1889-271517
www.puppetmaster.co.uk
Free parking available.
Wheelchair access

Visit our farm-based workshop where you can watch puppets being made and have a go yourself with our demonstration puppets. We specialise in **high quality puppets and models, hand made to our own unique designs**, using recycled wood. Our constantly expanding range of animal and people puppets includes glove, rod and strung puppets, fully articulated marionette people and a Punch and Judy range. We can also produce puppets to your individual specifications. For the ultimate gift we produce caricature marionettes from photographs so you can immortalise your friends and family. Prices range from £20 to £200. Mail order available through Website or e-mail: ian.redshaw@btopenworld.com

Directions: *on the A518 between Stafford and Uttoxeter opposite the Plough public house.* **Opening hours:** *10am-5pm Thurs-Mon.* **76**

SNOWY'S ARK, Unit D3, Maws Craft Centre, Ferry Road, Jackfield, Shropshire TF8 7LS

Est. 1995
Tel: +44 (0)1952-884540
Parking available
Wheelchair access
Credit cards

Alan Whitehead makes a large range of wooden items including toys for children of all ages, wildlife (out of hardwood and stained soft wood), fantasy **boxes, mushrooms, clocks and puppets and puppetry**, Noah's arks, boxes, mirrors, bookends, wooden marionettes and jigsaws, all of which can be personalised while you wait. Mail order available.

Directions: *south side of the New Bridge over river Severn between Ironbridge and Brosely. Turn left along river through Jackfield following signs for Maws Craft Centre.*

Opening hours: *usually Mon-Sun 10am-4pm.* **(77)**

Woodturning & Furniture

BEN CASSON, Wobage Farm Craft Workshops, Upton Bishop, Ross-on-Wye, Herefordshire HR9 7QP

Est. 1988
Tel/fax : +44 (0)1989-780495
Parking available
Credit cards

All kinds of furniture including chairs, tables, wardrobes, sideboards, wall cabinets, chests of drawers etc. designed and made to order. Influenced by the Arts and Crafts Movement and made in British and American hardwoods. Smaller items available in the showroom include trays, boxes and chopping boards. Prices £10-£5,000.

Directions: *on the B4224 between the A449 and A40, two and a half miles from Junction 3 on the M50.*

Opening hours: *from Apr-Sept Thurs-Sat; Sat & Sun rest of the year. For other times please make appointment.* **(14)**

THE CHAIR SHOP, Shop House, Llancloudy, Hereford HR2 8QP

Est. 1989
Tel/ fax: +44 (0)1981-580397
Parking available

We specialise in the making of **jointed furniture** in traditional and modern styles. Using the English hardwoods, primarily oak and ash, all furniture is designed by the maker. Client input is welcomed. Examples of our work including dining chairs, coffee tables and dresser are available for inspection. No stock is for sale.

Directions: *on the A466 in the centre of Llancloudy*

Opening hours: *prior appointment necessary.* **(78)**

CHRIS ARMSTRONG, Paddock House, Clifford, Herefordshire HR3 5HB

Est. 1990
Tel: +44 (0)1447-83156
www.chrisarmstrong.hayspace.co.uk
Parking available

I have been making **country furniture including ladderback chairs**, and tables for ten years. All work is in British hardwoods, locally sourced where possible. Other items produced include turned bowls and platters, chopping boards, CD storage racks, child's chair with or without rockers, and a dropside cot (conforms to British Standards 1753).

Directions: *workshop is on B4352 Hay-on-Wye to Bredwardine road, about five miles from Bredwardine, which is 15 miles from Hereford.*

Opening hours: *usually 9am to 5pm. Appointment necessary.* **(79)**

FROM THE WOOD, Studio 6, the Craft Centre, Hay-on-Wye, Hereford HR3 5DG

Est. 1985
Tel: +44 (0)1497 821355
www.fromthewood.co.uk
Parking available
Wheelchair access
Credit cards

The gallery has a reputation for exhibiting finely **turned wooden items** created by Britain's leading craftsmen. There are many turned pieces by David Woodward, who can be seen demonstrating in the adjacent workshop. The gallery and workshop are situated in the breath-taking surroundings of the Black Mountains. Mail order is available.

Directions: *at the top of the main car park in the craft complex in Hay-on-Wye.*

Opening hours: *Mon-Sun 9.30am-5.30pm.* **(80)**

GRAHAM RADLEY FINE FURNITURE, Holly Bank Workshops, Hemford, Minsterley, Shrewsbury, Shropshire SY5 OHN

Est.1980
Tel: +44 (0)1743-891481
Fax: +44 (0)1743-891481
www.grahamradley.co.uk
Parking available
Wheelchair access

Set high in the south Shropshire hills, Graham Radley specialise in fine **traditionally-made country furniture: dressers, tables, cabinets** etc., made to order. Work is made with character, solid native timbers, sourced locally where possible. Most furniture is made to order, but examples are on display in the showroom.

Directions: *on A488 Between Minsterley and Bishop's Castle by the Shelve/Hemford crossroads.*

Opening hours: *Mon-Fri 9am-5pm; Sat 9am-noon.*

IMAJINE, Frogmore Cottage, 3 Frogmore Road, Market Drayton, Shropshire TF9 3AX

Est. 1999
Tel: +44 (0)1630-653143
www.vanetwork.co.uk
Parking available

Two craftspeople making **furniture and hand-crafted textile 'paintings'.** Jim Sadler concentrates on the design and making of contemporary furniture based on traditional craft values using wood and aluminium. Maggie Allmark makes textile pictures using embroidery to create a two-dimensional effect. Most work is commissioned. Small stock of stitchings and furniture kept.

Directions: *centre of Market Drayton.*

Opening hours: *most times by appointment.*

JERRY BRYCE-SMITH, The Old School House, Station Street, Bishop's Castle, Shropshire SY9 5DD

Est. 1990
Tel/fax: +44 (0)1588-630006
Parking available

Situated in the historic market town of Bishop's Castle, I specialise in the making of **tables and chairs** by hand from selected native hardwoods. I undertake commissions for other furniture, designing each piece to specific requirements. Upholstered oak dining chairs cost from £265. Our 5' by 3' oak farmhouse table costs £395.

Directions: *at the top end of Station Street*

Opening hours: *prior appointment essential.*

LIVING WOOD, Greenwood Cottage, Bishops Frome, Worcester WR6 5AS

Est. 1985
Tel: +44 (0)1531-640005
Parking available
Wheelchair access
Credit cards

Mike and Tamsin Abbott use logs from their woodland, which they cleave and shave to produce **chairs** which retain all the strength, resilience and character of the tree. They also make baby-rattles from local apple-wood. Mike has been running courses and writing about green woodwork since 1985. Mail order available.

Directions: *half way between Hereford and Worcester, turn north onto B4214 to Bishops Frome. Half a mile after Hop Pocket Crafts turn right to Halmond's Frome. Greenwood Cottage is a mile along on the right.*

Opening hours: *prior appointment necessary.*

LYNN HODGSON, Wobage Farm Craft Workshops, Crow Hill, Upton Bishop, Ross-on-Wye, Herefordshire HR9 7QP

Est. 1989
Tel: +44 (0)1989-780495
Parking available
Credit cards

Lynn Hodgson makes **carved wooden furniture and other items**: coffee tables, chairs, candlesticks, mirror-frames, boxes, caskets, bookends, troughs carved with leaping hares, birds, fish, leaves and abstracted patterns. Prices start at £22 selling mainly through Wobage Makers' Gallery, with a large display for summer and Christmas exhibitions. Phone for details and dates.

Directions: *on the B4224 between A449 and A40, two and a half miles from Junc 3 on M50.*

Open: *Easter-Oct Thurs-Sun 10am-5pm. Oct-Easter Sat & Sun 10am-5pm.*

MICHAEL T. WOOD JOINERY, Unit 12, Glebe Farm Industrial Estate, Glebe Farm Road, Rugby, Warwickshire CV21 1GQ

Est. 1972
Tel: +44 (0)1788-576980
Fax: +44 (0)1788-550804
Parking available
Wheelchair access

Specialising in English **bespoke traditional joinery** products, we delight in producing exactly what our clients want. We guide them through the design stages of any commission and keep them informed during manufacture, advising on any advantageous variations. We pride ourselves on consistently achieving near perfection and pleased customers.

Directions: *from junction 1 on the M6 follow the signs to Rugby. The estate is signposted at the third traffic island.*

Opening hours: *Mon-Fri 7:45am to 4:45pm.* (85)

THE TOUCHWOOD STUDIO, Eccleshall, Staffordshire ST21 6JA

Est. 1994
Tel/fax +44 (0)1785-850176
Parking available
Credit cards

Seth Leach, a self-taught wood turner who is on the Register of the Worshipful Company of Turners, produces unique wood turning from his studio workshop in the heart of the Staffordshire countryside. **Working with aged fallen timber, the finished pieces often include naturally weathered surfaces**, wood with deep fissures, heavily knotted and with areas of unusual growth, all characteristics that provide potential for sensational turning. Visitors are welcome, by appointment, to view a range of finished items that are on display and for sale and to see for themselves the fascinating process of turning these unique pieces. Mail order available.

Directions: *please ring for directions.*

Opening hours: *Mon-Sat by appointment.*

Other Makers

BEAUMONT-MILLS, Unit 17, Chilvers Coton Craft Centre, Nuneaton, Warwickshire CV11 4LU

Est. 2000
Tel: +44 (0)7788-716478
Parking available
Wheelchair access

Lynne Beaumont and June Mills are **dressmakers offering a made-to-measure and design service**. They specialise in a range of bridal wear which can be individualised according to clients' wishes. Only highest quality fabrics used and workmanship is to a very high standard. They will also consider other commissions. Mail order available.

Directions: *M6 junction 3, then A444 towards Nuneaton. At large traffic island (before Nuneaton Centre) follow signposts to Craft Centre which is 100 yards from the 'Coton Arches' railway bridge.*

Opening hours: *Tues-Sat 10am-4pm.*

CASTLE PARK ARTS CENTRE, Castle Park, Frodsham, Cheshire WA6 6SE

Est. 1986
Tel: +44 (0)1928-735832
www.castle-park-arts.co.uk
Parking available
Wheelchair access

Castle Park Arts Centre was formerly a coach house and stables in the grounds of Castle Park, which was was owned by the Wright family until 1933. There are three **galleries exhibiting and selling work from local and national artists;** traditional and contemporary work. Exhibitions change every six weeks.

Directions: *approximately 13 miles from Chester. Follow signs for Frodsham. Turn into Castle Park and follow signs for the Arts Centre.*

Open: *Tues-Sat 10am/4.30pm (closed 12.30-2pm); Sun 2/4.30pm. Closed Mon.*

CROFT STUDIOS, Unit 6, 52 High Street, Stourbridge, Staffordshire DY8 1DE

Est. 1996
Tel: +44 (0)1384-392333
Fax: +44 (0)1384-393389
www.croftstudios.co.uk
Parking available
Wheelchair access
Credit cards

Sculptor Caroline Russell-Lacy's love of gardens inspired this **range of unique water features** including: lizard fountains, wall fountains, pools and bowls. Hand cast and finished in bronze, iron and faux lead metal/resin. Featured in show gardens at Chelsea and other flower shows, on televison and in numerous publications. Mail order available.

Directions: *hidden away in an alley off the High Street. Full directions given when making an appointment.*

Opening hours: *by appointment only.*

ETONE MODELS, Unit 5, Chilvers Coton Craft Centre, Avenue Road, Nuneaton, Warwickshire CV11 4LT

Est. 1989
Tel: +44 (0)7967 793183
Ample parking
Wheelchair access

Geoff Cook specialises in **model aircraft**. He offers a model aircraft building service, or you can buy hand made craft kits and build your own including Spitfire and Sea Fury power models, ASW19 and DG100 gliders. Also offers foam cutting service for veneered foam wings, deckings etc. Mail order available.

Directions: *M6 junc 3, then A444 towards Nuneaton. At large traffic island (before Nuneaton Centre) follow signs to Craft Centre which is 100 yds from the 'Coton Arches' railway bridge.*
Opening hours: *Mon-Sat 9am-5pm.*

③

EVERGREENS, Unit 4, Chilvers Coton Craft Centre, Avenue Road, Nuneaton, Warwickshire CV11 4LU

Est. 2000
Tel/fax: +44 (0)24-7634 1111
Carpark
Wheelchair access

Debbie Kendall and Zilla Cookes provide a comprehensive individual floral service for weddings, funerals, and for happy occasions (new babies, housewarmings etc.). Also helium balloons. Also **garden artefacts** including pot ornaments, willow planters, hanging baskets, twisted willow, wooden climbing frames and wrought iron work. Also seasonal decorative Christmas items.

Directions: *M6 junc 3, then A444 towards Nuneaton. At large traffic island (before Nuneaton Centre) follow signs to Craft Centre which is 100 yds from the 'Coton Arches' railway bridge.*
Opening hours: *Mon-Sat 10am-4PM.*

③

HEATHER HIGGINS, Westlands, Coven Road, Brewood, Staffordshire ST19 9DF

Est. 2000
Tel: +44 (0)1902-850949
www.wackyweddingsculptures.co.uk
Street parking

Heather has won many gold and silver awards in national and international sugarcraft competitions. She makes unique modern **ceramic and sugar sculptures for weddings, corporate events and collectors.** She prefers to deal one-to-one with her clients, designing bespoke sculptures as well as her own designs which are in caricature-style.

Directions: *Wolverhampton to Stafford main road. Turn left into Coven village. Follow signs for Brewood. 200 yards past Brewood sign.*
Opening hours: *please make appointment.*

89

IDIGBO FLYING MODELS, Amerton Farm, Stowe by Chartley, Staffordshire ST18 OLA

Est. 1999
Tel: +44 (0)1889-271517
Parking available
Wheelchair access
Credit cards

Makers of award-winning, **museum quality model aeroplanes** built from scratch for radio-controlled flying or static display. We also restore scale models either to fly again, or just for display purposes. Prices begin at £100. We are willing to be consulted on all your requirements: call in, telephone us or e-mail: ian.redshaw@btopenworld.com

Directions: *on the A518 between Stafford and Uttoxeter. Well signposted and opposite the Plough Pub.*
Opening hours: *10am-5pm daily (closed Tues and Wed).*

JOHN NEILSON LETTERCARVER, Pentrecwn, Llansilin, Oswestry, Shropshire SY10 7QF

Est. 1992
Tel/fax: +44 (0)1691-791403
Limited parking

John studied calligraphy before becoming a letter carver. Most of his work involves **hand lettercarving in stone and slate**, ranging from memorials, plaques and sculptural pieces to architectural lettering. All work is to commission and founded on a belief in the importance of strong and appropriate lettering design. Always happy to discuss commissions.

Directions: *given when appointment arranged.*
Opening hours: *by appointment.*

90

PROPPA TOPPA, Fairfields Cottage, School Lane, St. Martins, Oswestry, Shropshire SY11 3BX

Est. 1997
Tel/fax: +44 (0)1691-773752
Parking available
Wheelchair access
Credit cards

Clare and Sarah Butterton make **a range of unique hats** for summer and winter and all ages and sizes. Made from velvet, chenille, linen, silk and sinemay you can view their vast range of ready to wear or commission your own for the races, weddings and other special events. Mail order available.

Directions: *near the Primary School in St. Martin's village, one and a half miles off the A483 (Chester to Oswestry road).*
Opening hours: *please phone for appointment.*

91

REX M. KEY, Rotherhurst, Woodlands Road, Broseley, Shropshire TF1Z 5PU

Est. 2000
Tel: +44 (0)1952-882714
Parking available
www.broseley.pipes.co.uk

Maker of **clay tobacco pipes** in the traditional manner using Victorian cast iron equipment. More than 30 designs of pipes from small bubble pipes to elegant 22-inch churchwardens . Also eagle's claw, rustic, bulldog, masonic and football pipes. Prices from £1.99-£20. Also display cases can be commissioned. Mail order available.

Directions: *follow signs to Broseley Pipeworks Museum. Go past Museum, turn right into King Street, follow road for 400 yards then right into driveway signed Rotherhurst.*
Opening hours: *Sat & Sun 9am-noon.*   92

RODETTE INTERNATIONAL LTD, Orba Aromas, The Rhos, Hillhampton Lane, Shobdon, Leominster, Herefordshire HR6 9NE

Est. 1995
Tel: +44 (0)1568-708731
Fax: +44 (0)1568-708000
www.orba.co.uk

Orba Aromas room fragrances containing essential oils to perfume your room, caravan or boat for months, helping health and well-being. Skin care products include a goats milk range rich in natural vitamins kind to sensitive problem skin and which may help with eczema, psoriasis and allergic skin conditions, also gardeners' honey hand cream. Also body lotion and face cream for men. Available only by mail order.

ROSE ROYALE, Unit 13 Chilvers Coton Craft Centre, Avenue Road, Nuneaton, Warwickshire CV11 4LU.

Est. 1998
Tel: +44 (0)2476-374919
On-site parking
Wheelchair access

Jackie and Steve White supply a complete wedding day service and accessories for brides and the bridal party: **silk bouquets, posies, head-dresses, tiaras and table favours for guests** - all hand made to order. Unusual floral arrangements and home decor, general giftware and craft items available from stock. Mail order possible.

Directions: *M6 junction 3, then A444 towards Nuneaton. At large traffic island (before Nuneaton Centre) follow signposts to Craft Centre which is 100 yards from the 'Coton Arches' railway bridge.*
Opening hours: *Mon-Fri 10am-4pm; Sat 10am-4.30pm.*   3

STEPHEN HILL MONUMENTAL MASON, Unit 3, Chilvers Coton Craft Centre, Avenue Road, Nuneaton, Warwickshire CV11 4LT

Est. 1988
Tel: +44 (0)2476-353979
Fax: +44 (0)2476-712516
Parking available
Wheelchair access

Stephen Hill makes a large selection of memorials in varying traditional styles for churchyards and cemeteries. Details include hand-carved lettering and engraved designs. Although he specialises in **grave stones**, he also makes **commemorative plaques, kitchen worktops, fire hearths** and stone, house nameplates. Happy to discuss commissions. Mail order available.

Directions: *M6 junction 3, then A444 towards Nuneaton. At large traffic island (before Nuneaton Centre) follow signposts to Craft Centre which is 100 yards from the 'Coton Arches' railway bridge.*
Opening hours: *Mon-Sat 10am-4.30pm.*   3

Central England East

Bedfordshire, Derbyshire, Leicestershire, Northamptonshire, Nottinghamshire, Rutland

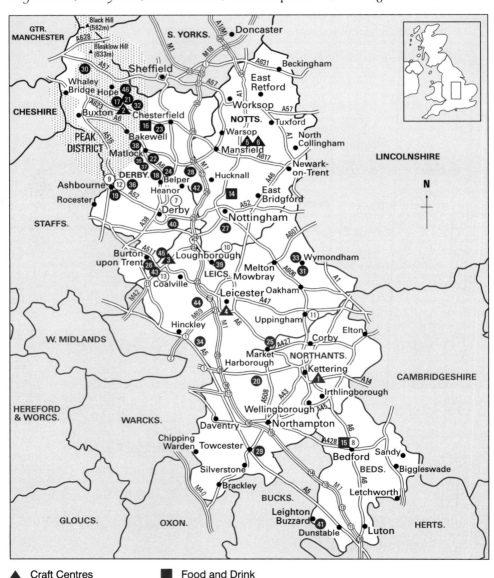

▲ Craft Centres   ■ Food and Drink

◯ Shops and Galleries   ● Makers' Workshops

The main Bedford village industry was clay brick-making. The tradition survives, albeit in factory form, at the Hanson brickworks in Stewartby.

Derbyshire in The Midlands, was part of the landscape of William Blake's blighted description 'dark satanic mills,' the result of the industrial revolution. Nowadays, Derbyshire is at the forefront of craft revival especially in the The Peaks tourist area, which has small craft galleries, craft shops and makers in abundance.

Leicestershire's biggest industry was hosiery but the last master hosier died in 1952. Stilton cheese, originated in the Middle Ages and has fared better; it is made around its birthplace of Melton Mowbray (and also in Nottinghamshire and Derbyshire).

Nottingham became synonymous with mass-produced lace in Victorian times. Some exponents of the hand made variety give occasional demonstrations in museums.

Craft Centres

CRANFORD ARTS, The Old Forge, Grafton Road, Cranford St Andrew, Kettering, Northhamptonshire NN14 4JE

Est. 1998
Tel: +44 (0)1536-330660
Fax: +44 (0)1536-330644
Parking available
Wheelchair access

The restored Old Forge, in the picturesque village of Cranford St Andrew, is the rural setting for Cranford Arts which produces individual ceramics (hand built, thrown, tiles and mosaics), flowercraft (floristry with fresh and artificial flowers for the home, weddings and corporate commissions). There is also a wide range of courses.
Directions: *A14 junction 10 or 11. Follow signs to Cranford. In Cranford follow signs to Grafton Underwood. Half mile on right, next to village hall.*
Opening hours: *Sun 11am-4pm. By appointment at other times.*　🔺**1**

EYAM HALL CRAFT CENTRE, Eyam Hall, Eyam, Hope Valley, Derbyshire S32 5QW

Est. 1996
Tel: +44 (0)1433-631976
Fax: +44 (0)1433-631603
Parking available
Wheelchair access
Credit cards (some makers)

Situated in the historic farmyard of Eyam Hall, a 17th century manor house, this is a genuine working craft centre with individual units producing a selection of unusual crafts including stained glass, fountains and garden sculptures, stringed musical instruments and more. Also a buttery serving homemade lunches and teas and gift shop.
Directions: *in the centre of Eyam village, which is off the A623 Baslow to Stockport road.*
Opening hours: *Tues-Sun 10.30am-5pm.*　🔺**2**

FERRERS CENTRE FOR ARTS AND CRAFTS, Staunton Harold, Ashby-de-la-Zouch, Leicestershire LE65 1RU

Est. 1974
Tel: +44 (0)1332-865408
www.ferrerscentre.co.uk
Parking available
Wheelchair access (mostly)
Credit cards (gallery and most makers)

Family-owned Centre located in the stable block of a the country estate of Staunton Harold. It provides workspace for sixteen artists and makers whose products include garden and domestic pottery, jewellery, bespoke furniture, bridal accessories, china restoration, replica Victorian automata, stone carving and picture framing. Tea-room and gallery. Mail order available.
Directions: *off the A42 between Ashby-de-la-Zouch and Melbourne. Follow signs for Staunton Harold.*
Opening hours: *most of the workshops are open to the public 11am-5pm. The centre is closed on Mondays.*

KNIGHTON LANE ARTISTS' GROUP, rear of 68 Knighton Lane, Aylestone, Leicestershire LE2 8BE

Est. 1982
Tel: +44 (0)116-2838564
http://beehive.thisisleicestershire
.co.uk/knightonlane
Parking available
Wheelchair access
Credit cards

Knighton Lane Artists' Group is a collectively run studio co-operative with space for practising artists and crafts people. We produce a range of arts and crafts including sculptures, ceramics, painting, collage and printing. Inquiries are welcome from local artists and craftspeople who may wish to join our co-operative.

Directions: *from Aylestone Road turn into Grace Road, above cricket ground. Take first left into Knighton Road. We are in the grounds of the neighbourhood centre on left.*

Opening hours: *prior appointment necessary.*

RUFFORD CRAFT CENTRE AND GALLERY, Rufford Country Park, Near Ollerton, Newark,

Nottinghamshire NG22 9DF

Est. 1981
Tel: +44 (0)1623-822944
Fax: +44 (0)1623-824702
www.ruffordcraftcentre.org.uk
Parking available
Wheelchair access
Credit cards

The Rufford Craft Centre comprises a gallery which stages exhibitions of contemporary craftwork and in particular contemporary ceramics, and the Rufford Ceramics Centre which offers a programme of residencies for international and national ceramists, to work in the fully equipped ceramics studio. Education programme, outdoor sculpture gallery, workshops and demonstrations.

Directions: *seventeen miles north of Nottingham on the A614.*

Opening hours: *Mar-Dec daily 10.30am/5pm; Jan-Feb daily 11am/4pm. The craft centre is open all year. Gallery closed between exhibitions.*

SHERWOOD FOREST ART AND CRAFT CENTRE, Forest Corner, Edwinstowe, Nottinghamshire NG21 9RN

Est. 1998
Tel: +44 (0)1623-825786
Fax: +44 (0)1623-655873
Parking on site
Wheelchair access
Credit cards (some studios)

Housed in a former Victorian coach house and stables offering crafts in eleven studios where you can visit the makers producing items suitable for home and garden in glass, copper and wrought iron etc. Items include cast nameplates, jewellery, pyrography, water features etc. Café and picnic area. Mail order some studios.

Directions: *in Edwinstowe, turn onto Church Street, turn first left. Centre and carpark are 100 yards on left.*

Opening hours: *Apr-Sept, Mon-Sat, 10am-5.30pm and Sun 10.30am-4.30pm. Oct-Mar, Wed-Sat, 10am-4pm and Sun.*

Craft Shops

THE BOTTLE KILN, High Lane, West Hallam, Derbyshire DE7 6HP

Est. 1985
Tel: +44 (0)115-9329442
www.bottlekiln.co.uk
Parking available
Wheelchair access
Credit cards

The Stone family's award-winning business is housed in a renovated pottery and offers a selection of contemporary art, crafts, gifts and cards. There is a constantly changing exhibition of paintings and ceramics, two shops and British crafts including jewellery. The Buttery Café and tea-garden provide a relaxed atmosphere.

Directions: *on a crossroads off the A609 at West Hallam, two miles west of Ilkeston and about 20/25 minutes from both Derby and Nottingham.*

Opening hours: *Tues-Sun 10am-5pm.*

GLAZED LOOKS, 8 Library Walk, Putnoe, Bedfordshire MK41 8HF

Est. 2000
Tel: +44 (0)1234-327231
Parking available
Wheelchair access

Glazed Looks offers a distinctive range of hand crafted pottery and ceramic items. Designed and created by the proprietor, Lindsey Rady. Orders are welcome for personalised and commemorative items for example birth plates, weddings and graduations. The current range includes over 600 line items. Visitors always welcome.

Directions: *in a small arcade of shops just off Putnoe Street in Putnoe, Bedford.*

Open: *Mon-Wed 9.30am-5pm, Tues 10am-5pm, Thurs closed, Fri/Sat 9.30am-1pm.*

MADE BY HAND, British Contemporary Craft and Design, 43, Church Street, Ashbourne, Derbyshire DE6 1AJ

Est. 1997
Tel: +44 (0)1335-300031
Parking available
Credit cards

A gallery shop within an eighteenth-century cottage, displaying a selection of British crafts: contemporary jewellery including embroidered silk necklaces, brooches, earrings and padded silk clocks, a changing range of ceramics, studio glass from several makers, wooden items (mainly bowls and small jewellery boxes). Established makers and new graduate designers.

Directions: *located along Church Street past the antique shops towards Ashbourne's Old Elizabethan Grammar School.*

Opening hours: *Thurs/Fri 10am-4pm. Sat 10am-5pm.*

WYMESWOLD COUNTRY FURNITURE, 17 Far Street, Wymeswold, Loughborough, Leicestershire LE12 6TZ

Est. 1983
Tel/fax: +44 (0)1509-880309
Parking available
Credit cards

Six showrooms on two floors in converted Georgian stables displaying original pine and local crafts (including unusual bags and character mugs and other pottery) together with carefully selected accessories and gifts. The range includes paintings, pottery, ironwork, needlework and cushions. A treasure chest of good taste, Wymeswold Country Furniture welcomes visitors.

Directions: *on the A6006 in the village of Wymeswold between Melton and Hathern.*

Opening hours: *Mon-Sat 9.30am-5.30pm, Sun 2-5pm.*

Galleries

THE GOLDMARK GALLERY, 14 Orange Street, Uppingham, Rutland LE15 9SQ

Est. 1972
Tel +44 (0)1572-821424
Fax +44 (0)1572-821503
www.gillrayprints.com
Parking available
Wheelchair access

The Goldmark Gallery has a huge range of the best in twentieth century prints from Picasso to Chagall, Moore to Miro, Piper, Sutherland and Hockney. We have a particular penchant for artists who think it of marginal importance to have learnt to draw. We're not stuck up and we'll give you coffee.

Directions: *Uppingham is a small market town on the A47 midway between Peterborough and Leicester. We are between the traffic lights and the market square.*

Opening hours: *9.30am-5.30pm Mon-Sat, 2.30-5.30pm Sun.*

OPUS GALLERY, 34 St John's Street, Ashbourne, Derbyshire DE6 1GH

Est. 2000
Tel/fax: +44 (0)1335-348989
Parking nearby
Wheelchair access
Credit cards

Opus opened in the millennium with a view to presenting a broad, fresh and accessible range of high quality contemporary British craft in a stylish modern setting. We specialise in jewellery and studio ceramics. Paintings in the rear of the gallery are changed monthly. All visitors are very welcome.

Directions: *from the top end of the market place, walk downhill to St John's Street at the bottom.*

Opening hours: *Mon-Sat 10am-5pm.*

Baskets & Wickerwork

COUNTRY CRAFTS OF MEASHAM, 20 North Walk, Ashby Road, Measham Derbyshire DE12 7JT

Est. 1984
Tel: +44 (0)1530-272469
Limited parking

Father and daughter Brian and Lynne Buckley-Sturgess specialise in the making of handmade **English willow basketware** of various shapes and sizes. Prices vary due to the uniqueness of their product, much of which is exported. They also specialise in cane, rush and Danish cord chair seating. All work is guaranteed.

Directions: *Measham is about one mile from junction 12 of the A42 in Leicestershire.*
Opening hours: *prior appointment necessary.*

13

Food & Drink

ALCAZAR BREWING COMPANY, 33 Church Street, Old Basford, Nottingham NG6 OGA

Est. 1999
Tel/fax +44 (0)115-978 2282
www.alacazarbrewingco.com;
www.midlandspubs.co.uk
Parking available
Wheelchair access
Credit cards

Alcazar Brewing Company was established in 1999 to create quality beers for the Fox & Crown Brewpub as well as the local, regional, national and international marketplace. The brewery is 12 barrel, full mash producing superb cask conditioned and bottled beers made to traditional recipes from the finest ingredients. Visitors are welcome to see the brewery in operation from our brewing gallery behind the Fox and Crown or, should they wish, can arrange to come along on guided brewery tours, normally conducted on Saturday afternoons. Mail order available for beer and brewery memorabilia. Visit our website for current selection and prices.

Directions: *two miles north of Nottingham city centre and two miles from junction 26 of the M1. Visit our website for detailed directions and maps.*
Opening hours: *Mon-Sat 12 noon-6pm.*

14

BROMHAM MILL AND GALLERY, Bridge End, Bromham, Bedfordshire MK43 8LP.

Est. 1984
Tel: +44 (0)1234-824330
Fax: +44 (0)1234-228531
www.borneo.co.uk/bromham_mill/
Parking available
W/chair access (ground floor)

Bromham Mill is a restored seventeenth century watermill grinding and selling fresh flour. When the mill was opened in 1984, part of the building was dedicated to fine art exhibition. The emphasis is now on contemporary crafts, particularly textiles in a much larger exhibition space. Activities including milling take place every Sunday.

Directions: *follow the brown waterwheel tourism signs from the A428 Bromham bypass. We are three miles to the west of Bedford.*
Opening hours: *Mar-Oct Wed-Sun 1am-5pm. Call for other times.*

15

THE VERY BEST OF BRITISH PRODUCE

The Farm Shop Courtyard

CHATSWORTH FARM SHOP

and

The Stud Farm Pantry Coffee Shop

Telephone:

01246 583392

CHATSWORTH FARM SHOP, Stud Farm, Pilsley, Bakewell, Derbyshire DE45 1UF

Est.1997
Tel +44 (0)1246-583392
Fax +44 (0)1246-582514
www.gustum.com
Parking for 80 cars
Wheelchair access
(restricted in courtyard)
Credit cards

Established in 1977 as a direct outlet for the estate's beef and lamb, Chatsworth Farm Shop has blossomed over recent years to become one of the best speciality food shops in Britain specialising in British food and drink. It has large kitchens producing fresh foods daily. Mail order available.

Directions: *1 3/4 miles from Chatsworth House in the village of Pilsey on the B6048 Bakewell road.*

Opening hours: *9am-5pm Mon-Sat 11am-5pm Sun.*

Glass

GLASSLIGHTS, Eyam Hall Craft Centre, Eyam, Hope Valley, Derbyshire S32 5QW

Est. 1991
Tel: +44 (0)1433-631662
Parking available
Wheelchair access
Credit cards

Stained and leaded glass windows designed and made to order using traditional techniques for domestic and ecclesiastical sites. There is also a range of unusual smaller items all handmade from stained glass on the premises, including jewellery, lamps and mobiles. See work in progress at the workshop all year round. Mail order.

Directions: *from A623 Chesterfield to Stockport road take turn to Eyam. Turn left in village past church and Eyam Hall.*

Opening hours: *usually 11am-5pm Tues-Fri, Sun and bank holidays.*

J-CRAFTS HANDPAINTED GLASS, Brook Street, Heage, Belper, Derbyshire DE56 2AG

Est. 1997
Tel: +44 (0)1773-513182
www.handpaintedglass.co.uk
Parking on road

Since 1997 we have been hand painting **original and beautiful designs on glassware** ranging from small candleholders to large vases. Samples of our work can be found in Heage Post Office/General Store and at the Lea Coach House Craft Centre near Matlock in Derbyshire. Commission work undertaken. Mail order leaflet available.

Directions: *in Heage village by the Post Office.*
Opening hours: *prior appointment necessary.* **(18)**

Jewellery

BEDAZZLE, 101 Mayfield Road, Ashbourne, Derbyshire DE6 1AS

Est. 1985
Tel +44 (0)1335-346253
www.peakdistrictproducts.co.uk
Parking available

Beadweaver and necklace maker. Chokers and necklaces of glorious **Venetian glass, crystal, pearls,** *cloisonné* **and minerals;** the world's finest and rarest beads brought together by Jinny Pound in an ever-changing collection of unique pieces. Examples of Jinny's work can be seen on the above website: see also adjoining advertisement.

Directions: *on the right of Mayfield Road, 500 yards from roundabout, travelling west towards Leek.*
Open: *visits by appointment only. Showlist and P.D.P. brochure upon request.* **(19)**

Bedazzle - beadweaver

Jinny Pound became fascinated with beadweaving over a quarter of a century ago. She established Bedazzle in 1985, and markets to a loyal customer base through major craft events. She specialises in chokers which, because of the technique, are strong, flexible, comfortable and completely adjustable.

These chokers, fashioned from the world's finest contemporary and antique beads, make an elegant and flattering statement. They are ideal for day, evening and special occasion wear. Jinny accepts

commissions, and can match fabrics, outfits or occasions.

Plain bands start at £30, fringed chokers between £80 and £250 depending on the quality and variety of the beads.

Jinny is a member of the prestigious group of Designer Makers living and working in the Peak District and further examples of her work can be found at

www.peakdistrictproducts.co.uk

101 Mayfield Road, Ashbourne, Derbyshire DE6 1AS. Tel 01335-346253

HELEN'S JEWELLERY WORKSHOP, 2 Newlands, Naseby, Northamptonshire NN6 6DE

Est. 1980
Tel: +44 (0)1604-740043
Fax: +44 (0)1604-743526
Parking available
Credit cards

Helen West individually makes creative decorative pieces of **gold and silver gemset jewellery** which include a variety of stones. She works on a variety of themes that she is continuously developing incorporating leaves and curls which contribute to a decorative and highly attractive texture. Helen also displays at New Studio in Olney.

Directions: *can't be missed in the centre of Naseby.*

Opening hours: *Mon-Fri 10am-5.30pm appointments only.*

Musical Instruments

ORB MUSIC, Eyam Hall Craft Centre, Eyam, Hope Valley, Derbyshire S32 5QW

Est. 1985
Tel: +44 (0)1433-630556
www.orbmusic.co.uk
Parking available

Makers, dealers and restorers of fine **violins, violas, cellos and banjos.** Our instruments are sold under the trade mark 'Orb'. Internationally acclaimed, our openback banjos are of the finest quality and inspired by the great classical era instruments. Our range includes the 'Concert Grand', 'Woodtone' and 'Old Time Mountain Banjo'. Mail order.

Directions: *from A623 Chesterfield to Stockport road take turn to Eyam. Turn left in village past church and Eyam Hall.*

Opening hours: *usually 11am-5pm Tues-Fri, Sun and bank holidays. Appointments advisable.*

Pottery & Ceramics

ALAN WARD POTTERY, Holloway House, Leashaw, Holloway, Matlock, Derbyshire DE4 5AT

Est. 1977
Tel: +44 (0)1629-534284
Parking on road

Ceramics in lovely shapes by Alan Ward are displayed in the roadside gallery adjacent to Holloway House. These are unique stoneware and porcelain items, often enhanced by subtle and beautiful glazes. The range includes bowls, jugs, planters and ceramic sculptures. Everything is reasonably priced. Visitors are welcome to browse or chat.

Directions: *turn off A6 at Cranford. We are situated at Holloway on the main road to Erich.*

Opening hours: *irregular so advisable to telephone first.*

ANN BATES - SCULPTURAL CERAMICS, Oak Cottage, Lumsdale, Matlock, Derbyshire DE4 5LB

Est. 1999
Tel: +44 (0)1629-55429
Fax: +44 (0)1
Parking available

I make one-off hand built **decorative ceramic pieces** rather than functional forms. Textures are inspired by the landscape and realised by pushing the plastic quality of clay to extremes. Colour from various oxides and carbonates provides endless possibilities for artistic expression. Prices from £20. Mail order for some items.

Directions: *given on request.*

Opening hours: *prior appointment necessary.*

CRICH POTTERY, Market Place, Crich, Derbyshire DE4 5DD

Est. 1975
Tel: +44 (0)1773-853171
Fax: +44 (0)1773-857325
www.crichpottery.com
On-site parking
Wheelchair access
Credit cards

Diana and David Worthy produce an extensive range of stoneware ceramics including **tableware, water feature/fountains, tiles, washbasins and special commissions.**Each piece is handthrown and decorated in rich, colourful unique glazes (blues, pinks, earth tones, black etc.), all individually hand drawn in floral and rural themes. Mail order available.

Directions: *M1 junction 28. A38 towards Derby. Take second exist at A610 towards Ambergate. Turn second right to Crich Market Place and John Lewis.*

Opening hours: *10am-6pm daily. Sundays please phone ahead.*

THE FRANK HAYNES GALLERY, 50 Station Rd, Great Bowden, Market Harborough, Leicestershire LE16 7HN

Est. 1987
Tel: +44 (0)1858-464862
Parking available
Wheelchair access
Credit cards

The gallery sells paintings and ceramics in two separate areas. The emphasis is on items made in the Midlands. I make blue and red glazed domestic stoneware and 'figure bowls'. We show **domestic, decorative and sculptural ceramics** by more than 40 makers. The emphasis is on pots to use.

Directions: *from Market Harborough train station take Great Bowden Road/Station Road. The gallery is signed on the right.*

Opening hours: *Thurs-Sun 10am-5pm. Tel for appointment on closed days.*

FURNACE LANE POTTERY, Unit 7, Furnace Lane, Moira, Swadlincote, Derbyshire DE12 6AT

Est. 1991
Tel/fax: +44 (0)1283-552218
Parking available
Wheelchair access

Louise Roe throws a range of very **handsome, rustic looking pottery.** All her pottery is fired in a woodburning kiln. The range includes teapots, mugs, jugs and bowls. All are intended for everyday use. Most work is glazed on the inside making it easy to clean. Prices from £2. Commissions undertaken.

Directions: *Moira Furnace on Moira Lane off the B5003, three miles from Ashby-de-la-Zouch and five miles from M42 junction 11.*

Opening hours: *Mon-Fri 9am-4pm, Sun 12pm-4.30pm (can vary).*

MIKE POWERS POTTERY, 1 Clifton Road, Ruddington, Nottinghamshire NG11 6DD

Est. 1981
Tel/fax: +44 (0)115-940 6968
www.powerspottery.co.uk
Parking available
Wheelchair access partly
Credit cards

Classic domestic stoneware, handthrown and decorated with colourful and vigorous brushwork. Suitable for oven, microwave and dishwasher, with a choice of three colours; plates, casseroles, tableware, soap dishes, cutlery drainers, grapedishes, planters, vases, olive dishes - over 90 separate items. 'Hand made pottery both practical and pleasing.' Mail order available.

Directions: *junction 24 (off M1). A453 (Nottingham South). After first roundabout (7 miles), pass Esso on right, take next right, signed Ruddington. In village go over railway bridge. Pottery on left.*

Opening hours: *Mon-Sat 10am-5.30pm (usually). Advise phoning in advance.*

RIDDINGS POTTERY, Greenhill Lane, Riddings, Derbyshire DE55 4AY

Est. 1995
Tel: +44 (0)1773-603187
www.riddingspottery.co.uk
Parking available
Wheelchair access to most areas
Credit cards

A working stoneware pottery, we throw **everything from thimbles to 24-inch bowls.** We run residential weekend courses and 'Saturday Specials'. Beginners are welcome. We dig for our clay locally and bake our work in a kiln we made ourselves. Visitors welcome to watch or talk pots. Mail order online.

Directions: *three miles from the M1 exit 28. Greenhill Lane is the main throughfare through Riddings.*

Opening hours: *reasonable hours on most days but telephone first.*

Textiles

PAM GARDNER, 1 Norton Crescent, Towcester, Northamptonshire NN12 6DW

Est. 1982
Tel: +44 (0)1327-350025
Parking available

I have twenty years' experience of spinning animal fibres including sheep fleeces, angora rabbit, mohair, alpaca and clients' longhaired pet combings and have a selection of **handspun, knitted scarves, hats, sweaters, jackets and baby garments** and handspun wool. £5-£150. 'A warm winter garment in all natural wool.' Mail order available.
Directions: *from A43 roundabout (Little Chef/Travelodge/MacDonalds) on edge of Towcester take town centre direction. At second roundabout take exit (Greenview Drive) leading to Norton Crescent.*
Opening hours: *by appointment only.*

THE SOFT CENTRE, Christine Waygood, 70 Charlestown Road, Glossop, Derbyshire SK13 8JN

Est. 1980
Tel/fax: +44 (0)1457-861549
Parking available
Wheelchair access
Credit cards

Individual handframed knitwear in natural yarns. We produce a range of coats, accessories and furnishings in felted lambswool. Work is inspired by the colours and textures from the local landscape and travels in Asia. I also make tufted rugs to commission. Mail order is available for most of the range.
Directions: *take A624 (Victoria Street) from the centre of Glossop towards Buxton. We are situated on the right hand side of the road opposite Whitfield House.*
Opening hours: *Oct-Feb Tues-Sat 10am-5pm, Mar-Sept Wed-Fri 10am-5pm. Telephone for appointment outside these times.*

Toys & Games

PLAYHOUSES BY NESS, The Windmill, Butt Lane, Wymondham, Melton Mowbray, Leicestershire LE14 2BU

Est. 2001
Tel/fax: +44 (0)1572-787584
Parking available
Wheelchair access

We specialise in **individually designed playhouses** built to the customer's own specifications. We are happy to include your own and your children's design ideas. Our playhouses are built using good quality timber to high safety standards. Visit our workshop and enjoy our play area and nearby teashop. Mail order available.
Directions: *follow B676 towards Saxby from Melton Mowbray for six miles. Turn right to Wymondham and left at the pub to the top of the hill.*
Opening hours: *Tues-Sun 10.30am-5pm.*

Woodturning & Furniture

ANDREW LAWTON FURNITURE, Goatscliffe Workshops, Grindleford, Hope Valley, Derbyshire S32 2HG

Est. 1980
Tel/fax: +44 (0)1433-631754
www.guildmark.co.uk
Parking available
Wheelchair access

For twenty years Andrew has been creating **contemporary bespoke furniture** and complete room schemes in beautiful woods. He is featured in the definitive book 'Furniture for the 21st century' by Betty Norbury. Work is mainly to commission. Clients are consulted at every stage to ensure usefulness and lasting pleasure. Mail order available.

Directions: *at the southern end of Grindleford village on the main road. Rail station one mile to the north.*

Opening hours: *Mon-Fri 9am-5pm.* (32)

DIFFERENT FURNITURE, 6 The Windmill, Butt Lane, Wymondham, Melton Mowbray, Leicestershire LE14 2BU

Est. 1997
Tel: +44 (0)1572-787300
Parking available
Wheelchair access

Different Furniture provides a personalised design service to produce a varied range of items including candlesticks, **tables, chairs and staircases.** Drawing inspiration from the art deco and avant-garde periods and utilising many techniques, striving to blur the line between art and function and achieving an element of Zeitgeist in metalwork. Mail order.

Directions: *B676 from Melton Mowbray. Right turn at signpost for Wymondham. Turn left at the Berkley Arms public house into Butt Lane. The windmill is on the left.*

Opening hours: *Mon-Sun 10am-6pm.* (33)

DOVETAIL FINE FURNITURE, The Carthouse Barn, Bittesby Farm, Bittesby, Lutterworth, Leicestershire LE17 4JH

Est. 1984
Tel/fax: +44 (0)1455-557773
www.dovetail-fine-furniture.co.uk
Parking available
Wheelchair access
Credit cards

Mike Faill creates **bespoke furniture** from his individual designs. Fine furniture is also created from customers' own ideas using traditional skills passed down through the years. Quality renovation of antiques is also undertaken. A Dovetail product will be the antique of tomorrow. Mail order is available upon request.

Directions: *M1 junction 20 take turning to Lutterworth. Keep on dual carriageway until A5 roundabout; right to Hincksey; then first right hand turning.*

Opening hours: *Mon-Sat 8am-5pm.* (34)

MALCOLM D. SMITH, 29 Market Place, Cromford, Matlock, Derbyshire DE4 3RE

Est. 1989
Tel/fax: +44 (0)1629-826620
www.malcolmdavidsmith.co.uk

Malcolm makes a range of **contemporary vernacular furniture,** mostly made in English hardwoods and inspired by natural forms (i.e. not with straight lines). Mostly seating and clock and music stands. Pieces are designed to have individual character. Each is part of a range that is continually developing and evolving. Mail order available.

Directions: *on foot: Cromford market place. Face away from Greyhound Hotel. Cross on crossing to right and 20 yards on the left is driveway of my workshop and gallery.*

Opening hours: *Thurs, Fri, Sat, Sun, Mon 10am-5pm. Please tel to confirm.*

MELVYN TOLLEY, The Old Post Office, Pinfold Lane, Bradley, Ashbourne, Derbyshire DE6 1PN

Est. 1988
Tel/fax: +44 (0)1335-370112
www.PeakdistrictProducts.co.uk/Tolley
Parking available
Wheelchair access

We make individual **hand made Windsor chairs** in yew, elm, cherry and ash. All are crafted in our timeless designs 'from tree to chair' in our small rural workshop. All chairs are as individual as the trees from which they came. Free quotations and brochures on request. Chair restoration work also undertaken.

Directions: *A517 Ashbourne to Belper. Approximately three miles east of Ashbourne turn into the lane signposted Bradley village.*

Opening hours: *most days 10am-5pm but advisable to phone first.*

NICHOLAS HOBBS, 1C Ravenstor Road, Wirksworth, Derbyshire DE4 4FY

Est. 1993
Tel: +44 (0)1629-823445
www.nicholashobbs.co.uk
Parking available

A Loughborough-trained craftsman with nearly ten years' experience I design and make **contemporary furniture** in distinctive architectural design styles in the arts and crafts tradition. Using a variety of British, American and tropical woods I make a range of furniture including entire dining-room and bedroom suites. Most work is to commission.

Directions: *Wirksworth is on the B5023 five miles south of Matlock. Ravenstor Road is at the southern end of the town.*

Opening hours: *prior appointment necessary.*

SIMMONS AND MILES, The Workshop Main Road, Wensley, Matlock, Derbyshire DE4 2LH

Est. 1988
Tel/fax: +44 (0)1629-734826
www.simmonsandmiles.co.uk
Parking available
Wheelchair access

Simmons and Miles are **antique furniture restorers** working to private commission. Services include cabinet and veneer repairs, sympathetic cleaning and traditional hand refinishing. We also offer day or week long individual tuition, perhaps as part of an activity holiday in the beautiful Peak District. Some work available for mail order.

Directions: *on the B5057 between Matlock and Bakewell.*

Opening hours: *prior appointment necessary.*

Other Makers

THE BELLFOUNDRY MUSEUM, Freehold Street, Loughborough, Leicestershire LE11 1AR

Est. 1784 bellmaker;
1986 as museum.
Tel: +44 (0)1509-233414
Fax: +44 (0)1509-263305
www.taylorbells.co.uk
Parking available
Partial wheelchair access
Credit cards

The world's largest, still working Bellfoundry. Makes **church and hand bells in bronze.** Tour of the works and bell casting viewing at selected times. Timetable is free on request. Allow one and a half hours for tour plus visit to museum and shop. Adults £3.80/children £1.90. No catering facilities. Mail order available.

Directions: *museum/shop on Cobden Street, off Freehold Street, which is off Queens Road between the A6 Leicester and A60 Nottingham roads in Loughborough east of town centre.*

Opening hours: *Tues-Fri 10am-12.30pm and 1.30-4.30pm plus some Sats and occasional Sundays. Please telephone first to avoid disappointment.*

BOB NEILL - BURNT OFFERINGS, 10 Long Croft, Aston on Trent, Derbyshire DE72 2UH

Est. 1985
Tel: +44 (0)1332-792036
Limited parking

Bob specialises in **burnt designs on wood** (pyrography) - personalised wooden items e.g. christening stool, wedding plate, small items for children, door plaques, egg cups, rolling pins, thimbles, spoons, trinket boxes, welly pegs. He also runs pyrography workshops and courses for those wishing to learn this craft. Mail order available.

Directions: *just off junction 23A of the M1. Details given when appointment is made.*

Opening hours: *by appointment only.*

DELOUNA, 41 Grasmere Way, Linslade, Leighton Buzzard, Bedfordshire LU7 2QN

Est. 1999
Tel/fax: +44 (0)1525-218136
www.delouna.co.uk
Parking available
Credit cards

A family-run business making various types of candles (e.g. entwined lovers paraffin candles), but specialising in **gel wax candles.** We make them in a range of glassware shapes, 15 colours and 35 scents. A choice of small blown glass embedded items can be included: hearts, shells, ships, animals etc. Also available 'glo' in the dark candles. £3.49-£35. Mail order only. Please ask for catalogue.

Directions: *outskirts of Leighton Buzzard off the A505.*

Opening hours: *direct sales not usual but possible. Appointment essential.*

FLIES BY WENDY, 47 Thorn Drive, Daisy Farm Estate, Newthorpe Common, Nottinghamshire NG16 2BH

Est. 1985
Tel/fax: +44 (0)1773-761645
Parking available
Credit cards

We specialise in **framing traditional trout and salmon flies.** We have a large selection and also frame to customers' requirements. Associated gifts such as brooches, earrings, and hat plumes are also available. We have collections of selected fly tying materials and fishing tackle including hand built cane rods. Mail order available.

Directions: *1 mile north of junction 26 of the M1. Follow signs for Ikea then continue to Eastwood. Look for Newthorpe Common and turn left, first left, last left.*

Opening hours: *prior appointment only.*

42

KARELDI STONE, Craft Workshop 3, Furnace Lane, Moira, Swadlincote, Derbyshire DE12 6AT

Est. 2000
Tel: +44 (0)1283-225986
Fax: +44 (0)1530-489822
www.kareldistone.co.uk

Karen Lee produces **sculptural stoneware for the garden/patio/conservatory.** She specialises in wall mounted animal masks, animals, troughs, planters and statues that are cast in 100 per cent frostproof stone, and which recreate the beauty of a natural stone finish. Choice of colours: sandstone, Portland/terracotta). Mail order available Commissions undertaken

Directions: *from A42 exit for Ashby-de-la-Zouch and follow the signs through Ashby for Moira and Moira Furnace Museum.*

Opening hours: *Mon-Fri 9am-5pm. Sat/Sun 10am-5pm.*

43

LEICESTERSHIRE EMUS, 31 Newbold Road, Kirkby Mallory, Leicestershire LE9 7QG

Est. 1997
Tel: +44 (0)1455-823344
Fax: +44 (0)1455-828273
www.leicestershireemus.com
Limited parking
Partial wheelchair access

Margaret Dover breeds emus as livestock producing meat, feathers, emu oil skincare products, eggs and eggshells. She also sells **carved emu eggs.** The eggs are an unusual colour and construction having three layers going from dark green on the outside, through blue/green to white on the inside. Mail order available.

Directions: *will be given when appointment is made.*

Opening hours: *flexible, but please make appointment first.*

44

SERENDIPITY CROWNS, TIARAS AND ACCESSORIES, Unit F14, Ferrers Centre, Staunton Harold, Near Ashby-de-la-Zouch, Leicestershire

Est. 2000
Tel: +44 (0)1332-862181
www.ferrerscentre.co.uk
Parking available
Wheelchair accessible

Samantha Gilmour's workshop is in a Craft Centre in the grounds of Staunton Harold Hall. She produces a range of exquisitely designed **occasion headwear: crowns and tiaras using silver and gold plate,** swarowski crystals, shells, pearls, feathers and semi-precious stones. Also hairpins, chokers, ring cushions and bridal bags. Commissions/mail order available.

Directions: *exit M1 at junction 24. Follow signs for A142 and Ashby-de-la-Zouch. At 'Nagstaff' roundabout take road for Staunton Harold. For the Ferrers Centre follow the brown anvil signs.*

Opening hours: *by appointment only.*

45

THE STENCIL SHOP, Eyam Hall Craft Centre, Eyam, Hope Valley, Derbyshire S32 5QW

Est. 1995
Tel: +44 (0)1433-639001
Parking available
Wheelchair access
Credit cards

We are a unique and specialist shop stocking the largest range of **stencils** in the area, along with products for decorative paint finishes. The range includes Fired Earth and Annie Sloan paints, earth pigments, varnishes, glazes, books, bespoke stencils, gilding and decoupage products. Commissions undertaken and mail order available.

Directions: *from A623 Chesterfield to Stockport road take turn to Eyam. Turn left in village past church and Eyam Hall.*

Opening hours: *Tues-Sun 10.30am-5pm.*

46

East Anglia

Cambridgeshire, Lincolnshire, Norfolk, Suffolk

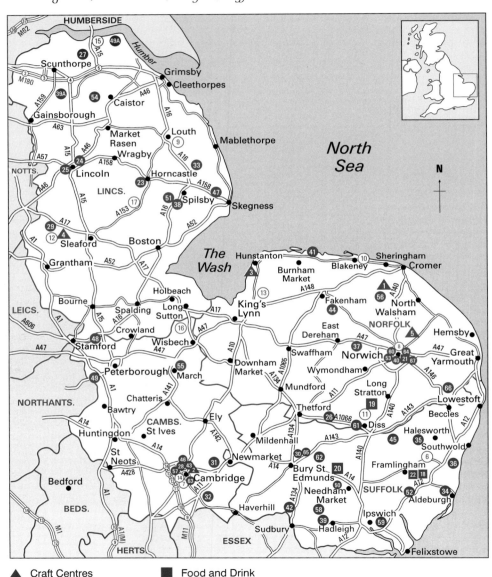

Craft Centres

Shops and Galleries

Food and Drink

Makers' Workshops

The rolling expanses and once prosperous wool towns of Suffolk and Lincoln contrast with the flatter, sparser counties of Cambridgeshire and Norfolk (the Fenlands) whose watery expanses were drained less than 200 years ago. The pottery traditions of Norfolk and Suffolk are widely carried on in contemporary times. Other local crafts perpetuated, include brewing, winemaking, corncraft and silk weaving. The influence of Eric Gill, the twentieth century calligrapher, and wood and stone carver, is evident in the products of the Cambridge workshop founded by David Kindersley, who was his apprentice.

Lincolnshire has a mainly agricultural, rather than craft, tradition; Boston was a centre of wode dye production, and reed cutting (for thatching) was the mainstay of the East Fen near Skegness.

Craft Centres

ALBY CRAFT CENTRE, Cromer Road, Erpingham, Norfolk NR11 7QE

Est. 1976
Tel: +44 (0)1263-761226
www.albycraftcentre.co.uk
Parking available
Wheelchair access
Credit cards

A collection of individual businesses set in restored farm buildings and four acres of gardens and ponds; includes a gallery of contemporary crafts, a giftshop and tearoom. Our range of crafts include furniture, woodturning, picture framing, leather harnesses, sculpture and stained glass. The centre and gardens are well worth a visit.

Directions: *halfway between Aylsham and Cromer on the A140 twenty five minutes from Norwich.*

Opening hours: *Tues-Sun 10am-5pm.*

ALL SAINTS GARDEN ART AND CRAFT CENTRE, c/o Markets Manager, Cambridge City Council, Cambridge CB2 3QJ

Est. 1970
Tel: (0)1223-457446
www.cambridge-art-craft.co.uk
Parking available
Wheelchair access
Some artists take credit cards

An open air art and craft market in the historic heart of Cambridge, with a reputation for quality at affordable prices. Our motto is 'we make what we sell.' With a wide range of stalls run by individual artists who all display their work on the internet on our website.

Directions: *in Trinity Street opposite Trinity College.*

Opening hours: *every Sat 10am-5pm and other selected days.*

LE STRANGE OLD BARNS, Antiques and Arts and Crafts Centre, Golf Course Road, Old Hunstanton, Norfolk PE36 6JD

Est. 1994
Tel: +44 (0)1485-534743
Fax: +44 (0)1485-533402
Parking available
Wheelchair access
Credit cards

The largest centre of its type in Norfolk, Le Strange offers a fine collection of antiques, original paintings and English crafts in one complex, in a beautiful location adjoining beach. A variety of craft demonstrations throughout every day including a potter, clockmaking, jewellery, glass and china painting etc.

Directions: *follow large brown signs in Old Hunstanton on A149. Hunstanton is approximately 15 miles north of Kings Lynn on A149.*

Opening hours: *summer 10am-6pm; winter 10am-5pm seven days.*

MANOR STABLES CRAFT CENTRE, Lincoln Road, Fulbeck, Grantham, Lincolnshire NG32 3JN

Est. 1987 (new owner 2000)
Tel: +44 (0)1400-272779
www.cuttinglane.com
Parking available
Credit cards
Wheelchairs: access ground
floor only.

A working craft centre set in a beautiful village and offering a relaxing and interesting day out. A variety of craftspeople work on site: blacksmith, saddler, clockmaker etc. Also available: dried flowers, interior accessories, furniture, gifts and upholstery. Three showrooms display a wealth of traditional and contemporary hand made items. Tearoom.

Directions: *on the A607 between Lincoln and Grantham.*

Opening hours: *Tues-Sun 10.30am-4.30pm plus bank holidays.*

Wroxham Barns
Norfolk's finest rural craft centre

- A collection of beautifully restored 18th century barns set in 10 acres of Norfolk countryside. 13 resident craftsmen specialising in traditional and contemporary crafts including wood turning, stained glass, cider and apple juice pressing, model shipbuilding, patchwork and quilting, pottery, botanical painting and jewellery making

- Buy that special something - for a friend or for yourself - in our gift, food and clothes shops

- Enjoy mouthwatering cakes, snacks and home cooked lunches in our tearoom

Wroxham Barns, Tunstead Road, Hoveton, Norfolk, UK NR12 8QU
Tel: 01603 783762 Web: www.wroxham-barns.co.uk

WROXHAM BARNS, Tunstead Road, Hoveton, Norfolk NR12 8QX

Est. 1983
Tel: +44 (0)1603-783762
Fax: +44 (0)1603-781401
www.wroxham-barns.co.uk
Parking available
Wheelchair access
Credit cards

Traditional and contemporary craft skills are practised in our converted barn workshops. Observe craftsmen creating unique items. The craftsmen will be pleased to chat to you about their work and many work to commission to produce original crafts to your design. See also:*Food and Drink, Glass, Jewellery, Pottery, Textiles, Woodturning, Other Makers.*

Directions: *take the A1151 from Norwich to Wroxham. Then follow brown and white tourist signs for one and a half miles on the Tunstead Road.*

Opening hours: *Mon-Sun 10am-5pm.*

Craft Shops

BOWLING GREEN CRAFTS, The Bowling Green, Badingham, Woodbridge, Suffolk IP13 8LX

Est. 1996
Tel: +44 (0)1728-638500
www.bgcrafts.co.uk
Parking available
Wheelchair access
Credit cards

We are a family business in rural Suffolk. Annie Taylor is a quilt designer/maker and Chris paints terracotta and ceramics to his own designs. We also showcase a huge variety of work by local craftspeople. For examples of our work, visit our shop or website. Various commissions undertaken. Mail order available.

Directions: *Badingham on the A1120 tourist route between Yoxford and Framlingham*
Open: *Tues-Sun 10am-6pm Apr-Dec; Tues-Sun 10am-4pm Jan-March.*

CAMBRIDGE ARTS AND CRAFTS, PO Box 82, Cambridge, Cambridgeshire CB2 2XQ

Est: 1991
Tel: +44 (0)1223-247370
Parking available
Wheelchair access
Credit cards at most stalls

We are a group of craftworkers from the East Anglia region who have joined to display work at this small but high quality enterprise. Unique gifts at affordable prices including jewellery, woodturning, original prints, hand made cards, *devoré* silks and pottery. We also accept work on a commission basis.

Directions: *display stalls are in Guildhall Place, Cambridge, between the Lion Yard car park and the marketplace.*
Opening hours: *Saturdays only 9.30am-5pm.*

JADE TREE, 39 Elm Hill, Norwich, Norfolk NR3 1HG

Est: 1998
Tel/ fax: +44 (0)1603-664615
Parking available
Wheelchair access limited
to ground floor shop

We are five artists and craftspeople who work and sell in a seventeenth century merchant's house. In our studios we produce ceramics, embroidered textiles, original artwork, handmade cards, sculpture and decorative boxes. Choose an unusual gift in our shop or come and meet us to discuss a commission.

Directions: *in Norwich's Elm Hill, two minutes walk from the cathedral.*
Opening hours: *Mon-Sat 10am-5pm.*

LOUTH CRAFT GALLERY, Unit 9, Newmarket Hall, Cornmarket, Louth, Lincolnshire LN11 9PU

Est. 1993
Tel: (0)1507-354884
www.louthcg.freeserve.co.uk
Parking available
Wheelchair access
downstairs only
Credit cards

We are a group of artists and craftmakers working together on a cooperative basis to bring an extensive range of beautiful and unusual, high quality, locally made crafts direct to the public. We staff the shop so we are able to discuss special commissions. Orders can be mailed if requested.

Directions: *in the corner of New Market Hall behind the Mason's Arms and near the tourist information centre in Louth Market Place.*
Opening hours: *Mon-Sat 9.30am-4.30pm.*

MADE IN CLEY, Starr House, Cley-next-the-sea, Holt, Norfolk NR25 7RF

Est. 1984
Tel: +44 (0)1263-740134
Fax: +44 (0)1263-740186
Limited parking available
Credit cards

Located in the centre of the village, we stock hand thrown domestic and sculptural pottery in stoneware, porcelain and raku. Also contemporary jewellery in silver and gold, prints and sculptures in marble and other stones. Everything is made on the premises and exhibited in a Regency shop which is of historical interest.

Directions: *on the A149 in the centre of the village.*
Opening hours: *June-Oct. Tues-Sun 10am/5pm. From Oct to June closed Weds and Suns open 11am-4pm.*

Galleries

2 FISH GALLERY, Gissing Road, Burston, Norfolk IP22 5UD

Est. 2001
Tel: +44 (0)1379-741796
Fax: +44 (0)1379-740711
Parking available
Limited wheelchair access

On show in the gallery are one-off pieces of furniture, such as tables, chairs, mirrors, wardrobes, chests, boxes, shelves, etc. by David Gregson. Other work (ceramics, textiles, jewellery, stained glass, sculpture, etc.) is by local and national craftsmen, all of a very high standard. Prices range from £5-£10,000.

Directions: *north on A140 from Scole. Left to Shimpling and Burston, over railway crossing, first right, 200 yards on right is gallery sign.*

Opening hours: *Tues-Sun and bank holiday Mondays 10am-5pm.*   ⑪

CUTTING LANE INTERIORS, Manor Stables Craft Centre, Lincoln Road, Fulbeck, Grantham, Lincolnshire NG32 3JN

Tel: +44 (0)1400-272779
www.cuttinglane.com
Parking available
W/chairs: ground floor only
Credit cards

Three showrooms full of many interesting and unusual arts and crafts produced by some of the finest artists and craftspeople. Many items are unique and cover both traditional and contemporary styles. We aim to promote those with real talent and make their work available at realistic prices. Tearoom.

Directions: *on the A607 between Lincoln and Grantham.*

Opening hours: *Tues-Sun 10.30am-4.30pm plus bank holidays.*   ⑫

DERSINGHAM POTTERY AND GALLERY, 46 Chapel Road, Dersingham, near King's Lynn, Norfolk PE31 6PN

Est. 1972
Tel: (0)1485-540761
Parking available
Wheelchair access
Credit cards

Pottery and paintings are displayed in our converted carrstone stables once belonging to the Sandringham Estate. The stoneware and porcelain domestic and individual pieces by June Mullarkey include a variety of coloured glazes, textures and shapes. The paintings by Ben Mullarkey, in watercolour and acrylic are of Norfolk and beyond.

Directions: *on the B1440 in the centre of the village of Dersingham one mile from Sandringham.*

Opening hours: *Tues-Sat 10am-5pm.*   ⑬

PRIMAVERA, 10 King's Parade, Cambridge, Cambridgeshire CB2 1SJ

Est. 1946
Tel: +44 (0)1223-357708
Fax: +44 (0)1223-576920
www.primaverauk.com
Car park nearby.
No w/chair access downstairs.
Credit cards

Primavera is the oldest contemporary art and crafts gallery in the country and has over 400 of the best contemporary artists in Britain. Exhibitions run alongside ever-changing displays of wonderful and unique jewellery, paintings, innovative modern furniture, ceramics, sculpture, glassware, clocks, watches, automata, woodwork, silverware, wrought iron, textiles and hand-made card and paper.

Directions: *since 1960 situated opposite the entrance to King's College Cambridge.*

Opening hours: *9.30am-5,30pm Mon-Sat; Sun 11am-5pm.*   ⑭

ROPEWALK CONTEMPORARY ART AND CRAFT, The Ropewalk, Maltkiln Road, Barton-on-Humber, North Lincolnshire DN18 5JT

Est. 2000
Tel/fax: +44 (0)1652-660380
www.the-ropewalk.com
Parking available
Wheelchair access
Credit cards

The Ropewalk in run by an artists' co-operative. The grade II listed building holds two galleries, artists' studios, a bespoke picture framing service and the Waterside Heritage Display. The Art Gallery changes shows every fortnight, while the Craft Gallery has a permanent selling exhibition of over 80 makers. Mail order available.

Directions: *situated on the south bank of the River Humber in the shadow of the Humber Bridge. Signposted from the A15.*

Opening hours: *Tues-Sat 10am-5pm; Sun 10am-4pm.*   ⑮

SKYLARK STUDIOS, Hannath Road, Tydd Gote, Wisbech, Cambridgeshire PE13 5ND

Est. 1993
Tel +44 (0)1945-420403
www.skylark.studios.dial.pipex.com
Car park at front.
Wheelchair access.
Credit cards

Skylark Studios is a unique privately owned gallery with a professional and friendly service. Specialising in a balanced range of accessible innovative work across a variety of media including ceramics, cards, jewellery, etchings, linocuts, screenprints and original paintings, representing a good selection of work of artists from all over the UK.

Directions: *just off the A1101, 6 miles north of Wisbech and 3 miles south of Long Sutton on the Lincolnshire/Cambridgeshire border.*

Opening hours: *10am-5pm Tues-Fri, 11am-5pm Sat.*

TATTERSHALL STATION GALLERY AND POTTERY, The Old Station, Sleaford Road, Tattershall, Lincolnshire LN4 4JG

Est. 1975
Tel: +44 (0)1526-344037
www.paintingsandpottery.co.uk
Parking available
Limited wheelchair access
Credit cards

Resident artist, Arthur Watson, presents a feast of watercolours, prints and ceramics, all displayed in the Old Station's booking hall and ticket office. Arthur is a full-time professional artist with 36 years' experience. He enjoys painting in both traditional and contemporary styles and also produces stoneware and handthrown ceramics. Mail order available.

Directions: *situated in Tattershall's Old Railway Station on the A153, a quarter of a mile west of Tattershall Castle.*

Opening hours: *Mon-Sun 10am-5pm.*   (17)

Food & Drink

BRUISYARD VINEYARD AND HERB CENTRE, The Winery, Church Road, Bruisyard, Saxmundham, Suffolk IP17 2EF

Est. 1974
Tel: +44 (0)1728-638281
Fax: +44 (0)1728-638442
Parking available
Wheelchair access
Credit cards

A vineyard with winery in traditional Suffolk farm buildings. We have tranquil water and herb gardens with a peaceful and wooded picnic area. Our country shop sells a range of wines and choice things to eat and drink. There is also a large variety of potted herbs and seeds for sale.

Directions: *follow the brown tourist signs from the A12/B1119 Saxmundham Bypass, A1120/B1120 to Badingham or B119/B1120 to Framlingham.*

Open: *winter Tues-Sun 11am-4pm, summer Tues-Sun 10.30am-5pm.*   **18**

BUFFY'S BREWERY, Rectory Road, Tivetshall St Mary, Norwich, Norfolk NR15 2DD

Est. 1993
Tel: (0)1379-676523
www.buffys.co.uk
Parking available
Wheelchair access
Credit cards

The brewery is situated in our own garage next door to our sixteenth century hall house. We produce a range of high quality beers and ales which are available in carry-home containers from the brewery door. Our beers are for sale in many local pubs and also in our own taproom.

Directions: *from Norwich take the A140 south towards Ipswich. After 12 miles Tivetshall St Mary and Rectory Road is signposted on the right.*

Opening hours: *Mon-Fri 9.30am-5pm. Generally open all weekend. Advisable to phone before any visit.*   **19**

NORFOLK CIDER COMPANY, Wroxham Barns, Tunstead Road, Hoveton, Norfolk NR12 8QU

Tel: +44 (0)1603-784876
Fax: +44 (0)1603-781401
www.craft-centre.org.uk
Parking available
Wheelchair access
Credit cards

Traditional cider-makers daily demonstrating apple milling and pressing on nineteenth century Norfolk equipment and producing pure, fresh apple juice. Also available, proper, award-winning cider and other apple-related products. Demonstration given by appointment. Trade enquiries welcome. Watch out for us demonstrating at shows across East Anglia and the South East.

Directions: *take the A1151 from Norwich to Wroxham. Then follow brown and white tourist signs for one and a half miles on the Tunstead Road.*

Opening hours: *Mon-Sun 10am-5pm.*

PALMERS BAKERIES, The Bakehouse, Old Street, Haughley, Near Stowmarket, Suffolk IP14 3NR

Est. 1869
Tel: +44 (0)1449-673286
Fax: +44 (0)1449-672376
www.palmersbakery.co.uk
Parking available
Wheelchair access can
be arranged

A high class family bakers and confectioners producing a wide range of fresh bread, confectionery and savouries made to centuries-old recipes handed down from generation to generation. Our goods are made with traditional ingredients by Master Baker craftsmen and baked on site in our unique and ancient brick ovens.

Directions: *off A14 just outside Stowmarket. The Bakehouse is at the top of Haughley Old Street (main street) on village green near Post Office and Pub.*

Opening hours: *Mon-Fri 8.30am-5pm; Sat 8am-1pm.*   `20`

RONALDO ICES, 2 Glenmore Gardens, Norwich, Norfolk NR2 4PH

Est. 1976
Tel: +44 (0)1603-633127
Fax: +44 (0)1603-765361
www.ronaldo-ices.com
Parking available.

Family business making real ice-cream using local ingredients, milk, cream, fruits, nuts and liqueurs. Most popular three flavours: vanilla; strawberry, chocolate rum and raisin; raspberry and champagne. Ice-cream barrows available for events. Also, commission your own flavour (minimum 25 litres). Direct sale to visitors (minimum half litre) or two to four litres local delivery.

Directions: between Grapes Hill (inner ring road) and Dereham road. First right off Dereham Road; immediately behind Jet garage.

Opening hours: Mon-Fri 9am-6pm. Sat by appointment.   `21`

SHAWSGATE VINEYARD Ltd, Badingham Road, Framlingham, Suffolk IP13 9HZ

Tel: +44 (0)1728-724060
Fax: +44 (0)1728-723232
www.shawsgate.co.uk
Parking available
Wheelchair access
Credit cards

Various award-winning white and red wines and ciders produced using modern machines. Open for sales, tours (specialised and general) and tastings. Picnic and children's play area. Shawsgate Vineyard is a fully operational vineyard offering contract winemaking and vine leasing. Visit us or our website for more details. Mail order available

Directions: *north-east of Framlingham and castle on B1120 - follow brown tourist signs.*

Opening hours: *Mon-Fri 9am-5pm; Sat-Sun 10am-5pm.*   `22`

Glass

CHAMELEON CRYSTAL, the Hopton Ironworks, the Wong, Horncastle, Lincolnshire LN9 6EB

Est. 1995
Tel/ fax: (0)1507-524460
Parking available
Wheelchair access

Chameleon Crystal make **hand blown lead crystal glass**. They specialise in producing replacement items for the antique trade, reproductions of antique glass and decorative works of art. Also for sale are antique silver plates with glass linings. More contemporary works are also available. These craftspeople work to clients' requirements in undertaking commissions.

Directions: *on the premises of a large furniture shop in the Wong. Look for the big chair.*

Opening hours: *by appointment.*   (23)

COASTAL STAINED GLASS, Wroxham Barns, Tunstead Road, Hoveton, Norfolk NR12 8QU

Est. 1995
Tel: +44 (0)1603-784825
Fax: +44 (0)1603-781401
www.craft-centre.org.uk
Parking available
Wheelchair access
Credit cards

Glassmaker Tim Foord specialises in stained glass giftware including **Tiffany lamps, decorative mirrors, terraria, trinket boxes and clocks**. Especially popular at time of press are window panels (both internal and external), firescreens made to customer wishes and specifications and a new range of picture frames (also customised). Commissions are especially welcome.

Directions: *take the A1151 from Norwich to Wroxham. Then follow brown and white tourist signs for one and a half miles on the Tunstead Road.*

Opening hours: *Mon-Sun 10am-5pm.*

JAQ McCAUGHERN, 30 Victoria Street, West Parade, Lincoln, Lincolnshire LN1 1HY

Est. 1996
Tel: (0)1522-539730
Parking available
Credit cards in the gallery

Jaq makes unique **wall panels, plaques and mirrors** made of wood and glass. The wood pieces are carved in wood with raised gesso detail. The glass is kiln formed and painted from the reverse. The result is translucent and very dramatic pieces. Commissions are undertaken and purchase by mail order is possible.

Directions: *follow signs for central Lincoln and then go north up Orchard Street from outside City Hall. Go across a little road and over a hill into Victoria Street. Prior appointment necessary.* 24

KEVIN WALLHEAD, 19 Grafton Street, Lincoln LN2 5LT

Est. 2000
Tel: (0)1522-821567
Parking available

Kevin is a home-based producer of **wall mounted and free-standing glass**. His work includes drawings in glass and simple figurative imagery which allow the viewer to subjectively explore and interpret the work with reference to their own ideology. Prices from £30 to £1,000. Commissions are welcome.

Directions: *half a mile from the city centre off Monk's Road. Turning onto Grafton Street opposite Monk's Abbey School.*

Opening hours: *please make appointment.* 25

VICTORIA BHOGAL, 1 Manor Cottages, Kenning Hall Road, Garboldisham, Diss, Norfolk IP22 2SJ

Est. 1992
Tel/fax: (0)1953-681049
Good parking

Victoria Bhogal trained in **fine art stained glass** at Central St. Martin's and works mainly to commission. Her work is about colour and sensuous, flowing lead line inspired by organic forms. Visitors can see her work in progress and learn about the techniques and the healing properties of coloured light.

Directions: *from the A1066, take the B1111 through Garboldisham. Turn right. The studio is a mobile home on the left.*

Opening hours: *by appointment only.* 26

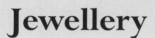

Jewellery

CAPRICORN JEWELLERY AND MINERALS, Wroxham Barns, Tunstead Road, Hoveton, Norfolk NR12 8QU

Est. 1983
Tel: +44 (0)1603-784082
Fax: +44 (0)1603-781401
www.capricornminerals.co.uk
Parking available
Wheelchair access
Credit cards

We use traditional skills to create unique jewellery using **lustrous gemstones/freshwater pearls** sterling silver and 9ct gold. Our range of necklaces, bracelets and earrings is shown to advantage against a backdrop of natural minerals, ornamental fossils, crystals and gems. Special gifts to give, or simply to spoil yourself.

Directions: *take the A1151 from Norwich to Wroxham. Then follow brown and white tourist signs for one and a half miles on the Tunstead Road.*

Opening hours: *Mon-Sun 10am-5pm.* 5

ELISE M RAMSAY, White House, 27 Low Road, Worlaby, Brigg, North Lincolnshire DN20 0LY

Est. 1968
Tel: +44 (0)1652-618341
Parking available
Credit cards

A full range of jewellery hall marked London. I have been designing and making jewellery for over half a century and although I am aware of trends in jewellery design, my work is largely inspired by the 1920s. Each item is designed/produced individually using traditional methods in silver, gold and semi-precious stones.

Directions: *given when appointment is made.*

Opening hours: *please ring after midday for an appointment.* 27

TANIA JAMES, 3 Felton Street, Cambridge, Cambridgeshire CB1 2EE

Est. 1975
Tel: +44 (0)1223-476400
Parking available
Credit cards

I make jewellery mainly from silver and some gold, using flowing shapes often elegantly enclosing semi-precious stones. Many pieces are individually designed: **flamboyant brooches and eminently wearable earrings,** necklets and bracelets. I enjoy having visitors to my workshop and am always happy to consider personal requirements and undertake some commissions.

Directions: *aim for Cambridge rail station, turn into Tenison Road; take the fourth left into Felton Street.*

Opening hours: *Mon-Fri 10am-5pm.*   **28**

Leatherwork

MARK BUSHELL (SADDLERS), Manor Stables, Craft Workshops, Fulbeck, Grantham, Lincolnshire NG32 7SN

Est. 1989
Tel: +44 (0)1400-273711
www.cuttinglane.com
Parking available
Credit cards

A Member of the Society of Master Saddlers, Mark makes **saddlery, harness and bridlework.** He provides new and secondhand saddlery, horse clothing, bridlework and driving harness; also a saddle fitting service. Repairs also carried out. Bespoke work has included rocking horse saddlery and a saddle for a veteran motorbike. Mail order possible.

Directions: *off A607. Fulbeck village halfway between Lincoln and Grantham. Craft Centre is well-signposted off the main (A607) road.*

Opening hours: *Tues-Sun 10am-6pm.*   **29**

Metalwork & Silversmithing

JWH McCAUGHAN, 19 The Stables, Timworth Green, Bury St Edmunds, Suffolk IP31 1HS

Est. 1997
Tel/fax: +44 (0)1284-754416
Parking available
Wheelchair access

I design and make **decorative usable furniture and sculptured items,** predominantly from steel and from wood. In achieving this, I am able to combine my facilities with my own traditional skills of blacksmithing, welding, sheetmetal-working and woodworking to produce contemporary and traditional articles. Work may be done to commission.

Directions: *3 miles north of Bury St Edmunds, turn right off the A134 Bury St Edmunds to Thetford Road.*

Opening hours: *Mon-Fri 9am-5pm. Prior appointment necessary.*   **30**

Musical Instruments

MIKE GILPIN HURDY GURDIES, Hill Cottage, Heath Rd, Swaffham Bilbeck, Cambs. CB5 OLS

Est. 1995
Tel +44 (0)1223-812378
Parking available

The hurdy gurdy is an instrument with a history going back to the 12th century, and is currently enjoying a renaissance in folk music circles. Having been a player for some years I then studied musical instrument technology at London Guildhall University, establishing my workshop in 1995. I make **four styles of hurdy gurdy** - the Bosch (a medieval-style instrument based on one featured in a painting by Hieronymous Bosch), a 19th century French guitar bodied, a19th century French lute-backed and also a less ornate model suitable for beginners. All are made using traditional woods with some decorative inlay work.

Directions: *from the A14 take the B1102 towards Burwell; in Swaffham Bulbeck follow signs to Newmarket. Hill Cottage is on junction of Heath Road and Quarry Lane.*

Opening hours: *visits by appointment only.*

31

Pottery & Ceramics

ABINGTON POTTERY AND CRAFT SHOP, 26 High Street, Little Abington, Cambridge, Cambridgeshire CB1 6BG

Est. 1964
Tel: +44 (0)1223-891723
Parking available
Credit cards

Originally a medieval open hall house, which was extensively restored when Abington Pottery was established. Hand made stoneware pottery is produced on the premises, including **tableware, garden pots and lamp bases.** Named mugs, plates and bowls can be commissioned for all anniversary occasions. House numbers and name-plates can be made to order.

Directions: *8 miles south-east of Cambridge on A1307 Cambridge-Colchester road.*
Opening hours: *Mon-Sun 9am-6pm.*

32

ALFORD POTTERY, Commercial Road, Alford, Lincolnshire LN13 9EY

Est. 1972
Tel: +44 (0)1507-463342
Parking available
Wheelchair access

Heather and Michael Dufos are makers of handthrown **pottery stoneware, tableware, kitchenware** as well as some giftware. They also make unusual commemorative and company mugs and tankards. Additionally, they specifically design practical tableware for disabled people. Commission and trade enquiries welcome. Personal reliable service and very reasonable prices.

Directions: *Alford is on the A1104 off the A16. Commercial Road is in the town off West Street (also A1104).*
Opening hours: *Mon-Fri 9am-5pm. Mon-Sat May-Dec.*

33

ANNIE LEE, Dunan House, 41 Park Road, Aldeburgh, Suffolk IP15 5EN

Est. 2000
Tel: +44 (0)1728-452486
Fax: +44 (0)1728-453454
www.annlee.co.uk
Parking available
Wheelchair access

I paint on **domestic ware ceramics, especially large plates.** These can be personalised with names and dates. I also make hand built pieces like garden pots and small-lidded containers. Prices from £10-£200. My ceramics make unusual gifts. They often have a seaside theme as I live by the sea. Mail order available.

Directions: at *Aldeburgh roundabout turn right down Park Road. It has a 'private road' sign and directions to hospital. House is on left before tennis courts. Workshop at back.*

Opening hours: *Mon-Sun 10am-5pm. Prior appointment recommended.*

CHEDISTON POTTERY, The Duke, The Green, Chediston, near Halesworth, Suffolk IP19 0BB

Est. 1982
Tel: +44 (0)1986-785242
Parking available
Wheelchair access but
please phone first
Credit cards

Mark Titchener has been making wood fired **slipware and sculptural pieces** since 1982. His sculpture is slip decorated, slab built and modelled. Influenced by Byzantine architecture and pagan symbolism, all are individual pieces. He also makes a range of frostproof terracotta garden pots which are all wheel thrown or slab built.

Directions: *take B1123 Harleston road from Halesworth. Chediston is two and a half miles from town. Follow the blue signs to the pottery on the right.*

Opening hours: *Tues-Sun 9am-5.30pm but advisable to ring first.*

GLYNN HUGO STUDIO POTTERY, The Old Stores, Darsham, Saxmundham, Suffolk IP17 3QA

Est. 1963
Tel/fax: +44 (0)1728-668274
Limited parking

The Pottery is a one-man studio producing a complete range of **domestic ware and sculptural pieces.** The work is predominantly hand thrown in stoneware, porcelain and basalt clays. It is fired in a propane kiln after a previous biscuit firing. The studio and showroom were converted from the former village stores.

Directions: *half a mile north of Darsham Station level crossing on the A12 turn right into Darsham village street. The Pottery is half a mile on the right.*

Opening hours: *Mon-Sun 10am-7pm.*

GRAHAME CLARKE PORCELAIN, The Old Hall, East Tuddenham, Near Dereham, Norfolk NR20 3NP

Est. 1990
Tel: +44 (0)1603-880439
Fax: +44 (0)1603-881340
www.grahameclarkeporcelain.co.uk
Parking available
Wheelchair access

Grahame's blue and white freehand porcelain is made and painted at his Norfolk studio. The **refined country porcelain** is designed to complement the table and home. In the English tradition, each piece is both unique and individual. Visitors are welcome to view the large selection. Colour catalogue on request. Mail order available.

Directions: *1 mile off A47, half a mile east of East Tuddenham on Mattishall road.*

Opening hours: *Mon-Sun 10am-dusk. Prior appointment recommended.*

JOHN AND JANE SNOWDEN, Thirtytales Cottage, Cul-de-Sac, Stickford, Lincs PE22 5EY

Est. 1975
Tel: +44 (0)1205-480848
Parking available
Wheelchair access

John uses home-made glazes to produce **illustrious and bright raku ceramics.** Basic domestic stoneware also made. Ceramic sculptures to commission are made for indoors and out (especially windchimes). Group and individual tuition given. Technical consultancy to schools and colleges available. Jane also does embroidery work. Prices from £5-£400. Mail order available.

Directions: *half a mile from A16 Stickford by-pass. 10 miles north of Boston and sign-posted 'Stickford.'*

Opening hours: *by appointment only.*

KERSEY POTTERY, the Street, Kersey, Ipswich, Suffolk IP7 6DY

Est. 1973
Tel: +44 (0)1473-822092
www.kerseypottery.com
Parking available
Wheelchair access
Credit cards

We make **highfired stoneware and ceramics** including jugs, bowls, teapots and dishes made as individual pieces. Most of our work is thrown on the wheel and square dishes are slabbed. Glazing is idiosyncratic with several layers built up and fired to 1340 centigrade. Prices range from £1.50-£50. Larger works £50-£200.

Directions: *next to the Watersplash in Kersey. Between Ipswich and Colchester turn onto B1070; round Hadleigh bypass on the A1071 and onto A1141; take first left to Kersey.*

Opening hours: *Tues-Sat 9.30am-5.30pm Sun 11am-5pm.* (39)

KIRTON POTTERY, 36 High Street, Kirton in Lindsey, Gainsborough, Lincs. DN21 4LX

Est. 1975
Tel +44 (0)1652-648867
Parking available

Peter and Christine Hawes make a large range of both **brightly coloured majolica and more subdued stoneware for domestic use**. Christine was trained as a painter at Sheffield College of art. Peter learnt from books such asMichael Cardew's 'Pioneer Pottery' when he and Christine worked to set up a pottery training workshop in Botswana. Images of their work are on www.axisartists.org.uk. Commissions are welcome, including commemorative plates and sculptural figures for the garden. Visitors can see both the making and decorating in the workshop and a wide range of items in the showroom.

Directions: *Kirton lies off the A15 between Lincoln and Scunthorpe: the pottery is just below the market square at the top of the town.*

Opening hours: *9.30am-5.30pm Wed-Sat; 2.30-5pm Sun.*

LUCY EDWARDS CERAMICS, The Jade Tree, 39 Elm Hill, Norwich NR3 1HG.

Est. 2000
Tel/fax: +44 (0)1603-664615
Parking available
Wheelchair access to
ground floor only

Lucy specialises in simple **hand-built ceramics in raku and stoneware** Pieces are both sculptural and functional, echoing the textures, curves and hollows found in natural forms. Prices start at £4. Lucy is always happy to demonstrate and discuss the making process in her studio above the shop. Commissions welcome.

Directions: *located on Elm Hill, cobbled street 2 mins walk from the Cathedral.*

Opening hours: *Mon-Sat 10am-5pm.*

THE OLD STATION POTTERY AND BOOKSHOP, The Old Station, 2-4 Maryland, Wells-next-the-sea,

Norfolk NR23 1LX
Est. 1978
Tel: +44 (0)1328-710847
Fax: +44 (0)1328-711566
Parking available
Wheelchair access

We spent many years producing cast animal figures. Now sanity has prevailed and we produce hand thrown domestic ware including mugs, jugs, bowls and containers as well as, earthenware pottery. We also make large hand built ceramic sculptures of **life size female torsos**. We also have an extensive second hand bookshop.

Directions: *from Burnham end of town drive along quay. Follow road around corner and over the hill past the police station. We are 50 yards further on left.*

Opening hours: *9am-5pm daily. Closed Thurs.*

POSTING HOUSE POTTERY, The Posting House, Hall Street, Long Melford, Sudbury, Suffolk C010 9JA

Est. 1997
Tel: +44 (0)1787-311165
Fax: +44 (0)1787-311164
Parking available
Wheelchair access
Credit cards

We hand make and sell **domestic and decorative pots in stoneware and porcelain;** bowls, jugs, mugs, plates, teapots and vases. Pieces can be made to order. We also sell work by three similar potteries. All our work is dishwasher and microwave proof, and food safe. Mail order available.

Directions: *centre of village, east side of main street (Hall Street) opposite Co-op store.*

Open: *Tues-Sat 10am-6pm, bank holiday Mondays and some Sundays.*

RACHEL DORMOR CERAMICS, White House Arts, 72 Fen Road, Chesterton, Cambridgeshire CB4 6AD

Est. 2000
Tel: +44 (0)1223-424000
Parking available
Wheelchair access

We have a range of hand built and wheel thrown **domestic ware in porcelain and stoneware**. There is a range of sculptural smoke fired and raku vessels. There are also paintings and textiles by our resident artists. Creative courses are run throughout the year at our riverside workshop. Telephone for details.

Directions: *follow the towpath out of the city by foot for a mile and a half. By car we are just over the level crossing on Fen Road.*

Opening hours: *daily 10am-5pm.*

43

RYBURGH POTTERY, May Green, Little Ryburgh, Fakenham, Norfolk NR21 0LP

Est. 1985
Tel: (0)1328-829543
Parking available

Stephen Parry specialises in making **pots for the kitchen and table.** All pots are hand thrown using both stoneware and porcelain clays which are ash glazed and fired to 1300 C in a wood fired kiln. Our stoneware pots and porcelain are all available mail order. Visitors are welcome.

Directions: *three miles south east of Fakenham, just off the A1067 Norwich Road. Look for signs saying 'Little Ryburgh only'*

Opening hours: *Mon-Sun 9am-6pm. Good idea to telephone first.*   44

SOENDERGAARD DESIGN, Fressingfield House, Church Street, Fressingfield, Suffolk IP21 5PA

Est. 1995
Tel/fax: +44 (0)1379-586200
Parking available
Wheelchair access

Lars Soendergaard Gregersen is Danish-born and has worked in pottery and ceramics for over 20 years. He specialises in contemporary handthrown **porcelain made in the Scandinavian tradition:** tableware and home accessories are finished in glazes using only natural pigments. Prices from £20-£60. Commercial production and individual pieces available.

Directions: *follow B1116 from either A12 or A143 to Fressingfield. Shop/studio is opposite the Fox and Goose Inn.*

Opening hours: *all week 10am-4pm.*   45

SUSAN CUPITT, 62 Humberstone Road, Cambridge CB4 1JF

Est. 1995
Tel: +44 (0)1223-311937
Parking available

I make wheel thrown **stoneware, ceramics and domestic pottery** placing emphasis on form and experimenting with dark muted glazes using oxides with wood ash. Pots range from sophisticated forms to simple vessels such as tea pots, bowls and jugs. I exhibit in various galleries including Peterborough's Guildenburgh and Broughton House in Cambridge.

Directions: *north of the city on Chesterton Road. Take De Freville Avenue then the second street on the left.*

Opening hours: *prior appointment necessary.*   46

THREEWAYS POTTERY, Common Lane, Burgh-le-Marsh, Lincolnshire PE24 5HH

Est. 1985
Tel: +44 (0)1754-8190756
www.burghlemarsh.com
Parking available
Wheelchair access

Threeways is a small pottery workshop, producing a range of **hand thrown domestic ware** and other items. The clay used is highfiring stoneware, suitable for oven-to-table use. Products include casserole and serving dishes, mugs and plates. Visitors are welcome to watch us work. Classes for all standards are run on Wednesdays.

Directions: *towards Skegness on A158, take first left after the Windmill onto Ingoldmells Road. Pottery is on junction with common.*

Open: *open most days on a flexible basis. Good idea to phone first.*   47

TRICIA FRANCIS, Wroxham Barns, Tunstead Road, Hoveton, Norfolk NR12 8QU

Est. 1981
Tel: +44 (0)1603-782171
Fax: +44 (0)1603-781401
www.craft-centre.org.uk
Parking available
Wheelchair access

Hand thrown terracotta pottery. Tricia makes practical, unusual pottery especially for kitchen and garden. A Tricia Francis house name plaque is a work of art - hand painted and caringly personalised to your requirements, then finished to the highest standards. Pots £4-£80. House name plaques from £18. Mail order from website.

Directions: *take the A1151 from Norwich to Wroxham. Then follow brown and white tourist signs for one and a half miles on the Tunstead Road.*

Opening hours: *Mon-Sun 10am-5pm.*   5

VINE FARM POTTERY, Vine Farm, Barnack Road, Bainton, Stamford, Lincolnshire PE9 3AE

Est. 1986
Tel: +44 (0)1780-740611
Parking available
Wheelchair access
Credit cards

Carlos Versluys is a studio potter making **carved stoneware vessels** and occasional domestic ware. Each piece is thrown then highly fired in a gas kiln with matt wood ash glazes. His work is widely exhibited. The adjoining gallery and 18th century stone barn also display selected work from other makers.

Directions: *the pottery is on the main road going through Bainton village opposite the church.*

Opening hours: *anytime by prior appointment.*   48

WOODNEWTON POTTERY, 43 Main St, Woodnewton, Oundle, Nr Peterborough PE8 5EB

Est. 1989
Tel: +44 (0)1780-470866
Fax: +44 (0)1780-470722
www.studiopottery.co.uk
Parking available
Wheelchair access
Credit cards

The Pottery is housed in a converted Methodist church. A wide range of **useful and colourful tableware and ovenware,** including pots, jugs, plates, etc. are made. All are decorated with fruits in various patterns. Prices range from £1-£150. Visitors can watch work in progress. Mail order available.

Directions: *100 yards from the White Swan pub - village centre.*

Opening hours: *by appointment.*

 49

Textiles

ELIZABETH OLDFIELD, Roseholme, Peploe Lane, New Holland, North Lincolnshire DN19 7PS

Est. 1984
Tel +44 (0)1469-530905
Parking available
Limited wheelchair access

Elizabeth has a smallholding and keeps a small flock of Jacob sheep whose wool is wonderful for hand-spinning, with colours ranging from cream through to black. She does not sell hanks of wool, preferring to make it up herself into finished items, mixing the colours she spins to create **interesting combinations of colour and texture.** Items range from small novelties such as miniature sheep through knitted hats, scarves and waistcoats, fine lace scarves, crochet fashion shawls and stoles to thickly spun wool woven into floor rugs. Visitors are welcome and can see the sheep but please ring first. Mail order available.

Directions: *on the south bank of the Humber 6 miles to the east of the Humber Bridge (B1206): first turning to right on entering the village.*

Opening hours: *by appointment only.*

 49a

HELEN RIPLEY, The Fields, Straight Road, Battisford, Stowmarket, Suffolk IP14 2HD

Est. 1998
Tel/fax: +44 (0)1449-613801
www.helenripley.co.uk
Parking available
Wheelchair access

My work explores the glowing colours of **dyes on silk, with some stitched texture** piping and pleating etc. and acrylic marks. I sell my studio pieces, and have undertaken some public commissions. The images are inspired by landscape, but are not realistic. Prices range from £200-£1,000. Mail order is available on website.

Directions: *from Stowmarket (off A14 Ipswich to Bury St Edmunds) towards Combs, turn left towards Combs Tannery. Continue for one and a half miles. At T-junction, turn left. House 200 yards left.*

Opening hours: *by appointment.*

 50

JANE SNOWDEN, Thirtytales Cottage, Cul-de-Sac, Stickford, Lincolnshire PE22 SEY

Est. 1975
Tel: +44 (0)1205-480848
Parking available
Wheelchair access

Jane graduated with a degree in tailoring and embroidery and has worked in these areas for over twenty years. Her applique method produces abstract patterns combining various colours and textiles on **waistcoats (£60+), cushions and hats (£15+)** in various natural fibres. Husband John works in ceramics. Commissions welcome. Mail order available.

Directions: *half a mile from A16 Stickford by-pass. 10 miles north of Boston and sign-posted 'Stickford.'*

Opening hours: *by appointment only.*

 51

LADS AND LASSES, Wroxham Barns, Tunstead Road, Hoveton, Norfolk NR12 2QU

Tel: +44 (0)1603-784060
Fax: +44 (0)1603-781401
www.ladsandlasses.co.uk
Parking available
Wheelchair access
Credit cards

We offer **children's clothes,** hand made in England and suitable for boys and girls from three months to ten years. Made from quality cotton fabrics in a range of exciting designs and colours. Our garments are fully washable, hardwearing and versatile and of course kids love to wear them. Website mail order.

Directions: *take the A1151 from Norwich to Wroxham. Then follow brown and white tourist signs for one and a half miles on the Tunstead Road.*

Opening hours: *Mon-Sun 10am-5pm.*

QUILTERS HAVEN, 68 High Street, Wickham Market, Suffolk IP13 0GU

Est. 1993
Tel: +44 (0)1728-746275
Fax: +44 (0)1394-610525
Parking available
Limited wheelchair access
Credit cards
www.quilters-haven.co.uk

We are one of the top **quilting and patchwork** centres in the United Kingdom. We have thousands of bolts of fabric and hundreds of books for hobbyists. During the summer we run a wide range of day-long courses in our teaching centre for both beginners and the advanced.

Directions: *we are at the centre of Wickham Market overlooking the square.*

Opening hours: *Mon-Sat 9am-5pm.*

SEW CREATIVE, Wroxham Barns, Tunstead Road, Hoveton, Norfolk NR12 8QU

Est. 1989
Tel: +44 (0)1603-781665
Fax: +44 (0)1603-781401
www.wroxham-barns.co.uk
Parking available
Wheelchair access
Credit cards

Patchwork quilting specialist plus cross stitch and tapestries. A limited number of hand made quilts for sale as making process is long-term. Also offers on-site quiltmaking workshops with national and international tutors suitable for beginners and more experienced craftspeople. Also fabric, quilters' haberdashery and books. Mail order available.

Directions: *take the A1151 from Norwich to Wroxham. Then follow brown and white tourist signs for one and a half miles on the Tunstead Road.*

Opening hours: *Mon-Sun 10am-5pm.*

TAMARA RAMPLEY, The Jade Tree, 39 Elm Hill, Norwich, Norfolk NR3 1HG

Est. 1998
Tel/fax: +44 (0)1603-664615
Parking available
Wheelchair access

I create original illustrative designs for hand-cut **embroidery decoration on couture scarves, wraps and clothing.** Layers of silk and transparent fabrics are overlaid, embroidered and cut away to let the light shine through areas of the design. Accessories or garments created to commission for that special occasion. Mail order available.

Directions: *Elm Hill is the medieval cobbled street close to the River Wensum and the Cathedral.*

Opening hours: *Mon-Sat 10am-5pm.*

Woodturning & Furniture

KEVIN P BURKS, The Old School, Cadney Road, Howsham, North Lincolnshire LN7 6LA

Est. 1976
Tel: +44 (0)1
Fax: +44 (0)1
Parking available
Wheelchair access to
some areas

We are primarily **cabinet makers** using English oak and chestnut wood. We also make domestic and office furniture. Our work is usually of traditional design though we also undertake more contemporary pieces. Most work is on a commission basis for private individuals. Prices start at £95 for an octagonal table or stool.

Directions: *just off the B1434.*

Open: *Mon-Fri 8am-5pm, Sat 9am-4pm, by appointment at other times.*

RICHARD CARPENTER, 22A Wisbech Road, March, Cambridgeshire PE15 8ER

Est. 1996
Tel: +44 (0)1354-650942
Parking available

Richard Carpenter is a designer and craftsman producing high quality **domestic and ecclesiastical furniture** in English hardwoods (cherry, ash, sycamore etc). Direct sales or to commission. Clients throughout the UK and Europe. Designs are produced in close co-operation with the client to meet their specific ideas, needs and budget.

Directions: *on the right hand side of the road into March from the Northern Roundabout.*

Opening hours: *by appointment only.*

RON LYONS, Wroxham Barns, Tunstead Road, Hoveton, Norfolk NR12 8QU

Est. 1990
Tel: +44 (0)1603-784245
Fax: +44 (0)1603-781401
www.wroxham-barns.co.uk
Parking available
Wheelchair access
Credit cards

I specialise in turning English and exotic hardwoods producing **large bowls and platters (up to 60cm diameter), ringstands, lace bobbins, lightpulls** and I am happy to take private commissions. Also pyrography done on breadboards, chopping boards etc. Also, a variety of small items, beautifully crafted in different woods - ideal holiday gifts.

Directions: *take the A1151 from Norwich to Wroxham. Then follow brown and white tourist signs for one and a half miles on the Tunstead Road.*

Opening hours: *Mon-Sun 9.30am-4.45pm; closed Wednesdays.*

TURNING POINT, Unit 6, Alby Crafts, Cromer Road, Erpingham, Norfolk NR11 7QE

Est. 1989
Tel: +44 (0)1263-761400
www.kdewick.co.uk
Parking available
Wheelchair access
Credit cards

Turning Point is a workshop that produces contemporary **one-off turnings and commissioned furniture,** mostly in native hardwoods. Turned stock is always available. Prices range from £2-£2000. Furniture commissions are undertaken with the client's ideas being fundamental to the finished piece. Furniture restoration projects are also willingly taken on.

Directions: *halfway between Aylsham and Cromer on A140, 25 mins from Norwich.*

Opening hours: *Tues-Sun 10am-5pm.*

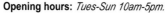

Other Makers

CARDOZO KINDERSLEY WORKSHOP, 152 Victoria Road, Cambridge CB4 3DZ

Est. 1976
Tel: +44 (0)1223-362170
www.kindersleyworkshop.co.uk
Parking available
Wheelchair access
Credit cards accepted
on website

Lettercutters, mainly in stone, we continue the workshop that David Kindersley started in 1946 after having been apprenticed to Eric Gill. We make one-offs to special individual needs and for institutions. We cut stone, engrave glass, publish books and have started a range of lettered items including postcards, porcelain, calendars, scarves, ties and T-shirts.

Directions: *Victoria Road begins at the junction of the Huntingdon and Histon roads (A1307 and B1049, respectively), half a mile north of Cambridge city centre.*

Opening hours: *by appointment only.*

CHARLES FREEMAN - HISTORIC MODEL SHIPWRIGHT, Wroxham Barns, Tunstead Road, Hoveton, Norfolk NR12 8QU

Est. 1999
Tel: +44 (0)1603-783762
Fax: +44 (0)1603-781401
www.hmsmodel.co.uk
Parking available
Wheelchair access
Credit cards

My aim is to promote the skill of **wooden boat building in miniature**. I offer an extensive range of tools, materials and modelling kits, as well as ready-made ships, half hulls, clocks barometers and other nautical giftware. I also offer full back up and advice for model makers. Commissions undertaken. Mail order available.

Directions: *take the A1151 from Norwich to Wroxham. Then follow brown and white tourist signs for one and a half miles on the Tunstead Road.*

Opening hours: *Mon-Sun 10am-5pm.*

CHRIS HUTCHINS NORFOLK SKETCHES, Wroxham Barns, Tunstead Road, Hoveton, Norfolk NR12 8QU

Est. 1984
Tel: +44 (0)1603-784221
Fax: +44 (0)1603-781401
www.wroxham-barns.co.uk
Parking available
Wheelchair access
Credit cards

Artist and printmaker Chris Hutchins works mainly in pencil producing highly detailed drawings of Norfolk, Suffolk and 'Constable Country.' He has a range of over 100 views which he prints from original drawings on an old offset litho machine. Every print is personally signed by the artist. Prints from £3. Originals from £300.

Directions: *take the A1151 from Norwich to Wroxham. Then follow brown and white tourist signs for one and a half miles on the Tunstead Road.*

Opening hours: *Mon-Sun 10am-5pm. Closed Weds in winter.*

CORNCRAFT, Bridge Farm, Monks Eleigh, Ipswich, Suffolk IP7 7AY

Est. 1973
Tel: +44 (0)1449-740456
Fax: +44 (0)1449-741665
www.corncraft.co.uk
Parking available
Wheelchair access
Credit cards

Corncraft is situated on a farm specialising in growing materials to make their extensive range of **corn dollies and floral art.** Other specialities include a vast range of crafts and gifts for sale in the gift shop, and the adjoining tea room, which serves delicious home-made food. Mail order available.

Directions: *in the heart of rural Suffolk, situated on the A1141 between Hadleigh and Lavenham.*

Opening hours: *Mon-Sat 10am-5pm; Sun 11am-5pm.*

58

COTTAGE FLOWERS, Wroxham Barns, Tunstead Road, Hoveton, Norfolk NR12 8QU

Est. 1983
Tel: +44 (0)1603-783762
Fax: +44 (0)1603-781401
www.craft-centre.org.uk
/blanch.html
Parking available
Wheelchair access
Credit cards

Janet Blanch's Cottage Flowers produces an exclusive range of **botanical prints, stationery, wrapping paper, and greetings cards** for all types of occasion from watercolour paintings by the owner/artist Janet Blanch. Many items produced on recycled paper. Original paintings also available; and painting workshops. Mail order available.

Directions: *take the A1151 from Norwich to Wroxham. Then follow brown and white tourist signs for one and a half miles on the Tunstead Road.*

Opening hours: *Mon-Sun 10am-5pm.*

FERIAL ROGERS, 1 Holly Cottages, Little Bealings, Woodbridge, Suffolk IP13 6PN

Est. 1990
Tel: +44 (0)1473-624141
Fax: +44 (0)1473-630451
Limited parking

Ferial's main work is in **one twelfth and one twentyfourth scale furniture miniatures** for collectors. She is also interested in painting on silk in a number of styles and covers a number of themes. Additionally, she undertakes some heraldic work for institutions and individuals. Mail order is available upon request.

Directions: *in Little Bealings turn down Holly Close (off Holly Lane); turn right at end. Park cars in open space then walk to house; the last on the path.*

Opening hours: *appointment necessary.*

59

JACQUI FENN DESIGNS, The Jade Tree, 39 Elm Hill, Norwich, Norfolk NR3 1HG

Est. 1998
Tel/fax: +44 (0)1603-664615
Parking available
Wheelchair access to
ground floor
Credit cards

Beautiful range of **stylish hand made cards** that may be customised (names or dates written onto the cards). Individually hand painted and one-off designs are made, especially for weddings: choose from the range of designs in our album or commission your own design for a wedding or other special occasion.

Directions: *located in Elm Hill, medieval cobbled street 2 mins walk from Cathedral.*

Opening hours: *Mon-Sat 10am-5pm.*

60

JO HINCKS, The Old Chapel, Fair Green, Diss, Norfolk IP22 4BG

Est. 1989
Tel: +44 (0)1379-643925
Parking available
Wheelchair access

Jo Hincks' **paper vessels and reliefs** are constructed using the laminating technique of papier-mâché. Acryllic glazes, collage elements or prints are then applied. Works are varied in scale and form and may be table or wall pieces. Each vessel is unique. Commissioned work is undertaken. Prices start at £40.

Directions: *situated on the south side of Fair Green just off the A1066 Thetford to Diss road.*

Opening hours: *By appointment.*

MICKY BOLTON, Boltons, The Street, Badwell Ash, Bury St Edmunds, Suffolk IP31 3DH

Est. 1990
Tel: +44 (0)1359-259575
www.weldartist.com
Parking available
Wheelchair access

Micky converted from antique car restorer to weld artist around ten years ago. He now specialises in producing lifelike animal **sculptures made from recycled cars and agricultural parts,** from snails to ostriches. Some contemporary and abstract sculptures are also made. Prices from £50-£10,000. Commissions undertaken. Images of work on website.

Directions: *A14 Elmswell/Norton exit. A1088 towards Ixworth. Through Norton. Turn right towards Walsham le Willows. 3 miles to Badwell Ash. Opposite St Mary's Crescent.*
Opening hours: *by appointment.*

MYERS PRINTS, Fisher Hall, Guildhall Place, Cambridge CB2 3NH

Est. 1980
Tel: +44 (0)1223-247370
Parking available
Wheelchair access
Credit cards

I make original prints and cards. My style of painting involves delicate and complex use of fine lines. I produce **cat portraits and engravings** and also accept commissions on houses, working from drawings done on site. I particularly enjoy half timbered, flint and haphazard rural buildings such as old barns.

Directions: *in central Cambridge opposite 'Toxic 8' near the Lion Yard car park.*
Opening hours: *Sat 9.30am-5pm.*

REBECCA SPRAGGE, 520 Earlham Road, Norwich, Norfolk NR4 7HR

Est 1998
Tel: +44 (0)1603-502172
Parking available
Wheelchair access

A theatrically trained designer costumier, Rebecca makes decorative embroidered traditionally **boned corsets, bustiers, costume fantasy and historic and wedding dresses.** She also creates sculptures, wall hangings and paintings using mixed media. Her work has been demonstrated at the Victoria and Albert Museum. Visitors welcome to see her studio. Commissions undertaken.

Directions: *follow signs for Sainsbury Centre (University of East Anglia) on B1108 situated by the Fiveways roundabout.*
Opening hours: *visits by appointment only please.*

STEPHEN BUSHELL, Barns and Stables, Timworth Green, Bury St Edmunds, Suffolk IP31 1HS

Est. 1999
Tel: +44 (0)1359 241879,
+44 (0)777-3060703
Parking available
Wheelchair access

I have spent several years training and working with master craftsmen in Newcastle, London and Switzerland on the manufacture and restoration of time pieces. Recently, I have started making my own **gold and silver clocks and watches** according to traditional methods but employing contemporary designs. Estimates available by phone.

Directions: *off A134 Bury St Edmunds to Thetford road, to Barns and Stables, Timworth.*
Opening hours: *Mon-Sat 9am-3pm. Prior appointment necessary.*

VERENA MURTAGH, Orchard Farm, Hales Green, Hales, Norfolk NR14 6QJ

Est. 1992
Tel: +44 (0)1508-548967
Parking available
Wheelchair access

Large and small sculptures in clay are semi-figurative and made for both indoors and the garden. Verena's work aims for clear lines and solidity in a contemporary context. Tiles and flower pots of various types are also produced. Visitors can watch work in progress. Commissions are happily undertaken.

Directions: *directly off A146 between Beccles and Hales, 600 yards before Shell garage a track on the left leads to the house.*
Opening hours: *by appointment.*

WINDOW CARDS BY JULIE BERNICE, The Jade Tree, Elm Hill, Norwich NR3 1HG

Est. 1996
Parking available

Julie started making her **cards and decorative boxes** six years ago after working on dolls' house restoration. The cards have a diamond-shaped window and Julie creates an unusual visual effect by using cut-outs of flowers, animals and scenery pictures on the inserts of the cards. Prices vary from £1.75 to £3.50.

Directions: *Elm Hill Tourist Street is close to Cathedral, St Andrews Hall and River also fairly close to city centre.*
Opening hours: *Mon-Fri 10am-5pm.* 67

Yorkshire, Lancashire

and Humberside

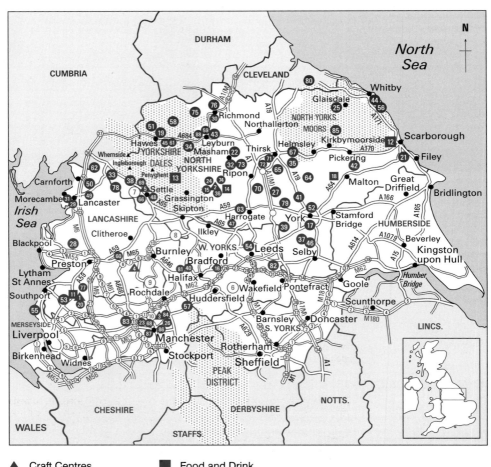

▲ Craft Centres   ■ Food and Drink

○ Shops and Galleries   ● Makers' Workshops

These counties represent the heartland of nineteenth century industrial Britain. In particular, the area from Lancashire in the west, through southern Yorkshire, to the docks of Humberside, was densely industrial. The mill workers of Yorkshire and Lancashire used to wear clogs to work, and even today you may hear their descendants referred to as 'cloggies.' North Yorkshire is a place to fill your lungs with fresh air and 'get away from it all'; agriculture has always been dominant there, and it is home to The Dales and the National Park that contains them. North Yorkshire is where you will find most of the craft makers of Yorkshire. Traditional craft industries include cheesemaking, (especially in the Wensleydale area), brewing and rope-making; Manchester Craft Centre is at the forefront of modern craft and design.

Craft Centres

ART@CEDARFARM, Back Lane, Mawdesley, Ormskirk, Lancashire L40 3SY

Est. 1998
Tel: +44 (0)1704-822101
Fax: +44 (0)1704-822616
www.cedarfarm.net
Parking available
Wheelchair access
Credit cards (some makers)

Art@Cedarfarm is an exciting new development in the heart of rural west Lancashire. Consisting of art and design based businesses, there are nine working craftspeople producing a wide range of high quality innovative work. The selection includes baskets, glass, textiles, sculptural ceramics, stained glass and jewellery.

Directions: *from A59 between Ormskirk and Southport follow signs to Mawdesley. From Rufford follow brown tourist board signs to 'Cedar Farm Galleries'.*

Opening hours: *Tues-Sun 10am-5pm and Mon bank holidays.*

KING STREET WORKSHOPS, King Street, Pately Bridge, North Yorkshire HG3 5LE

Est. 1993
Tel: +44 (0)1423 712877
www.afct30.ukgateway.net
Parking available
Wheelchair access on
ground floor
Some credit cards

King Street Workshops contain 8 businesses, seven of which are craft based. The converted buildings used to be a workhouse and council depot. Glass, jewellery, ceramics and wood furniture are sold. The main building houses award winning Nidderdale Museum (check times before going). There are several pubs and cafés on nearby streets.

Directions: *King Street turning is between High Street and Bridge (at low end of High Street). Follow signs for workshop and museum.*

Opening hours: *Mon-Sat 9am-5pm but varies. Tel to check on individuals.*

MANCHESTER CRAFT AND DESIGN CENTRE, 17 Oak Street, Northern Quarter, Manchester M4 5JD

Est. 1983
Tel: +44 (0)161-8324274
Fax: +44 (0)161-8323416
www.craftanddesign.com
NCP parking Church/High St
Limited wheelchair access
Credit cards

Located in a Victorian style market building, Manchester Craft and Design Centre is the Northwest's largest centre for the production and retail of contemporary craft and design. Visitor's can enjoy the excellent café, view the changing exhibition programme and choose from an array of 18 different shops on two floors.

Directions: *five minutes on foot from bus interchange and metrolink at Piccadilly Gardens. Go up Oldham Street, second left Hilton Street, second right to Oak Street.*

Opening hours: *Mon-Sat 10am-5.30pm.*

OSWALDTWISTLE MILLS LTD, Collier Street, Oswaldtwistle, Accrington, Lancashire BB5 3DE

Est. 1992
Tel: +44 (0)1254-871025
Fax: +44 (0)1254-770790
www.o-mills.co.uk
Parking available
Wheelchair access
Credit cards

Oswaldtwistle Mills has a wide range of crafts and goods including encaustic art, rubber-stamping, stencilling and more. The complex that houses the craft centre is located in the grounds of a fully working mill from which flour is available. Craft workshops are regularly held. Mail order is available upon request.

Directions: *from junction 7 of the M65 follow the signs to Oswaldtwistle Mills*

Opening hours: *Mon-Sat 9am-5pm, Thurs until 8pm, Sun 11am-5pm.*

WATERSHED MILL VISITOR CENTRE, Watershed Mill, Langcliffe Road, Settle, North Yorkshire BD24 9LR

Est. 1993
Tel: +44 (0)1729-825111
Fax: +44 (0)1729-825202
www.dalesmeade.co.uk
Parking available
Wheelchair access
Credit cards

A nineteenth-century former cotton mill, Watershed Mill is in the Dales by the River Ribble and houses the Dalesmeade Centre which sells products from 45 craft makers under the Dalesmade label (woodwork, pottery, leatherwork, paintings, prints and textiles etc). Other shops on site (golf, rock and fossil, factory outlet). Tearoom. Mail order available.

Directions: *from A65 travel into Settle market town, follow brown and white tourist signs. Mill is 400 yards on B6479. Look for Mill chimney.*

Opening hours: *Mon-Sat 10am-5.30pm. Sun 11am-5pm.*

Craft Shops

BOTHY SHOP AND GALLERY YORKSHIRE SCUPLTURE PARK, West Bretton, Wakefield, Yorkshire WF4 4LG

Est. 1993
Tel: +44 (0)1924-830125
Fax: +44 (0)1924-830044
www.ysp.co.uk
Parking available
Wheelchair access
Credit cards

The Bothy Shop brings together talented new designers with established makers to combine and contrast textures and media in a variety of styles, ranging from the traditional to the innovative. The range includes jewellery, textiles, leatherwork, ceramics and toys. Prices range from £25 to £2,000. An art loan scheme is available.

Directions: *1 mile from junction 38 of the M1.*

Opening hours: *Mon-Sun winter 11am-4pm, summer 11am-5pm.*

DALESMADE CENTRE, Watershed Mill, Settle, North Yorkshire BD24 9LR

Est. 1991
Tel: +44 (0)1729-825111
Fax: +44 (0)1729-825202
www.dalesmade.co.uk
Parking available
Wheelchair access
Credit cards

Housed in a cotton mill dating from the 1820s, the Dalesmade Centre is a shop within a craft complex offering a superb choice of crafts made in the Yorkshire Dales. Visitors will also find a wide range of fashion, knitwear, golf equipment, accessories and gift ideas in the rock and fossil shop. Homemade food is available in the coffee shop. Mail order.

Directions: *on leaving the A65 go through the Market Town of Settle Mill, situated on the B6479 signposted Hawes.*

Opening hours: *Mon-Sat 10am-5.30pm, Sun 11am-5pm.*

⑦

Galleries

BRENT GALLERY DAVID BINNS FINE ART, 60A Keighley Road, Cowling, Near Keighley, Yorkshire BD20 8BL

Est. 1979
Tel: +44 (0)1535-636892
Fax: +44 (0)1535-632774
Parking available
Wheelchair access possible
Credit cards

Brent Gallery sells works by David Binns. Original watercolours, limited edition prints and a range of miniatures depicting British wildlife, greetings cards and commercial products, many designed by David Binns including jigsaws, plates, beakers and music cards. Also ceramic animals and birds by Stephen Binns. Mail order available.

Directions: *on the A6068 road at Cowling. This is the main route from Keighley to Colne.*

Opening hours: *10.30/noon and 2/5pm. Closed all day Wednesday and Sat pm.*

THE LAST DROP GALLERY, The Last Drop Village, Bromley Cross, Bolton, Lancashire BL7 9PZ

Est. 1976
Tel/fax: +44 (0)1204-593528
www.wildlifesculptures.co.uk
Parking available
Wheelchair access
Credit cards

Established at the Last Drop Village for over 25 years, I produce one-off painted ceramic, bronze or precious metal wildlife sculptures to commission. The gallery offers a huge range of art and gifts at prices to suit every pocket and taste. Refreshments at the tea shop or pub. Mail order is available.

Directions: *A666 from Bolton. 4 miles to Egerton then turn right at traffic lights/war memorial. Left at the next traffic lights then 300 yards.*

Opening hours: *Mon-Sun 10am-5pm.*

THE SMITHFIELD GALLERY, Unit 61, 44 Tib Street, Northern Quarter, Manchester M4 1LA

Est. 2001
Tel: +44 (0)161-8324242
Fax: +44 (0)1229-585396
Parking available
Wheelchair access by arrangement
Credit cards

We have fourteen artists, all showing original works. Three of them djsplay around the world. The Gallery has three levels on two floors. We specialise in creative metalworks from mirrors to sculptures and also from chairs to cushions. Paintings also exhibited. Prices from £60-£600. Commission work is considered. Mail order available.

Directions: *100 yards from Piccadilly Railway Station. Behind Debenhams at the corner of Church St and Tib St, opposite Afflecks Palace.*

Opening hours: *Tues-Sat 10.30am-4.30pm; prior appointment preferred.* ⑩

Baskets & Wickerwork

BRITISH BASKETS, Studio 8, Art@Cedarfarm, Back Lane, Mawdesley, Ormskirk, Lancashire L40 3SY

Est. 1993
Tel/fax: +44 (0)1704-822358
www.britishbaskets.co.uk
Parking available
Wheelchair access
Credit cards

With 39 years' experience, I make **baskets in willow** using the traditional methods outlined on my website. I draw on the full history of the craft to make a wide range of baskets in regional, British and international styles. I often work on commission developing customers' ideas. Mail order available.

Directions: *from A59 between Ormskirk and Southport follow signs to Mawdesley. From Rufford follow brown tourist board signs to 'Cedar Farm Galleries'.*

Opening hours: *Tues-Sun 10am-5pm and Mon bank holidays.*

Food & Drink

THE HONEY FARM, Race Course Road, East Ayton, Scarborough, North Yorkshire YO13 9HT

Est. 1989
Tel: +44 (0)1723-864001
Fax: +44 (0)1723-862455
www.BeeHeath.com
Parking available
Wheelchair access
Credit cards

Recommended in the Sunday Telegraph as a 'taste guide to honey', The Honey Farm offers a range of tasting tours and honeys gathered from the Yorkshire Dales. There is also a range of honey related products including pure beeswax candles. All available mail order. Also a farm bakery, shop, tearoom and restaurant.

Directions: *on the A170 Scarborough to Pickering road.*

Opening hours: *Mon-Sun 9am-5pm.*

12

WENSLEYDALE DAIRY PRODUCTS, Gayle Lane, Hawes, North Yorkshire DL8 3RN

Est. 1992
Tel: +44 (0)1969-667664
Fax: +44 (0)1969-667638
www.wensleydale.co.uk
Parking available
Wheelchair access
Credit cards

The makers of 'real Wensleydale cheese'. Visit the museum portraying the history of cheesemaking in Wensleydale. Then see the cheese being made from our viewing gallery. Sample a selection from the delicatessen, ending your visit with a mouth-watering treat in the restaurant. 'A grand day out.' Mail order available.

Directions: *Take A684 to Hawes, then follow signs for Kettlewell - entrance 150 yards at top of hill.*

Opening hours: *Mon-Sat 9.30-5pm; Sun 10am-4.30pm.*

13

YORKSHIRE COUNTRY WINES, Riverside Cellars, The Mill, Glasshouses, Harrogate, North Yorkshire HG3 5QH

Est. 1989
Tel/fax: +44 (0)1423-711947
Parking available
W/chair access with notice

Country wines are produced in the vaulted cellars of a 19th century flax mill. Join one of our winery tours, or just sample the wines (including Elderberry, Elderflower, Parsnip and Raisin and Cherry and Dandelion) in our tasting room which houses an impressive water turbine. Mail order is available.

Directions: *signed from the crossroads off the B6165 Harrogate to Pately Bridge road,*
Opening hours: *Easter-Christmas Wed-Sun 11.30am-4.30pm, Christmas-Easter Sat/Sun 11.30am-4.30pm. Tours Fri/Sat 11:45am.*

14

Glass

ANDREW SAUNDERS AND DAVID WALLACE GLASSMAKERS, 4 King Street Workshops, King Street, Pately Bridge, North Yorkshire HG3 5LE

Est. 1981
Tel/fax: +44 (0)1423-712570
www.yorkshire.co.uk
/glassmakers
Parking available
Wheelchair access

We are a small workshop producing a wide range of **functional and decorative glassware** in recycled lead crystal. Using traditional techniques and inspired by historical artefacts, we produce a range including vases, candleholders, paperweights, drinking glasses and perfume bottles. Glassblowing can be seen most days. Mail order available.

Directions: *King Street turning is between High Street and Bridge (at low end of High Street). Follow signs for workshop and museum.*

Opening hours: *Mon-Fri and alternate weekends 9.30am-5.30pm.*

DESIGN GLASS, Grove Works, Hind Street, Wyke, Bradford, Yorkshire BD12 8JT

Est. 1989
Tel/fax: +44 (0)1274-605454
www.designglass
Parking available

We produce **stained glass, painted and fired glass,** fused and etched glass and slumped glass to the specification of clients. We welcome people to look around our showroom and busy workshop to see how things are done, and we are pleased to give quotations for work. Mail order available.

Directions: *junc 26 M62; take A58 towards Halifax, through crossroads (lights) to second crossroads (lights, Red Lion pub), turn right. Travel under a mile towards Bradford; on right.*
Opening hours: *Mon-Fri 8.30am-5pm; Sat 8.30am-noon.*

GREEN GLASS STUDIOS, 144 Albemarle Road, South Bank, York, North Yorkshire Y023 1HB

Est. 2000
Tel +44 (0)1904-645298
Parking available

We specialise in the production of coloured designed kiln-formed **glass combined with enamels to give beautiful landscape images** on glass panels. Panels are available as pictures, framed in English oak. We also have a colourful range of ceramic agate ware for table use. Also, leaded glass, bowls and tiles. Mail order available.

Directions: *from Leeds via A64 into York. Follow signs to racecourse. Right at bottom of Tadcaster Road. Pass the racecourse and third left opposite telephone booths.*
Opening hours: *flexible. By appointment only.*

JORVIK GLASS, Castle Howard, York, North Yorkshire YO60 7DA

Est. 1995
Tel/fax: +44 (0)1653-648555
Parking available
Wheelchair access
Credit cards

Situated in the grounds of Castle Howard. Traditional techniques of glassblowing can be viewed at close quarters in the company's hot glass studio. A wide range of**functional and decorative glassware** is manufactured on the premises, along with commission work, corporate incentives and repairs. Mail order catalogue available.

Directions: *from York take the A64 Scarborough Road. Castle Howard is six miles before Malton signed to the left. Located in the courtyard of Castle Howard.*
Opening hours: *Mar-Dec Mon-Sun 10am-5pm. Winter months by appointment.*

ORANGE GLOW WORKSHOPS, The Penn House, Off Market Place, Hawes, North Yorkshire DL8 3QX

Est. 1997
Tel: +44 (0)1969-667668
Fax: +44 (0)1969-667094
Parking available
Wheelchair access
Credit cards

The workshop is open all year round and caters for all needs. Visitors are welcome to come and browse in the shop or watch the glassmaker at work. We design and produce high quality **handmade hot glass** products that are exported throughout the USA and Far East. Mail order available.

Directions: *behind the Spar shop on the High Street.*
Opening hours: *Mon-Sun no Sat 10am-4pm.*

SLY GLASS, Studio 9, Art@Cedarsfarm, Back Lane, Mawdesley, Lancashire L40 3SY

Est. 1999
Tel/fax: +44 (0)1704-823360
Parking available
Wheelchair access
Credit cards

We are makers of **hand blown studio glass;** designed, blown and finished on the premises by Leona Murtagh and Stephen Linders. All the work is freeblown without the use of moulds so that each piece is unique. Fresh colours and elegant forms make the work both collectible and contemporary. Mail order available.

Directions: *from A59 between Ormskirk and Southport follow signs to Mawdesley. From Rufford follow brown tourist board signs to 'Cedar Farm Galleries'.*
Opening hours: *Tues-Sun 10am-5pm and Mon bank holidays.*

THE STAINED GLASS CENTRE, Killerby Lane, Cayton, Scarborough, North Yorkshire YO11 3TP

Est. 1985
Tel: +44 (0)1723-581236
Fax: +44 (0)1723-585465
www.stainedglass-centre.co.uk
Parking available
Wheelchair access
Credit cards

Valerie Green is a fourth generation member of the Lazenby family to be working in the stained glass craft. The centre houses a showroom, workshops, exhibitions of**stained glass** and a tearoom. Our experts repair damaged stained glass and leaded windows. Residential courses are available. Mail order available upon request.

Directions: *A165 Scarborough/ Filey Road. Turn at roundabout onto B1261. Turn left at sign.*
Opening hours: *Mon-Sun 10am-5pm.*

UREDALE GLASS, 42 Market Place, Masham, near Ripon, North Yorkshire HG4 4EF

Est. 1981
Tel/fax: +44 (0)1765-689780
www.uredale.co.uk
Parking available
Wheelchair access
Credit cards

Tim and Maureen Simon have created a worldwide reputation for their distinctive style of glass making. Their extravagant use of colour and traditional techniques ensure the individuality of each piece. The range includes **lighting, stained glass and collectors' items.** Corporate and private commissions are undertaken. Mail order available. .

Directions: *Uredale is 10 mins offA1. Walk under King's Head Archway and 50 yds beyond.*

Opening hours: *Mon-Sun 10am-5pm.*   (22)

Jewellery

COLETTE HAZELWOOD - CONTEMPORARY JEWELLER, Jelly Studios, Manchester Craft Centre, 17 Oak Street, Northern Quarter, Manchester M4 5JD

Est. 2000
Tel: +44 (0)161-8191108
Fax: +44 (0)161-8323416
www.craftanddesign.com
Parking available

Contemporary jewellery for people who dare to be different. I use both precious and non-precious materials to create **art you wear.** This is a different view of jewellery design often using stark machine age materials. 'Throw away your diamond ring and join me outside the jewellery closet'. Mail order available.

Directions: *five minutes on foot from bus interchange and metrolink at Piccadilly Gardens. Go up Oldham Street, second left Hilton Street, second right to Oak St.*

Opening hours: *Mon-Sat, all week in Dec, 10am-5.30pm.*   (23)

DEBBY MOXON AND IAN SIMM, 1 King Street Workshops, Pately Bridge, North Yorkshire HG3 5LE

Est. 1982
Tel: +44 (0)1423-712044
Parking available

Debby Moxon and Ian Simm have created several unique ranges of **contemporary jewellery** using different materials and techniques. The range includes silver with opal and 18ct gold, varying precious and semi-precious stones, silver with imprinted and oxidised patterning and a heat coloured titaniun range. Commissions welcome. Mail order catalogue available.

Directions: *King Street turning is between High Street and Bridge (at low end of High Street). Follow signs for workshop and museum.*

Opening hours: *Mon-Sat 9am-5pm but telephone first.*   (24)

LYNNE GLAZZARD - JEWELLERY DESIGNER, Low Gill Beck Farm, Glaisdale, Whitby, North Yorkshire YO21 2QA

Est. 2000
Tel: +44 (0)17811-528781
Parking available

I work on two scales: small pieces of jewellery and large wall panels (up to a metre diameter). However, I specialise in **jewellery incorporating colour,** usually vitreous enamel or dyed-anodised aluminium. Each piece is individually made and inspired by the local landscape and history. I also make clocks. Mail order available.

Directions: *from Glaisdale, take road marked 'Dale only'. After one mile take left turn and continue for a further mile.*

Opening hours: *open most days, but please make appointment.*   (25)

R.A. DESIGNER JEWELLERY, Studio 5, Manchester Craft Centre, Oak St, Northern Quarter, Manchester M4 5JD

Est. 1986
Tel/fax: +44 (0)161-8317613
Parking available
Wheelchair access
Credit cards

A selection provided by in-house and other leading British designers. See work being carried out at the bench; designers create fine pieces from a range of **precious metals and stones** such as fine or chunky silver, wedding and engagement rings. All to suit you and your budget.

Directions: *five minutes on foot from bus interchange and metrolink at Piccadilly Gardens. Go up Oldham Street, second left Hilton Street, second right to Oak Street.*

Opening hours: *Mon-Sat 10am-5.30pm. Closed first Mon of month.*   (26)

VIN BOOTLE, Rohan Cottage, Back Street, Aldborough, York, North Yorkshire YO51 9EX

Est. 1990
Tel: +44 (0)1423-324108
www.vinbootle.co.uk
Parking available
Credit cards

Vin Bootle is a gold and silversmith designer. Based mainly on Celtic designs, every piece is genuinely handcrafted. Every item is totally individual, especially when the customer is involved in the design. **Celtic weave wedding rings** are Vin's speciality. Mail order is available upon request. Visit website to view examples.

Directions: *one mile from Boroughbridge off the A1(M) junction 48, North Yorkshire.*

Opening hours: *Mon-Sun 9am-6pm.*

Metalwork & Silversmithing

IRON GARDEN, Locking Stoops, Wharles, Preston, Lancashire PR4 3SN

Est. 1998
Tel: +44 (0)1772-690339
Parking available
Wheelchair access

We design and make **ironwork for the garden.** Our range includes potholders, sculptures, birdtables, obelisks, footscrapers, flower supports and flower arrangement stands etc. Prices from £3 to £500. If you are looking for something unusual, original and not mass produced or can't find a supplier, then give us a call. Mail order is available upon request.

Directions: *turn off the A583 to Clifton Village, past the BNFL. At pub junction turn left then first right. 2 miles further then right after M55 bridge.*

Opening hours: *Mon-Sat 10am-5pm.*

MERRIMAN SILVER, 834 Harper's Mill, White Cross, Lancaster, Lancashire LA1 4XQ

Est. 1985
Tel/fax: +44 (0)1524-382323
www.british-silver.com
Parking available
Wheelchair access
Credit cards

Using traditional techniques such as hand raising and forging, to make **tableware,** our style is of clean, flowing lines with minimal decoration and often incorporating wood and horn. We have completed several prestigious commissions and won numerous awards for our designs. The range includes sterling silver tableware and gifts. Mail order.

Directions: *M6 junction 33; follow signs to Lancaster; just before town centre turn right at Lancashire Enterprise/Granade sign. Reception on left.*

Opening hours: *Mon-Fri 8am-4pm.*

Musical Instruments

MILNER AND HALLOWS, 28 The Green, Richmond, North Yorkshire DL10 4RG

Est. 1980
Tel: +44 (0)1748-822284
Parking available
Wheelchair access

A small, friendly and traditional business, we provide a good range of student instruments. Prices range from £95 to £3,000 for **violins, violas and cellos**, as are available. We also have strings, bows and cases and many other accessories. All repairs are carried out on the premises. Mail order available.

Directions: *out of Richmond on the A6108 towards Reeth. 150 yards past Fina petrol station turn left. Shop at bottom of hill on left.*

Opening hours: *Mon-Sat 9am-5pm.*

ROBERT DEEGAN HARPSICHORDS, Tonnage Warehouse, St George's Quay, Lancaster, Lancashire LA1 1RB

Est. 1971
Tel/fax: +44 (0)1524-60186
Parking available
www.deeganharpsichords.com

Robert Deegan has been making harpsichords since 1969 and has a well deserved international reputation for high quality craftmanship and reliability. Robert also makes **harpsichords spinets, virginals and clavicords.** His harpsichords have been chosen for concerts, recordings and broadcasts by notable leading musicians worldwide. Instruments to commission, or occasionally from stock.

Directions: *two blocks from the Maritime Museum on St George's Quay.*
Opening hours: *Mon-Fri 9am-5pm. Sat by arrangement. Prior appointment necessary.*

Pottery & Ceramics

BEE TAYLOR, Clifton House, Park Street, Masham, Near Ripon, North Yorkshire HG4 4HN

Est. 1989
Tel: +44 (0)1765-689349
www.beetaylor.com
Parking available
Wheelchair access

Personalised, high quality tableware using porcelain from different sources, which Bee then decorates with her own designs, or to commission, producing 'Quirky, fun and useful pieces for adults and children.' Her trademark animals are already collectible. Wedding and christening pieces, children's tea services and play sets. Mail order brochure.

Directions: *will be given when appointment is made.*
Opening hours: *by appointment only.*

BENTHAM POTTERY, Oysterber Farm, Burton Road, Low Bentham, Near High Bentham, Via Lancaster, North Yorkshire LA2 7ET.

Est. 1970
Tel: +44 (0)15242-61567
Fax: +44 (0)15242-62885
www.yorkshirenet.co.uk
/benthampottery/index.htm
Parking available
Credit cards

Kathy and her son Lee run their Pottery producing **pots** in the traditional manner, mainly on the wheel and fired in a gas kiln to stoneware temperatures. Visitors welcome to browse and watch the potters in action. Pottery courses from half a day to a week. Holiday cottages are available for rent.

Directions: *Turn off A65 for Bentham. We are betwen Low Bentham and Burton-in-Lonsdale, halfway between B6480 and A65 just inside North Yorkshire.*
Opening hours: *Mon-Sat 9am-5pm.*

THE CAT POTTERY, Moorside, West Burton in Wensleydale, North Yorkshire DL8 4JW

Est. 1982
Tel: +44 (0)1969-663273
www.catpottery.co.uk
Parking available
Wheelchair access
Credit cards

A hidden waterfall, a beautiful village green; idyllic surroundings in which to discover **ceramic Moorside Cats** created by sculptors Sarah and Shirley Nichols, a mother and daughter team. Their own cats have, over the years, been the models for their unique range of ceramic cats. Mail order available.

Directions: *one mile from A684 on B6160 mid way between Leyburn and Hawes, one mile from Aysgarth Falls.*
Opening hours: *Mon-Fri 9am-4.30pm, Sat/Sun 10am-2pm.*

COXWOLD POTTERY, Coxwold, York, Yorkshire YO61 4AA

Est. 1965
Tel: +44 (0)1347-868344
Parking available
Wheelchair access
Credit cards

Coxwold Pottery is a small country workshop and gallery. We produce a wide range of **slip-decorated wares** for use in the home and garden. We also sell garden pots which have been made by other English potters as well as herbs in season. Prices range from £3-£300. Mail order available.

Directions: *Coxwold is twenty miles north of York, four miles south-east of Thirsk, midway along road between A170 and A19.*
Opening hours: *Tue-Fri 2pm-5.30pm all year; Sun 2pm-5.30pm Jul-Aug.*

DIANNE CROSS CERAMICS, King Street Workshops, Pately Bridge, North Yorkshire HG3 5LE

Est. 1981
Tel: +44 (0)1423-712054
Parking available
Wheelchair access
Credit cards

At my workshop in the Yorkshire Dales I make both usable decorated **contemporary stoneware pottery** and also matt glazed pieces. Widely on display, my work is wheelthrown and the functional pots are decorated with abstract designs. The range includes mugs, jugs, teapots, bowls and vases. Mail order available.

Directions: *King Street turning is between High Street and bridge (at low end of High Street). Follow signs for workshop and museum.*

Opening hours: *10am-5pm Mon/Tues, Thurs-Sat. Telephoning first advisable.*

GAIL FOX, Green View, The Green, Stillingfleet, York, Yorkshire Y019 6SH

Est. 1984
Tel: +44 (0)1904-728273
www.gailfox.ceramics.
btinternet.co.uk
Parking available

Hand-built coil pots in red earthenware clay, coloured with slips. Sawdust fired to give striking crazed and marbled patterning. Decorative pots and bowls inspired by the weathered surfaces of ancient pots; also by African and South American pottery. Elegant and minimal work. Not suitable for food use. £40-£180. Mail order available.

Directions: *from York on A19 southbound, take B1222 to Sherburn-in-Elmet. Stillingfleet is 5 miles from junction. Turn right opposite the church.*

Opening hours: *by appointment only.*

INGLETON POTTERY, Bank Botton, Ingleton, North Yorkshire, LA6 3HB

Est. 1969
Tel: +44 (0)15242-41363
www.ingletonpottery.com
Parking available
Wheelchair access

Hand thrown, high fired traditional stoneware using our own clays and glazes. Our extensive range includes **tableware, electric and oil lamps** and terracotta gardenware in season. Occasional 'make your own pot' days are also run. We can always be seen at work in the workshop. Organised workshop visits by appointment.

Directions: *down by the river, under the huge viaduct that crosses the village.*

Opening hours: *Mon-Sun 10am-5pm.*

ISA K-J DENYER, Wighill House, Wighill, Tadcaster, North Yorkshire LS24 8BG

Est. 1989
Tel +44 (0)1937-835632
Fax +44 (0)937-836171

My work is functional domestic **pottery designed for use as well as beauty**. It is reduction fired in stoneware and porcelain using traditional glazes. Life drawing and print making have also led me to experiment with print making techniques onto paper porcelain. My greatest delight is to know that my work is being used every day in many parts of the world. My pottery is an integral part of my life: I have made pots in Montego Bay in Jamaica, London, Virginia, USA and Cape Town South Africa as well as in Yorkshire. Mail order available.

Directions: *from A64 take A659 through Tadcaster and over bridge: left down Wighill Lane and after 2 miles enter the village; 200 yards down from the church.*

Opening hours: *at any time, by appointment only.*

MILL POTTERY, Bridge Mill Workshops, St George's Square, Hebden Bridge, West Yorkshire HX7 8ET

Est. 1989
Tel: +44 (0)1422-844559
Parking available
Credit cards

Jan Burgess makes handthrown domestic stoneware, **pots for eating, drinking and cooking** at reasonable prices. A wide range of my stock is on sale in the showroom. Prices for pots range from £5 to £70. Pots are frequently made on a commission basis. Mail order is available upon request.

Directions: *on the top floor of Bridge Mill in the centre of Hebden Bridge.*

Opening hours: *Mon-Fri 9.30am-5pm, Sat 11am-5pm, Sun closed.*

RUTH KING, Rose Cottage, Main Street, Shipton-by-Beningborough, Yorkshire YO30 1AB

Est. 1979
Tel: +44 (0)1904-470196
www.ruthkingceramics.com
Parking available
Wheelchair access
Credit cards

Over the last 20 years Ruth King has developed a widely displayed, unique style of handbuilt ceramics combining high quality workmanship with the simple elegance of form and decoration to produce individual items of distinction in **saltglazed stoneware.** Visitors welcome to the studio and small showroom by prior appointment. Mail order available.

Directions: *5 miles north of York on A19 to Thirsk in centre of Shipton-by-Beningborough, next door but one to the Dawnat Arms.*

Opening hours: *prior appointment necessary.*　

SOPHIE HAMILTON, The Pottery, High Marshes, Malton, North Yorkshire YO17 6YQ

Est. 1991
Tel/fax: +44 (0)1653-668228
www.sophiehamilton.co.uk
Parking available
Wheelchair access
Credit cards

Established in 1991, we produce an exciting range of **contemporary hand made pots.** The pots are all functional and decorated with rich coloured glazes and patterns. The range includes mugs, jugs, bowls, plates, platters, vases, plant pot holders etc. Prices vary from £5 to £90. Mail order available.

Directions: *turn off A169 between Malton and Pickering and follow signs to High Marshes and Thorton Dale. The pottery is at the first farm on your right.*

Opening hours: *Mon-Fri 10am-6pm, Summer Sun 2pm-5pm.*　42

THE TEAPOTTERY, Leyburn Business Park, Leyburn, North Yorkshire DL8 5QA

Est. 1979
Tel: +44 (0)1969-623839
Fax: +44 (0)1969-624079
www.teapottery.com
Parking available
Wheelchair access
Credit cards

Watch from a visitor walkway with information points, as craftspeople make **unique, collectible teapots** including haywains, beds, lava lamps, microphones, jukeboxes, caravans, radios, cameras, agas, pianos etc. Browse in the teapot shop and take tea from a very unusual teapot in the refreshment area. Sister teapottery in Keswick, Cumbria. Mail order worldwide.

Directions: *follow A684 eastwards (towards A1). Leyburn Business park is half a mile from the town centre. Follow white/brown signs from Market Place.*

Opening hours: *Mon-Sun 9am-5pm.*　43

WASH HOUSE POTTERY, 4 Blackburns Yard, Church Street, Whitby, North Yorkshire YO22 4D5

Est. 1984
Tel: +44 (0)1947-604995

The pottery employs a number of assistants to create a wide range of products including **customised tiles, brightly coloured majolica ware,** house plaques, garden planters and commemorative plates. The pottery's styles and designs reflect images of the Southern Western USA. A mail order service is available upon request.

Directions: *on east side of Whitby off the old part of Church Street. Second yard on right once old Market Square is passed.*

Opening hours: *Mon-Sun 10am-5pm.*　44

THE WENSLEYDALE POTTERY, Market Place, Hawes, North Yorkshire DL8 3QX

Est. 1983
Tel: +44 (0)1969-667594
Parking available
Wheelchair access
Credit cards

We make beautiful and **practical domestic pottery** in stoneware with cream glazes, blue glazes and earth coloured glazes. We are also the home of 'Wensleydale cheese dishes'. All pottery is made on the premises and visitors are welcome to watch us work. Promotional ware available on a commission basis. Mail order available.

Directions: *through the entry beside the rock and gem shop on the south side of the market place. Follow signs.*

Opening hours: *Mon-Sat 10am-5:50pm.*　45

Textiles

ALISON BRAMLEY - TEXTILE DESIGN, Dove Cottage, Riccall Lane, Kelfield, Yorkshire Y019 6RE

Est. 2001
Tel/fax: +44 (0)1757-249295
Parking available

Alison Bramley makes unique, unusual, **brightly coloured, wall hangings** in any size, small or large and made to her own designs. They are made in dopion silk, with frayed edges giving stained glass window effect. Prices range from £25-£2,500 more or less depending on size. Commissions welcome - any size any colours.

Directions: *turn off the A19 (York to Selby) road at Riccall. Follow sign to Kelfield. Second new house coming into the village on the right hand side.*

Opening hours: *usually 10am-5pm. Appointment necessary.*

BUTTERCUP KNITWEAR, Willow Cottage, Rigton Hill, North Rigton, North Yorkshire LS17 ODJ

Est. 1982
Tel/fax: +44 (0)1423-734166
www.buttercup-knitwear.com
Parking available
Wheelchair access

Diana Birtwistle designs and produces a range of hand framed **designer waistcoats, jackets, jumpers and hats** in natural fibres. She uses a gleaming palette of colours, and often embellishes their natural form, to give the garments a distinct and special English 'country' look. Mail order is available upon request.

Directions: *3 miles south of Harrogate off main Bradford Road; into village and past school and pub; left at 14% incline sign onto bumpy track; second house on left.*

Opening hours: *prior appointment necessary.*

CHRISTINE CARRADICE, 18 Craven Terrace, Settle, North Yorkshire BD24 9DB

Est. 1997
Tel: +44 (0)1729-822945
Fax: +44 (0)1729-825202
www.dalesmade.co.uk
Parking on road

Christine Carradice is a silk painter and designer working from her studio in Settle. She produces a wide range of **hand painted pure silk items** including scarves, ties, pictures and cards using her skill with different techniques and beautiful colours. She also creates attractive and very wearable designs. Velvet scarves are also available with *devoré*, embossed or textured motifs.

Directions: *will be given when appointment is made.*

Opening hours: *by appointment only.*

THE DECORATIVE STITCH, Escowbeck House, Crooke O' Lune, Caton, Lancashire LA2 9HS

Est. 1990
Tel: +44 (0)1524-770224
Parking available

As an individual craftsmaker working from home, I specialise in creative **embroidery panels** depicting ruined abbeys and church windows and also hand made embroidered books. For the last eight years I have also taken commissions for bridal embroidery, working in traditional or contemporary stitching. Limited stock for sale.

Directions: *exit 34 M6 then 2 miles along A683 towards Kirkby Lonsdale. First right after Scarthewaite Hotel.*

Opening hours: *prior appointment necessary.*

ELIZABETH COTTAM, Far Barn, Gressingham, Lancaster, Lancashire LA2 8LW

Est. 1992
Tel: +44 (0)15242-21658
Parking available

Elizabeth makes **fleece embroidery wall hangings.** She describes her technique as highly textured painting in wool in glowing shades produced from reliable plant dyes. Prices from £50 to £1000. This unique and easy-to-carry product has gone around the world. I organise workshops in my technique for seven to 15 people.

Directions: *junction 35 off the M6, take B6254 for 3 miles; turn right (signed Gressingham); turn right at Church, then right again. Far Barn is second on left.*

Opening hours: *prior appointment necessary.*

FOCUS ON FELT, Bushby Garth, Hardraw, Hawes, North Yorkshire DL8 3LZ

Est. 2000
Tel: +44 (0)1969-667644
www.focusonfelt.co.uk
Parking available
Wheelchair access
Credit cards

My workshop gallery adjacent to our house holds my range of **contemporary felt artwork.** Evocative images of the surrounding countryside are created within the felt. I also sell and exhibit unique hand made gifts and cards. In addition I run workshops for adults and children (booking is essential). Mail order available.

Directions: *take A684 to Hawes in Wensleydale, then follow signs to Hardraw, which is a mile and a half from Hawes.*

Opening hours: *prior appointment necessary.*

JACQUELINE JAMES - HANDWOVEN RUGS, 4 Rosslyn Street, York, Yorkshire Y030 6LG

Est. 1989
Tel: +44 (0)1904-621381
www.handwovenrugs.co.uk
Parking available

I specialise in making **individually designed, hand-woven rugs and wall hangings** for sale and exhibition. Constructed as durable floor rugs, their decorative quality makes them equally appropriate as wall hangings. I take commissions and am able to design and weave a unique rug to co-ordinate with any setting. Mail order available.

Directions: *will be given when appointment is made.*

Opening hours: *by appointment.*

JOANNE EDDON, Studio 3, Art@Cedarfarm, Cedarfarm, Mawdesley, Lancashire L40 3SY

Est. 1986
Tel: +44 (0)1704-821429
www.j-eddon.freeserve.co.uk
Parking available
Wheelchair access

I have been producing and selling my range of **hand painted silk scarves, ties** and associated products since 1986. My designs are usually in a wide range of rich and vibrant colours and the unusual monoprint technique of hand painting gives a unique painterly style to my work. Mail order available.

Directions: *from A59 between Ormskirk and Southport follow signs to Mawdesley. From Rufford follow brown tourist board signs to 'Cedar Farm Galleries'.*

Opening hours: *Tues-Fri 10am-3pm, Sat/Sun 12-5pm.*

MUSHROOM DESIGNS, 1 Pasture Grove, Leeds, Yorkshire L57 4QP

Est. 1998
Tel: +44 (0)113-2693955
Fax: +44 (0)113-2953469
www.mushroomdesigns.co.uk
Parking available
Credit cards online only

Andrew Jacobs and Michelle Lipman make a range of exciting, original and often highly coloured **hand painted silk** ties, waistcoats, bows, cushions and scarves. Commissions are readily available for any occasion. Please ring for craft fair event details in your area. Order online from our website. Mail order catalogue available upon request.

Directions: *complicated; please telephone.*

Opening hours: *Mon-Sun 9am-9pm.*

PAULA'S ART ON SILK, Wicks Lane, Formby, Merseyside L37 3JE

Est. 1989
Tel: +44 (0)1704-875655
www.paulasartonsilk.co.uk
Parking available
Credit cards

Hand-painted silk using the Gutta technique to produce **defined designs on scarves, ties, cushions,** framed pictures, brooches, keyrings, umbrellas, handbags, lamps, greetings cards etc. Use of different types and weights of silk to produce quality work. Member of West Lancashire Craft Guild and Guild of Silk Painters. Also workshops. Mail order available.

Directions: Formby is between the A565 and the Irish Sea. Detailed directions when appointment made.

Opening hours: by appointment only.

RAW FIBRES, The Old Signal Box, Station Workshops, Robin Hood's Bay, North Yorkshire Y022 4RA

Est. 2001
Tel: +44 (0)1947-880632
www.brigantia.co.uk

Producer/supplier of natural and hand-dyed fibres and yarns for creative embroideries, feltmakers, spinners and students. Own range of handspun yarns, handwoven/knitted textiles - cushions, rugs, garments, handfelted slippers, own Shetland fleeces, mohair, alpaca, silk, linen, cotton, books, equipments, commissions, tuition in handspinning, dyeing and feltmaking. Demonstrations and talks. Mail order available.

Directions: *behind the village hall, adjacent to the carpark.*

Opening hours: *most days. Ring to check opening times.*

RUTH GILBERT, Peel Street Workshops, Marsden, Huddersfield HD7 6BW

Est. 1976
Tel: +44 (0)1484-843879
Parking available

I am a **cloth weaver** with years of experience. Items include curtains and clothing and small articles such as bags, purses, table mats and cushion covers. I also offer a variety of talks and workshop sessions. Style is modern but 'my skill is as old as ancient Egypt and Peru.' Commission work considered.

Directions: *on A62 Huddersfield-Oldham, follow 'village centre' signs. Above 'Pennine Tea Rooms,' door in Brougham Road.*

Opening hours: *Any time by appointment.*

SWALEDALE WOOLLENS LIMITED, Muker, Richmond, North Yorkshire DL11 6QG

Est. 1974
Tel/fax: +44 (0)1748-886251
www.swaledalewoollens.co.uk
Parking available
Some wheelchair access
Credit cards

In the midst of the rolling hills of Swaledale, the shop supplies all types of **woollen clothing from stockings to hats**. Items are made by nearly forty local home workers, aged from 20 to 90 years. Wools on the cone are also sold. Mail order available from illustrated brochure.

Directions: *On B6270, 20 miles west of Richmond, located in centre of village of Muker, next to Farmers Arms Pub.*

Opening hours: *Mon-Sat 10am-5.30pm.*

WENSLEYDALE LONGWOOL SHEEPSHOP, Cross Lanes Farm, Garriston, Leyburn, North Yorkshire DL8 5JU

Est. 1989
Tel/fax: +44 (0)1969-623840
www.wensleydalelongwool sheepshop.co.uk
Parking available
Wheelchair access
Credit cards

Supplies **products made from the wool of the Farm's rare Wensleydale sheep**: 'soft and silky, with a natural sheen, the spun wool produces garments with very special qualities.' Items available include hand-knitting yarns and patterns, sweaters, cardigans and jackets, fleeces and combed tops for spinners and craft enthusiasts. Mail order available.

Directions: *leave Leyburn on A6108 or A684 after 1 mile. Follow signpost to Garriston and Barden. Shop is on next crossroads.*

Opening hours: *Tue-Sat 10am-5pm Apr-Oct; Tue 10am-5pm Nov-Mar. Prior appointment recommended.*

WOOLLIBACKS, Eastgate Cottage, 1a King Street, Whalley, Clitheroe, Lancashire BB7 9SP

Est. 1986
Tel: +44 (0)161-4852551
Fax: +44 (0)161-4828212
Parking available
Wheelchair access

Handspinner, designer and weaver of knitwear, specialising in environmentally friendly yarns. Natural, organically grown rare breed wools, Lancashire-spun unbleached cotton, naturally dyed and recycled fibre yarns handknit into sweaters, shawls, hats and throws. Also handwoven fabrics, calico from Lancashire looms and natural wool travel rugs. Commissions are undertaken. Mail order available.

Directions: *follow signs to ruined Whalley Abbey. From Abbey courtyard through gateway on left. Left again. Eastgate cottage is at end of the lane.*

Opening hours: *all hours but phone to avoid disappointment.*

Toys & Games

LONGBARN ENTERPRISES, Low Mill, Bainbridge, Leyburn, North Yorkshire DL8 3EF

Est. 1970
Tel: +44 (0)1969-650416
Parking available

Christopher Cole makes **dolls' houses and accessories** that are sold all over the world. All are made from MDF and built to a 1:12 scale. The majority of houses are inspired by existing buildings. Most work now is on commission basis for reproductions of customer's houses. Mail order is available.

Directions: *the public toilet on the Village Green is at the top of our drive.*

Opening hours: *prior appointment necessary.*

TOBILANE DESIGNS, Newton Hulme Farm, Whittington, Carnforth, Lancashire LA6 2NZ

Est. 1985
Tel/fax: +44 (0)15242-72662
www.commander.clara.
net/tobilane:htm
Parking available
Credit cards

We are specialist makers of **model farms and castles.** All are made from MDF and range in price from £65 to £95. Many farms are made on a commission basis as reproductions of customers' farms and include outbuildings. We also restore old toys such as rocking horses and teddy bears. Mail order available.

Directions: *3 miles south of Kirkby Lonsdale on the B6254 near Whittington.*

Opening hours: *Mon-Sat 10am-5pm, Sun 11am-4pm.*

Woodturning & Furniture

A + A STUDIO/WORKSHOP, rear of 19/21 Mayfield Grove, Harrogate, North Yorkshire HG1 5HD

Est. 1992
Tel: +44 (0)1423-880762
Parking available

Adrian Lister enjoys **carving frames and heads** and other small items. His frames show adapted and modified geometric patterns inspired by different cultures of the world: the South Pacific, Africa, the Americas, the Orient; ancient, primitive and modern. His heads are sometimes quirky, sometimes realistic, mostly tactile objects. Mail order available.

Directions: *five minutes' walk from town centre and bus/train stations. In back road between Franklin Road and Mayfield Grove.*

Opening hours: *by appointment.*

ACORN INDUSTRIES, Brandsby, York YO61 4RG

Est. 1958
Tel: +44 (0)1347-888217
Fax: +44 (0)1347-888382
www.acornindustries.co.uk
Parking available

Alan Grainger claims to make any kind of **domestic furniture** and has specialised in making **traditional oak furniture** for over forty years. Most work is on commission basis working closely with customers both at the design and production stages. Mail order is available and much work is exported to the USA.

Directions: *on the B1363 York to Helmsley Road in the middle of Brandsby village.*

Opening hours: *Mon-Fri 8am-5pm, Sat 9am-12.30pm.*

ALBERT JEFFRAY, Sessay, Thirsk, North Yorkshire YO7 3BE

Est. 1966
Tel/fax: +44 (0)1845-501323
Parking available

The business started in 1966 using a carved eagle as a trade mark. We make **dining, occasional and ecclesiastical furniture** which is produced along with individual carvings and gifts in various woods, English oak being a speciality. Orders are taken for stock sizes or from customers' own designs.

Directions: *at the north end of the village next to the post box. The village is 2 miles from the A19 and 6 miles from the A1(M) junction 49.*

Opening hours: *Mon-Fri 8.30am-5pm.*

BENJAMIN THOMAS WOODWORK, 2 Chapel Street, Settle, North Yorkshire BD24 9HS

Est. 1985
Tel: +44 (0)1729-822760
www.btwoodwork.co.uk
Parking available
Credit cards

Individual woodturnings and one-off bespoke items of furniture made from English hardwoods or reclaimed pine (antique effect). In our showroom we also sell other local crafts including glassware (ornamental, handpainted tumblers and glasses etc). Wooden items include candle holders, lamps, clocks, vases, candlesticks and platters. Mail order available.

Directions: *adjacent the police station in Settle.*

Opening hours: *closed Sun and Mon.*

BOB HUNTER - WREN CABINET MAKERS, Pear tree House, Thirlby, Thirsk, North Yorkshire YO7 2DJ

Est. 1980
Tel: +44 (0)1845-597453
Limited roadside parking

Small family business where, with the exception of a few basic machines, all the work is done by hand, incorporating a lot of **traditional hand carving.** Visitors welcome to our small showroom where we have a range of oak furniture and gifts, all bearing our trademark - a small carved wren. Delivery Service.

Directions: *one mile from Sutton-under-Whitestonecliffe which is on the A170 Thirsk-Scarborough road (4 miles from Thirsk).*

Opening hours: *Mon-Fri 9am-5pm; Sat 9am-12pm; other times by appointment.*

CASEMENTS THE CABINET MAKERS, Slack Lane, Pendlebury, Greater Manchester M27 8QU

Est. 1965
Tel: +44 (0)161-7941610
Parking available
Wheelchair access

A cabinet maker with nearly 50 years of experience, I specialise in **one-off pieces and copies.** There is a showroom on site where a range of my work is always on display. Gold tooled leathers are always supplied and fitted. Antique restoration is also carried out on the premises.

Directions: *off the A666 at Pendlebury.*

Opening hours: *Mon-Fri 8am-6pm, Sat 8am-1pm.*

DALESBREAD CONTEMPORARY FURNITURE, The Smithy, Austwick, Near Lancaster, Lancashire LA2 8BA

Est. 1993
Tel/fax: +44 (0)15242-51798
www.dalesbred.co.uk
Parking available
Wheelchair access

Our range of contemporary furniture covers **everything from a dining suite to a breadboard.** We specialise in incorporating beautiful native burrs. Each piece is numbered, recorded and inlaid with the Dalesbred ram's head. All pieces are unique and an investment for the future. We also upholster, and sell ironwork.

Directions: *in the centre of Austwick village on the village green opposite the pub.*

Opening hours: *Mon-Fri 8am-6pm.*

DAVID A WARDINGLEY, Corner Croft, Staveley, Knaresborough, North Yorkshire HG6 9JY

Est. 1981
Tel: +44 (0)1423-340432
Parking available

A professional turner, David specialises in making **vessels, bowls and hollow forms,** all from English timbers and often using natural irregularities found in the wood. David is keen to work with the environment. One of his main sources of wood is fallen timber. Prices range from £6-£600. Commission work undertaken.

Directions: *Staveley is off the A6055, midway between Knaresborough and Aldborough. In village 150 yards from the green on Arkendale Road.*

Opening hours: *All hours every day. Prior appointment necessary.*

DESIGN IN WOOD, The Old Coach House, Chapel Street, Thirsk, North Yorkshire YO7 1LU

Est. 1993
Tel: +44 (0)1845-525010
Fax: +44 (0)1845-523092
www.designinwood.co.uk
Parking available
W/chairs to workshop only
Credit cards

Design in Wood makes imaginatively designed high quality **contemporary furniture and architectural joinery.** Each piece, from a fitted kitchen to a jewellery box, is specially commissioned and tailored to the requirements of the customer and situation. Particular care is taken over individual design and use of materials, primarily temperate hardwoods.

Directions: *behind the market place, adjacent to the swimming pool in the centre of Thirsk.*

Opening hours: *Mon-Fri 8.30am-5.30pm or by appointment.*

ENGLISH HARDWOOD FURNITURE, The Workshop, Mill Yard, Catton Lane, Topcliffe, Thirsk, North Yorkshire YO7 3RZ

Est. 1985
Tel/fax +44 (0)1845-578172
www.furniture-designers.co.uk
Parking available
Wheelchair access

All visitors are welcome at our showroom on the banks of the river Swale just outside Topcliffe. Paul Bulmer works in all the English hardwoods and specialises in tables and chairs. Table styles include: refectory, farmhouse, extending, circular, oval, drop leaf etc. Chairs include Windsor, ladder-back, high-back, contemporary. Nigel Dixon works mainly in native oak producing all types of furniture in a variety of contemporary and traditional designs. One-off commissions are a speciality; **each piece is truly unique and built to last centuries.** Nigel signs his work with a woodworm motif. Products available by mail order from the above address.

Directions: *Topcliffe Village is 3 miles from the A1M, just off the A168; in Topcliffe take the A167: after 200 yards see sign at start of Catton Lane.*

Opening hours: *10am-5pm, Mon-Sat.*

HENKI FURNITURE BY DESIGN, Tower Hill, Grewelthorpe, Ripon, North Yorkshire HG4 3DS

Est. 1998
Tel +44 (0)1765-630331
Fax +44 (0)1423-528079
www.henki.co.uk
Parking available

Henki Furniture by design was set up three years ago by Niall Hawkridge to meet the needs of discerning clients wanting **hardwood furniture for today's lifestyle** but made using traditional techniques. Using modern designs Henki's team of craftsmen can design and make you antiques of the future. As well as specialising in free-standing furniture, i.e. dining suites, Henki also design and build outstanding one-off kitchens and bedrooms. Our prices range from £150 to £20,000. The workshop is based in the country, but Henki will also be opening a shop/showroom in Harrogate early in Spring 2002: also see the Website.

Directions: *from Ripon take the Kirby Malzeard/Grewelthorpe road for 6 miles: 1 mile before Grewelthorpe turn right on Mickley Road, then 100 yards on the right.*

Opening hours: *8am-5pm, Mon-Sat.*

OAK AND COUNTRY FURNITURE, 9 King Street Workshops, King Street, Pately Bridge, North Yorkshire HG3 5LE

Est. 1993
Tel: +44 (0)1423-712877
Parking available
Wheelchair access
Credit cards

I specialise in making **bespoke furniture in British hardwoods** such as oak and ash. Each piece is carefully crafted to suit your individual requirements, in natural, polished or painted finish. I can also supply kitchen cabinets and fitted furniture. Furniture can be viewed at the workshop.

Directions: *King Street turning is between High Street and Bridge (at low end of High Street). Follow signs for workshop and museum.*

Opening hours: *Mon-Sat 10am-5pm.*

PHILIP BASTOW CABINET MAKER, Reeth Dales Centre, Silver Street, Reeth, North Yorkshire DL11 6SP

Est. 1982
Tel/fax: +44 (0)1748-884555
Parking available
Wheelchair access
Credit cards

Philip Bastow specialises in the design and manufacture of **individual furniture commissions using mainly oak, ash, elm and sycamore.** Browse around his furniture display where you will see examples of complete pieces and small wooden gifts including book ends, bud vases, chopping boards, stools, lamps, decanter trays etc. Mail order available.

Directions: *follow Gunnerside road out of Reeth; the workshop is the last turnoff on the right and is signposted.*

Opening hours: *Mon-Sat 9am-5pm; Sun and evenings by appointment.*

SIMON ANDREW CABINET MAKER, 30A Firby Road, Gallowfields Trading Estate, Richmond, North Yorkshire DL10 4ST
Est. 1990
Tel: +44 (0)1748-826706
Parking available

Specialising in **bespoke furniture,** Simon works in a variety of British, European and North American timbers. Each piece is designed and crafted to reflect the natural beauty of the wood. Commissions are welcome for free standing or fitted furniture with a traditional or contemporary style. Ecclesiastical work is also undertaken.

Directions: *A1608 from A1 to Richmond. At traffic lights turn right for Gallowfields Trading Estate. Second left onto Green Howards Street then second left to Firby Road.*

Opening hours: *prior appointment necessary.* **76**

Other Makers

ARTS UNLIMITED, Studio 5, Art@Cedarfarm, Cedarfarm, Back Lane, Mawdesley, West Lancashire L40 3SY
Est. 1996
Tel: +44 (0)1772-734636
www.cedarfarm.net
Parking available
Wheelchair access

Arts Unlimited is based at the Fizzy Pink Studios at Cedar Farm. Julie and Sharon, both trained artists, are dedicated to the production of refreshing and original **hand made cards and art work** using a varied range of materials, from wire and painted silk to pressed flowers and tin cans.

Directions: *from A59 between Ormskirk and Southport follow signs to Mawdesley. From Rufford follow brown tourist board signs to 'Cedar Farm Galleries'.*

Opening hours: *Tues-Sun 10am-5pm.* **77**

BIJOUX/BALME STUDIOS, Bentham Lodge, High Bentham, near Lancaster, Lancashire LA2 7LQ.
Est. 1991
Tel/fax: +44 (0)15242-61404
www.dalesmade.co.uk
Ample parking

Juliet Allen of Bijoux, produces **limited edition prints from hand-carved blocks**. Also greetings cards for all occasions (including Christmas) featuring her own 100% recycled, hand made paper. Simon Balme of Balme studios makes limited edition prints from his paintings and can work to commission. Also some watercolours for sale. Mail order available.

Directions: *postal address Lancaster, Lancashire, but situated in North Yorkshire. Details given when appointment made (Balme Studios only).*

Opening hours: *Balme studios by appointment only. Bijoux not open to public.* **78**

CHARLES SMITH STONECARVER, The Old Police House, Main Street, Great Ouseburn, York YO26 9RQ
Est. 1983
Tel: +44 (0)1423-330799
Fax: +44 (0)1423-339084
Parking available
Wheelchair access

Charles Smith is a sculptor of letters, **stonecarver** and designer. Sculptures are regularly commissioned as either free-standing pieces or as coats-of-arms, inscriptions etc for public and private buildings. All work is in new stone and on a commission basis. Photographs of Charles' work are available from the Craft Council.

Directions: *2 miles off the B6265 on the Boroughbridge to Green Hammerton Road.*

Opening hours: *Mon-Fri 9am-6pm, appointment preferable.* **79**

D.H. TAXIDERMY, Redlands, Reid Terrace, Guisborough, Cleveland, Yorkshire TS14 6EB
Est. 1998
Tel/fax: +44 (0)1287-630940
Parking available
Credit cards

Dave Hornbrook, a Department of Environment Registered Taxidermist, produces extremely high standard **bird and mammal taxidermy.** He is qualified and accredited by the Guild of Taxidermists (only 20 members in the UK). Various specimens are always on display, mostly in glass cases with impressive scenery. Commission work welcome. Mail order available.

Directions: *in town centre behind the High Street.*

Opening hours: *anytime day or evening.* **80**

HANNAH'S HAND MADE CARDS, Northlights Art Space, Melbourne St, Hebden Bridge, West Yorkshire HX7 6AS

Est. 2000
Tel: +44 (0)1422-843519
www.hannahscards.f2s.com
Limited parking

Northlights Artspace is a shared studio with 17 working artists and craftspeople situated in the picturesque mill town of Hebden Bridge. I have been working here for a year making **handmade cards** using intricate papercut designs. I also make personalised cards of your own house using the same techniques. Mail order available.

Directions: *up Hangingroyd Road and take second left. Go to large mill and through green doors to top of the stairs.*

Opening hours: *Mon-Fri 9:15am-3pm.*

KING WILLIAM FIREPLACES, King William IV Hotel, Aketon Road, Cutsyke, Castleford, West Yorkshire WF10 5HJ

Est. 1989
Tel: +44 (0)1977-511611
Fax: +44 (0)1977-511797
Ample on-site parking

Carl Clayton has a workshop and showroom where he produces **Adam-style fire surrounds.** Can also work to customer's own designs and colour match to existing furniture and interior decoration etc. There is a huge selection of fire grates, marble, tiles and cast iron inserts to choose from to complement the fire surround.

Directions: *from M62 eastbound, junction 31. Follow signs for Castleford. After one and a quarter miles right at roundabout. On the left at traffic lights.*

Opening hours: *Mon-Sat 10am-5pm.*

MARTYNE RAVEN (STARRY EYES DESIGNS), 14 Doefield Avenue, Ellenbrook, Worsley, Manchester M28 7GT

Est. 1992
Tel/fax: +44 (0)161-703 8651
www. starryeyes.co.uk
Parking available
Wheelchair access

I make and sell **framed textiles** produced using fabric paint and hand embroidery. Prices start at £60 including frame. I also make a range of **silver jewellery.** Popular fantasy designs include angel pendants and brooches in the shape of flying cats. Also a range of hand made cards and prints. Mail order available.

Directions: *given when appointment is arranged.*

Opening hours: *by appointment only.*

MOSAIC WORK, Manchester Craft and Design Centre 17 Oak Street, Northern Quarter, Manchester M4 5JD

Est. 1996
Tel: +44 (0)161-2240794
Fax: +44 (0)161-8323416
Parking available
Wheelchair access
Credit cards

I use traditional methods to make **modern mosaics.** I cut and combine various materials; tesserae, Venetian smalti, stained glass, ceramics and stone or marble. I also use gold and silver leaf to make my own mosaics. I work mainly on a commission basis. Mail order is available upon request.

Directions: *five minutes on foot from bus interchange and metrolink at Piccadilly Gardens. Go up Oldham Street, second left into Hilton Street, second right to Oak Street.*

Opening hours: *Mon-Sat 10am-5.30pm.*

MOORWAX CANDLE WORKSHOP, Wood View, Hutton-le-Hole, Near Kirkbymoorside, North Yorkshire YO62 6UA

Est. 1995
Tel: +44 (0)1751-417233
Fax: +44 (0)1751-417233
www.yell.com
Short-term parking available
Credit cards

Chris has been making high quality, long-burning candles since 1972. He aims to raise the level of **candlemaking to an art form** and is influenced by modern ceramic glazes and natural colours and textures. Commissions and special orders undertaken (churches, hotels, special candles, etc.). Prices range from £2.95-£45. Mail order available.

Directions: *2.5 miles north of the A170 Thirsk-Scarborough road. The workshop is situated at the southern end of the village of Hutton-le-Hole.*

Opening hours: *Apr-Dec, Tue-Sun 11am/5pm; by appointment at other times.*

PUTTI, Studio 1 and 2, Manchester Craft and Design Centre, 17 Oak Street, Manchester M4 5JD

Est. 1989
Tel: +44 (0)161-8390100
www.putti.co.uk
Parking available
Wheelchair access
Credit cards

Putti is a sculpture studio at Manchester Craft and Design Centre. As well as the popular and quirky **concrete animals**, we are also involved in **architectural restoration**, having worked on the Natural History Museum and the Savoy. We also undertake **portrait modelling.** Mail order is available upon request.

Directions: *five minutes on foot from bus interchange and metrolink at Piccadilly Gardens. Go up Oldham Street, second left Hilton Street, second right to Oak Street.*

Opening hours: *Mon-Sat 10am-5.30pm.*

TRACEY BIRCHWOOD, Manchester Craft and Design Centre, 17 Oak St, Northern Quarter, Manchester M4 5JD

Est. 1996
Tel: +44 (0)161-8327476
Fax: +44 (0)161-8323416
Parking available
Credit cards

Tracey designs, produces and sells **contemporary ceramics and jewellery.** Her ceramics are unique and glazed in bright primary colours. Prices range from £12-£500. Other craft/design work is on sale in the Craft Centre, including metalwork, wood, textiles, glass and cards. Café and take-away with extensive menu. Mail order available.

Directions: *Manchester city centre. From Picadilly Gardens go down Oldham Street, take second left down Hilton Street, second right down Oak Street.*

Opening hours: *Mon-Sat 10am-5.30pm; Sun 11am-5pm Dec.*

WHITE ROSE CANDLES, Wensley Hill, Wensley, Leyburn, North Yorkshire DL8 4HR

Est. 1971
Tel/fax: +44 (0)1969-623544
Parking available
Wheelchair access
Credit cards

Our small family business, run from an 18th century watermill has a reputation for high quality longburning candles in a wide range of colours, shapes, sizes and perfumes. We **specialise in candles for churches and weddings**; also a comprehensive range of candle-holders and flower-pots. Prices from £1. Mail order available.

Directions: *in Wensley, one and a half miles from Leyburn on the A684 to Hawes, next to the Three Horseshoes pub.*

Opening hours: *Mon/Tues/Thurs/Fri/Sun 10am-5pm.*

The North

County Durham, Cumbria, Northumberland

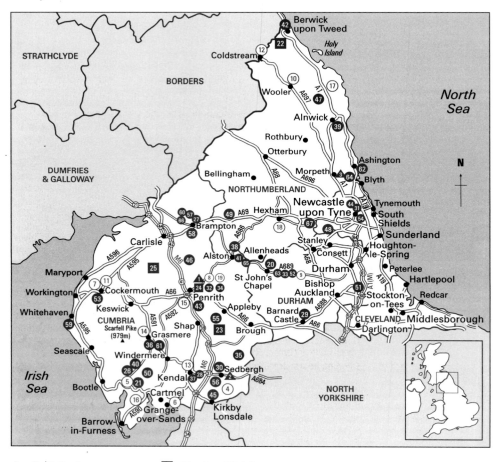

▲ Craft Centres   ■ Food and Drink
○ Shops and Galleries   ● Makers' Workshops

Cumbria's Lake District, is one of Britain's tourist hotspots, and now home to a growing number of contemporary craft makers and craft galleries.

Northumberland and Durham are both justly proud of their pasts. County Durham has 're-created' history at Beamish open air museum (near Chester-le-Street) by moving buildings there from around the county. Crafts have traditionally played a part in home-life where women carried out lace-making and quilting; both crafts are still practised by enthusiasts and demonstrated at the Museum.

Northumberland of the wild and craggy landscapes is associated with mysticism, spirituality and pipe playing and making. Northumbrian pipes have their own museum in Morpeth. More practical are crafts including kipper making (thought to be a Northumbrian invention) around Craster and Seahouses, and the weaving of Northumberland tweed.

Craft Centres

BROUGHAM HALL CRAFT CENTRE, Brougham Hall, Penrith, Cumbria CA10 2DE

Est. 1987
Tel/fax: +44 (0)1768-868184
Parking available
Wheelchair access
Credit cards

Brougham Hall, built in the fifteenth century, is England's largest country house restoration project. It has a craft centre, two museums and a Cromwellian chapel. For sale are French clothing, smoked foods, chocolates, carved stone, soft furnishings, art metalwork and paintings. Mail order for some goods is available.

Directions: *one mile south of Penrith just off the A6. Brougham Hall is signposted 500 yards south of Eamont Bridge.*

Opening hours: *Mon-Sun 9am-dusk.*

DENT CRAFTS CENTRE, Helmside, Dent, Cumbria LA10 5SY

Est. 1979
Tel: +44 (0)1539-625400
www.dentcraftcentre.co.uk
Parking available
Some wheelchair access
Credit cards

Converted from an eighteenth century hay barn, the Centre provides an appropriate setting for a splendid display of local craftwork and watercolours, hand made cards, preserves and many other unusual gifts of high quality. Visitors can also enjoy fresh, homebaked food in a delightful tearoom adorned with tools of yesteryear.

Directions: *on the main road between Sedbergh and Dent, eight miles from exit 37 of the M6.*

Opening hours: *Weds-Mon 10.30am-5.30pm.*

NORTHUMBRIA CRAFT CENTRE, The Chantry, Bridge Street, Morpeth, Northumberland NE6 11PD

Est. 1985
Tel: +44 (0)1670-511323
Fax: +44 (0)1670-511326
www.castlemorpeth.gov.uk
Parking at nearby car park
Wheelchair access
Credit cards

Northumbria is home to a fine tradition of craftwork. The Northumbria Craft Centre sells over 65 hand made regional crafts made by some of the Northumbrian craftsmen who display their unique and reasonably priced work. Most days will also see a number of craftspeople demonstrating their skills. Mail order available.

Directions: *take A197 off A1 north of Newcastle. Cross River Wansbeck and turn left. See Chantry building immediately on left.*

Opening hours: *Mon-Sat 10am-5pm, in summer also Sun 11am-5pm.*

Craft Shops

BEST CELLARS, The Hill Studio, Dent, Sedbergh, Cumbria LA105 5QL

Est. 1998
Tel: +44 (0)1539-625354
Parking available

The shop is located in the beautiful Dales village of Dent. I stock hand made British crafts made using all mediums. Many of these interesting and unusual pieces are made in the local area. Work on show includes jewellery, pottery, textiles, metal and glass. I provide a very different range of goods.

Directions: *take the first left after Dent Post Office.*

Opening hours: *10.30am-5.30pm Mon-Sat. Summer 7 days a week. During winter it is advisable to tel first.*

(4)

THE BROUGHTON CRAFT SHOP/LAKESLATE, Griffin Street, Broughton-in-Furness, Cumbria LA20 6HH

Est. 1990
Tel: +44 (0)1229-716413
Parking available
Wheelchair access
Credit cards

A shop and studio showing a wide range of quality craftwork. The owner can also be seen making his distinctive and unique range of polished slate and silver jewellery inspired by the beautiful colours and patterns of Lake District slates. Mail order is available upon request. Ceramics, glass and cards also availble.

Directions: *in the centre of Broughton-in-Furness, 100 yards from the square.*

Opening hours: *Tues-Sat 9.30am-5.30pm.*

(5)

CUMBRIA CRAFT GUILD, Anyang, Fernleigh Road, Grange-Over-Sands, Cumbria LA11 7HP

Est. 1989
Tel: +44 (0)1539-533957
Parking available
Wheelchair access

Cumbria Craft Guild exhibits various Cumbrian craftwork, including woodwork, ceramics, textiles, and metalwork - wrought iron and jewellery. The stunning scenery of the Lake District, coasts and the Borders provide inspiration for members. A full list of members is available on application. Our annual exhibition is held at different venues. Mail order available.

Directions: *junction 41 of M6 to Penrith East/Brough/Appleby. Left to town centre at next roundabout. Park in Soughend Road car park.*

Opening hours: *Tues-Sun 10am-4pm.*

(6)

COCKERMOUTH CRAFT AND GIFT CENTRE, Crown Street, Cockermouth, Cumbria CA13 OEH

Est. 1995
Tel: +44 (0)1900-824662
Parking available
Wheelchair access
Credit cards

3,000 square feet of crafts in one of Cumbria's largest craft outlets. Sells a very wide range of items including papier-mâché, knitwear, stained glass, woodturned bowls, carved mirror frames and tables, crackle glaze pots, jewellery, hand made cards, painted cupboards, doughcraft. Also crafts by the disabled, books, imported giftware. Coffee shop.

Directions: *by mini-roundabout at the end of main street, opposite Wordsworth House (Wordsworth birthplace, National Trust).*

Opening hours: *Mon-Sun 9.30-5pm.*

(7)

EDEN CRAFT GALLERY, St Andrew's Churchyard, Penrith, Cumbria CA11 7YE

Est. 1982
Tel: +44 (0)1768-867955
Fax: +44 (0)1768-863518
www.btinternet.com/~viv.marston
Parking available
Wheelchairs ground floor
Credit cards

We stock a wide range of locally produced crafts including Lilliput Lane Cottages which are made in Penrith. We also have a full picture framing service which includes all needlework. Come and visit the shop and enjoy a cup of coffee upstairs.

Mail order is available for all our goods.

Directions: *in St Andrew's Churchyard at the centre of Penrith by the monument clock (go between Natwest and Barclays banks).*

Opening hours: *Mon-Sat 9am-5pm. Closed Weds during winter.*

(8)

FROSTERLEY CRAFTS, Roseli Cottage, 68 Front Street, Frosterley, Weardale, Co Durham DL13 2QS

Est. 1990
Tel: +44 (0)1388-526488
Parking available
Wheelchair access

We sell a wide range of quality hand made goods including candles, painted glass, jewellery, children's clothing, clippiemats, wrought iron and dolls' houses. We will also make specialised gifts and personalised products. There are regular demonstrations, tea rooms and an antiques corner. Mail order is available upon request.

Directions: *head west out of Durham on the A690 joining the A689. Frosterley is situated between Wolsingham and Stanhope Journey.*

Opening hours: *Mon-Fri 1.30pm-5.30pm.*

THE POTTERY STUDIO AND SHOP, 56 High Street, Wooler, Northumberland NE71 6BG

Est. 1985
Tel +44 (0)1668-281623
www.potterwaller.co.uk
Parking available
Wheelchair access

Vanessa Waller is a **specialist in Mocha Ware decoration;** she is one of only three professional Mocha artists in the UK. The decoration forms tree-like dendritic patterns and is landscaped. Her products include hand thrown pots for the home and garden, a sheep range, castles, inlaid glass, seahorses and butterflies, animal toast racks and note holders, sculptured birds - puffin etc., clocks, and commemorative plates. The tableware is both dishwasher and microwave safe. Demonstrations can be arranged by appointment. Special commissions are most welcome. Vanessa's work is also available from Paxton House, the Hirsel Gallery, the Coquetdale Gallery and elsewhere.

Directions: *Wooler is located on B697 from A1 between Newcastle-upon-Tyne and the Borders.* **Open:** *April-Oct 10am-5pm Mon-Sat: Nov-Mar 10am-4pm Tues-Sat. Closed Thurs pm.*

SKYLARK STUDIO, 9 South Street, Cockermouth, Cumbria CA13 9QF

Est. 1994
Tel: +44 (0)1900-823521
www.skylarkstudio.co.uk
Parking 200 yards away in town car park
Wheelchair access
Credit cards

Established in 1994, Skylark Studio is the gallery of artist Rolf Parker, whose etchings and watercolours depict the local landscape and streetscape. The shop also stocks a large range of fashion jewellery made on the premises, as well as a collection of British crafts which offer value for money. Mail order available.

Directions: *From main street in Cockermouth, walk up Station Street and take first left into South Street at the Tithe Barn pub.*

Opening hours: *Tues-Sat 9am-5pm. In Feb advisable to telephone first.*

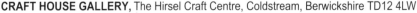

Galleries

CRAFT HOUSE GALLERY, The Hirsel Craft Centre, Coldstream, Berwickshire TD12 4LW

Est. 1984
Tel/fax: +44 (0)1890-882965
Parking available
Wheelchair access
Credit cards

Wilma Bannink's well-established gallery is surrounded by a beautiful woodland park and is filled with a range of crafts; excellent as gifts: jewellery, paintings, glass, wood sculptures and silk-covered boxes and books, furniture, fire irons and more, all hand made and mostly by local craftspeople. Adjacent tea-rooms. Mail order available.

Directions: *turn right just north of Coldstream off the A697 Newcastle to Edinburgh Road, signposted Hirsel Country Park.*

Opening hours: *Mon-Sun 10.30am-5pm, all year.*

GREEN DOOR STUDIOS, 112 Highgate, Kendal, Cumbria LA9 4HE.

Est. 1995
Tel: +44 (0)1539-721147
Parking available

Green Door Studios is an artists' and craftspeople's co-operative. Members of the studio can exhibit as a group whilst also getting support from fellow artists, some of whom are very well known locally and nationally. Paintings, textiles, ceramics and sculpture are exhibited and can be purchased from individual makers.

Directions: *park at the Brewery Arts Centre in Highgate, walk up Highgate 100 yards, Studio entrance is above a decorating shop.*

Opening hours: *Mon-Sun 9am-7pm. Prior appointment necessary.*

THE HEATON COOPER STUDIO LTD, The Studio, Grasmere, Cumbria LA22 9SX

Est. 1939
Tel: +44 (0)15394-35280
Fax: +44 (0)15394-35797
www.heatoncooper.co.uk
Parking available
Wheelchair access
Credit cards

The gallery houses exhibitions of paintings, prints, sculpture and cards of four generations of the Heaton Cooper family, from the watercolours of Alfred (1863-1929) and William (1903-1995) to the present day members. Artists' materials, including specialist drawing and painting materials and paper are for sale. Mail order available.

Directions: *in the centre of Grasmere village opposite the village green.*

Opening hours: *Easter-Oct Mon-Sat 9am-6pm, winter Mon-Sat 9am-5pm, Sun all year 12pm-5pm.*

LABURNUM CERAMICS GALLERY, Yanwath, near Penrith, Cumbria CA10 2LF

Est. 1995
Tel: +44 (0)1768-864842
www.laburnumceramics.co.uk
Parking available
Wheelchair access
Credit cards

This is a small friendly gallery specialising in high quality contemporary studio ceramics and glass from 100 leading artists and craftsmen from Cumbria, the rest of the UK and Europe. There are exciting exhibitions as well as a peaceful sculpture garden adjoining the owner's seventeenth century cottage. Prices from £2-£1000.

Directions: *junction 40 M6; A66 east 1 mile. Next roundabout: take A6 south; right onto B5320. After 1 mile; right to Yanwath, Gate Inn; bear right, then 100 yards.*

Opening hours: *Tues-Sat and bank holidays 10am-4.30pm.*

MOONSHADOW GALLERY AND CAFE, 46 Market St, Ulverston, Cumbria LA12 7LS

Est. 1998
Tel: +44 (0)1229-588828
Parking available
Wheelchair access
Credit cards

Moonshadow Gallery is arranged on three floors of a restored Georgian listed building. The Gallery presents high quality and innovative craft of all types from local and nationally renowned makers. The Gallery Café serves a varied menu throughout the day - homemade soup, light meals, speciality coffees, baked goods, etc. Mail order available.

Directions: *centre of town at the lower end of Market St; two minutes from either of the two main car parks.*

Opening hours: *Tues-Sat 10am-5pm.*

NORSELANDS GALLERY, The Old School, Warenford, Belford, Northumberland NE70 7HY

Est. 1980
Tel: +44 (0)1668-213465
Fax: +44 (0)1668-219056
www.norselands.co.uk
Parking available
Wheelchair access
Credit cards

Norselands Gallery is home to Studio Two where Veronica Rawlinson handcrafts the famous 'faceless ladies' in stoneware. For over twenty years the gallery has specialised in quality British crafts, watercolours and prints with prices ranging from £20 to £200. Light refreshments are available from Easter through to September. Mail order available.

Directions: *right off A1 10 miles north of Alnwick for Warenford. Brown tourist signs for Craft Gallery and Workshop.*

Opening hours: *Mon-Sun 9am-5pm.*

THE PINFOLD, 10 Market Street, Hexham, Northumberland NE46 3NU

Est. 1982
Tel/fax: +44 (0)1434-607621
Parking available
W/chair access to ground floor
Credit cards

Exhibiting locally made pottery and other work by local artists, we are a design-led gift shop also stocking furniture and furnishings which are mainly made by British small craft makers placing an accent on quality and originality. The work of several local artists is also on display.

Directions: *Market Street is directly off the main Market Square.*

Opening hours: *Mon-Sat 10.30am-5pm, closed Thurs.*

THE RUHM GALLERY AND CAFE, 15 Victoria Road, Penrith, Cumbria, CA11 8HN

Est. 2000
Tel: +44 (0)1768-867453
Fax: +44 (0)1678-866621
www.ruhm.co.uk
Parking available
Wheelchair access
Credit cards

The Ruhm Gallery opened in response to approaches from local artists and craftspeople. It provides them with exhibition space within a gallery that draws attention for its quality and variety. We show the work of many local and national ceramic artists, sculptors, glass-makers, painters and print-makers. Exhibitions change every six-eight weeks.

Directions: *M6 junction 40. Take A66 towards Brough. At next roundabout take first left into Penrith. half a mile down on left-hand of side street. Car park at rear.*

Opening hours: *Mon-Sat 9am-6pm; Sun 10am-4pm.* ⑲

Baskets & Wickerwork

CURLEW BASKETS, The Vicarage, Burnfoot, St John's Chapel, Upper Weardale, Co Durham DL13 1QH

Est. 1988
Tel: +44 (0)1388-537822
Parking available
Wheelchair access

I weave **rustic frame baskets** from willow and rush which are traditional to the old gardening, agricultural and fishing industries. They all have English hardwoods frames such as beech and oak and are coracle shaped. Log, shopping and gardening baskets are also for sale. Mail order is available upon request.

Directions: *turn right off the Dale Road by the village church and we are just down the lane.*

Opening hours: *daytime seven days a week.* ⑳

OWEN JONES, Spout Meadow. High Nibthwaite, Ulverston, Cumbria LA12 8DF

Est. 1988
Tel: +44 (0)1229-885664
Parking available
Wheelchair access

Owen is a maker of **oak swill baskets** which are traditional in the Lake District and were used on the farm, in industry and wherever a tough durable basket was needed. They are made by weaving thin strips of coppiced oak around an oval hazel rim. Prices from £30-£50. Mail order available.

Directions: *one of ten houses in High Nibthwaite at the southern end of Coniston Water.*

Opening hours: *Open any time by appointment.* ㉑

Food & Drink

CHAIN BRIDGE HONEY FARM, Horncliffe, Berwick-on-Tweed, Northumberland TD15 2XT

Est. 1966
Tel: +44 (0)1289-386362
Fax: +44 (0)1289-386763
www.chainbridgehoney.co.uk
Parking available
Wheelchair access

The Honey Farm and Visitor Centre own 1500 beehives in the surrounding countryside. The main crop is heather honey from the moors and the main speciality is comb honey. Over 60 honey and beeswax products including hand cream and candles, are made at the Honey Farm. Prices range from 70p-£6.95. Mail order available.

Directions: *signposted on A1 at East Ord roundabout. Also from A698 1 mile from A1.*

Opening hours: *1 Apr-31 Oct; Mon-Sat 10.30am-5pm and Sun 2-5pm. Nov-Mar weekdays only 9am/5pm.* 22

KENNEDY'S FINE CHOCOLATES, The Old School, Orton, Penrith, Cumbria CA10 3RU

Est. 1991
Tel/fax: +44 (0)15396-24781
Parking available
Wheelchair access
Credit cards

We are a small chocolate factory making a wonderful assortment of handmade chocolates. Our factory shop has a full display of our chocolate products. We also have a coffee house and ice cream parlour with home made baking and ice cream making. Mail order is available upon request.

Directions: *on B6260 Tebay to Appleby Road, 2 miles from junction 36 on the M6. At the centre of the village opposite the village hall.*

Opening hours: *Mon-Sat 9am-5.30pm, Sun and public holidays 11am-5pm.*   23

THE OLD SMOKEHOUSE AND TRUFFLES, Brougham Hall, Brougham, near Penrith, Cumbria CA10 2DE

Est. 1987
Tel/fax: +44 (0)1768-867772
Parking available
Wheelchair access

Set in an English country house, the Old Smokehouse takes pride in producing fine smoked food, made to perfection, using mainly Cumbrian meat, fish and cheese. Truffles' handmade chocolates are made from fresh cream and real alcohol. Also available is smoked fish, game, poultry and sausages. All available by mail order.

Directions: *one mile south of Penrith just off the A6. Brougham Hall is signposted 500 yards south of Eamont Bridge.*

Open: *Oct-Apr Mon-Fri usually 10am-4.30pm, Easter-Oct 10am-5pm.*   24

THE WATERMILL RESTAURANT, Priests Mill, Caldbeck Wigton, Cumbria CA7 8DR

Est. 1986
Tel/fax: +44 (0)16974-78267
www.watermillrestaurant
.sagehost.co.uk
Parking available
Wheelchair access

Specialising in jams, chutneys, cakes, puddings and rum butter, the Watermill is a restaurant focusing on vegetarian cuisine. Food is made on the premises each day from the best quality produce. The restored mill includes a working waterwheel, interesting shops and workshops including a hand made pine showroom.

Directions: *Caldbeck is on the B5299.*

Opening hours: *Mon 11am-4pm, Tues-Sun 10am-5pm.*

25

General Gifts

ARTISTRY, 1 Devonshire Terrace, Coniston, Cumbria CA21 8HG

Est. 1989
Tel: +44 (0)15394-41305
Fax: +44 (0)15394-41773
Parking available on road
below house

Rachell Arnett works in various mediums and styles, from highly detailed naturalistic studies to more contemporary abstract work. Her subjects include flowers, pets, houses and landscapes. She works from clear photos when undertaking commission work. Her pictures are usually A4. Also collages and embroideries. Mail order available.

Directions: *from petrol station on left turn right at crossroads; left into Old Furness Road; park in car park; up stairs to next terrace; left to second house on right.*

Opening hours: *prior appointment necessary.*[maker 26]   26

Glass

ALEX HAYNES ALBION GLASS, Unit 3, Old Union Art Studios, Union Lane, Brampton, Cumbria LA8 1BX

Est. 1991
Tel/fax: +44 (0)1697-73780
www.albionglass.co.uk
Parking available
Credit cards

A small studio producing only handmade work using traditional methods. **Leaded glass table and pendant lamps** are made to Tiffany patterns and Alex Haynes' own designs. Prices from £50. Albion Glass also design and make stained glass windows and doors for houses and churches and offer full restoration services.

Directions: *A69 to Brampton. At T junction turn right; at Methodist Church turn left. 100 yards on left.*

Opening hours: *Mon-Sat 9am-6pm but advisable to phone first.*

JO VINCENT DESIGNS, Unit 10A, Hall House Industrial Estate, New Hutton, Kendal, Cumbria LA8 OAH

Est. 2000
Tel: +44 (0)7957-232908
Parking available

Jo Vincent designs and makes a unique range of **kiln-formed glass for the interior environment.** Her range of products includes vessels, wall panels, mirrors, screens and lighting. As each piece is hand made, no two pieces are exactly the same. Commissions from private and corporate clients welcome. Mail order available.

Directions: *junction 36 off M6. From Kendal A684 to Sedburgh, past Holme Park School on right. At top of hill turn right into the estate.*

Opening hours: *by appointment only.*

Jewellery

ICE DESIGNS, 1 Galgate, Barnard Castle, County Durham DL1R 8EQ

Est. 1999
Tel +44 (0)1833-660935
Parking available

ICE Designs specialise in **design led, quality made jewellery** in gold, silver and platinum, either set with precious stones or just in beautifully crafted metal. ICE Designs first take an idea then sketch, theme and develop it into a final design then select the stones and metal transforming the idea into a high quality piece of hand-crafted jewellery. Our other services include the restoration of antique jewellery to its original beauty and high-class jewellery repairs. Go on – search through your jewellery box for those old out-of-date pieces and have them transformed into a new family heirloom.

Directions: *situated at the bottom of Galgate on the corner with the market place.*

Opening hours: *9.30am-5pm Tues-Sat.*

SEED BEAD DESIGNS, 99 Main Street, Sedbergh, Cumbria LA10 5AD

Est. 1998
Tel/fax: +44 (0)15396-21489
Parking available

Using **Japanese Delica beads** and original designs, I make rings, earrings and pendants. These materials and designs are unique in the United Kingdom. Commissions are accepted and purchase by mail order is available upon request. There is a good range of designs at various prices.

Directions: *M6 junction 37, route A685 to Sedbergh (5 miles). Last shop on right in main street.*

Opening hours: *Mon-Sun 9.30am-4.30pm.*

WILLIAMSON BROWN, 20a Clayton Road, Jesmond, Newcastle-upon-Tyne NE2 4RP

Est. 1995
Tel: +44 (0)191-2818273
Fax: +44 (0)191-2818287
Parking available
Wheelchair access for
narrow chairs
Credit cards

Leading contemporary jeweller's with **work from silver and goldsmiths** from all over Great Britain beautifully displayed in handmade maple cabinets. Two **working jewellers** **on site** work on commissioned items in the workshop at the rear of premises: visitors are welcome to watch the production work or browse over the range of jewellery.

Directions: *from A1 motorway - after Tyne Bridge and underpass - bear right toward Whitley Bay 'Coast.' Left at roundabout up Osborne Road, left at traffic lights into Clayton Road.*

Opening hours: *Mon-Sat 10am-5pm.*

Metalwork & Silversmithing

JOHN HARRISON ART METALWORK, Unit 8 Brougham Hall, Penrith, Cumbria CA10 2DE

Est. 1989
Tel: +44 (0)1768-890558
Fax: +44 (0)1768-881395
Parking available
Limited wheelchair access
Credit cards

The workshop is in the historic Brougham Hall. All articles are entirely handmade in **copper, brass and stainless steel** and include plates, dishes, coasters, letter racks, brooches and vases. Commissions and commemorative items are undertaken. John also carries out antique copper and brass repairs. Mail order is available.

Directions: *one mile south of Penrith just off the A6. Brougham Hall is signposted 500 yards south of Eamont Bridge.*

Opening hours: *Mon-Fri 9.30am-5pm. By appointment at weekends.*

RB AYRE, 58 Front Street, Frosterley, Weardale, Co Durham DL13 2QS

Est. 1998
Tel: +44 (0)1388-526488
Parking available

RB Ayre works to clients' requirements to make **wrought ironwork** such as candelabras, candlesticks, gates, hanging baskets and rose arches. He also makes garden ornaments, planters and seat benches. Doubling as a gardener, this designer and wrought iron worker has the specific knowledge to provide a comprehensive service.

Directions: *upon request.*

Opening hours: *prior appointment necessary.*

SMALLFAB (LES HARRISON), Unit 6 Brougham Hall, Penrith, Cumbria CA10 2DE

Est. 1997
Tel: +44 (0)1768-865905
Parking available
Credit cards

Les Harrison, a native of Cumbria, served his apprenticeship with a local engineering company and now makes a range of goods including **gates and fencing, fire grates** and fireside furniture, weather vanes, curtain poles, bed heads, four poster beds, candlesticks and commissions. All for the discerning customer.

Directions: *one mile south of Penrith just off the A6. Brougham Hall is signposted 500 yards south of Eamont Bridge.*

Opening hours: *winter Mon-Fri 10am-5pm, summer Mon-Sun 10am-5pm.*

STEVE HOPPS BLACKSMITH, Sandbed, Fellend, Kirkby Stephen, Cumbria CA17 4LP

Est. 1999
Tel/fax: +44 (0)15396-23327
Parking available

Steve Hopps handforges **wrought iron and steel**. He works with clients to achieve their own ideas and requirements. Steve specialises in traditional designs from different historical periods. All pieces are finished by quenching in hot beeswax to give a deep natural lustre. He also runs blacksmithing courses. Mail order available.

Directions: *on main road (A683)from Sedbergh to Kirkby Stephen. 7 miles from Sedbergh and 8 miles from Kirkby Stephen.*

Opening hours: *prior appointment necessary.*

Pottery & Ceramics

AMBLESIDE STUDIO POTTERY, Ambleside Studio, Unit C Dixon's Court, 101 Lake Road, Ambleside, Cumbria LA22 0DB

Est. 2000
Tel: +44 (0)15394-34120
www.madeincumbria.co.uk
then Abigail Jacobs link
Parking available

Abigail Jacobs produces a quirky and decorative range of **press moulded hand painted tableware** in high fired stoneware. Her work includes bowls, teapots, platters and soup tureens. Sue Bartholomew makes planters, urns, pitchers and platters, combining classic shapes with textured clay to produce an original range of stoneware pottery.

Directions: *situated at the end of the courtyard between Young's Furnishings and the Football Museum on Lake Road.*

Opening hours: *Mon-Sun 10am-6pm.*

HELM GROVE, Helmgrove Burton Road, Oxenholme, Kendal, Cumbria LA9 7EP

Est. 2000
Tel: +44 (0)1539-734539
www.helmgrove.btinternet.co.uk

Art and craft products including **ceramic Celtic images and plaques.** Ceramic pieces are individually hand made, fired and glaze fired, then smoke fired. Real gold leaf used to highlight the relief giving a unique 'artifact' appearance. Also: a series of twenty ogham greetings cards showing the Celtic meanings for native British trees. Online mail order.

Directions: *telephone for directions.*

Opening hours: *by appointment only.*

THE PENNINE POTTERY, Alston, Cumbria CA9 3NG

Est. 1992
Tel: +44 (0)1434-382157
Parking available
Wheelchair access
Credit cards

Peter Lascelles specialises in **Leach tradition studio pottery,** domestic hand thrown stoneware, including mugs, vases, bread crocks, blackware and flowerpots. Visitors are welcome to watch Peter working. Commissions are undertaken. The pottery also houses a gift shop and café for which fresh food is made daily. Mail order also available.

Directions: *going north east from Alston look for signs two and a half miles from Alston.*

Opening hours: *Tues-Sun 10am-4.30pm.*

SHIRE POTTERY GALLERY AND STUDIOS, Millers' Yard, Prudhoe Street, Alnwick, Northumberland NE66 1UW

Est. 1982
Tel/fax: +44 (0)1665-602277
www.porcelain-shirepottery.co.uk
Parking available
Wheelchair access
Credit cards

Exhibition space features Ivar Mackay's **studio porcelain:** 'I am less interested in decorative embellishment and prefer to allow the quality of the glaze and the purity of the thrown form convey my message.' A varied programme of contemporary art, sculpture, wood and glass also on show. Crafts Council recommended. Mail order available.

Directions: *follow 'Shire Pottery Gallery and Studios' brown signs as you enter Alnwick from the A1 south of Rothbury.*

Opening hours: *Mon-Sat 10am-5.30pm; Sun by appointment.*

SPIRAL POTTERY, 1 Devonshire Terrace, Coniston, Cumbria LA21 8HG

Est. 1982
Tel: +44 (0)15394-41305
Fax: +44 (0)15394-41773
Parking on terrace below house

Mike Labrum has been producing a wide range of quality **hand thrown pottery** in the area for 23 years. Prices range from £2-£60. He also paints numerous themes but mainly landscapes and abstracts primarily in watercolours. Prices for paintings range from £50. Mail order is available upon request.

Directions: *from petrol station on left turn right at crossroads; left into Old Furness Road; park in car park; up stairs to next terrace; left to second house on right.*

Opening hours: *prior appointment necessary.*

SUE SHARP, Whitewell Farm, Alston, Nenthead Road, Cumbria CA9 3LD

Est. 1991
Tel: +44 (0)1434-381879
www.suesharp.co.uk
Parking available
Credit cards

Pots are wheelthrown from a smooth, white ballclay and decorated using brightly coloured slips, covered by a transparent glaze and fired to a high temperature to create robust, usable wares: **candle holders, oil burners, mugs, plates,** etc. Prices £7.50-£25. Workshops and demonstrations for 8-10 people. Mail order (sale or return) by arrangement.

Directions: *from Alston take A689 to Nenthead. At approximately 1.5 miles, Whitewell Farm is on the right.*

Opening hours: *Mon-Sun 9am-5pm. Prior appointment recommended.*

TOWER HOUSE POTTERY, Tower House, Tweedmouth, Berwick-upon-Tweed, Northumberland TD15 2BD

Est. 1977
Tel: +44 (0)1289-307314
Parking available
Wheelchair access

I hand throw **colourful decorative earthenware** which is also useful. Using 'sgraffito', a traditional English slipware technique which involves scratching through the slipware, I produce numerous designs. Commissions are undertaken; many for large tile panels depicting landscapes and buildings. All produce is oven and microwave proof. Mail order is available.

Directions: *follow brown tourist signs from the centre of Tweedmouth.*

Opening hours: *Mon-Fri 10am-5pm. Other times by appointment.*

42

WETHERIGGS COUNTRY POTTERY LTD, Clifton Dykes, Penrith, Cumbria CA10 2DH

Est. 1855
Tel +44 (0)1768-892733
Fax +44 (0)1768-892722
www.wetheriggs-pottery.co.uk
Ample parking
Wheelchair access
Credit cards

Wetheriggs has been a working pottery since 1855 and is now the only **steam powered country pottery** in the UK. The traditional working pottery offers the chance to see how a pot is thrown, slip trailed with a traditional cow horn and goose quill or painted and decorated. Visitors have a chance to have a go themselves in the 'Pots of Fun' studio. Other attractions at the pottery include a children's play area, a country café, rare breed farm animals, birds of prey, a natural newt pond, a collectibles shop and a shop selling country gifts and local Cumbrian crafts.

Directions. Exit M6 junction 40; A66 towards Scotch corner; A6 south towards Kendal: a mile after Eamont Bridge turn left towards Cliburn for one and a half miles.

Opening hours: *10am-5.30pm Weds-Mon summer: 10am-5pm Thurs-Mon winter, daily in school holidays.*

43

Textiles

ALMOST UNWEAROUTABLE, The Old Gun Room, Blagdon Estate, Seaton Burn, Northumberland NE13 6DB

Est. 1974
Tel: +44 (0)1670-789786
Fax: +44 (0)1670-789784
www.almostunwearoutable.com
Parking available
Wheelchair access

Victoria Robertson has specialised in **socks, stockings and other knitwear** for over 25 years using tried and tested machine-washable woollen yarn, to produce durable items for country and sporting pursuits. A huge range of other knitwear items can be produced to the style, pattern, colour and lettering required; mail order available.

Directions: *will be given when arranging appointment.*

Opening hours: *Any time by appointment.*

ANNETTE BENSON, Fell Yeat, Casterton, near Kirkby Lonsdale Cumbria LA6 2JW

Est. 2000
Tel: +44 (0)15242-71340
Parking available

I make **hand dyed, felted and embroidered bags** from the wool of our own sheep on the Pennines. Inspiration for the colours and embroidery come from the seas around Australia and also the garden. Prices start from £20. Photographs of my work are available as is mail order upon request.

Directions: *follow the Brownthwaite Nursery signs on the A65 between Kirkby Lonsdale and Cowan Bridge.*

Opening hours: *prior appointment necessary.*

EDEN VALLEY WOOLLEN MILL, Front Street, Armathwaite, Carlisle, Cumbria CA4 9PB

Est. 1988
Tel/fax: +44 (0)16974-72457
Parking available
Wheelchair access
Credit cards

Steve Wilson designs, weaves and knits **coloured fabrics for clothing** and other products. His enterprise is small scale and prices are very reasonable. Trained in Galashiels, he has been weaving for over 20 years. He also runs courses for interested individuals and groups. Mail order is available upon request.

Directions: *two miles off the A6, follow signs from midway between Penrith and Carlisle.*

Opening hours: *Mon-Sat 9.30am-5.30pm.*

ELIZABETH ANN KNITWEAR, Warden's Cottage, Chillingham, Alnwick, Northumberland NE66 5NP

Est. 1984
Tel/fax: +44 (0)1668-215250
Parking available
Wheelchair access at
Lowick workshop

I mainly make **Shetland wool knitted jackets** in a beautiful range of shades. Garments are made to order or available from a small stock in the workshop. The surface patterns are inspired by the intricate knotwork to be found in the Lindisfarne Gospels. Mail order is available upon request.

Directions: *from A1 turn west onto B6353. The workshop is on the right opposite the war memorial. Phone for clear directions.*

Opening hours: *most afternoons April to October. Tel before noon to be sure.*

KAREN VICKERS, 1 Dene Crescent, Rowlands Gill, Tyne and Wear NE39 1DS

Est. 1996
Tel: +44 (0)1207-542374
Fax: +44 (0)1207-549100
Parking available

I specialize in rich, lively coloured textiles. A plethora of techniques is employed - **embroidery, silk painting, patchwork, quilting,** etc. - to produce a variety of items including pictures, hangings, scarves and banners. I run workshops in crafts ranging from candlemaking to batik, patchwork to painting and retreats in spirituality and creative arts.

Directions: *off the A1 at Whickham, Swallwell junction. A694 to Consett and Rowlands Gill. In Rowlands Gill take B6315 to Ryton. Then take second left - Dene Crescent.*

Opening hours: *by appointment only.*

48

RACHEL PHILLIMORE, Matties Green, Kellah, Haltwhistle, Northumberland NE49 0JN

Est. 1998
Tel: +44 (0)1434-320706
Parking available
Wheelchair access

Rachel specialises in the making of colourful **hooky and proggy rugs and wall hangings.** Hooky and proggy is an old traditional English technique involving placing hessian on a frame then hooking and prodding it into finished garments. Other materials, including felts and plastic are incorporated into designs, which are mainly of flowers.

Directions: *necessary to phone as the workshop is located in a very rural area.*
Opening hours: *prior appointment necessary.*

THE STUDIO BY THE LAKE, Lake Bank, Water Yeat via Ulverston, Cumbria LA12 8DL

Est. 1995
Tel: +44 (0)1229-885629
Parking available
Wheelchair access
Credit cards

Denise Huddleston is a nationally acclaimed textile artist and jeweller, working in her private studio to produce **contemporary embroidered textiles and jewellery** inspired by the surrounding landscape. The studio also includes a sales and exhibition area. Workshops and courses are available. Prices range from £15-£500. Mail order is available.

Directions: *Lake Bank is at the southern end of Coniston Water on the main A5084. Coniston to Ulverston road - ring for details.*
Opening hours: *Any time by appointment.*

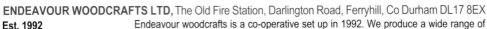

Toys & Games

ENDEAVOUR WOODCRAFTS LTD, The Old Fire Station, Darlington Road, Ferryhill, Co Durham DL17 8EX

Est. 1992
Tel: +44 (0)1740-657676
Limited parking
Wheelchair access

Endeavour woodcrafts is a co-operative set up in 1992. We produce a wide range of hand made **quality wooden items** and individual designs. Examples include animal desk tidies (£3.75), farms and garages (bright colours in child safe paint £39), garden trugs and planters (from £39). Mail order is available.

Directions: *on the A167 between Darlington and Durham; at the south end of Ferryhill on the right just before the right hand fork signposted town centre B6287.*
Opening hours: *Mon-Fri 9am-4pm.*

TOYS AND THINGS, Parish Hall, Frosterley, Weardale, Co Durham DL13 2QS

Est. 1995
Tel: +44 (0)1388-526488
Parking available
Wheelchair access

For Martin Hutchinson making toys and things has been a lifelong hobby. He makes **dolls' houses, cots and swinging cradles,** Wild West forts and castles (figures supplied if required), bird tables with tiled roofs and carved birds attached. He also makes crackets (traditional stools). Mail order available.

Directions: *from Durham city head west for approximately 18 miles.*
Opening hours: *Easter-Oct 1.30am-5.30pm and school holidays.*

Woodturning & Furniture

BARRY PORTER, Crosthwaite House, Pardshaw, Cockermouth, Cumbria CA13 0SP

Est. 1995
Tel: +44 (0)1900-824671
www.barryporter.cjb.net
Parking available

Visit the studio of a professional woodcarver and furniture maker who produces **carved oak furniture** to commission. From felling and conversion of local oak to the handforging of hinges and catches, all is carried out by me at the studio. Visitors are welcome to see carving work in progress. Carving courses available.

Directions: *from A66 at Cockermouth, take the A5086 Egremont for two miles - signposted Pardshaw village on the left.*

Opening hours: *Mon-Sun 9am-6pm.*

BEN ATKINSON FURNITURE, 192 Heaton Road, Newcastle-upon-Tyne, NE6 5HP

Est. 1999
Tel: +44 (0)7930 324 498
www.furnituredesigns.
freeserve.co.uk
Parking available

Commissioned contemporary furniture ranging from **mirrors and coffee tables to dining sets and fitted cupboards.** I offer my clients freshly designed concepts to enhance their living environment using native hardwoods from sustainable sources. I wish to expose the dormant personality and elegance found in wood to create simple, functional, yet beautiful furniture.

Directions: *given when appointment is made.*
Opening hours: *by appointment only.*

CABBAGES AND KINGS, The Grainstore, Meaburn Hall Farm, Maulds Meaburn, Penrith, Cumbria CA10 3HW

Est. 1999
Tel: +44 (0)1931-715097
Limited parking available
Wheelchair access
Credit cards

We design and hand make **original wooden furniture for outside the house.** We incorporate hand made glass, copper and green oak. We work across the United Kingdom with clients to produce one-off pieces of furniture, unfitted kitchens, beds and just about anything in wood. Mail order available.

Directions: *10 miles south of Penrith at the end of the village at the junction to King's Meaburn.*

Opening hours: *prior appointment necessary.*

THE CHAIR WORKSHOP, 99 Main Street, Sedbergh, Cumbria CA10 5AD

Est. 1993
Tel: +44 (0)15396-21489
www.sedbergh.org.uk/
ChairWorkshop
Parking available
Wheelchair access

Sandra Cotterell makes a range of things to put bottoms on including stools and children's chairs. Her **seats** are made from a range of materials including cane, rush, cords, rope, seagrass and Danish cord. Chair repairs and reseating are also carried out. Craft supplies and tuition are available. Mail order available.

Directions: *junction 37 off M6, A685 to Sedbergh (five miles). Last shop on the right in the main street.*

Open: *Mon-Sat 9.30am-4.30pm, Sun by appointment. Advisable to ring first.*

PETER AND JANE WALMSLEY, Hill Head Farm, Walton, Brampton, Cumbria CA8 2DX

Est. 1996
Tel/fax: +44 (0)1697-72024
Parking available
Wheelchair access
Credit cards

Peter Walmsley produces **fine hand crafted miniature furniture** from oak and other native hardwoods. Tropical and exotic hardwoods are used, if favourable, from renewable resources. Prices range for cabinets from £200 to £800. Peter accepts commissions and will gladly discuss your own designs. Mail order is available upon request.

Directions: *from Walton take left fork to Hethersgill/Leaps Rigg. Follow road one mile. After stone bridge, on brow of hill take farm track on right.*

Opening hours: *Mon-Sun 10am-dusk.*

PETER LLOYD, The Old School House, Hall Bankgate, Brampton, Cumbria CA8 2NW

Est. 1989
Tel/fax: **+44 (0)16977-46698**
Parking available
Credit cards

I search out unusual and beautiful pieces of wood to create **boxes:** jewellery chests, workboxes, writing boxes, christening and chess boxes. Made entirely from wood, including the hinges, each is signed, numbered and totally unique. Special presentation or celebration pieces can be made to commission e.g. bible box, bridge box. Prices from £180. Mail order available.

Directions: *from village centre take Talkin Road at the Belted Will pub. The studio is 50 yards on the right.*

Opening hours: *7 days but appointment necessary.*   **58**

RAM WORKSHOP, 42 Irish Street, Whitehaven, Cumbria CA28 7BY

Est. 1996
Tel: **+44 (0)1946-63331**
Parking available in town
centre car park

We design and produce **hardwood furniture, large and small.** Using local windblown timber and painted woodwork we make trays, cupboards, jewellery boxes, chests etc. Also the famous 'house-box' of your own home. We also have a range of greeting cards produced from our own paintings. Commissions welcome. Mail order available.

Directions: *private house at the end of the market place. Our workshop is in the garden.*

Opening hours: *prior appointment necessary.*   **59**

THREE HORSE SHOES WOOD CRAFTS, Three Horse Shoes, Irthington, Carlisle CA6 4PT

Est. 1988
Tel: **+44 (0)1228-675657**
www.threehorseshoeswoodcrafts.com
Parking available
**For wheelchair access to
workshop please phone first**
Credit cards

We make **high quality wood turnery,** small furnishings, needlework frames and stands for the stitchcraft enthusiast. Made to measure in oak, mahogany, beech and other hardwoods with optional padded tops or lids. We are also specialists in wood finishing, repolishing and reproduction furniture. Mail order available upon request.

Directions: *M6 exit 43 (east), A69 to Brampton, A6071 towards Longtown, turn right after four miles (signposted Hethersgill/ Roadhead), after half mile turn right at crossroads. Workshop on left.*

Opening hours: *Mon-Fri 10am-4pm. Phone call desirable.*   **60**

Other Makers

HIDE AND HORN, 101 Lake Road, Ambleside, Cumbria LA22 0DB

Est. 1984
Tel/fax: **+44 (0)15394-33052**
Parking available
Can visit wheelchair users
Credit cards

Peter Hodgson has long experience of working in **leather, horn and antler.** He also does repairs. His range includes car seats, dog boots, handbags and bellows. From beautiful horn, which Peter calls the 'natural plastic', he makes spoons, brooches, powder horns, bugles etc. Individual enquiries/orders are always welcome. Mail order available.

Directions: *in town next to Young's furniture shop. Phone for more specific directions.*

Opening hours: *Mon-Sat (not Thurs) 9am-5pm.*   **61**

ILLUSTRATED CALLIGRAPHIC MAPS, Stonewood, Woodhorn Village, Ashington, Northumberland NE63 9YA

Est. 1970
Tel: **+44 (0)1670-817521**
Parking available

Thomas Fleming makes illustrated hand-crafted calligraphic **maps of Border Battlefields and Reiver Families, Lindisfarne, Burns Country,** Isle of Mull, Warwickshire, Northumberland. Priced as prints or framed £3-25. Also exquisite calligraphic passages with gold leaf. Commissions include county council work for permanent display using coats of arms, heraldry etc. Mail order available.

Directions: *follow A19 and continue north towards Woodhorn village. Right at crossroads. Bungalow 100 yards on right.*

Opening hours: *flexible. By appointment only.*

LAURA HARTSHORNE, Frosterley House Cottage, Frosterley-in-Weardale, County Durham DL13 2RF

Born 1917
Tel +44 (0)1388-527595
Parking available nearby

Laura Hartshorne specialises in the old craft of **hairpin crochet** and has been involved crafts all her life. She retired from the craft centre she ran in the Old Church Hall in 1996, however she continued to receive enquiries from previous customers and so decided to work from home. Everything she makes is individual and of her own design and is therefore not available elsewhere. Ms Hartshorne also provides demonstrations, conducts day and half day workshops and offers individual tuition. Her work can be seen in a small display in Stanhope, which is a main stop for holidaymakers.

Directions: *in the village of Frosterley in Weardale, the main road of which is a popular road to the lakes.*

Opening hours: *visits by prior appointment.*

LINDISFARNE SUNDIALS, 43 Windsor Gardens, Bedlington, Northumberland NE22 5SY

Est. 1955
Tel: +44 (0)1670-823232
Fax: +44 (0)1670-823232
www.lindisun.demon.co.uk
Parking available

Tony Moss makes **sundials in brass or bronze** to individual order. Each dial is a solar timepiece being calculated for the client's precise latitude and executed to jewellery standards with any required logo or inscription incorporated into the design. Replacement parts for damaged or broken dials can be re-created. Mail order available.

Directions: *100 yards off Bedlington main street to the south. A road on the right of the war memorial lawn is marked 'leading to Windsor Gardens.'*

Opening hours: *By appointment only.*

MOORLANDS DIPPED CANDLES, Unit 1E, Skelgillside Workshops, Nenthead Road, Alston, Cumbria CA9 3TR

Est. 1981
Tel/fax: +44 (0)1434-382738
www.moorlands-candles.co.uk
Parking available
Wheelchair access but limited in workshops

Inspired by the work of Danish candlemaker Kurt Saybe, Moorlands candles started life in 1981. We have a wide range of **quality burning dipped candles** in varying sizes and colours. We also make and sell garden flares, beeswax and vegetable oil dips. Mail order is available on request.

Directions: *at top of Alston's Front Street turn left towards Nenthead on the A689. The workshops are the last buildings in Nenthead on the right.*

Open: *Mon-Fri (not Thurs) 9am-5.30pm. By appointment at other times.*

SARK CHAPEL, Quarry Grove, Hethersgill, Carlisle, Cumbria CA6 6ES

Est. 1980
Tel: +44 (0)1228-675347
www.meirian.freeserve.co.uk
Parking available
Credit cards

Our works are figurative **embroidered textile panes** based on landscape, the human figure and animal studies. Commissions including portraits accepted. Artist designed needlepoint, appliqué and cross-stitch, pictures, oils and watercolours are all for sale. All products are on display in our chapel conversion. Mail order is available upon request.

Directions: *junction 44 M6 via Scaleby and Smithfield. From A6071 Brampton to Longtown, 4 exits to Hethersgill.*

Opening hours: *prior appointment necessary.*

THE STENCIL LIBRARY, Stocksfield Hall, Stocksfield Hall, Stocksfield, Northumberland NE43 7TN

Est. 1988
Tel: +44 (0)1661-844844
Fax: +44 (0)1661-843984
www.stencil-library.com
Parking available
Wheelchair access
Credit cards

We **design and manufacture stencils.** Our shop stocks lots of stencil-related goodies along with supplies for paint effects, gilding and decoupage enthusiasts. Finished items, home furnishings and the work of local craftspeople are also available. For courses and tours of Stocksfield Hall ring for a full brochure. Mail order available.

Directions: *on the B6309 between the river Tyne and Stocksfield railway station. Five minutes from the A69 Carlisle to Newcastle road.*

Opening hours: *Mon-Sat 9.30am-5.30pm.*

Scottish Lowlands

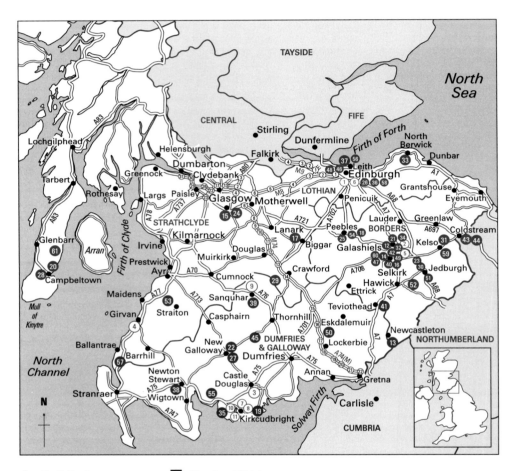

▲ Craft Centres ■ Food and Drink
○ Shops and Galleries ● Makers' Workshops

The Scottish Lowlands contain Scotland's two premier cities Edinburgh and Glasgow. Edinburgh has some of the finest kilt and Highland clothes makers, while Glasgow was the generator of the 'Glasgow style' of Art Nouveau led by the Scottish architect and designer Charles Rennie Mackintosh. Many craftspeople of today cite him as influencing their work, particularly furniture makers, stained glass producers and jewellery designers. At Pencuik, seven miles from Edinburgh you can see glass being blown at Edinburgh Crystal Visitors' Centre; while Galashiels is the traditional centre of the woollen-weaving and tartan industries. Kircudbright in Dumfries and Galloway, is known as 'the artists' town, famous for Scottish artists including the painter Edward Hornel of 'The Glasgow Boys', and now for its many galleries.

Craft Shops

CELTIC ART AND TRAVEL CENTRE, 207 High Street, Edinburgh EH1 1PE

Est. 1996
Tel: +44 (0)131-2263133
Fax: +44 (0)131-2257028
www.scottishmemories.com
Parking available
Credit cards

The Celtic Art and Travel Centre seeks to promote Scottish culture and Scotland's burgeoning cottage industries. All products reflect the varied and beautiful artwork of both ancient and modern Celtic artists. The gifts range in style and price to suit all tastes, interests and budgets. Mail order available upon request.

Directions: *on the High Street/Royal Mile between North Bridge and George IV Bridge on the north side and upstairs at the Exchange.*

Opening hours: *Mon-Sun Oct-Apr 9am-5pm, May-Sept 9am-8pm.*

(1)

THE CRAFTERS, High Street, Melrose, Scottish Borders TD6 9PA

Est. 1998
Tel: +44 (0)1896-823714
Parking available
Wheelchair access
Credit cards

A co-operative of craft workers and artists from the Scottish Borders which is continuously growing. The group includes amongst its members potters, painters, jewellers, knitters, silk artists and metal workers. The shop is manned in turn by all the members who are willing to discuss their craft and possible ideas on special commissions.

Directions: *half way up the High Street.*

Opening hours: *Mon-Sat 10am-5pm.*

GALLOWAY CRAFT GUILD CRAFTS, 76 King Street, Castle Douglas Dumfries and Galloway DG7 1AP

Est. 1995
Parking available
Wheelchair access up step

The Gallery Craft Guild has 140 members who promote their work at exhibitions and craft fairs. Their shop has two rooms filled with a selection of beautiful crafts of all types and to suit all pockets. Commissions are also undertaken. Mail order is available upon request and by negotiation.

Directions: *from the Market Hill car park we are 100 yards down the street on the right.*

Opening hours: *Mon-Sat summer 10am-5pm, winter 10.30am-4pm.*

GIRVAN POTTERY, The Wave Craft Gallery, 4 Knockcushan Street, Girvan, Ayrshire KA26 OAG

Est. 1988
Tel: +44 (0)1465-712897
Parking available
Wheelchair access
Credit cards

The Pottery, one of Girvan's oldest buildings, is the workshop of potter and owner Winifred Wright. The front part is a shop selling her work and that of local craftworkers in wood, metal, art textiles, pottery etc. She also gives pottery classes for an hour, day or week. Mail order available.

Directions: *centre of Girvan town.*

Opening hours: *Mon-Fri summer and Tues-Sun in winter.*

THE OLD SCHOOL, Bowden, Melrose, Scottish Borders TD6 0SS

Est. 2000
Tel: +44 (0)1835-822228
www.theoldschooltearoom.
fsnet.co.uk
Parking available
Wheelchair access
Credit cards

We sell a wide range of genuine local Borders crafts, from ceramics to pictures and silver to silks. We also have a good stock of quality secondhand and antiquarian books, many of Scottish interest. Our award-winning licensed tearoom serves fine teas and coffees, homemade cakes and light meals using local produce.

Directions: *from Melrose leave by the B6359 sign posted Lilliesleaf. After two miles turn left onto the B6398 sign posted Bowden.*

Opening hours: *Tues-Fri 10am-5pm, Sun 12-2pm.*

SCOOSH, 30 St Mary's Street, Edinburgh EH1 1SU

Est. 1999
Tel/fax: +44 (0)131-5576600
www.scoosh.net
Parking available
Credit cards

A bright and airy shop, Scoosh holds a visual feast of unique clothing and knitwear for adults and children. The shop also stocks an abundance of scarves, other accessories, jewellery and gifts. Mail order is available to customers on request. Please visit our website or telephone for details.

Directions: *travelling down from Edinburgh Castle, St Mary's Street is the first left on the Royal Mile.*

Opening hours: *Mon-Sat 10am-6pm, Sun 11am-5pm.*

SCOTTISH GEMS, 162 Morningside Road, Edinburgh EH10 4PX

Est. 1986
Tel/fax: +44 (0)131-4475579
www.scottish-gems.co.uk
Parking available
Credit cards

We are a long established retailer of Scottish made jewellery and crafts with an extensive range of silver jewellery and giftware in both traditional and contemporary designs. A wide range of glass, wood, and ceramic wares are also available. Prices range from £15 to £500. A mail order catalogue is available.

Directions: *follow A702 from the City Centre which brings you to Morningside. Buses 5, 11, 15, 16, 17 and 23 bring you there from the south side of the city.*

Opening hours: *Mon-Sat 9.30am-5.30pm.*

Galleries

CASTLE DOUGLAS ART GALLERY, The Stewartry Museum, St Mary Street, Kirkcudbright, Dumfries and Galloway DG6 4AQ

Est. 1938
Tel/fax: +44 (0)1557-331643
Parking available
Wheelchair access

The gallery forms an excellent venue which plays host to an annual programme of exhibitions ranging from fine art to photography. Much of the art and crafts on display are for sale. In addition touring exhibitions are regularly displayed at the gallery. Please contact us with any enquiries.

Directions: *in the older part of Kirkcudbright at the angle of the High Street. Gallery has a prominent steeple.*

Opening hours: *variable. Please telephone for current programme.*

EUCHAN HOUSE GALLERY, Sanquhar, Dumfries and Galloway, Scotland DG4 6LG

Est. 2001
Tel/fax: +44 (0)01659-50224
Parking available
Wheelchair access to
ground floor only

Situated on the outskirts of the village in a beautiful location close to Euchan Falls and Well, Euchan House Gallery exhibits a varied selection of unusual and original silk paintings and wallhangings by artist Noelle Stevenson, who works from the adjoining studio. A small, friendly gallery with reasonable prices. Commissions accepted.

Directions: *towards Sanquhar on A76; follow signs for Blackaddie House Hotel - turn into Blackaddie road, pass hotel, cross bridge, past golf course and first house on left.*
Opening hours: *Mon-Sat 10am-4pm; Sun by appointment.* ⑨

HIGH ST GALLERY, 84 High Street, Kirkcudbright, Dumfries and Galloway DG6 4JL

Est. 1997
Tel: +44 (0)1557-331660
www.kirkcudbright.co.uk
Parking available
Wheelchair access
Credit cards

A gallery run by two graduates of the Glasgow School of Art and Edinburgh College of Art. It exhibits the work of contemporary Scottish painters, continuing the tradition of Kirkcudbright, the artists' town. Also for sale are cards, silk, wood and antiques. Mail order is available upon request.

Directions: *opposite the Court House near the Tolbooth in Kirkcudbright.*
Opening hours: *Mon-Sun 10am-5pm, May-Sept 10am-7pm.* ⑩

TOLBOOTH ART CENTRE, The Stewartry Museum, St Mary Street, Kirkcudbright, Dumfries and Galloway DG6 4AQ

Est. 1991
Tel/fax: +44 (0)1557-331643
Parking on street
Wheelchair access

The Tolbooth Art Centre is based in Kirkcudbright's 17th Century Tolbooth which served previously as the Sheriff Courts and prison. The lives of Kirkcudbright's best-known artists (EA Hornel, Jessie M King, EA Taylor and Charles Oppenheimer) are commemorated there and their works displayed. The Centre's gift shop sells prints, paintings, crafts and art books.

Directions: *in the older part of Kirkcudbright at the angle of the High Street. It has a prominent steeple.*
Opening hours: *Mon-Sat 11am-4pm.* ⑪

General Gifts

BEES KNEES, 6/8 Market Street, Galashiels, Scottish Borders TD1 3AA

Est. 1997
Tel: +44 (0)1896-759995
Fax: +44 (0)1896-660935
Parking available
Wheelchair access

We stock a wide range of giftware and original artwork as well as our own brand of fragrant products, including pot pourri, fragrant terracotta, confetti and *bonbonnières*. Our prices range from under £1 to over £250 for an original painting by a local artist. Mail order is available.

Directions: *follow the one way system around Galashiels. We are on the right hand side after the cinema.*
Opening hours: *Tues-Sat 10am-5pm.*

MOUSE HOUSE ARTWORK, Riccarton Mill, Newcastleton, Roxburghshire TD9 0SN

Est. 1992
Tel: +44 (0)13873-76738
www.mouse-house-artwork.co.uk
Parking available

I specialise in drawing and painting animals and birds - domestic animals and wildlife. Pictures concentrate on the subject's vitality and spirit, avoiding sentimentality. Artwork is available as original portraits, limited edition prints, greetings cards and various stationery. In-house mounting and framing available. Commissions welcome. Prices from £1. Brochure on website.

Directions: *six and a half miles north-east of Newcastleton, in the Scottish Borders, on the B6357 Jedburgh Road.*
Opening hours: *by appointment.*

TROLL'S EYE CRAFTS, Unit 4 Venture Centre, St Mary's Mill, Level Crossing Road, Selkirk, Scottish Borders TD7 5EQ

Est. 1995
Tel: +44 (0)1750-21668
Parking available
Wheelchair access
Credit cards

Craftswoman Danielle Ray designs and makes fine leather bags and belts, jewellery and accoutrements for 'living history.' Also for sale are Celtic, Viking and medieval designs, horn and leather drinking vessels, historical footgear, battle gear, penannular brooches and more. A mail order price list is available upon request.

Directions: *next to the Borders Central Library in Selkirk.*
Opening hours: *Mon-Fri 11am-5pm.*

Glass

P.M. STAINED GLASS, 56 Manchester Drive, Glasgow G12 0NQ

Est. 1996
Tel: +44 (0)141-3346768
www.pmstainedglass.co.uk
Parking available
Credit cards

We specialise in the **design and restoration** of stained glass and the manufacturing of glass products. Work is carried out by Phil Melville, an award winning craftsman. We also build one of a kind, and reproduction panels to suit individual tastes, styles and budgets for domestic and commercial settings. Mail order available.

Directions: *available with map on website, or on request.*
Opening hours: *Mon-Sun 9am-5pm, but appointment necessary.*

SELKIRK GLASS VISITOR CENTRE, Selkirk, Scottish Borders TD7 5EF

Est. 1977
Tel: +44 (0)1750-20954
Fax: +44 (0)1750-22883
Parking available
Wheelchair access
Credit cards

Visitors are welcome to watch our skilled craftsmen at work creating **art glass paperweights**. Browse through the many items created in our factory. All are in the showroom and many are sold at factory prices. Relax in our coffee shop which serves light lunches, snacks and homebakes. Mail order available upon request.

Directions: *on the north side of Selkirk on the main A7 route.*
Opening hours: *Mon-Sat 9am-5pm, Sun 11am-5pm.*

SMASHING GLASS, Upper Drochil Cottage, Newlands, West Linton, Scottish Borders EH46 7DD

Est. 1989
Tel: +44 (0)1721-752650
www.smashingglass.com

We are a family run business based in the rolling borders' hills. We make original and unique designs in pottery and metal, sea-washed glass and coal. We also make **bees and dragonflies in stained glass** and fish mobiles in colourful glass and gorsewood. Mail order through website only.

TWEEDSMUIR GLASS, Tweedsmuir, Biggar, Lanarkshire ML12 6QN

Est. 1993
Tel/fax: +44 (0)1899-880282
Parking available
Wheelchair access
Credit cards

Chris Dodds is a master glassmaker with 34 years of experience. He designs and makes several ranges of ornamental hand made glass including **vases, perfume bottles, animals and paperweights**. Visitors can watch and speak to him as he works and browse in the adjoining shop. Mail order available upon request.

Directions: *along the A701 from Moffat to Edinburgh. Pull into the Crook Inn car park after the village of Tweedsmuir.*
Opening hours: *Mon-Sat 10am-4pm.*

Jewellery

CENTAUR DESIGN, 3 Bear Gates, Traquair, Innerleithen, Scottish Borders EH44 6PN

Est. 1989
Tel: +44 (0)1896-831376
Fax: +44 (0)1896-830947
www.centaurdesign.co.uk
Parking available
Wheelchair access
Credit cards

Casting in silver and bronze, we are a partnership which etches to art quality. We specialise in **Celtic art products and tiaras** as well as other jewellery, belts, buckles and other traditional Scottish Highland dress. Mail order is available upon request. Please telephone or check on website for details.

Directions: *6 miles from Peebles, signposted 'for Traquair House' approximately 45 minutes from Edinburgh in the Scottish Borders.*

Opening hours: *10am-6pm.*

 18

M. GILL JEWELLERY, 80 Old High Street, Kirkcudbright, Dumfries and Galloway DG6 4JL

Est. 1958
Tel/fax: +44 (0)1557-339111
Parking available

We are a hand made jewellers offering a **design and production service** using customers' stones or our own. There is a wide range of jewellery on sale in our shop set in the heart of this well-known artists' town. Prices range from £10 to £10,000. Repair and restoration work taken on.

Directions: *on Kirkcudbright Old High Street opposite the Sheriff Court.*

Opening hours: *Mon-Fri 10am-6pm.*

 19

R. GRANT LOGAN, Glenramskill, Campbeltown, Mull of Kintyre, Argyll PA28 6RD

Est. 1978
Tel/fax: +44 (0)1586-553588

Grant Logan is a goldsmith born in Campbeltown and trained in Glasgow. His love of Kintyre, the Atlantic and nature inspires him in producing **handmade gold jewellery,** often incorporating precious stones. His range includes: brooches, bracelets, pendants, chokers, earrings, cufflinks, tie-tacks, dress rings, signet, wedding and engagement rings. Commissions undertaken. Mail order available.

Directions: *the workshop is alongside The Heatherhouse, 1.5 miles from Campbeltown, en route to Davaar Island on the south side of Campbeltown Loch.*

Opening hours: *Mon-Fri 8am-1pm and 2-5.30pm; 8am-12.30 Sat.*

 20

STEEL CRAFT SCOTLAND, 90 Woodstock Avenue, Galashiels, Scottish Borders TD1 2EG

Est. 1971
Tel: +44 (0)7946-278932
Parking available

Colin Campbell specialises in modern designs. Each piece is a one-off utilising **stainless steel with precious stones** set in silver mounts, pendants, brooches, tie, lapel and kilt-pins. Customers can commission their own designs. Prices start at £14.50. He markets his work throughout the UK, USA and Australia.

Directions: *from Galashiels town centre, one mile east towards Melrose on the B6574. Take Langlee Drive on right and follow to Woodstock Avenue. First block on right.*

Opening hours: *Sat-Sun 10.30am-4.30pm.*

 21

Leatherwork

THE CLOG AND SHOE WORKSHOP, Balmaclellan, Castle Douglas, Dumfries and Galloway DG7 3QE

Est. 1977
Tel: +44 (0)1644-420465
Fax: +44 (0)1644-420777
www.clogandshoe.co.uk
Parking available
Wheelchair access
Credit cards

The Workshop is located in a beautiful and forgotten part of Scotland (the original home of the Gaels). Ongoing work can be watched. There is a showroom for ready-made items. **Footwear can be made to personal requirements** and sent out. Leathergoods from 25p; adult footwear from £54. Mail order available.

Directions: *13 miles north of Castle Douglas on A713 towards Ayr. Right at the Ken Bridge Hotel onto A712 and follow thistle tourist signs - "The Clog and Shoe Workshop".*

Opening hours: *Mon-Fri 9am-5pm; by appointment at other times.*

 22

CUERO BAGS, Cuero Workshop, Harestanes Visitor Centre, Ancrum, by Jedburgh, Scottish Borders TD8 6UQ

Est. 1989
Tel: +44 (0)1835-830742
Fax: +44 (0)1835-830742
www.cuero.co.uk
Parking available
Wheelchair access
Credit cards

Cuero is run by Caroline Marr and based in the Scottish Borders. Her principle products include a range of hand crafted **soft leather bags and jackets**. Each item is beautifully designed and carefully cut and sewn to make the most of the soft leather. Commissions are welcome and mail order is available.

Directions: *on the A68, 3 miles north of Jedburgh*

Opening hours: *Apr-Oct Mon-Sun 12am-5pm.*

 23

Metalwork & Silversmithing

SHONATSO CREATIVE METALWORK, 15 MacKenzie Gardens, East Kilbride, South Lanarkshire G74 4SA

Est. 1998
Tel/fax: +44 (0)1355-222109
www.shonatso.co.uk
Parking available
Wheelchair access
Credit cards

Paul King creates items to suit his customers' requirements. He has a small selection of **metal furniture, sculptures and mirrors** on display. Some of his work is very unusual such as a table showing the moons of Saturn, rose glass mirrors with diamond-cut frames and speaker and television stands. Mail order available.

Directions: *the workshop is on a farm in Newton Mearns and directions will be given when an appointment is made.*

Opening hours: *any time by appointment.*

 24

Musical Instruments

JULIAN GOODACRE, 4 Elcho Street, Peebles, Scottish Borders EH45 8LQ

Est. 1986
Tel: +44 (0)1721-722539
www.goodacrepipes.mcmail.com
Parking available

I make and play a wide range of quality **Scottish and English bagpipes** from British hardwoods. These are based on my own playing, researching and copying of museum examples. Bagpipes include Scottish smallpipes, Border pipes, Leicestershire smallpipes, English Greatpipes and Cornish double pipes. I also publish tune books and CDs. Mail order available.

Directions: *given when appointment made.*
Opening hours: *prefer by prior arrangement.*

Pottery & Ceramics

THE ADAM POTTERY, 76 Henderson Row, Edinburgh EH3 5BJ

Est. 1997
Tel: +44 (0)131-557 3978
On-street parking & free
at weekends
Credit cards

Janet Adam runs a one-woman pottery, although work and showroom space is made available for other ceramists. Her **wheelthrown stoneware and porcelain** is enhanced by subtly colourful reduction-fired glazes. Most pieces are one-offs encompassing a variety of forms and functions for indoors and out. Visitors welcome to watch work in progress.

Directions: *one mile north of Princes Street down Hanover Street, then Dundas Street. Turn left at Henderson Row, on right on corner of Saxe-Coburg Street, in basement.*
Opening hours: *10am-6pm except Sundays.*

ANNE HUGHES POTTERY, The Pottery, Balmaclellan, Kirkcudbrightshire DG7 3QB

Est. 1984
Tel: +44 (0)1644-420205
Parking available
Some wheelchair access

Our wide range of colourful ceramics is unusual, varied and reasonably priced. Featured in our showroom are **fountains, wine coolers, flower discs** and many designer household items. A popular pottery, our visitors are welcome to watch work in progress. Mail order is available upon request but only for certain items.

Directions: *above Balmaclellan village on the A712, 23 miles from Dumfries and two miles from New Galloway.*
Open: *Easter-Sept/Oct, Mon-Sun 9.30am-6pm. By appointment in winter.*

CAMPBELTOWN POTTERY, 34 Union Street, Campbeltown, Mull of Kintyre, Argyll PA28 6HY

Est. 1997
Tel: +44 (0)1586-553550

Established for nearly five years in Campbeltown, in the Mull of Kintyre, Simon Rochford's pottery makes **tableware, decorative pieces and tiles**. He uses a white stoneware porcelain fired to 1,295 degrees. Each piece is hand thrown/made, and decorated with brass rollers, stamps, glass and classic Eastern glazes. Mail order available.

Directions: *in town centre next to Eaglesome Whisky Shop.*
Opening hours: *Mon-Sat 9am-5.30pm.*

DRAKELAW POTTERY AND SHOWROOM, near Crawfordjohn, Lanarkshire ML12 6SQ

Est. 1992
Tel/fax: +44 (0)1864-502748
www.sadta.co.uk
/crawfordjohn.html
Parking available
Credit cards

Liz Cameron designs and makes a range of **functional and decorative stoneware pots** including mugs, jugs, bowls, casseroles and serving dishes. Each piece is thrown and decorated to produce individual pieces that are all oven, microwave and dishwasher proof. Visitors always welcome. Prices from £3. Mail order available.

Directions: *M74 junction 13. Follow signs for B7078 and take it north for half a mile. Turn left (signed Crawfordjohn). After two miles the pottery is signposted on right.*

Opening hours: *times vary but open most days. Telephone first.*

HUNTER ART AND TILE STUDIO, Harestanes Ancrum, Scottish Borders TD8 6UQ

Est. 1982
Tel: +44 (0)1835-830328
Parking available
Wheelchair access
Credit cards

Douglas Hunter set up this small ceramic studio in the heart of the rural Scottish Borders and has nearly twenty years' experience. Visitors welcome to watch the **hand painting of tiles and plates**. Much of the work on sale has a traditional, almost Victorian look. Single tiles from £7. Mail order available.

Directions: *3 miles north of Jedburgh off the A68 next to the well sign-posted Harestanes Visitor Centre.*

Opening hours: *Mon-Sun 10am-5pm.*   (30)

THE KELSO POTTERY, The Knowes, Kelso, Scottish Borders TD5 7BH

Est. 1970
Tel +44 (0)1573-224027
Parking available
Wheelchair access
(one step).
Credit cards

The Kelso Pottery was set up by Ian and Elizabeth Hird: both studied at Edinburgh College of Art and drew on their knowledge of potting in Portugal and studies of 18th and 19th century Scottish pottery to create a range of simple, practical stoneware pottery, including **mugs, jugs, bowls, cover jars, piggy-banks, vases**. Also a range of low-fired earthenware 'time tablets', 'feelies' and votive figures fired in the Kelso pit-kiln, for which pieces are wrapped in oats, barley etc. before being fired; the kiln smothers and traps the ash 'flashing' new patterns into the clay.

Directions: *100 yds behind Kelso Abbey in the large Knowes car park.*

Opening hours: *10am-1pm and 2-5pm, Monday-Saturday.*   (31)

MARIANNE FINLAYSON, 31 Earlstow Road, Stow, Galashiels, Scottish Borders TD1 2RL

Est. 1996
Tel: +44 (0)7947-821297
www.MariannesPottery.co.uk
Parking available

Marianne Finlayson makes large and small items of **stoneware pottery decorated with applique design** which reflects the borders countryside. She also makes hand painted tiles and porcelain jewellery to customers' specifications. Mail order is available upon request. Please visit our website or telephone for further details concerning mail order or otherwise.

Directions: *from the north, take the second right, then the first left. The house is on the right after the bend.*

Opening hours: *Mon-Fri 9am-5pm.*

SHAPE SCAPE CERAMICS, The Pottery, Station Hill, North Berwick, East Lothian EH39 4AS

Est . 1982
Tel/fax: +44 (0)1620-893157
Parking available

Elaine Dick designs and manufactures a unique selection of **semi-porcelain ceramic plates, vases, table lamps** and clocks all of which are decorated with a range of subtle colours. Her work is both decorative and functional. Mail order is available upon customers' request. Please telephone for further details.

Directions: *on Station Hill on the A198 23 miles east of Edinburgh in the seaside resort of North Berwick.*

Opening hours: *Tues/Wed/Fri/Sat 10am-1pm. Other times by appointment.*

SHEENA'S CLAYTHINGS, Tweedswood Cottage, Newstead, Melrose, Scottish Borders TD6 9DA

Est . 1989
Tel: +44 (0)1896-822076
Parking available

I make **unusual pottery objects** mainly for hanging on walls. My speciality is making masks but I also make dolphins and sunflowers. Rugby players are made in their own team colour jerseys. Melrose is the heart of Rugby with the famous Greenyards. Prices from £5 to £20. Mail order available.

Directions: *Newstead is one and a quarter miles from Melrose. At top of village turn left into Rushbank. I am off Rushbank in house with odd roof.*

Opening hours: *when home; open in the mornings. Best to telephone first.*

Textiles

JO GALLANT - TEXTILE ARTIST, Ironstones 70 High Street, Kirkcudbright, Dumfries and Galloway DG6 4JL

Est .1987
Tel: +44 (0)1557-331130
Parking available
Wheelchair access
Credit cards

I use combinations of dye-painting, construction, appliqué and machine embroidery to make **cushions, light-hangings and wall-hangings.** A love of colour and texture leads to luscious and highly coloured combinations of fabrics, in designs ranging from abstract through to depictions of local flora, fauna and landscape. Mail order available.

Directions: *near centre of Kirkcudbright. Follow signs for Tolbooth Art Centre. I am three doors away.*

Opening hours: *Mon-Sat 10am-5pm.*

JOYCE FORSYTH SCOTTISH DESIGNER KNITWEAR, 42 Candlemaker Row, Old Town, Edinburgh EH1 2QE

Est. 2000
Tel: +44 (0)131-2204112
Street parking (short stay)
Wheelchair access
Credit cards

Edinburgh Old Town is the location for Joyce's exclusive range of knitwear. Trained at Grey's School of Art in Aberdeen, Joyce is now designing and producing easy-to-wear knitwear in 100% natural fibres. Her collection ranges from **simple box jackets to extravagent flared coats.** Come and enjoy colour and style.

Directions: *up the Mound near Chamber Street and the New Museum of Scotland. The shop is located just down from the Greyfriars Bobby statue.*

Opening hours: *Tues-Sat 10am-5.30pm.*

KINLOCH ANDERSON, Commercial Street/Dock Street, Leith, Edinburgh EH6 6EY

Est. 1868
Tel: +44 (0)131-555 1355
Fax: +44 (0)131-555 1392
www.kinlochanderson.com
Customer parking
Wheelchair access
Credit cards

Highland Dress and accessories. Kiltmakers by Appointment to the Royal Family. Family-owned over five generations. Renowned for quality Scottish clothing and textiles. Shop specialising in Highland Dress including sporrans, sgian dubhs, kilt pins, brogues and brooches. Professional advice and personal service. Unique Heritage Museum with viewing window to kiltmaking. Mail order available.

Directions: *in Leith, historic port of Edinburgh; immediately opposite Scottish Executive building in Commercial St; close to Ocean Terminal - Edinburgh's newest retail and leisure destination.*

Opening hours: *Mon-Sat 9am-5.30pm.* 37

MERRICKNITS, 80 Queen Street, Newton Stewart, Dumfries and Galloway DG8 6JL

Est. 1979
Tel: +44 (0)1671-403842
Parking available
Wheelchair access

Merricknits is a small **local knitwear co-operative** producing a wide range of individual styles and patterns, both new and traditional, in natural and man made fibres, although the emphasis is on wool. Customer's own yarn can be knitted up. Prices start at £8. A mail order brochure is available upon request.

Directions: *on A75 take Newton Stewart exit from roundabout towards town. Merricknits is about 400 yards from roundabout on right near Bruce Hotel.*

Open: *Mon/Wed 10am-1pm. Other days 10am-1pm and 2-5pm. Closed Sun.*

ORIGINAL SANQUHAR JERSEYS (SCOTLAND), 30 High Street, Sanquhar, Dumfries and Galloway D94 6BL

Est. 1989
Tel: +44 (0)1659-58264
Parking available
Wheelchair access

Keen to promote Scottish knitting traditions, Alison Thomson researched and developed the indigenous patterns knitted in Sanquhar, Scotland since 1700. She knits her **Sanquhar jerseys** on a handframed knitting machine using modern techniques. Her high quality work, with historical significance is exported to many parts of the world. Mail order available.

Directions: *on the A76 (Dumfries to Kilmarnock), in the centre of the High Street near Tolbooth museum in Sanquhar.*

Opening hours: *Mon-Sat 10am-5pm, closed Thurs/Sat afternoons.*   **39**

SUE ELLIOT, River Cottage, Riverside Road, Selkirk, Scottish Borders TD7 5DY

Est. 1998
Tel/fax: +44 (0)1750-22243
Parking available
Wheelchair access
Credit cards

Sue Elliot lives and works by the river in the historic border town of Selkirk. She makes **silk and velvet goods** including silk and velvet scarves, wraps and cushions, mirrors, silk covered notebooks and silk and velvet embroidered brooch cushions. Prices range from £7.50 to £80. Mail order available.

Directions: *follow signs in Selkirk for swimming pool; pass pool; turn left; when you reach the river turn right. Workshop 300 yards along.*

Opening hours: *Mon-Fri 9.30am-4.30pm, closed 12.30-2.30pm.*   **40**

TEVIOTDALE ARANS, Dryden, Teviothead, Hawick, Scottish Borders TD9 0PP

Est. 1988
Tel/fax: +44 (0)1450-850205
Parking available
Wheelchair access

Teviotdale Arans make **hand-knitted Aran sweaters,** jackets and accessories. They also make two-ply hand knitted baby shawls which are a speciality. All types of hand knitting are undertaken. Commissions for one-off garments are always welcome. Mail order is available upon request. Please telephone for further details.

Directions: *Teviothead is 10 miles south of Hawick on the A7.*

Opening hours: *prior appointment necessary.*   **41**

Toys & Games

BORDER BRUINS AND COZY BEAR, Craft Centre, Tweedbank, Galashiels, Scottish Borders TD1 3RJ

Est. 1990
Tel/fax: +44 (0)1896-752934
Parking available
Wheelchair access
Credit cards

Sue Nicholl, makes **Scottish bruin' teddy bears** from mohair and cashmere. Their handsome looks reflect their origins in the Scottish Borders. Sue also designs and makes a range of 'Cozy Bear' cuddly clothes and pram accessories in plastic and vibrant colours to complement her range of teddy bears. Mail order available.

Directions: *from Melrose follow directions to Tweedbank Industrial Estate. Follow road past industrial estate and into a residential area about one mile. Craft Centre on right.*

Opening hours: *Mon-Fri 10am-4pm.*   **42**

RONNIE HEK, Unit 3, Coldstream Workshops, Home Place, Coldstream, Scottish Borders TD12 4DT

Est. 1989
Tel/fax: +44 (0)1890-882527
www.tartangift.co.uk
Parking available
Credit cards

We design and manufacture a range of **Scottish tartans and gifts**. Tartan teddy bears are our speciality. Our newest bear is Hamish, a fully jointed plush teddy bear wearing a knitted sweater, plumed tartan tam and scarf in any tartan of your choice. Mail order is available upon request.

Directions: *left at the petrol station on the Main Street and left again at the top of the hill.*

Opening hours: *Mon-Thurs 8.30am-5pm, Fri 8.30am-2pm.*   **43**

TOPTOISE DESIGN, Dove Cottage, The Hirsel Homestead, Coldstream, Scottish Borders TD12 4LW

Est. 1992
Tel: +44 (0)1890-883385
www.toptoise.com
Parking available
Wheelchair access
Credit cards

We are makers of **collectors' dolls' houses** specialising in Charles Rennie Mackintosh Furniture and houses (endorsed by the Glasgow School of Art) in 1:12, 1:24 and 1:48 scales. Victorian vernacular dolls' houses and shops and copies of customers' own houses on a commission basis are also made. Mail order available.

Directions: *we are within the Homestead at the Hirsel Country Park in Coldstream.*

Opening hours: *Mon-Sun 10am-5pm but please telephone first.*

WOOD 'N' THINGS, Gravel Pit Cottage, Kirkland, Moniaive, Thornhill, Dumfries and Galloway DG3 4HB

Est. 1984
Tel: +44 (0)1848-200345
Parking available
Wheelchair access
Credit cards

We make **small wooden-wheeled toys** ranging in price from £2.10. Toy aircraft are our speciality. We also make special toys such as Noah's ark, a roll-on, roll-off ferry with vehicles, and nativity sets. Other products include pepper mills, lidded trinket boxes and wooden handled cutlery. Mail order available.

Directions: *our shop is at the junction of the A702/B729 at Kirkland, 14 miles from Dumfries, 6 miles from Thornhill and two miles before Moniaive.*

Opening hours: *Summer 10am-5pm, winter 10am-4pm, closed Tues am and Thurs except July and August.*

Woodturning & Furniture

CHRIS HOLMES CABINET MAKERS, Gogar Cabinet Makers, 194 Glasgow Road, Edinburgh EH12 9BR

Est. 1973
Tel: +44 (0)131-317 7240
Parking available
Wheelchair access

For over a quarter of a century, I have specialised in the design and making of **furniture in native hardwoods**. Work is done on a commission basis for private, corporate and public clients. My joint aims are always to demonstrate the highest standards of progressive design, materials, construction and workmanship.

Directions: *on eastbound carriageway of A8 (main Edinburgh-Glasgow road) between Edinburgh airport and city. Turn left 500 yards after 40mph sign.*

Open: *Mon-Fri 9am-6pm. Appointment needed. Other times possible by arrangement.*

C.S.K. WOODTURNING, The Old School House, Bowhill, Selkirk, Scottish Borders TD7 5ET

Est .2000
Tel: +44 (0)1750-76258
Parking available

Calum Flanders' small workshop produces various turned items from reclaimed and home grown timbers (pine, oak, elm, yew, cherry etc.) including bowls (plain and bark edged), **goblets, candlesticks, cheeseboards, plates and 'lazy susans.'** Also items in jadewood (Australian soapstone). Furniture repairs undertaken. Commissions welcome. Please telephone for details.

Directions: *4 miles west of Selkirk on the A708 turn left for Bowhill at General Bridge then turn right, continue for one mile.*

Opening hours: *prior appointment necessary.*

J.M.K. DESIGNS, Gogar Cabinetworks, Gogar Old Church, 194 Glasgow Road, Edinburgh EH12 9BR.

Est. 2000
Tel/fax: +44 (0)131-317 7240
www.jmkdesigns.co.uk
Limited parking
Wheelchair access

JMK Designs specialises in **modern, organic one-off furniture pieces** in combinations of solid timber and veneered, turned and chamfered plywood, which may have inlays of metal foil, ivory, mother-of-pearl, bone or horn substitutes, glass, perspex and other materials. Also sculpture in the round in solid timber. Mail order possible.

Directions: *on eastbound carriageway of A8 (main Edinburgh-Glasgow road) between Edinburgh airport and city. Turn left 500 yards after 40mph sign.*

Opening hours: *Mon-Fri 9am-6pm. Appointment necessary.*

ROB ELLIOT FURNITURE, River Cottage, Riverside Road, Selkirk TD7 5DU
Est .1988
Tel/fax: +44 (0)1750-22243
www.robelliotfurniture.com
Parking available
Wheelchair access
Credit cards

High quality furniture inspired by the natural forms of burr elm from the Scottish Borders. Only trees which have died naturally are used to create our one-off and unique pieces. The range includes dining tables and chairs, beds, cabinets, dressers, rockers, desks and many other items. Mail order available.

Directions: *follow signs in Selkirk for the swimming pool, pass pool and turn left. Turn right at river. Workshop is 300 yards along.*

Opening hours: *Mon-Fri 8am-12pm, 1-4.30pm, Sat 9am-12pm.*

SCULPTURAL WOODTURNING, Riverhouse, Boreland, Lockerbie, Dumfries and Galloway DG11 2PA
Est .1989
Tel: +44 (0)1576-610388
http://webite.lineonenet/~samvado
Parking available
Wheelchair access
Credit cards
-

Samvado places a less utilitarian emphasis on his pieces, instead letting his woodturning express the beauty of the trees. He makes **bowls, balls, plates, clocks and carvings.** The workshop/gallery is on a scenic route past Samye Ling Tibetan temple through the Moffat Hills to Edinburgh. Mail order available.

Directions: *from M74 at Lockerbie north to Borland (8 miles); in village take right turning for Corrie. After quarter mile; right through Gall Farm and on for one mile.*

Opening hours: *9am-6pm if in. Advisable to make an appointment.*

THOMAS HAWSON DESIGNER/MAKER, 7 Upper Nisbet, Ancrum, Jedburgh, Scottish Borders TD8 6TS
Est. 1998
Tel/fax: +44 (0)1835-850754
www.thomashawson.com
Parking available

Thomas Hawson provides an intimate, innovative and adaptable design and make service. Products range from small scale, high quality, batch produced pieces to large public commissions. His wide and varied works range **from toothpicks to rocketships in wood.** Design development and prototype production is available to other producers. Please telephone for details.

Directions: *given once visit arranged.*

Opening hours: *workshop not visitable on spec. Prior appointment necessary.*

TOBY VINT FURNITURE, Wester Fodderlee, Bonchester Bridge, near Hawick, Scottish Borders TD9 8JE
Est. 1997
Tel/fax: +44 (0)1450-860225
Parking available

I produce quality **furniture in local hardwoods.** I admire the simplicity of line and construction in early furniture. The influence of this is reflected in my work but structured in keeping with modern interiors. The range of previous commissions includes display cabinets, bookshelves, tables, stools and knife blocks etc.

Directions: *on the B6357 between the A68 to Jedburgh and Bonchester Bridge.*

Opening hours: *Mon-Fri 9am-5pm.*

WOODARTS, 38 Patna Road, Kirkmichael, Ayrshire KA19 7PJ
Est. 1986
Tel: +44 (0)1655-750386
www.woodarts.co.uk
Parking available
Wheelchair access

Alan Lees specialises in **large indoor and outdoor woodcarvings** made to commission, sometimes in situ. New ventures include hand carved solid body guitars and religious statuary. Our workshop is very small, so work is best viewed in situ or on website. Also, carving courses by arrangement. Mail order available.

Directions: *in the small conservation village of Kirkmichael, 3 miles off A77, turn left at Minishant.*

Opening hours: *by appointment only.*

WOODWORKS, 8 Newby Court, Peebles, Scottish Borders EH45 8AL
Est. 1985
Tel/fax: +44 (0)1721-724442
Parking available
Wheelchair access
Credit cards

Bruce Frost specialises in **turning wooden lamps and carvings.** He also makes hand carved signs for homes and businesses. All are made from home grown timbers such as elm, ash, beech and sycamore. Work is often by commission. Bruce provides both galleries and interior decorators with his work. Mail order available.

Directions: *off High Street.*

Opening hours: *Mon-Sat 10am-5pm.*

Other Makers

ALEXANDRA WOLFFE - ANIMALS, Tollhouse, Gatehouse-of-Fleet, Castle Douglas, Dumfries and Galloway
DG7 2JA
Est. 1981
Tel: +44 (0)1557-814300
Fax: +44 (0)1557-814344
Parking available
Wheelchair access

Alexandra's background in ceramics and anatomy combined with a love of animals is expressed in her exquisite **small sculptures of pets, domesticated animals and champion stock.** Subjects can be sculpted from photographs, which don't have to be professional, but photos from all round are useful especially for non-symetrical colouring. Mail order worldwide.

Directions: *the Tollhouse is at the top of Gatehouse-of-Fleet High Street. The studio/ gallery is behind the main buildings, facing carpark and mill pond.*

Opening hours: *Mon-Sat 10am-4.30pm.*

55

CARBERRY CANDLES LTD, Carberry, Musselburgh, East Lothian EH21 8PZ
Est. 1970
Tel: +44 (0)131-6655656
Fax: +44 (0)131-6532720
www.carberry-candles.com
Parking available
Wheelchair access
Credit cards

Carberry Candle Cottage has a visitor centre where production can be seen in action. **Demonstrations and a factory video** add to the experience. Visitors can even carve their own candle. A wide variety of candles are on display in the shop, including Christmas selection and bargain corner. Coffee shop. Mail order available.

Directions: *from A1 take 'Dalkeith' exit. Follow brown signs for Carberry Candles.*

Opening hours: *Mon-Sat 9am-5pm; Sun 12pm-5pm.*

56

CERAMIC HOUSE MINIATURES, Kilandtringan House, Glenapp by Girvan, Ayrshire KA26 OPE
Est. 1991
Tel: +44 (0)1465-831211
www.sujo.com/CT/Potting.
Shed.htm

Shirley Risdon makes **models of individual houses and other buildings** by commission. The base, including immediate garden, is approximately A4 size. I work from my own sketches and photographs so I visit the premises personally. Models are hand built, fired in the kiln and hand decorated. Presentation case included. Mail order available.

Directions: *three and a half miles south of Ballantrae off the A77, look for 'Pottery and Plants' signs; or 15 miles north of Stranraer off the A77, look for similar sign.*

Open: *variable, but open most days. Please tel ahead if travelling much distance.*

57

CRAIG MITCHELL, c/o Adam Pottery, 76 Henderson Row, Edinburgh EH3 5BJ
Tel: +44 (0)131-557 3978
On-street parking & free at weekends
Credit cards

Figurative ceramic sculptures and clay caricature portraits to commission. Former are energetic visual puns about the human condition or everyday life refracted through Craig's imagination. Small for table-tops, or can be five feet high. Example: Roller Coaster Emotions, 'a big guy in a tiny carriage at the top of a roller coaster.'

Directions: *one mile north of Princes Street down Hanover Street, then Dundas Street. Turn left at Henderson Row, on right on corner off Saxe-Coburg Street.*

Opening hours: *10am-6pm except Sundays.*

58

KELSO CANDLES, Craignethan House, Jedburgh Road, Kelso, Scottish Borders TD5 8AZ
Est. 1990
Tel: +44 (0)1573-224818
Parking available
Wheelchair access two steps

We produce a **full range of candles** including geometric shapes, floating candles, fruit, animals, birds, castles, scented and decorated candles, Christmas candles, personalised applique candles for weddings and other special events and will match colour requirements exactly. We also make gold candles using gold lacquer. Prices from 60 pence. Mail order available.

Directions: *from Kelso Square follow Bridge Street and cross the River Tweed. Keep to left up the hill; turn right at Jet Garage. 200 metres along on right.*

Opening hours: *Mon-Sun 9am-6pm. Advisable to telephone first.*

59

RAY BROWN DESIGN, Laundry House, Bowhill, Selkirk, Scottish Borders TD7 5ET

Est. 1993
Tel/fax: +44 (0)1750-20430
www.raybrowndesign.com
Parking available
Credit cards

We design and manufacture the most detailed and to scale **statuettes available to military enthusiasts** collectors and connoisseurs. Themes include historical, native American, equestrian, natural history, sporting, portraiture and miniature collections. We also offer a contract casting and molding service in addition to our sculpting service to other companies. Mail order available.

Directions: *three miles west of Selkirk, follow signs to Bowhill Estate. Ask for directions to Bowhill Design.*

Opening hours: *Mon-Fri 9am-5pm but appointment necessary.*

TORRISDALE CASTLE ORGANIC TANNERY, Torrisdale Castle, Carradale, Campbeltown, Argyll PA28 6QT

Est. 1994
Tel/fax +44 (0)1583-431233
www.torrisdalecastle.com
Parking available
Wheelchair access
Credit cards

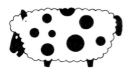

Established in the 1960s as Grogport Rugs by Molly Arthur, the Tannery was opened at Torrisdale in 1994 by her daughter Mary Macalister Hall. The Tannery uses a traditional tanning method using tree bark instead of modern chemicals and produces **beautiful sheepskins, deer and goatskins** in a variety of natural colourings. Visitors are welcome to look round the tannery, which has no nasty smell! In addition to the skins, the small shop sells a variety of gifts from all over the country including jumpers, slippers, handbags, belts and soft toys. Skins are also available by mail order from the above address.

Directions: *2 miles south of Carradale and 13 miles north of Campbeltown: turn in at the gates and follow the signs.*

Opening hours: *10am-6pm Mon-Fri, 2-6pm Sat-Sun.*

Scottish Highlands

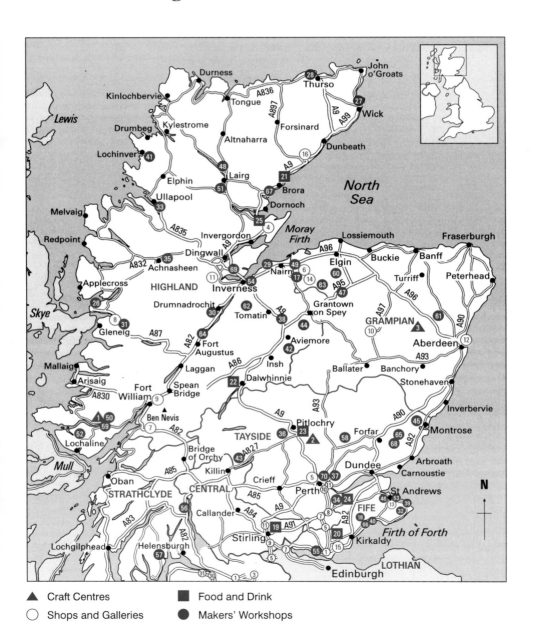

▲ Craft Centres   ■ Food and Drink
○ Shops and Galleries   ● Makers' Workshops

Steeped in history, The Highlands are a world apart; a land of mists and lochs, crofts, smokeries and whisky distilleries and the true heart of Scotland. Most of the distilleries are happy to welcome visitors and offer them a tour and a dram. Celebrated in song and verse, the Highlands have a long tradition of creative arts and now also of applied arts and many crafts. Near the Ochil Hills in the West Highlands, textile production has been a craft industry for generations. Scottish music plays a large part in many communities and there is no shortage of bagpipe makers should you want to learn to play, or kilt and weapon makers if you want to dress the part.

Craft Centres

ARIUNDLE CENTRE, Strathview, Strontian, Argyllshire PH36 4JA

Est. 1990
Tel: +44 (0)1967-402279
Parking available
Wheelchair access
Credit cards

Catherine Campbell's Centre comprises various craft workshops: batik, decorative glass, spinning from her own sheep and goats' wool, and natural dyeing. She also offers weekend courses in batik, weaving, stained glass, beginners' watercolour painting, pottery, basket and felt making and patchwork for £55 including lunch and tea. Accommodation can be arranged.

Directions: *Ardnamurchan Peninsula. Cross on Corran Ferry which is 8 miles east of Fort William and drive to Strontian.*

Opening hours: *7 days 9am-5pm (later in summer).*

DOWALLY CRAFT CENTRE, Dowally, by Pitlochry, Perthshire PH9 ONT

Est. 1983
Tel: +44-(0)1350-727604
Parking available
Wheelchair access to craft shop but not restaurant upstairs
Credit cards

Dowally Craft Centre and Restaurant was opened in 1983 and has become an established centre where customers are delighted to discover an Aladdin's cave of quality crafts, gifts, knitwear and clothing plus pottery, quilted wall hangings and stencilled pine chests which are made on the premises and exclusive to this oasis on the A9 North Road. Climb the rainbow stairs to the wood-lined restaurant where you can enjoy a selection of home-cooked meals and delicious home baking all day. The centre is set in its own grounds in the country, 5 miles north of Dunkeld, a place not to be missed.

Directions: *17 miles north of Perth on the A9, signposted and located 7 miles south of Pitlochry.*

Opening hours: *10am-6pm seven days a week March December.*

THE MONYMUSK ARTS TRUST, Monymusk, Aberdeenshire AB51 7HJ

Est.1990
Tel: +44 (0)1467-651220
Fax: +44 (0)1467-651250
Parking available
Wheelchair access

The Arts Trust is housed in a former stone-polishing works dating from the mid-18th century. Throughout the summer local makers and artists are in residence making and selling a variety of crafts. There are also regular art exhibitions from further afield. Concerts are held summer and winter. Tea-room and walled garden.

Directions: *Monymusk is 18 miles west of Aberdeen and is signed off the A944 after Dunicht.*

Opening hours: *1 May-30 Sept. 10am-4pm.*

Craft Shops

ALDIE WATERMILL, Craft and Gift Shop, Aldie, Tain, Ross-shire IV19 1LZ

Est. 2001
Tel: +44 (0)1862-893786
Parking available
Wheelchair access (ground floor sales)
Credit cards

An historic watermill dating from 1860 and still mechanically in working order. The Craft and Gift Shop is located inside the mill and sells all manner of local and/or Scottish hand made products including tinned haggis, pottery, local textiles (scarves, shawls, travel rugs) and small items from local woodturners. Mail order available.

Directions: *35 miles north of Inverness on the A9 towards Tain. Follow brown tourist signs for Aldie Watermill which is half a mile before Tain.*

Opening hours: *Mon-Sat 10am-5pm; Sun 10am-4pm Apr-Oct.*

BUTH BHEAG, 5 Watergate, Perth, Perthshire PH1 5TF

Est. 1993
Tel: +44 (0)1738-442263
Street parking
Wheelchair access
Credit cards

Arlene Baird's small shop, sells the work of over twenty Scottish-based, contemporary craft makers. Items include refurbished furniture, ceramics, papier-mâché, glass, textiles, lampshades, bags, clocks, mirrors, jewellery and hand made cards, from Perthshire and further afield in Scotland. Colourful revamped furniture and wooden framed mirrors to order.

Directions: *located adjacent to George Street at the bottom of Perth's High Street, close to the River Tay.*

Opening hours: *Mon-Sat 10am-5.30pm (Wed 12.30pm-5.30pm).*

THE CLAY PEOPLE - Ceramics and Silk, Units 5 & 6, Logie Steading, Forres, Morayshire IV36 2QN

Est. 1989
Tel +44 (0)1309-675587
www.theclaypeople.co.uk
Parking available
Wheelchair access
Credit Cards

Unusual ceramics and silk textiles. Innovative and practical kitchenware with hand-painted designs and sculpture incorporating mixed media, made on the premises by Allan Dixon. Rosie Logan textiles include original painted and stitched silk and luxurious velvets for rich panels in bodices. Customised picture framing also available. Mail order available.

Directions: *6 miles south of Forres signed 'Logie Steading' off the A940.*

Opening hours: *Tues-Sun 11am-5pm.*

CRAFTS AND THINGS, Glencoe, Argyllshire

Est. 1968
Tel: +44 (0)1855-811325
Fax: +44 (0)1855-811483
www.glencoe.u-net.com
Parking available
Wheelchair access
Credit cards

Crafts and Things is housed in a converted barn and comprises a craft shop, coffee shop and a woollen shop. It specialises in hand made goods of 'distinction and quality' mostly sourced from Scotland. Hand made items include pottery, jewellery, clothes, books, woodware, leather goods, soft toys, toiletries etc. Mail order available.

Directions: *between Glencoe and Ballachulish on the A82, just past Glencoe crossroads heading north.*

Opening hours: *Mon-Sat 9am-5pm (later in summer months).* ⑦

HIGHLAND ORIGINS, Ardelve, Dornie, by Kyle, Ross-shire IV40 8DY

Est. 2000
Tel: +44 (0)1599-555444
www.highlandorigins.com
Plenty of parking
Wheelchair access
Credit cards

Located in a converted barn by Loch Duich overlooking Eilean Donan Castle, Highland Origins offers selected contemporary crafts from Skye and the West Highlands including soaps, stained and painted glass, woollen tunics with Celtic knotwork designs, funky spiky hats and bags, driftwood products, cards, stationery and gift packaging.

Directions: *on the A87.*

Opening hours: *Mon-Sat 10am-6pm (plus late nights and Sun in July/August).*

LOCHABER SIDING, Railway Station, Fort William, Inverness-shire

Est. 2001
Tel: +44 (0)7759 604325
Parking available
Wheelchair access
Credit cards

A retail outlet for the Lochaber Craft and Food Producers Association whose isolated dwellings mean they are not easily able to welcome visitors to their homes. The Siding sells the work and produce of 50 members and includes woodwork, knitwear, wool, pottery, silk scarves, cards, walking sticks and garments. Also coffee shop.

Directions: *located at the Railway Station in Fort William.*

Opening hours: *Mon-Sat 9am-5.30pm.*

THE LUMSDEN BOTHY, Boghead Farm, Lumsden by Huntly, Aberdeenshire AB54 4LE

Est. 1989
Tel: +44 (0)1464-861735
www.bonnysocks.co.uk
Parking available
Credit cards

Lumsden Bothy craft and gift shop is located on a working farm which includes a pedigree herd of angora goats producing quality mohair made into socks, scarves, blankets and jumpers that are sold in the shop with a large selection of other quality crafts from local craftspeople. Demonstrations. Tearoom. Mail order available.

Directions: *from Aberdeen A944 from the centre, through Alford and follow A994 right for nine miles into Lumsden. Lumsden Bothy is on right, next to Scottish Sculpture Workshops.*

Opening hours: *10am-10pm, Mon-Sun.*

THE MADE IN SCOTLAND SHOP LTD, Station Road, Beauly, Inverness-shire IV4 7EH

Est. 1991
Tel: +44 (0)1463-782821
Fax: +44 (0)1463-782409
www.made-in-scotland.co.uk
Parking on site
Wheelchair access
Credit cards

The purpose-built Made in Scotland shop is a large (6000 sq. feet) shop and showroom for a multiplicity of Scottish crafts and is located in landscaped gardens in the scenic village of Beauly. Most goods are hand made and include textiles, jewellery, ceramics, glass, wood turning, bespoke furniture etc. Mail order available.

Directions: *12 miles north of Inverness on the southern edge of Beauly on the A862*

Opening hours: *7 days.*

Galleries

ABERDEEN ART GALLERY, Schoolhill, Aberdeen AB10 1FQ

Est. 1885
Tel +44 (0)1224-523700
Fax +44 (0)1224-632133
www.aberdeencity.gov.uk
Car parks nearby
Wheelchair access with
assistance from staff
Credit cards (in shop)

The North of Scotland's premier local authority-funded art gallery with a long-established reputation for promoting crafts. Collections include work by Bernard Leach, Michael Cardew, textiles by Tadek Beutlich and jewellery from Susanna Heron. A wide range of ceramics, glass, jewellery and other crafts is available from the Gallery Shop.

Directions: *From Aberdeen's main thoroughfare, Union Street, walk through Belmont Street. Aberdeen Art Gallery faces you at the end of Belmont Street.*

Opening hours: *10am-5pm Mon-Sat, 2-5pm Sun.*

CRAWFORD ARTS CENTRE, 93 North Street, St Andrews, Fife KY16 9AD

Est. 1978
Tel: +44 (0)1334-474610
Fax: +44 (0)1334-479880
www.crawfordarts.free-online.co.uk
Parking available
Wheelchair access

Originally founded by St Andrews University, we are now an independent charitable company. We provide exciting exhibitions of all kinds of visual and applied art. Further examples of which are available in the foyer shop. Residencies and art classes offered. More information on the website and in catalogue. Mail order available.

Directions: *proceed along North Street towards the Cathedral ruins. We are halfway along, on the left, past the cinema and opposite the police station.*

Opening hours: *Mon-Sat 10am-5pm; Sun 2pm-5pm.*

LOGIE STEADING ART GALLERY, Logie Steading Visitor Centre, Forres, Moray IV36 2QN

Est. 1994
Tel: +44 (0)1309-611378
Fax: +44 (0)1309-611300
www.logie.co.uk
Parking available
Wheelchair access
Credit cards

Logie Steading was a model farm, built in the 1920s and is located in the Findhorn Valley. The gallery offers a changing exhibition of work from nearly a hundred contemporary artists: textiles, pottery, sculpture, prints, glass, cards, watercolours and oil paintings. Various short courses offered. Tea-room. Mail order available.

Directions: *six miles south of Forres on A490. Follow brown tourist signs.*

Opening hours: *March-Christmas 10.30am-5pm every day.*

SHORELINE STUDIO, 2 Shore Road, Aberdour, Fife KY3 0TR

Est. 1997
Tel/fax: +44 (0)1383-860705
Parking available
Wheelchair access
Credit cards

The Shoreline Studio is a compact gallery which promotes quality works of art. The gallery is situated in the centre of an historical conservation village in south Fife. It exhibits and sells original paintings, prints, ceramics, stained glass sculpture, jewellery and cards. Please visit our website for a taste of our range.

Directions: *at Forth Road Bride, follow the A921 east to Aberdour via Inverkeithing and Dalgety Bay. We are at the top of Shore Road off the High Street.*

Opening hours: *Mon-Fri 10am-5pm, Sat 11am-5pm, Sun 2pm-5pm.*

TIMESPAN HERITAGE CENTRE AND ART GALLERY, Dunrobin Street, Helmsdale, Sutherland KW8 6JX

Est.1997 (museum 1987)
Tel: +44 (0)1431-821327
Fax: +44 (0)1431-821058
www.timespan.org.uk
Parking available
Wheelchair access
Credit cards

Purpose-built, Timespan's buildings house a museum of Victorian life depicted in tableaux and a fine and contemporary applied arts gallery. Exhibitions change monthly and include sculpture, pottery, jewellery, installations etc. and are accompanied by a programme of events. The centre also includes a herb garden, craft units, gift shop and café.

Directions: *just off the A9, 70 miles north of Inverness in Helmsdale village.*

Opening hours: *Apr-Oct Mon-Sat 9.30am-5pm, Sun 2-5pm. Nov-Mar appointment necessary.*

Baskets & Wickerwork

GILES PEARSON, Unit 7, Logie Steading, Forres, Morayshire IV36 2QN

Est. 1987
Tel: +44 (0)1309-611280
Parking available
Wheelchair access
Credit cards

Giles Pearson offers a wide range of country, antique and folk art furniture. He also does **restoration specialising in cane and rush-seated chairs.** Materials used include rush, split cane, seagrass, straw pine, oak and ash. He also buys and sells furniture. On site furniture showroom and tea-room. Mail order available.

Directions: *6 miles south of Forres on the A940, Grantown Road.*

Opening hours: *7 days 11am-5pm.*

WILLOW AND WOOD, 27 Glenwood Road, Leslie, Fife KY6 3EN

Est 1998
Tel: +44 (0)1592-743502

Andrew Vedmore and Jane Wilkinson make both **traditional and contemporary willow baskets, hurdles and furniture**. They also create willow work sculpture. Their work is widely displayed throughout Scotland. Jane is an experienced teacher and organises regular basketry workshops. Please ring for details of the courses. Mail order is available upon request.

Directions: *will be given when appointment is made.*

Opening hours: *by appointment only.*

 18

Food & Drink

BRIDGE OF ALLAN BREWERY, The Brewhouse, Queens Lane, Bridge of Allan, Stirling, Stirlingshire FK9 4NY

Est. 1997
Tel +44 (0)1786-834555
Fax +44 (0)1786-833426
www.bridgeofallan.co.uk
Parking available
Wheelchair Access
Credit Cards

The Brewery and Visitor Centre was founded in 1997 and offers visitors the chance to meet the brewer, learn the secrets of preparing traditionally crafted beers and see the care and skill that goes to making a fine hand brewed Scottish real ale pint using 100% natural ingredients with no additives or preservatives. Entry is free and our friendly staff will offer you samples of our cask ales, stouts, bitters and lagers. Browse around the memorabilia, tour the working brewery, savour the aromas, taste the range of malted barley and enjoy true Scottish hospitality. Internet and mail order case orders are welcomed.

Directions: *located at the rear of the Queen's Hotel which is on Henderson Street, Bridge of Allan, situated between the Wallace Monument and Dunblane Cathedral.*

Opening hours: *10am-5pm daily (not Christmas/New Year).* **19**

THE BUTTERCHURN AND SCOTTISH FOOD AND CRAFT CENTRE, Cocklaw Mains Farm, Kelty, Fife KY4 0JR

Est. 1979
Tel: +44 (0)1383-830169
Fax: +44 (0)1383-831614
www.butterchurn.co.uk
Parking available
Wheelchair access
Credit cards

Housed in renovated farm buildings, we have a collection of some of the best Scottish foods and crafts. All are sourced in Scotland. Our 'Taste of Scotland' restaurant is open all day. There is also a play park and animal farm for the children. Gallery exhibitions change monthly. Mail order available online.

Directions: *just off junc 4 of the M90 motorway. Follow brown signs from top of slip road.*

Opening hours: *Mon-Sun 9.30am-5.30pm.* **20**

CLYNELISH DISTILLERY, Brora, Sutherland KW9 6LR

Est. 1819
Tel: +44 (0)1408 623000
Fax: +44 (0)1408 623004
www.highlandescape.com
Parking available
Wheelchair access to shop and Visitor Centre
Credit cards

Visitors to the Distillery are given a warm welcome. Guided tour to see the ancient process of distilling. Knowledgeable guides explain the process. At the end of the tour there is a taste of a fourteen-year-old single malt. Entrance fee for tour. Shop sells whisky, sweaters and glassware. Mail order available.

Directions: *one mile north of coastal holiday village of Brora.*

Opening hours: *Mon-Fri 9am-5pm. Last tour 4pm.* **21**

DALWHINNIE DISTILLERY VISITOR CENTRE, Dalwhinnie, Inverness-shire PH19 1AB

Est. 1898
Tel: +44 (0)1540-672219
Fax: +44 (0)1540-672228
Parking available
W/chair access (not distillery)

Dalwhinnie Distillery is Scotland's highest distillery situated in splendid isolation at the meeting place of the old drove roads. Visitors can watch the distillers at work making one of Scotland's six 'classic malts' before it is casked and matured for fifteen years. There is a charge for tours. Mail order available.

Directions: mid-way on the A9 between Perth and Inverness. Follow A889 for one mile to Dalwhinnie. It is visible and well-signed.

Open: *Mar-Dec, Mon-Fri 9.30am/4.30pm; June-Oct: also Sat (same hours) and Sun 12.30/4.30pm. In winter (Dec-Mar) hours restricted and appointment is advisable.*   `22`

EDRADOUR DISTILLERY, Pitlochry, Perthshire PH16 5JP

Est. 1825 (Visitor Centre 1986)
Tel: +44 (0)1796-472095
Fax: +44 (0)1796-472002
www.edradour.co.uk
Parking available
Partially w/chair accessible
Credit cards

Scotland's smallest distillery nestles in hills east of Pitlochry. The last Scottish distillery to produce a handcrafted malt in limited quantity (12 casks a week) by traditional methods. See how the whisky is made then browse in the shop with a wide range of gifts. Free tour and tasting. Mail order available.

Directions: *from Pitlochry take A924 Braemar/Blairgowrie road through Moulin village. After climbing hill and passing over a small bridge you will see Edradour signed.*

Opening hours: *Mar-Oct, Mon-Sat 9.30am-5pm; Sun midday/5pm.*   `23`

ELLA DRINKS LIMITED, Alloa Business Centre, Alloa, Clackmannanshire FK10 3SA

Est. 1999
Tel: +44 (0)1259-721905
Fax: +44 (0)1259-834074
www.bouvrage.com
Credit cards (on-line)

We make Bouvrage Raspberry Drink, which contains a pound of Scottish raspberries to every 750ml and has a wonderful bitingly fresh taste and smell of raspberries. 'All natural ingredients, real juice drink.' Bouvrage is available from Sainsbury, Waitrose and some delicatessens nationwide but can also be ordered direct from the website. Cost from £1.19 for a slimline can. Private premises not open to public.

FLETCHERS OF AUCHTERMUCHTY, Reediehill Deer Farm, Auchtermuchty, Fife KY14 7HS

Est. 1976
Tel +44 (0)1337-828369
www.fletchersscotland.co.uk
Parking available
Two low steps for w/chairs
Credit cards

John and Nicola Fletcher produce venison and handmade venison products with no artificial ingredients. Britain's first deer farm, free range - everything done on farm. Venison cuts and joints; also veniburgers, oak smoked venison, venison haggis, venison pies and a range of venison sausages including venison with whisky. Recipes provided. Mail order available.

Directions: *take B936 north in Auchtermuchty and look out for small 'Venison, 2m' sign on a white gable end. Bear left there and follow signs for venison.*

Opening hours: *any time to suit by appointment only.*   `24`

GLENMORANGIE DISTILLERY, Tain, Ross-shire, IV19 1PZ

Est. 1843
Tel: +44 (0)1862-892477
www.glenmorangie.com
Parking on site
Limited wheelchair access
Credit cards

Glenmorangie Distillery forms a clutch of barns and outbuildings on the shores of Dornach Firth half a mile from Tain. Visitors can see the whisky making: mashing, fermentation and distillation. The on-site shop sells a range of Glenmorangie whiskies: single malt, vintage etc. plus pottery and locally produced preserves. Mail order available.

Directions: *on the A9, 2 minutes north of Tain, 45 minutes from Inverness.*

Opening hours: *Mon-Fri 9am-5pm all year; Sat 10am-4pm; Sun midday-4pm June-August.*   `25`

General Gifts

GRAMARYE STUDIO, An Cuilionn, Achmore, Stromeferry, Ross-shire IV53 8UU

Est. 1995
Tel/fax: +44 (0)1599-577264
www.gramaryestudio.co.uk
Parking available
Wheelchair access

In a small, friendly, working studio Annie Coomber prints offbeat, limited edition linocuts and produces papier-mâché items made from, or finished with, fine papers. Items include dishes and boxes. Notelets, gift packaging, tags and cards also available as are ceramics and painted silk. Mail order UK only via website.

Directions: *just off the Plockton to Stromeferry Road, north of Achmore Village.*
Opening hours: *Apr-Oct Mon-Sat 9.30am-5pm.*

Glass

BOWER GLASS DESIGNS, 49 Dunnett Avenue, Wick, Caithness KW1 4DY.

Est. 1998
Tel: +44 (0)1955-602567
Fax: +44 (0)1955-661344
www.caithnessstainedglass.co.uk
Parking available

Jean Anderson of Bower Glass produces stained glass artwork ranging from large individually designed panels to small items. Her speciality is **traditional leaded window and door panels** using the copper foil method. Also, painted glass panels, decorated mirrors, lamps, frames, gifts, candle-holders and furniture panels, glass mosaic work, all to original designs.

Directions: *the studio is located in the small town of Wick, just off main road northwards.*
Opening hours: *by appointment only.*

GLASS CREATIONS, Thurso Glass Studio, Riverside Road, Thurso, Caithness KW14 8BV

Est. 1990
Tel/fax: +44 (0)1847-894017
www.glasscreations.ukf.net
Parking available
Wheelchair access
Credit cards

From his studio on Scotland's northern coast, Glass Creations' glass artist and designer Ian Pearson produces a wide range of glassware to suit every requirement from **animals and flowers to presentation pieces** and sculptures. Functional items include bowls, candlesticks and holders. Wedding favours and cake tops a speciality. Mail order available.

Directions: *entering Thurso, take first right over road bridge, past tourist office on the right. Continue 200 yards and Glass Creations is the white building on left.*
Opening hours: *Mon-Sat 10am-5pm; Sun 2-5pm.*

HALF-A-MOON, Station Road, Ardersier, Inverness-shire IV2 7SU

Est. 1987
Tel: +44 (0)7774-842598
Fax: +44 (0)1463-238941
www.halfamoon.hypermart.net
Parking available
Wheelchair access

We design and manufacture **stained glass, fused glass and wrought iron** to our own unique designs. We can make anything from a small light catcher to a large panel, a candlestick to a weather vane and anything else you care to think of or commission. Mail order available.

Directions: *from the A96 Inverness to Aberdeen road B9006 to Ardesier; we are on the left at the 30mph sign.*
Opening hours: *Mon-Sat 11am-4.30pm. Other times by appointment.*

ICEBERG GLASSBLOWING STUDIO, Victoria Buildings, Drumadrochit, Inverness-shire IV63 6TX

Est. 1982
Tel: +44 (0)1456-450601
Parking available
Credit cards

Douglas Wilson and Julie Snowdon's studios offer lamp-worked glassblowing demonstrations and a range of glass products. You will see glass being heated, shaped and blown to form **contemporary jewellery and Scottish souvenirs,** vases, hanging decorations and life-like blue cats. The glass used is tough borosilicate. Mail order available.

Directions: *on the A82, between the two Loch Ness Monster exhibitions.*
Opening hours: *Mon-Sun 9am-8pm summer; 10am-5pm winter.*

WATERGLASS, The Old Exchange, Torran Donn, Ardelve by Wyle, Ross-shire IV40 8DY

Est. 1990 USA/2000 UK
Tel: +44 (0)1599-555452

Waterglass is a small stained glass studio producing **original and individually crafted leaded glass designs with primarily Celtic themes.** Items vary from small to large panels, along with faeries and dragons. A range of clan crests are also available to commission and by mail order. Enquiries are welcome.

Directions: *A87 towards Kyle, pass Eilean Donan Castle, left into Ardelve; small white building by telephone box.*
Opening hours: *Mon-Sat 10am-4pm.*

Jewellery

CAMAC JEWELLERY, 10 East Shore, Pittenweem, Anstruther, Fife KY10 2LE

Est. 1997
Tel/fax: +44 (0)1333-312465
Parking available
Credit cards

Camac Jewellery is run by David Mackin who makes sterling **silver pieces set with semi-precious stones** including Russian and Lithuanian amber, garnet, river pearls, amethyst, iolite and tourmaline, and is based in a fishing village near St Andrews. Designs include contemporary, Celtic and Art Nouveau. Commission work and mail order available.

Directions: *on the harbour front in Pittenweem.*
Opening hours: *prior appointment necessary.*

KNOCKAN STUDIO, Argyle Street, Ullapool, Ross-shire IV26 2UB

Est. 1994
Tel/fax: +44 (0)1854-613365
www.knockanstudio.com
Parking available
Wheelchair access
Credit cards

'The first and only' working Scottish jewellery and gemcutting studio specialising in **Scottish gold and Scottish gemstones.** Our other work includes abstract and contemporary designs in silver chosen for their artistic merit, use of colour and texture. We also carry a range of pottery and textiles by Scottish designers. Mail order available.

Directions: *directly opposite the police station in Ullapool.*
Opening hours: *Mon-Sat 9.30am-5pm.*

NICOLA FLETCHER, Reediehill Farm, Auchtermuchty, Fife KY14 7HS

Est. 1975
Tel: +44 (0)1337-828369
www.nicolafletcher.co.uk
Parking available
Assistance needed for w/chairs
Credit cards

Nicola produces **designer jewellery and silverware.** Everything is done to commission. One-off designs made of precious metals including titanium, usually inlaid with precious or semi-precious stones or exotic woods, or patinated metals. Public collections include the Victoria and Albert Museum and the Royal Scottish Museum, Edinburgh. Private and corporate work undertaken.

Directions: *take B936 north in Auchtermuchty and look out for small 'Venison, 2m' sign on a white gable end. Bear left there and follow signs for venison.*
Opening hours: *any time to suit by appointment only.*

THE STUDIO JEWELLERY WORKSHOP GALLERY AND CAFE, Achnasheen, Wester Ross IV22 2EE

Est. 1998 (gallery)
1979 (workshop)
Tel/fax +44 (0)1445-720 227
www.studiojewellery.com
Parking easily available
Wheelchair access

The Studio Jewellery Workshop has been established for twenty two years and has built up a reputation for the quality of jewellery and silverware produced by Susan Plowman. Also on show is the largest selection of contemporary jewellery in the Highlands, fine art prints, glass, designer clothing and ceramics. Fabulous wholefood café.

Directions: *From Inverness take the A9 north, then the A835, then the A832 to Achnasheen: Gallery is in the centre next to the railway station.*

Opening hours: *9.30am-5pm, 7 days a week. (6 days Sept-April).*

Metalwork & Silversmithing

METALWORK AND SILVERWARE, Aultbeag, Grandtully, by Aberfeldy, Perthshire PH15 2QU

Est. 1968
Tel: +44 (0)1887-840484
Fax: +44 (0)1877-840785
Parking available
Wheelchair access

Exceptional designer and engraver, Malcolm Appleby is a goldsmith and silversmith. He has worked for the V & A, The British Museum, The Royal Armouries, The Worshipful Company of Goldsmiths' Hunterian Museum, the National Museum of Finland, The Fitzwilliam Museum in Cambridge and private collections. He does **jewellery, medals, beakers, candlesticks and engraving.**

Directions: *off the A9 (Ballinluig turn off), then Aberfeldy. Aultbeag road on left at Grandtully. Yellow house at end of the road.*

Opening hours: *by appointment only.*

ORNAMENTAL IRONWORK, 83 Abbey Road, Scone, Perthshire PH2 6JS

Est. 1993
Tel: +44 (0)1738-552925
Street parking
Wheelchair access

Garden and Eileen Morrison specialise in wrought ironwork in various designs: **patio planters, house plant stands,** wine racks, candle stands, house nameplates, window and door grilles. Also available are a large range of floral art stands a selection of which are always available for viewing on the premises.

Directions: *take the A94 from Perth. Turn left at The Scone Arms pub which leads on to Abbey Road.*

Opening hours: *Mon-Thurs 9am-5pm. Appointment preferred.*

Pottery & Ceramics

CARRBRIDGE POTTERY STUDIO, Station Road, Carrbridge, Inverness-shire PH23 3AN

Est. 1992
Tel/fax: +44 (0)1479-841247
www.carrbridgestudios.com
Parking available
Wheelchair access
Credit cards

Pottery studio and workshop of potter/sculptress Alice Buttress, with a unique and varied selection of original work. She produces handthrown and handbuilt **decorative pottery, ceramic jewellery, raku,** animal and figure sculptures. Also watercolour prints. Visitors can watch a pot being thrown or have a go themselves. Mail order available.

Directions: *23 miles south of Inverness off the A9. In Carrbridge, turn into Station Road (opposite Post Office) half way up road on right.*

Opening hours: *Mon, Wed, Fri 10am-6pm. Other times by appointment.*

CRAIL POTTERY, 75 Netaergate, Crail, Fife KY10 3TX

Est 1965
Tel: +44 (0)1333-451212
www.crailpottery.com
Parking available
Wheelchair access
Credit cards

Set in a flower filled courtyard at the heart of Crail, this is a family pottery of three generations standing. We produce a diverse range of **stoneware and decorated earthenware;** from mugs to salad sets and cookery pots to planters. Every piece is hand thrown, decorated and glazed in our workshops.

Directions: *in the centre of Crail follow the sign on the chemists down Rose Wynd to the pottery.*

Opening hours: *Mon-Fri 9am-5pm, Sat/Sun 10am-5pm.*

EARTHEN IMAGES, Unit 27b, Hawkslaw Trading Estate, Riverside Road, Leven, Fife KY8 4LT

Est. 1990
Tel/fax: +44 (0)1333-421165
www.made-in-fife.co.uk
Parking available
Wheelchair access
Credit cards

We specialise in making **pottery cats and friends** using stoneware clay. 'Methil Moggie' is our main product which now has a collectors' following and comes with its own legend. Visitors are welcome at the workshop to see the selection of moggies, mutts, moos and many more affordable gifts. Trade enquiries welcome.

Directions: *the industrial estate is opposite Sainsbury's supermarket.*

Opening hours: *Mon-Fri 8.30am-5pm.*

HIGHLAND STONEWARE, Lochinver, Sutherland IV27 4LP.

Est. 1974
Tel: +44 (0)1571-844376
Fax: +44 (0)1571-844626
www.highlandstoneware.com
Parking available
W/chair access (if assisted)
Credit cards

High quality hand made decorative ceramic stoneware, **tableware, cookware, gifts and tiles.** All making processes can be viewed at our Ullapool potteries. The decorating artists are inspired by their beautiful surroundings: scenery, flora and fauna and fish are painted on to the pottery. 'Art pottery - designed to be used.' Mail order available.

Directions: 96 miles north west of Inverness. Take A897 via Ullapool to Lochinver then follow signs for the Pottery.

Opening hours: *weekdays all year 9am-6pm. Mon-Sat Easter to Oct.*

LOCH-AN-EILEIN POTTERY, Rothiemurchus, Aviemore, Inverness PH22 1QP

Est. 1980
Tel/fax: +44 (0)1479-810837
www.scotland2000
Parking available
Wheelchair access

Penny Weir makes **glazed terracotta domestic ware.** She specialises in jugs of all sizes from cream jugs to pitchers, and in large breakfast cups, teapots, mugs, storage jars and garden pots. Thursday is 'throw-your-own' day and for a small charge your pot can be glazed and fired. Mail order available.

Directions: *take the B970 to Cairngorm out of Aviemore, right at T-junction, first left signed to Loch-an-Eilein. 2 miles from Aviemore.*

Opening hours: *Tues-Sun 10am-5pm. Closed Mon.*

LOCH TAY POTTERY, Lawers View, Fearnan, Aberfeldy PH15 2PF

Est. 1983
Tel: +44 (0)1887-830251
Parking available

Andy Burt produces a wide range of **functional and decorative stoneware pottery.** Domestic items are robust and durable and include egg cups, amphorae, casseroles, tattie pots, bread crocks, vases, large jugs and urns. Visitors, buyers and browsers always welcome to visit the showroom. Demonstrations and/or instruction by arrangement.

Directions: *at Ballinluig on the A9. Take the A827 to Fearnan, passing through Aberfeldy and Kenmore.*

Open: *Open all year round. Mon-Sun 9am-5pm. Advisable to tel in advance.*

NETHYBRIDGE POTTERY, Grantown-on-Spey, Morayshire PH26 3NH

Est. 1998
Tel: +44 (0)1479-821114
www.nethybridge.com/pottery
Parking available
Wheelchair access
Credit cards

Rob Lawson makes **chunky functional dinnerware:** plates, bowls, serving dishes, goblets, mugs, teapots, jugs etc. in blues and greens. Other pieces such as candlesticks, lampbases, bottles, vases, plates and platters all vary in design and glaze colour and patterns. All making processes can be viewed at various times. Mail order available.

Directions: *on B970, one and a half miles from Nethybridge and three and a half miles from Grantown-on-Spey. Easy access from A9 and Aviemore.*

Opening hours: *Mon-Fri 10am-5pm.*

RUTHERFORD'S WHISKY CERAMICS, Montrose Pottery, Brechin Road, Montrose, Angus DD10 9LU

Est. 1834
Tel: +44 (0)1674-677733
Fax: +44 (0)1674-673132
www.thespiritofscotland.co.uk
Large car park
Wheelchair access
Credit cards

Rutherford's have been producers of fine whiskies since 1834. These are now available in a range of **ceramic bottles and decanters** made in our own pottery. We specialise in small, limited editions to commemorate important events and can also personalise individual decanters to mark a wedding, retirement etc. £6-£150. Mail order available.

Directions: *one mile west of Montrose on the A935 to Brechin.*

Opening hours: *weekdays usually 9am-5pm. Weekends 10am-5pm. Telephoning ahead advised.*

ST ANDREWS POTTERY SHOP, 4 Church Square, St Andrews, Fife KY16 9NN

Est 1984
Tel/fax: +44 (0)1334-4777444
Parking available
Wheelchair access
Credit cards

At the St Andrews Pottery Shop in the centre of St Andrews we have a wide range of **decorative pottery,** made by proprietor George Young, to suit the needs of visitors and locals alike. The selection of pots changes regularly. We are very happy to discuss commissions. Mail order available.

Directions: *in town centre behind ladies' toilets and Doll's House Restaurant in Church Square.*

Opening hours: *Mon-Sat 9.30am-5.30pm. Seasonal Sun opening.*

SPEYSIDE POTTERY, Ballindalloch, Banffshire AB37 9BJ

Est 1989
Tel: +44 (0)1807-500338
www.users.globalnet.co.uk
/-tgough
Parking available
Credit cards

The pottery produces both **domestic ware and display pieces.** All pottery is oven, dishwasher and microwave proof. The pots are all handmade from stoneware clay and are fired to a temperature of 1,300 C in a wood-fired kiln. Mail order is available upon request. Please visit website or telephone for further details.

Directions: *on A95 16 miles north east of Grantown-on-Spey; 5 miles south west of Aberlour and near Glenfarclas Distillery.*

Opening hours: *mid-Mar-Oct Mon-Sun 10am-5pm.*

SUTHERLAND POTTERY, Shinness, Lairg, Sutherland IV27 4DN

Est. 1974
Tel: +44 (0)1549-402223
Parking available
Wheelchair access
Credit cards

Hubert Corbett makes hand thrown stoneware pottery produced and decorated on site. Each item is unique, i.e. never two the same. **Ceramic clocks are a speciality** and unique to this pottery. Also for sale are sheepskins, deerskins, woollens etc. all locally produced. Coffee lounge with home baking. Mail order available.

Directions: *follow A836 north from Lairg until you come to signs for pottery two miles further.*

Opening hours: *Mon-Sun 8am-9pm.*

VERONICA NEWMAN, Wester Golford, Moyness, Nairn, Inverness-shire IV12 5QQ

Est. 1997
Tel: +44 (0)1309-641203
www.veronicanewman.co.uk
Parking available

I make hand thrown porcelain specialising in a range of fine **porcelain bowls, boxes and vases** as well as domestic ware and 1/12th scale miniatures for dolls' houses. Many pieces are translucent, some painted with on-glaze lustre using precious metals requiring a third kiln firing. Commissions welcome. Mail order available.

Directions: *from Auldearn (nr. Nairn on A96) take road by war memorial to Moyness. After 2 miles first left. Pottery is half a mile on right.*

Opening hours: *by appointment.*

WOODLAND POTTERY, Strontian Village Centre, Strontian, Ardnamurchan, Argyll PH36 4HZ

Est. 1993
Tel: +44 (0)1967-402175
www.strontian.fsnet.co.uk
Parking available
Credit cards

Pottery was a hobby before I became established and opened my own workshop. All the pottery is made on site. I specialise in **slip cast and hand-decorated pottery** with a wide range of designs. I also sell locally made items including wooden toys, garden ornaments and walking sticks. Mail order available.

Directions: *centre of Strontian, next to the main village store and tourist office and police station.*

Open: *Easter-Nov daily 9.30am-5pm. Appointment needed for Jan/Feb.*

Textiles

ABHRAS, 1, Altass by Lairg, Sutherland, IV27 4EU

Est. 1988 (Skye)
Tel: +44 (0)1549-441256
Parking available

Abhras is Gaelic for woolwork. Sonia Bidwell specialises in **dramatic woven pictures/ wall hangings** depicting stories from Gaelic and Norse culture. She also does unusual, unique knitwear from handspun wools and sheepskin fur fashion. She will work from customers' own designs and ideas. Very competitive prices. Worldwide mail order.

Directions: *given when appointment is made*
Opening hours: *flexible, by appointment.*

CLAGGAN CRAFTS, Claggan, Lochaline, Morvern, Argyll PA34 5XB

Est. 1987
Tel: +44 (0)1967-421240
Fax: +44 (0)1967-421281
Parking available
Assisted wheelchair access

Attractive knitwear workshop and gallery situated in beautiful Morvern countryside, selling a variety of locally-produced crafts and a **large range of knitwear** from plain or cable to picture knits. We can create a design of your pet knitted on a jumper or wall-hanging. Colour mail order brochure available.

Directions: *4 miles north of Lochaline on A884.*
Opening hours: *11am-4pm daily (closed Tues & Sat).*

DI GILPIN HANDKNITWEAR, Burghers Close, 141 South Street, St Andrews, Fife, Scotland KY16 9UN

Est. 1983
Tel: +44 (0)1334-476193
www.handknitwear.com
Parking available
Limited wheelchair access
Credit cards

Design Studio in the heart of St Andrews stocks high quality **contemporary clothing, knitwear, jewellery and accessories.** Also specialist Handknitting Studio with a glorious range of handknitting yarns and patterns from Di Gilpin, Rowan, Jaeger, Colinette and Jamieson's of Shetland. Workshops are available all year alongside a mail order catalogue and website.

Directions: *Burghers Close is in the centre of St Andrews just off South Street.*
Opening hours: *Mon-Sun 10am-6pm.*

JAMES PRINGLE WEAVERS OF INVERNESS, Holm Woollen Mill, Dores Road, Inverness IV2 4RB

Est. 1798
Tel: +44 (0)1463-223311
Fax: +44 (0)1463-231042
Parking for coaches and cars
Wheelchair access
Credit cards

After two hundred years of manufacturing textiles, the Mill is still producing today. Factory tour, tartan exhibition and 'have a go' at weaving tartan on a hand loom. On site shop sells knitwear and clothing, gifts, golf clothing and equipment. Pure new wool **tartan travel rugs** made on site. Mail order possible.

Directions: *on Bridge Street in Inverness.*
Opening hours: *Mar-Oct Mon-Sun 9am/5.30pm; Oct-Mar 10am/5pm.*

McCALMAN KILTS, 6 North Roundall, Limekilns, Fife KY11 35Y

Est. 1988
Tel/fax: +44 (0)1383-872677
www.mccalman-kilts.co.uk
Parking available
Credit cards

Laura Hepplewhite, proprietor of McCalman Kilts, has been established as a **kilt maker** for many years. All of her kilts are handstitched in the time-honoured way using traditional methods. All kilts are produced by Laura in her premises attached to the family home. Mail order enquiries welcome from all over world.

Directions: *two miles up river from Forth Road Bridge, north (Fife) side. Take first left at village 30 mph limit sign; then second left. Door under car port.*
Opening hours: *appointment necessary.*

SANDY MACPHERSON, Inverhoullin, Tarbet, Arrochar, Loch Lomond, Argyll G83 7DN

Est. 1973
Tel: +44 (0)1301-702685
Fax: +44 (0)1301-702269
Parking available
Wheelchair access
Credit cards

Sandy Macpherson does handloom weaving on site using a 150-year-old loom. Visitors are welcome to observe the work while gazing over Loch Lomond. He specialises in **tartan blankets and plaids.** Also on sale are handknitted Arran sweaters in cream, fawn, navy blue and grey. Mail order available. Adjacent restaurant.

Directions: *just over a mile north of Tarbet on the A82.*

Opening hours: *Mon-Sun 9am-5pm.*

Toys & Games

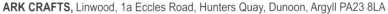

ARK CRAFTS, Linwood, 1a Eccles Road, Hunters Quay, Dunoon, Argyll PA23 8LA

Est. 1992
Tel: +44 (0)1369-706157
Fax: +44 (0)1369-706157
Parking available
Credit cards

We specialise in the design and manufacture of wooden toys: **vehicles and animals** to stimulate creative play. Vehicles: trains, fire engine, horse box, lorries and vans, digger and cars. Animals: cats and teddy bears and a range of animals on wheels. Bright colours or plain. Colour brochure for mail order available.

Directions: *from Western Ferries turn right; first left, then at the top of the hill turn right. First house on left, approx. 100 yards from ferry.*

Opening hours: *Mon-Sat 10am-4pm.*

THE CAMINO WORKSHOP LTD, 19 Commercial Street, Alyth, Perthshire PH11 8AF

Est. 1988
Tel/fax: +44 (0)1828-633632
Parking available
Wheelchair access
Credit cards

We make handcrafted **dolls' houses, shops and miniature furniture** for collectors of all ages. Exclusive makers of 'Coronation Street' range; also Charles Rennie Mackintosh. Additionally we offer a design service and commissions are welcomed (your own house in miniature?), wooden toys and nursery furniture also produced. Catalogue and mail order available.

Directions: *over the stream running adjacent to the town square; approximately 10 miles north-west of Dundee.*

Opening hours: *10am-5pm daily. Closed Wed & Sun.*

NESS CRAFTS, Ness Cottage, Scotstown, Strontian, Acharacle PH36 4JB

Est. 1995
Tel: +44 (0)1967-402028
Parking available
Wheelchair access difficult

Jane and Tim Collins run their small workshop specializing in wood and wool crafts individually made and finished. Tim, a retired woodwork teacher makes wooden toys: **trains, trucks, lorries, tractors, animal jigsaws and puzzles.** Jane machine and hand knits jumpers, hats etc. plus hand spinning yarn. Demonstrations given.

Directions: *from Strontian take Polloch road for approx. two miles. On the left, 200 yards past red telephone box.*

Opening hours: *Easter-December. Closed Thurs & Sun.*

Woodturning & Furniture

BURNSIDE BALLINTOMB FURNITURE MAKERS, Archiestown, Aberlour, Moray AB38 7QT

Est. 1987 this address
Tel/fax: +44 (0)1340-810495
www.gvis.co.uk/ballintomb-furniture
Parking available

Over 56 years of craftsmanship are built into every piece of **quality hardwood furniture,** designed and constructed here on Speyside by father and son team Henry and Julian Schmechel. Traditional mortice and tenon joints and dovetails used throughout. Visitors welcome to discuss their requirements. Mail order and delivery worldwide.

Directions: *one mile out of Archiestown on left hand side of road to Knocklands Road.*

Opening hours: *weekdays 9am-5pm. Weekends by appointment.*

LETHENTY MILL FURNITURE, Lethenty Mill, Inverurie, Aberdeenshire AB51 OHQ

Est. 1977
Tel: +44 (0)1467-622489
Fax +44 (0)1467-629631
www. lethenty-mill.com/
www.wood-shop.co.uk
Parking available.
Wheelchair access
Credit cards

Established in 1977, Lethenty Mill Furniture is a traditionally run and family owned business specialising in **handcrafted kitchens and furniture** made from locally grown hardwoods. We carefully select local ash, elm, oak and beech wood which we then cut and season at our mill. Our skilled craftsmen can assist with design or we can work from customer's own designs, ensuring each piece of furniture made is unique and of the highest quality. We also sell a range of woodworking tools, finishing products, books, wood blanks and our own local hardwood. Please view our Website www.wood-shop.co.uk for more details: mail order available.

Directions: *from Aberdeen take the A96 to Inverness: at Inverurie turn right on to the B9170, follow road for about 2 miles then right at our sign.*

Opening hours: *9am-5pm Mon-Fri; 10am-5pm Sat.*

PETER TYLER - WOODTURNER, Milton of Tordarroch, Dunlichity, Farr, Inverness IV2 6XF

Est. 1996
Tel: +44 (0)1808-521414
www.petertyler.fsbusiness.co.uk
Parking available
Wheelchair access
Credit cards

Locally sourced hardwoods are used to make a **wide range of domestic turned woodware, o**rnamental articles, and small items of furniture. The pieces are designed to be practical and beautiful. The craft shop next to the workshop stocks willow basketwork, pottery, weaving, jewellery and stationery - all hand made locally.

Directions: *south of Inverness, five miles west of the A9 on the Daviot to Dunlichity and Loch Duntelchaig Road (unclassified).*

Opening hours: *April-Dec Mon-Sat 10am-5.30pm.*

RON PARKER SCULPTURE, Beachens Two, Dunphail, Forres, Moray IV36 2QH

Est. 1990
Tel: +44 (0)1309-611273
Parking available
Wheelchair access
Credit cards

Hand made wood sculpture. Each piece individually worked and unique. Subjects include **birds, animals, figures and abstracts,** large and small using local hardwoods obtained from managed sites. Oak, elm, yew, laburnum, rhododendron etc. or customer provides the raw material for the sculptures. A wide range of work is always available. Commissions undertaken.

Directions: *situated just off the A940 midway between Forres and Grantown-on-Spey. Signposted 'Sculpture Workshop.'*

Opening hours: *daily 9am-6pm. Weekends by appointment.*

Other Makers

THE CLANSMAN CENTRE, Fort Augustus, Loch Ness, PH32 4BD

Est. 1995
Tel/fax: +44 (0)1320-366444
www.scottish-swords.com
Parking available
Wheelchair access
Credit cards

The Centre, run by Alistair Stoddart comprises live presentations of 17th century Highland life, Celtic craft shop selling jewellery and locally produced work, and a Scottish armoury selling weapons made on the premises: **swords, dirks, sgians, targes (shields)** axes and clothing and leatherware (sporrans, belts, cuarans etc). Mail order available.
Directions: *centre of Fort Augustus, on western point of Loch Ness beside the A82 and the Caledonian Canal swing bridge; a two-minute walk from the carpark.*
Opening hours: *Mon-Sun 10am-6pm (reduced hours in winter).*

COLLECTAIR 2000, 32 West Hemming Street, Letham, Angus DD8 2PU

Est. 1995
Tel/fax: +44 (0)1307-818494
Parking available
Credit cards

Peter Fergusson makes mainly **aircraft models cast in pewter** or resin. Products are supplied to aircraft preservation groups, aviation museums etc. and are provided as cast or polished, available plain as fridge magnets or keyrings, or on a stand. Fellow aviation enthusiasts always welcome to discuss their requirements. Mail order.
Directions: *from Forfar take Arbroath road. After five miles turn right (signposted Letham). In Letham take a right at crossroads. No 32 is 500 yards on left.*
Opening hours: *by appointment only.*

EMBROIDERED ORIGINALS, The Embroidery Workshop, Blacketyside, Largo Road, Leven, Fife KY8 5PX

Est. 1989
Tel: +44 (0)1333-423985
Fax: +44 (0)1333-439158
www.made-in-fife.co.uk
Parking available
Credit cards

We design and produce hand made gifts for special occasions, using our unique blend of **embroidery, applique and hand lettering.** The compact showroom displays the full range, plus our Scottish keepsakes and Christmas designs (all year round). A mail order catalogue is available upon request. Please telephone for details.
Directions: *one mile out of Leven on the A915 (St Andrews) Road. We are directly opposite Silverburn Park.*
Opening hours: *Tues-Sat 10am-5pm, Sun 1-5pm.*

ORCADIAN STONE COMPANY LTD, Main Street, Golspie, Sutherland KW10 6RH

Est. 1970
Tel/fax: +44 (0)1408-633483
Parking available
Partially w/chair accessible
Credit cards

A family business, which sells jewellery and **giftware made from gemstones and natural stone.** The stone range includes clocks, lamps, vases, paperweights, pens and table tops. There is also a large exhibition of Highland and worldwide geology: rocks, minerals and fossils, including model, diorama and interpretive panels. Mail order available.
Directions: *on the A9 about an hour's drive north of Inverness. Situated on the left, 100 yards north of Golspie Post Office.*
Opening hours: *Mon-Sat 9am-5.30pm; Sun 10am-4pm in season.*

SHIRLEY I. FERGUSON CRAFTS, 30 West Hemming Street, Letham, Angus D08 2PU

Est. 1971
Tel/fax: +44 (0)1307-818494
Parking available
Credit cards

Graphic designer Shirley Ferguson **hand paints round stones with miniatures** of Scottish animals, birds, flowers and ancient monuments. Each one is signed and dated. She also makes jewellery (including pendants, brooches and scarf rings) using white quartz and agate hand painted with tiny designs. Prices are from £6-£100 and commissions are welcome.
Directions: *A90 to Forfar, East on to the A932. After 5 miles turn south to Letham. Studio on main street in village.*
Opening hours: *most times but appointment necessary.*

TARGEMAGER, Balquhidder, Main Street, North Kessock, Inverness IV1 3XN

Est. 1989
Tel: +44 (0)1463-731577
www.targemaker.co.uk
Parking available

Joe Lindsay's interest in the Jacobite era led to his business of hand crafting high quality **reproductions of original Scottish Highlander shields** (targes). These are about 19 inches diameter and covered with hide and deerskin with the front decorated with brass studs. Designs according to clan or maker's own. Mail order available.

Directions: *cross Kessock Bridge heading north from Inverness on A9. First junction left after bridge and follow road through Kessock to 150 metres E of hotel.*
Opening hours: *Mon-Sun 9am-7pm.*   (69)

WILLIAM MANSON PAPERWEIGHTS, Unit 2, Nether Friarton, Friarton Road, Perth, Scotland PH2 8DF

Est. 1997
Tel/fax +44 (0)1738-441007
Parking for cars and coaches
Wheelchair access
www.williammanson.co.uk
Credit cards

William Manson Paperweights was founded in July 1997 by William snr. and his wife Joyce and joined by their daughter Carolyn and son William jnr., also a paperweight artist. William snr. has 35 years glassmaking experience behind him and is regarded as Scotland's leading glass artist. We create **limited edition highly collectable paperweights.** Designs include flowers, fish, reptiles and insects, each signed by the artist. Special commissions are undertaken. Prices start from £55.00. Try our Masterclass, a unique opportunity to come to our studio to learn the art of paperweight making under the tuition of William snr and William jnr. E-mail williammanson@btconnect.com.

Directions: *exit M90 at junction 10; after passing sign for Scone Palace take first right; we are approx. 200 yards ahead on left.*
Opening hours: *9am-6pm Mon-Sat.*

Scottish Islands

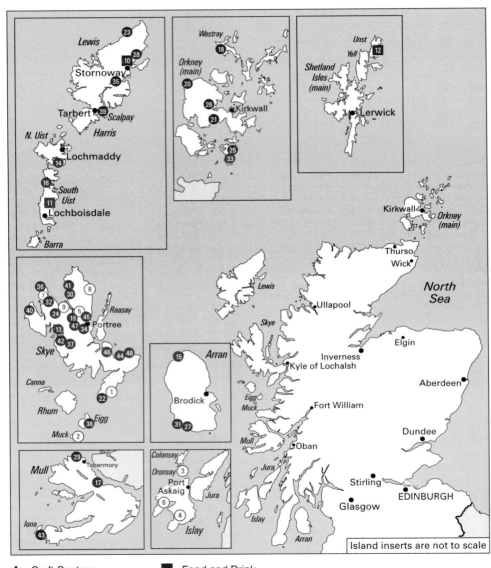

▲ Craft Centres **■** Food and Drink

○ Shops and Galleries **●** Makers' Workshops

Island inserts are not to scale

Romanticism is a luxury in the Islands; but then life has always been tough for the small island communities, especially in winter. Tourism income can be supplemented by the artefacts and craft products which many of them make.

The Isle of Skye in particular has become a haven for craft makers of all kinds, many of them originally from other parts of Britain. Even the small islands like Eigg, Colonsay and Scalpay have potters and jewellery designer/makers, dairies making hand made cheeses and others have toymakers and tapestry and cloth weavers.

The Western Isles, Orkney, and Shetland produce all the above, and in addition hand-knitted items made from the oiled wool of local sheep are much sought after. Shetland has Britain's northernmost brewery.

Craft Shops

ARMADALE POTTERY, Armadale, Ardvasar, Sleat, Isle of Skye IV45 8RS

Est. 1985
Tel: +44 (0)1471-844439
Parking available
Wheelchair access
Credit cards

A large variety of pottery is made on the premises: crystal glazed earthenware, stoneware, plus porcelain buttons. We also sell the work of three other Skye potteries, and other local crafts: paintings, cards, photographs, woodturning, pewter jewellery, gem-set silver jewellery, dolls and tote bags. Also minerals and fossil specimens. Mail order available.

Directions: *at the junction of the Armadale and Ardvasar Roads, 200 metres from the ferry terminal at Armadale.*

Opening hours: *7 days a week Easter-Nov 9.30pm-5.30pm.*   ①

CRAFTSHOP/TEAROOM ON ISLE OF MUCK, Gallanach, Isle of Muck PH42 4RP

Est. 1990
Tel: +44 (0)1687-462362
No car landing
Wheelchair access
Credit cards

Muck has a population of 28 and two Landrovers. The shop stocks quality local crafts including handknits (jumpers, socks, gloves etc), embroidered wall hangings and patchwork, leatherwork, homemade jams, marmalade and fudge, hand painted cards and slate paintings and clocks, silver jewellery and hand spun wools. The tearoom serves home baking.

Directions: *5 minutes walk from the harbour pier, or a one and a half mile walk from the second boat landing stage.*

Opening hours: *from May to October and flexible.*   ②

HEAVEN'S OCEAN, Barabhaig, Cruard, Camus Croise, Isle of Oronsay IV43 8QT

Est. 2001
Tel: +44 (0)1471-833475
Parking available
Wheelchair access

A studio on the shore, overlooking Camus Croise Bay to Sandaig Lighthouse which specialises in watercolour paintings and driftwood craft. Offers landscape paintings and pen and ink drawings and mirrors and frames made from driftwood. Also, collages, boxes and hand made cards. Coffee and tea provided. Children welcome.

Directions: *follow signs for Camus Croise and take the road along the shore. Our studio is next to the first house after the end of the public road.*

Opening hours: *Mon-Sun 10am-6pm.*   ③

ISLAY HEATHERS, Glenegedale House, Glenegedale, Isle of Islay, Argyll PA42 7AS

Est 1990
Tel: +44 (0)1496-302147
Fax: +44 (0)1496-302210
Parking available
Wheelchair access
Credit cards

A well-stocked shop selling a range of hand made and Scottish produced goods. Hand made items include patchwork quilts and cushions, teddy bears, pot-pourris, flower baskets, staghorn objects and walking sticks, plus hand painted pottery and wooden items. The shop also stocks woollens, candles, soaps, cosmetics etc. Mail order available.

Directions: *halfway on road between Bowmore and Port Ellen directly opposite the Islay airport.*

Opening hours: *Mon-Sun 9am-5pm.*　(4)

OVER THE RAINBOW, Quay Brae, Portree, Isle of Skye, Inverness-shire IV51 9DB

Est 1976
Tel/fax: +44 (0)1478-612555
Parking available
Credit cards

Uniquely situated above the harbour, Over the Rainbow Studio Design makes and sells knitwear and some jewellery. Our attractive, high quality Isle of Skye knitwear is internationally recognised as a leader amongst Scottish rural products. Colour predominates through complementary ranges of Scottish textiles including tweeds and tartans. Mail order worldwide.

Directions: *at the top of the Brae leading down to the Pier.*

Opening hours: *7 days 9am-9pm summer; Mon-Sat 9am-6pm winter.*　(5)

TORMISDALE CROFT CRAFTS, Tormisdale Croft, by Port Charlotte, Isle of Islay, Argyll PA48 7UE

Est 1986
Tel/fax: +44 (0)1496-860239
Parking available
Wheelchair access
Credit cards

The shop is on a working croft. We make all the crafts at the croft and wherever possible use recycled materials, driftwood and natural dyes. Visitors can see crafts being made including hand-spinning, staghorn carving, silk painting, patchwork etc, every day. All crafts are one-off designs. Commissions welcome. Mail order available.

Directions: *turn right in Port Charlotte by telephone box and continue for about four and a half miles to sign and turn right. Follow signs to shop.*

Opening hours: *Mon-Sun 9am-6pm. Other times by appointment.*　(6)

Galleries

DANDELION DESIGNS & IMAGES GALLERY, The Captain's House, Stein, Waternish, Isle of Skye IV55 8GA

Est. 1995
Tel: +44 (0)1470-592218
Parking available
Wheelchair access
Credit cards

Craft workshop and gallery specialising in quality hand made local crafts including our own distinctive woodcrafts with unique designs utilising pyrography and watercolour painting techniques. Original designs are inspired by Celtic art, Art Nouveau and the environment and landscape of the Hebrides: boxes, clocks, plaques, jewellery, clothing and more. Mail order available.

Directions: *take Dunvegan-Portree road, turn off on to B886 at Faery Bridge (4 miles from Edinbane) and travel 4 miles to·Stein.*

Open: *seven days 11am-5pm Easter to Oct. Other times by appointment.*　

THREE HERONS GALLERY, Old Mission Church, Culnacnoc, 4 miles south of Staffin, Trotternish, Isle of Skye

Est 1998
Tel: +44 (0)1470-562755 gallery
Tel: +44 (0)1471-822152 studio
www.isleofskye.net/threeherons/

The gallery sells fine art photographic prints, paintings by Ken Bryan and textiles by Polly Bryan. Polly makes hand woven and batik scarves and hangings. Other items on sale include hand made cards and small gifts. Mail order available. The Bryans also have a studio (Three Herons Studio, High Road, Broadford, Skye).

Directions: *gallery is 4 miles south of Staffin on A55. Studio is next to Broadford Hospital - take road opposite The Bank of Scotland.*

Open: *gallery 10am-5.30pm Mon-Fri Apr-Oct. Studio same hours plus 9am-1.30pm Sat.*

STUDIO FANKS, Fanks, by Portree, Isle of Skye IV51 9PX

Est 2001
Tel: +44 (0)1470-582330
Parking available
Wheelchair access
Credit cards

Studio Fanks opened in order to sell directly to the public. It is a small working artist's studio where Caroline Dear produces contemporary artworks. Her work includes basket forms, for which only local materials are used, black and white abstract landscape photography and also artists' books. Mail order available.

Directions: *12 miles from Portree on A850, turn right for Fanks. Studio Fanks is the first house on the left by the sea.*

Opening hours: *Mon-Sat 1pm-6pm.*

Food & Drink

HEATHER ISLE MEATS, The Abattoir, Rigs Road, Stornoway, Isle of Lewis H51 2RF

Est. 1993
+44 (0)1851-706733
Fax: +44 (0)1851-706803
Parking available

Lamb and beef products from black-faced sheep and Highland cattle naturally bred and reared on the crofts of the Outer Hebrides and grazed on machair (coastal grassland fertilised by shell sand thrown up from the sea) and hill top, heather and wild flower pasture, giving a unique tasting meat. Mail order available.

Directions: *Ullapool to Stornoway ferry and 5 minutes walk from ferry terminal or Skye to Tarbert (on Harris) then 40 minutes drive.*

Opening hours: *Mon-Thurs 9am-5pm; Friday closing at 4pm.*

SALAR FLAKY SMOKED SALMON, The Pier, Locarnan, Isle of South Uist, Outer Hebrides HS8 5PD

Est. 1983
Tel/fax: +44 (0)1870-610369
www.salar.co.uk
Parking available
Wheelchair access
Credit cards

Award-winning flaky smoked salmon from a process which cooks and smokes the fish producing a succulent and versatile product that can be eaten in pasta and other cooked dishes, in sandwiches, with salad, and hot or cold. Available direct from the smokehouse, ordered or bought from delicatessens, and national/international mail order.

Directions: *on the pier at Locarnan.*

Opening hours: *Mon-Fri 9am-5pm.*

VALHALLA BREWERY, Baltasound, Unst, Shetland ZE2 9DX

Est 1997
Tel/fax: +44 (0)1957-711658
www.valhallabrewery.co.uk
Parking available
Wheelchair access
Credit cards

Valhalla Brewery is Britain's most northerly brewery. We currently produce three cask-conditioned real ales and have recently added a fourth. These ales are all also available in bottles. Our ales are Auld Rock (4.5% ABV), White Wife (3.8%), Simmer Dim (4.0%) and New Stout (5.0%). Mail order available.

Directions: *follow main road (A968) north through Unst and you will find the Valhalla Brewery on your left as you approach the village of Baltasound.*

Opening hours: *Prior appointment necessary.*

General Gifts

AURORA CRAFTS, 2 Ose, Isle of Skye IU56 8FJ

Est 1984
Tel: +44 (0)1478-572208
Parking available
Credit cards

Situated in an attractive wildlife garden, we make bobbin lace and knitwear. We also sell woodturning, embroidery, beadwork and other crafts. Lace makes an ideal gift or souvenir. It is light and easy to pack. Mail order is available to customers on request. Please telephone for details.

Directions: *off A863, 6 miles south of Dunvegan. 600 yards along side road at Ose and then signposts to Aurora Crafts.*

Opening hours: *Mon-Sun 9am-7pm.*

13

ISLAND CRAFTS, Cnoc Ard, Grimsay, North Uist, Western Isles H56 5HU

Est 1956
Tel: +44 (0)1870-602418
Parking available
Credit cards

Lachlan Macdonald worked in the Harris tweed industry and now does a limited amount of hand weaving on the traditional four shaft wooden loom making chair backs with an emphasis on colour and texture. The shop also sells island pottery,books, knitwear cards, quality souvenirs and tweed. Mail order available.

Directions: *from south on A865, cross Long Benbecula and North Uist Causeway; then take signposted second turning on right.*

Opening hours: *Mon-Sun 10am onwards.*

14

THE WHINS - CRAFTS WORKSHOP, The Whins, Lochranza, Isle of Arran KA27 8JF

Est 1970
Tel: +44 (0)1770-830650
www.arran.uk.com
Parking available

We sell hand-painted stone characters and animals, hand-painted candles and wooden boxes. Visitors are welcome to look around our on-site workshop and watch our working craftsmen. We are sited in a crofter's cottage with beautiful scenic views over the Mull of Kintyre. Children welcome. Walking access only. Mail order available.

Directions: *Lochranza village is in north Arran.*

Opening hours: *Mon-Sun 10am-6pm.*

15

Jewellery

HEBRIDEAN JEWELLERY, Isle of South Uist, Iochdar, Western Isles HS8 5QX

Est. 1974
Tel: +44 (0)1870-610288
Fax: +44 (0)1870-610370
Parking available
Wheelchair access
Credit cards

Hebridean Jewellery began in a disused cowshed and now has a purpose-built workshop and shop, and shops in Fort William and Stornoway. **Silver and gold jewellery in Celtic style** including, small charms and bangles, earrings, cufflinks, rings, torques and pendant crosses. Also craft gifts, books and music. Mail order jewellery brochure available.

Directions: *half a mile south of the Benbecula/South Uist Causeway. Turn west off the A865 into Iochdar (Hebridean Jewellery Signboard). Right after one and a half miles.*

Opening hours: *Mon-Sat 9.30am-5.30pm.*

16

SALEN SILVER/AIRGIOD GU LEOR, Willow Cottage, Aros, Isle of Mull PA72 6JB

Est 1989
Tel: +44 (0)1680-300494
Fax: +44 (0)1680-300671
Parking available
Wheelchair access
Credit cards

The Assay hallmarking office credits Salen Silver with being one of the largest makers of **gold and silver Celtic crosses.** Crosses are plain, diamond cut or embossed with either a replica pattern of the Irish Kildalton cross or Celtic depictions of everyday life. Prices range from £10 to £295. Mail order available.

Directions: *follow the signs in Salon.*
Opening hours: *Mon-Sat 9:30am-5pm.*

WEST-RAY JEWELLERY, Mid-Ouseness, Westray, Orkney, Scotland KW17 2DW

Est 2000
Tel/fax: +44 (0)1857 677400
www.westrayjewellery.com
Parking available
Wheelchair access

West-ray Jewellery is based on the Orkney Island of Westray. The shop is run by George and Fiona Thomson who make **silver and gold jewellery.** The workshop is in a converted crofter's cottage. All items are hand finished with some being completely hand made. Mail order is available upon request.

Directions: *follow the craft trail signs.*
Opening hours: *Mon-Sat 9am-5pm; or by appointment.*

Metalwork & Silversmithing

CASTLE KEEP, Lisigarry Place, Portree, Isle of Skye IU51 9BD

Est 1991
Tel/fax: +44 (0)1478-612114
www.castlekeep.co.uk
Parking available

Rob Miller is a self-taught traditional bladesmith making **handforged blades for swords, and knives** including dirks and sgian dubhs. He works solely to commission making blades for collectors and re-enactment societies. He can make claymores or reproduce antique swords such as rapiers and Japanese martial arts swords. Mail order available.

Directions: *from Portree centre take Dunvegan Road out of town, pass Co-Op on left, Royal Mail sorting office on right. Next turn on to industrial estate.*
Opening hours: *Mon-Fri 10am-4.30pm.*

ORKNEYINGA SILVERSMITHS, Holland Cottage, Marwick, Birsay, Orkney Islands KW17 2NB

Est. 1989
Tel: +44 (0)1856 721359
Parking available
Credit cards

Kevin and Liz Allen make **jewellery and silverware.** Kevin was apprenticed to a master craftsman and Liz graduated in silversmithing and jewellery design. Tableware includes tumblers, quaichs (drinking cups), pill boxes, letter-openers and candle snuffers. Jewellery is affordable and decorated with Pictish and Celtic designs and symbols. Mail order available.

Directions: *on the B9056 Stromness to Birsay Road, between Skaill Bay and Marwick Head. Signposted on the Orkney Craft Trail route.*
Open: *10am-5pm (closed Tues and Sun). Other times by appointment.*

PETER ROWLAND HROSSEY SILVER, Crumbrecks, Orphir, Orkney KW17 2RE

Est. 1995
Tel/fax +44 (0)1856-811347
Parking available
Wheelchair access
Credit cards

Designer/silversmith specialising in the production of one-off commissions and ecclesiastical ware in silver and gold. Individual pieces, corporate and small batch production. **Tea services, chalices, candlesticks, flatware and holloware** etc etc. Each piece is hand-made from silver sheet using a variety of silversmithing techniques, e.g. raising, forging, chasing. My work can be seen at galleries and exhibitions throughout the UK. There is a small gallery adjoining my workshop where a limited amount of work is for sale; customers are always welcome to discuss commissions.

Directions: *A964 from Stromness, left at Scorradale road, then right into Petertown road at Hydro Station; then first track on left.*

Opening hours: *open most days but advisable to telephone first.*

Pottery & Ceramics

BAY POTTERY, Armadale Pier, Sleat, Isle of Skye IV45 8RS

Est. 2001
Tel/fax: +44 (0)1471-844442
Parking available
Wheelchair access
Credit cards

Maggie Zerafa's Bay Pottery produces hand made **stoneware tableware and gift pieces**. Her work is strongly influenced by the Japanese style and includes rice bowls and teapots, handleless teacups etc. She also produces different shaped vessels for arranging flowers, painting brush holders, salt shakers, large bowls. Glaze textures more important than decoration.
Directions: *50 metres from Armadale Pier on Skye.*
Opening hours: *weekdays 9am-5.30pm and Saturdays from Easter.*

BORGH POTTERY, Fivepenny House, Borgh, Isle of Lewis HS2 0RX

Est 1974
Tel/fax: +44 (0)1851-850345
www.borghpottery.com
Parking available
Credit cards

All our pottery: **domestic ware, vases, lampbases** etc is handthrown or handbuilt using traditional techniques. Particular attention is paid to the glazes, textures and surfaces to create patina and erosion reflecting the influence of the surrounding land and seascape. Considerable scope in size and design. Commissions welcomed. Mail order available.
Directions: *follow A857 to Ness. The Pottery is by the old bridge at Borgh.*
Opening hours: *Mon-Sat 9.30am-6pm.*

EDINBANE POTTERY, Edinbane, Isle of Skye IV51 9PW

Est 1971
Tel: +44 (0)1470-582234
www.edinbane-pottery.co.uk
Parking available
Wheelchair access
Credit cards

We are specialists in both **woodfired and saltglazed hand made pottery**. Our work is inspired by the landscape, colours and wildlife of Skye and the surrounding sea. All our pottery is extremely functional. Mail order is available to customers upon request. Please telephone for details or check our website.
Directions: *just off the A850, 14 miles from Portree, 8 miles from Dunvegan and 48 miles from the Skye Bridge.*
Opening hours: *Mon-Fri 9am-6pm. Open Mon-Sun Easter-Oct.*

ELLI PEARSON STUDIO POTTER, Church Road, St Margaret's Hope, Orkney, KW17 2SR

Est 1978
Tel: +44 (0)1856-831811
Parking available
Wheelchair access
Credit cards

We are a working pottery with a showroom and gallery. Visitors are always welcome and will see work in progress. We make **decorative and functional handmade pots** in both stoneware and porcelain. Mail order is available upon request. Potential customers are welcome to telephone us for details and prices.

Directions: *in the centre of St Margaret's Hope village.*

Opening hours: *Mon-Sat 10am-5.30pm.*

FURSBRECK POTTERY, Harray Potter, Fursbreck Pottery, Harray, Orkney KW17 2JR

Est. 1976
Tel/fax: +44 (0)1856-771419
www.@applepot.co.uk
Parking available
Wheelchair access

Andrew Appleby creates **pottery from Neolithic Bronze Age styles**: unglazed bowls, beakers, urns and pigmy vessels, through to modern, totally practical, coloured, glazed dinner services. Prices are from 95 pence. 'We demonstrate the art of pottery for visitors to our workshop.' Also: 'goblets of fire' made to commission. Mail order available.

Directions: *on the A986, close to the Harray Post Office.*

Opening hours: *daily 10am-6pm.*

ISLAND PORCELAIN LTD, Old School, Kilmory, Isle of Arran KA27 8PQ

Est 1988
Tel/fax: +44 (0)1770-870360
Parking available
Wheelchair access
Credit cards

We manufacture hand made **miniature porcelain figures, mainly birds, dolphins** and cats. Our work draws heavily on the bird and sea life of the Highlands and Islands. Our retail prices range from £5 to £20. In our seconds shop you can view the full range and other gifts. Mail order available.

Directions: *follow the South Road after leaving Brodick Pier. Kilmory is 16 miles from Brodick. Pottery clearly signposted.*

Opening hours: *Mon-Fri 9am-5pm.*

SCOTIA CERAMICS, Coll Pottery, Back, Isle of Lewis HS2 0JP

Est 1980
Tel: +44 (0)1851-820219
Fax: +44 (0)1851-820565
www.scottishpottery.com
Parking available
Wheelchair access
Credit cards

At the pottery we make one of the **widest range of ceramics** available anywhere in Scotland. Our work includes the Hebridean range of marbled gift and teaware, Island figurines, Scottish wildlife (including Hairy Highland cows), traditional and embossed thistleware, conical mugs, brooches, fridge magnets and Scottish giftware. Mail order available.

Directions: *6 miles from Stornoway Centre on the B895 Tolastadh (North Tolsta) road in the township of Coll.*

Opening hours: *Mon-Sat 9am-6pm.*

STARFISH CERAMICS, Unit 3, Baliscate, Tobermory, Isle of Mull, Argyll PA75 6NS

Est. 1998
Tel: +44 (0)1688-400374
www.chanonrypoint
/starfish ceramics
Parking available
Wheelchair access
Credit cards

Kate Carruthers suggests you 'pop into Starfish Ceramics for a fresh look at pottery' including **tableware, hand made tiles and one-off pieces**. All pottery is made in the studio by Kate. Batik and oil paintings are also on display and paint-a-pot workshops take place every Thursday. Mail order from the website.

Directions: *on the road out of Tobermory towards Salen, go half a mile up the hill after the roundabout. Studio clearly signposted on right.*

Opening hours: *Mon-Fri 10am-5pm. Workshops Thurs 10am-6pm.*

UIG POTTERY, The Pier, Uig, Isle of Skye IV51 9XY

Est 1993
Tel/fax: +44 (0)1470-542421
www.uigpottery.co.uk
Parking available
Credit cards

Uig Pottery is a small family business set up by Alan Freestone in the early 1990s. Most of Alan's work is hand thrown and decorated in a unique way using the surrounding land and seascape as inspiration. Alan uses a high fired porcellanous **stoneware suitable for food use** and dishwashers.

Directions: *next to the ferry terminal to the Outer Hebrides at the end of the A87.*

Opening hours: *Oct-Mar Mon-Sat 9am/6pm; Apr-Sept Mon-Sun 9am/6pm.*

Textiles

ARRAN FINE ART SILKS, Studio Wishing Well, Lagg, Isle of Arran KA27 8PQ

Est 1990
Tel: +44 (0)1770-870344
www.arran-art.co.uk
Parking available
Credit cards

We are an open studio practising silk painting in its many and varied forms. Our creations range from **silk jewellery to wallhangings**. We produce other textiles and sell silk accessories. Commissions are undertaken and mail order is available upon request. Please telephone or see our website for details.

Directions: *Lagg village is on the west side of Arran, 20 minutes drive south of Brodick.*

Opening hours: *Mon-Sat 10am-5pm.*

DUNHALLIN CRAFTS, 8 Dunhallin, Waternish, Isle of Skye N55 8GR

Est 1960
Tel: +44 (0)1470-592271
Parking available
Credit cards

Dunhallin Crafts make a wide **range of knitwear**, all made on the premises. They have many sorts of sweaters: fishribs, patterned, plain and children's named sweaters. They also make plain and patterned hats, wool and crochet work. A small selection of other crafts is also available. Mail order available.

Directions: *just off Waternish road (B866), 400 yards past the war memorial at Hallin and 100 yards to the right and up the hill.*

Opening hours: *Easter-Oct, Mon-Sun 10am-5pm. Other times by appointment.*

HOXA TAPESTRY GALLERY, Nevi Holm, Hoxa, St. Margaret's Hope, Orkney KW17 2TW

Est. 1996
Tel/fax: +44 (0)1856-831395
www.hoxatapestrygallery.co.uk
Parking available
Wheelchair access
Credit cards

Leila Thomson welcomes visitors to her gallery to see her **large, hand-woven tapestries** inspired by the rhythm of life and the local landscapes. You can watch her working at her loom. Small selection for sale and four-year waiting list for commissions. Cards and prints are also available to purchase. Mail order available.

Directions: *3 miles from St. Margaret's Hope Village; follow Craft Trail signs.*

Opening hours: *Summmer Mon-Fri 10am-5.30pm; Sat & Sun 2-6pm. Oct-Mar appointment necessary.*

OVER THE RAINBOW; ISLAND OF SKYE KNITWEAR, Quay Brae, Portree, Isle of Skye, Argyll IV51 9DB

Est. 1976
Tel: +44 (0)1478-612555
www.skye-knitwear.com
Parking available
Credit cards

Uniquely situated above the harbour, Over the Rainbow Studio Design make and sell **attractive, luxury, quality clothing**. Internationally recognised leading, rural Scottish producers. Colour predominates through contemporary ranges of Scottish textiles, knitwear and tartans. Also for sale is a wide range of jewellery, watches, prints, gifts and gadgets. Mail order available.

Directions: *top floor of first building on Quay Brae, the only road to and from harbour.*

Opening hours: *summer Mon-Sun 9am-9pm. Winter Mon-Sat 9am-6pm.*

P.Q.A., 27 Achmore, Lochs, Isle of Lewis H52 9DU

Est 1998
Tel: +44 (0)1851-860551
Main road parking

We produce crafts made from high quality locally made **Harris Tweed** using patterned and plain tweed, adding appliqué for pictorial or abstract designs, beadwork and embroidery. We make a wide variety of products such as rucksacks, handbags, toys, shoulder bags, cushion covers and various beaded, plain and applique drawstring bags.

Directions: *from Stornoway take the A859 to Cameron Terrace, take a left turn, we are the second house on your left after Cameron Terrace.*

Opening hours: *May-Sept Mon-Thurs 10am-5pm.*

SHILASDAIR,THE SKYE YARN COMPANY, Carnach, Waternish, Isle of Skye, Argyll IV55 8GL

Est. 1992
Tel: +44 (0)1470-592297
Fax: +44 (0)870-1351431
www.shilasdair-yarns.co.uk
Parking available
Wheelchair access
Credit cards

We specialise in natural dyed and coloured **knitting yarns, original handknits, knitkits,** unique resist-dyed garments, individual felted textiles and designer handspuns, all made from Scottish yarn using our own sheeps' wool. 'See the sheep, visit the dye house, browse in the shop.' From £6.75 (yarn)-£295 (garment). Mail order catalogue.

Directions: *follow sign for Shilasdair from Faery Bridge on A850 between Portree and Dunvegan. 7 miles from Faery Bridge on Waternish peninsula.*

Opening hours: *Easter-Oct Mon-Sun 10am/6pm. Other times by appointment.*

WERESHEEP, 2 Forestry Houses, Eynort, Carbost, Isle of Skye IV47 8SQ

Est 1998
Tel: +44 (0)1478-640422
www.weresheep.co.uk
Parking available
Credit cards

I design and construct **home and fashion accessories** using knitted and felted textiles in natural and man made fibres. My inspiration comes from micro-organisms, plants and animal forms. This shows in the fabric, construction and details of my work. Mail order is available upon request. Please telephone for details.

Directions: *in north west Skye 15 minutes from Sligachan Hotel; five minutes from Talisker Whisky Distillery.*

Opening hours: *Prior appointment necessary.*

Toys & Games

THE ROCKING HORSE WORKSHOP, Isle of Eigg, Small Isles, Inverness-shire PH42 4RL

Est. 2000
Tel: +44 (0)1687-7482402;
Fax: +44 (0)1687-7482486
www.isle of eigg.org
Parking available
Wheelchair access

We make to commission, quality **rocking horses in polished hardwood or traditional dapple** with a wide range of sizes and optional extras. All horses come complete with full leather saddle, tack, real horsehair, brass fittings and pillar safety stand. We also welcome old and much loved horses for restoration. Mail order available.

Directions: *we are located at the Island's pier.*

Opening hours: *are flexible by appointment only.*

SCALPAY BEARS, Rose Bank, Scalpay, Isle of Scalpay, Harris, Western Isles H54 3YG

Est 1989
Tel: +44 (0)1859-540222
Parking available

Rachel Macsween makes **bears, seals and scarves** from pure Harris Tweed. She also makes Castaway Bears. This range of bears takes its inspiration from the Island of Taransay, popularised by a recent BBC fly-on-the-wall documentary 'Castaway.' Mail order is available to customers upon request. Please telephone for details and prices.

Directions: *from Stornoway on Harris cross the bridge to Scalpay. I am in the Outend area of the island.*

Opening hours: *any time except Sundays.*

TOY MUSEUM GLENDALE, Holmisdale House, Glendale, Isle of Skye IV55 8WS

Est. 1987
Tel: +44 (0)1470-511240
www.toy-museum.co.uk
Parking available
Wheelchair access

Award winning visitor attraction/craft shop. Handmade crafts: **mini-books, wind-up dogs and mice, cube puzzle etc.** from £1.50. Also, world famous **Lewis Chess Sets** cast in resin/ground stone from £45. Also handknitted tams, hats, children's wear and dolls' house miniatures. Maker of Crokinole board game. Mail order available.

Directions: *7 miles from Dunvegan Castle on the Glendale Visitor Route in northwest Skye.*

Opening hours: *Mon-Sat 10am-6pm.*

WHYTE-WOODS CRAFTS, Uig, 22 Idrigill, Uig, Isle of Skye IV51 9XU

Est 1991
Tel: +44 (0)1470-542417
www.craftsonskye.org.uk
Parking available

Ron Whyte is a quality craftsman making **wooden gifts, games and toys**. Commissions are taken for anything in wood. Additionally, he can have tapestries blocked, stretched, mounted and framed. Similar work can be done for embroidery. All types of framing are undertaken. Boxes and frames can be commemoratively carved. Mail order available.

Directions: *location is signed from Uig Village.*

Opening hours: *Mon-Sat 9am-5pm. Closed Friday pm.*

Woodturning & Furniture

CARBOST STUDIO, Tigh Na Bruach, Carbostbeag, Carbost, Isle of Skye IV47 8SE

Est 2000
Tel: +44 (0)1478-640467
www.carbost.com
Parking available
Wheelchair access

Small craft workshop specialising in **turned wooden articles using native timber**, also unique embroidered needleart with an emphasis on nature and the Celtic culture. Also pens made using a decorative timber, and small furniture to commission. Visitors staying in the adjacent B&B can enjoy free demonstrations of woodturning. Mail order available.

Directions: *500 yards past Talisker Distillery on road to Portnalong.*

Opening hours: *Mon-Sat 10am-6pm.*

MULL FURNITURE, Shore House, Fionnphort, Isle of Mull, Argyll PA66 6BL

Est 1992
Tel: +44 (0)1681-700631
www.isleofmull-uk.co.uk
Parking available

Ian Slade specialises in the restoration and repair of antique furniture as well as upholstery. Ian also produces **wood turning** to gallery standard and gives individual tuition in woodturning with accommodation available in Shore House, on a Bed and Breakfast basis. Please refer to our website for further details.

Directions: *Shore House is on the Mull to Iona Ferry Slipway.*

Opening hours: *Mon-Sat 9am-5pm.*

Other Makers

BOREALIS PRODUCTS, Old Pier Road, Broadford, Isle of Skye IV49 9AE

Est. 1985
Tel: +44 (0)1471-822669
www.borealisskye.co.uk
Parking available
Credit cards

Jemina Copping makes this unique range of **body and hair care products** with high quality oils, waxes, herbal extracts and essential oils, for beautiful healthy skin and hair. She believes that 'making our products in the simplest way and in small batches preserves the natural goodness of the ingredients.' Mail order available.

Directions: *located by the Old Pier in Broadford, across the road from Skye Jewellery.*

Opening hours: *Mon-Sat 9.30am-5.30pm.*

ISLE OF SKYE CRAFTS/THISTLE STITCHES, Torr Park, Torvaig, Portree, Isle of Skye IV51 9H4

Est 1994
Tel/fax: +44 (0)1478-612361
www.isleofskyecrafts.com
Parking available
Credit cards

We offer a wide range of Scottish counted **cross-stitch kits** suitable for the beginner and the experienced stitcher. Our designs are all original and are produced in our own workshop where visitors can view each completed design. Please telephone or visit our website for catalogue and prices. Mail order available.

Directions: *Torvaig is two miles out of Portree along the A855 towards Staffin.*

Opening hours: *Mon-Fri 9.30am-5.30pm, Sat/Sun 10:30am-4:30pm.*

 45

SKYE IN FOCUS, The Skye Picture House, Ard Dorch, Broadford IV49 9AJ

Est. 1997
Tel: +44 (0)1471-822264
Fax: +44 (0)1471-820025
www.skyeinfocus.co.uk
Parking available

Steve Terry specialises in **hand-printed, original photographs** (colour and monochrome) featuring the landscape of Skye; everything from sunsets and blue skies to atmospheric shots of storm clouds over mountain peaks etc. Accepts commissions for particular location shots for overseas clients. Postcards and greetings cards are also available. Mail order.

Directions: *Steve's small gallery is 6 miles north of Broadford on the road to Portree.*

Opening hours: *Mon-Sun 10am-5pm. Appointment necessary in winter.* 46

SKYE ORIGINAL PRINTS, 1 Wentworth Street, Portree, Isle of Skye IV51 9EJ

Est. 1984
Tel: +44 (0)1478-612544
www.skyeprints.demon.co.uk
Parking available
Credit cards

Tom Mackenzie produces **colour etchings and mezzotints** of the Skye and Highland (Wester Ross) landscapes including the Cuillin Ridge and The Old Man of Storr. Etchings are multi-plated colour and 22 inches x 30 inches. Mezzotints are 6 inches x 4 inches. All are limited editions 40-70 copies. prices from £80-£250. Mail order available.

Directions: *on the main street of Portree.*

Opening hours: *Mon-Sat 9am-1pm & 2-5pm.* 47

WOODCARVER - MANDY SILVER, Bayhead, Lower Breakish, Isle of Skye IV42 8QA

Est. 1998
Tel +44 (0)1471-822521
Parking available

Working from her studio on the Isle of Skye, using traditional methods Mandy Silver carves **Celtic relief wallhangings and crosses** influenced by traditional designs together with **decorative spoons** which are original designs influenced by the Celtic culture. Mandy uses a variety of woods grown in the Scottish Highlands. Prices start from £20. Apart from commissions, much of her work relates to the landscape and natural history. Carvings are exhibited in galleries throughout the country and can be found in private collections in the USA, Canada and Japan. Mandy also demonstrates carving at various events in Scotland. Mail order available. E-mail mandysilveruk@yahoo.com.

Directions: *the studio is 20 minutes from Skye Bridge: further directions will be given when appointment is made.*

Opening Hours: *by appointment.* 48

Late Entries

The following entries were received too late for inclusion in the regional sections of *Hand Made in Britain*.

STARFALL POTTERY, Sheldon, Chippenham, Wiltshire SN14 ORH

Est. 1973
Tel: +44 (0)1249-713293
Parking available
Wheelchair access

Gordon Whittle has his studio and pottery in this attractive old farmhouse, where you can see to purchase a wide range of **domestic pottery and individual pieces.** Also commemorative pottery for weddings, christenings, anniversaries, etc. An interesting range of hand made greetings cards also available and herb plants in season.
Directions: *'Cross Keys' to Biddestone, turn right at 30mph sign, Chippenham Lane, Pottery half a mile on left.*
Opening hours: *Mon-Sun 9am-6pm.*

CAROLINE WHYMAN, 2 Iliffe Yard, Crampton Street, London SE17 3QA

Est.
Tel/fax: +44 (0)207-708 5904
Parking available
Wheelchairs: one small step

Caroline makes **bright blue and turquoise hand thrown porcelain** decorated with inlaid geometric patterns (square, circle, triangle) and embellished with gold or platinum lustres. She works with strong simple forms and geometric patterns. Other patterns are created using a fascinating grid system laid over the surface of the porcelain.
Directions: *six minutes walk from Kennington tube. Turn right out of tube station, take first right, then second left on Amelia Street and through black iron gates.*
Opening hours: *by appointment only.*

SUE HOAR CERAMICS, Studio 21, Iliffe Yard, Crampton Street, London SE17 3QA

Est. 1995
Tel: +44 (0)207-5826552
Fax: +44 (0)207-5825667
Parking available
Wheelchair access

I specialise in the technique of slab-rolling to make **sculptural *trompe-l'oeil* pieces** such as ceramic 'bags' whch are really vases. They come in all shapes and sizes and each one is unique as real ferns and leaves are impressed into the clay and coloured with oxides. Commissions accepted. Also garden urns and lights.
Directions: *five minutes walk from the Elephant and Castle tube station.*
Opening hours: *ring for appointment. Iliffe Yard Studios has an annual open weekend, the first weekend of December.*

SUE SHAW, 1 Stokehills, Farnham, Surrey GU9 7TE

Est. 1994
Tel/fax: +44 (0)1252-726684
www.axisartists.org.uk/all
/ref6456.htm
Parking available
Credit cards

Sculptural and Chalsis glass jewellery and glass bowls. Sue captures the magic of glass in **colourful earrings and pendants.** Some glass jewellery stunningly electroformed with copper and silver enriched by oxidising and gilding with gold leaf. Also fused and slumped glass bowls, some electroformed with metals. Mail order available.
Directions: *A325 to B3007 signed 'town centre' to traffic lights. Right into St. James, left into Stokehills.*
Opening hours: *by appointment only 10am-5pm.*

TONY BUNCE, Techlink, 17 Hazell Way, Stoke Poges, Slough, Berkshire SL2 4BW

Est. 1975
Tel: +44 (0)1753-643509
Parking available

Tony has been turning wood for over half a century but has only been doing it professionally since 1975. He specialises in fluted and hollow form work with a practical use such as **bowls and platters.** He also produces vases of all shapes including urns. Mail order available.
Directions: *from A40 at Gerrards Cross, take B416 to Stoke Poges. Turn right at Six Bells public house. Hazell Way at bottom of that road (200 yards).*
Opening hours: *10am-6pm. Please make an appointment.*

MIKE DAVIES WELSH LOVESPOONS, Model House Craft and Design Centre, Bullring, Llantrisant, Rhondda Cynon Taff CF72 8EB

Est. 1970
Tel: +44 (0)1443 228226
Fax: +44 (0)1269-597626
www.mikedavieswelshlovespoons.com
Parking available
Wheelchair access
Credit cards

I hand carve authentic, very high quality **Welsh lovespoons**, each piece being both unique and hand made. I use British hardwoods: walnut, cherry, lime, yew, sycamore etc. and then polish to a fine finish with beeswax. A huge array of designs are available from the elaborate and historical to the symbolic and Celtic art. Mail order available.

Directions: *from the M4, west of junction 34, follow signs to Llantrisant. The Model House Centre is off Heol y Sarn Street, off High Street.*

Opening hours: *Mon-Sat 10am-4.30pm. Appointment necessary.*

CAROLINE BENNETT, Wills Cottage, 64 Britons Lane, Linley Brook, Bridgnorth, Shropshire WV16 4TH

Est. 1998
Tel: +44 (0)1746-765078
Fax: +44 (0)1746-764909
Parking available

A **sculptor and ceramicist** working in a variety of media including clay, bronze, concrete, plaster and resin to create free-standing and wall-mounted figurative and abstract sculptural pieces for indoors and gardens. Ceramic ware includes functional and abstract forms using hand building, slip casting or throwing techniques. From £8-£1,100.

Directions: *four miles north of Bridgnorth on B4373. Turn left for 'The Smithies.' 150 yards on left is a driveway with a white stone signed 'Wills Cottage.'*

Opening hours: *prior appointment necessary.*

TERESA GREEN TEXTILE DESIGN, 2nd Floor, Alfred House, Ashley Street, Nottingham, Nottinghamshire NG3

Est. 2000
Tel: +44 (0)1509-558124
Fax: +44 (0)1509-558122
Parking available

Teresa Cole has recently established a printed textile workshop. She produces **unique, functional textiles with a composition print detail**. She works mainly with natural fibres and subdued colours. Items include bags, napkins and table linen, bed linen, deckchairs and blinds. Limited stock for sale as works to commission. Mail order available.

Directions: *from railway station head towards the ice rink; follow Carlton Road and then take third right (Ashley Street).*

Opening hours: *Mon-Fri 10am-4pm. Appointment necessary.*

DENNIS WOOLLEY, Tubhole Barn, Dent, Sedbergh, Cumbria LA10 5RE

Est. 1956
Tel: +44 (0)1539-625361
Parking available
Wheelchair access
Credit cards

I have been building instruments of the **harpsichord family, including spinets and virginals**, and latterly fortepianos in many different styles. Such instruments are now to be found throughout the world, in many colleges and university music departments. It is important to telephone first to make an appointment or discuss commissions.

Directions: *through Dent village, taking a right hand fork past the Post Office and then 2 miles along on this road.*

Opening hours: *9am-5.30pm but prior appointment necessary.*

SCOTTISH WALKING STICKS, 7 Torinturk, Tarbert, Argyll PA29 6YE

Est. 1993
Tel: +44 (0)1880-820714
Fax: +44 (0)1880-821163
Parking available
Wheelchair access
Credit cards

Horn-handled walking sticks and shepherd's crooks. This traditional country craft requires skill and patience to create a well-balanced article of great quality and excellence. The black buffalo horn handles are fashioned to traditional patterns. There are mounted on either striped Mexican bocote or black ebony shafts with a silver collar. Mail order available.

Directions: *located in the small hamlet of Torinturk, 5 miles from Tarbert on the B8024 road to Kilberry.*

Opening hours: *Mon-Sun 9am-7pm.*

THE SCALPAY WOODTURNER, Gillian Broughton, Keepers Cottage, Scalpay Island, Broadford, Isle of Skye IV49 9BS

Est. 1983
Tel: +44 (0)1471-822526
/0788 4280816
Website: www.scalpay.plus.com
Parking available
Credit cards

Gillian has been turning wood for fifteen years on the small island of Scalpay off the Isle of Skye. She uses Scalpay's own timber, turning **bowls both ornamental and functional**. Sizes range from four inches diameter to an impressive nineteen and a half diameter, up to six inches deep. £5-£100. Mail order available.

Directions: *will be given when appointment is made.*

Opening hours: *most sales via website, but visitors to workshop welcome by appointment only.*

Glossary

Amphora: pottery - a vessel with two handles and a narrow neck used by the Romans and Greeks for transporting liquids such as oil and wine

Appliqué: textile decoration - ornamenting fabric, knitwear etc by cutting out designs in fabric and attaching them, usually by sewing to the surface of another fabric to form pictures or patterns

Art Deco: style - design and interior decoration of 1920s and 30s. Derives from Art Nouveau but shapes were stylised and geometric rather than naturalistic

Art Nouveau: style - European art style of the late 19th century, characterised by flowing naturalistic forms epitomised by posters by Mucha (German) and Klimt (German/Austrian).

Arts and Crafts Movement: design/style - a reform movement to revive handicrafts and improve standards of decorative design in the wake of the 1851 Great Exhibition of London and as an antidote to falling standards due to mass-production. Spread to the USA in the 1870s. Takes its name from The Arts and Crafts Exhibition Society (founded 1882) and the Chicago Arts and Crafts Society (founded 1897).

Assemblage: composition - art work formed by grouping together found or unrelated objects

Avante-garde: adjective to describe ultra-modern art or literature or as a noun for leaders of such a movement

Batik: textile decoration - a way of applying design to textiles by applying wax to the parts left uncoloured. Originally from Java, Indonesia etc.

Bevel: cabinet-making - making a square edge into a sloping edge

Biscuit firing: pottery - dried pots are biscuit fired to 1000 degrees centigrade to pre-shrink and harden the clay, enabling them to be handled for the next stage - dipping in glaze

Bonbonière - dish for sweets

Bustier: strapless, close-fitting bodice, usually boned

Carrstone: a type of building stone from Norfolk

Chamfered: cabinet-making: bevel symetrically a right-angled edge or a corner

Champlevé: enamelling - enamels are poured into grooves engraved on surface of silver, bronze, copper etc. to be decorated and polished down to the same level as surrounding metal.

Charles Rennie Mackintosh (1868-1928): design - architect/designer and founder of the Glasgow style of Art Nouveau mainly for furniture and interior design but which avoided the exaggerated floral embellishment of Art Nouveau.

Cloisonné: enamelling - enamel is poured into cloisons (compartments) formed by a network of metal bands on the surface. The tops of the bands remain exposed dividing one area of colour from another

Collage: composition - technique of creating a pictorial composition in two-dimensions or very low relief by glueing all manner of objects/materials to a canvas or panel

Crackle or Craquelure: pottery - glaze involving deliberate 'crazing' for decorative effect. First used in China (Song Dynasty) in Kuan wares. Initiated in the West from the 19th century, especially by studio potters

Crockinole - traditional Canadian board game.

Cuaran - sandal-type shoe worn by poor people (Scottish)

Découpage: decoration - decoration of a surface by covering it completely with cutout paper figures or designs; can be used as a two-dimensional effect and framed as a picture; also an object so decorated.

Diamanté - decorated with powdered crystal or other sparkly substance for decorating costume jewellery, garments, shoes etc.

Engobes: pottery: French term for coating of slip applied all over a piece of pottery to cover its natural colour. Also provides ground through which grafitto decoration may be incised or on to which glazes or painted decoration may be applied.

Etching: prints - process of decorating metal with patterns bitten into the surface by acid originally used for armour; now used for print-making.

Feldspathic glazes: pottery - pottery glaze made from mineral feldspar which fuses at a high temperature (1,550 C) used on hard paste porcelain. Originated from China. Spread to The West in the 18th century

Gesso - gypsum or plaster of Paris used for painting and sculpture

Gill, Eric (1882-1940): stone-carver, typographer, engraver who was born in Brighton, Sussex and lived and worked in Wales in the 1920s

Grafitto: pottery - incising through the slip to reveal darker body before glazing. See also Sgraffiato.

Gouache: painting technique using opaque pigments ground in water and thickened

Gutta technique - way of painting on silk using a barrier to create defined designs (as opposed to swirling patterns)

Hardwood - the wood of most deciduous trees birch, oak etc. Denser and harder than the wood of evergreens e.g. pine.

Ladderback chair - type of upright chair with a slatted back resembling a ladder

Leach, Bernard 1887-1979 - probably the most famous British ceramicist of the twentieth century. Moved to St. Ives, Cornwall in the 1920s. Became part of the loosely structured artists and painters of the St. Ives Group.

Majolica: ceramic - earthenware with coloured decoration on an opaque white glass

Mead - drink made from fermented honey and water

Mezzotint: way of printing/engraving in which the surface of a plate is scraped to roughen it thereby producing tones and half-tones

Mochaware: pottery - tree and fern-like pattern on pottery made by blending herbs and metal oxides. Origins not known, but probably dates from 1700s

Morris, William (1834-96): writer, painter, designer, craftsman and social reformer founded a manufacturing and decorating firm in 1861 based on the idea of a mediaeval guild. Founder of the British Arts and Crafts Movement (see *Arts and Crafts Movement* above).

Windsor chair: furniture - traditional style of wooden dining chair with splayed legs and a semi-circular back supported by upright rods

Papier-mâché: a moulding material made from paper torn into strips or pulped and soaked in starch or flour paste or dextrin. Used to make decorative and functional objects, usually painted and varnished. Means chewed paper in French

Penannular - ring-like

Planter: ceramic - large container for decorative plants

Plique-a-jour: enamelling - transparent effect that resembles miniature stained glass

Pyrography: design - designs burnt on wood; poker work

Raku: pottery: a type of Japanese pottery originally made exclusively as tea ceremony ware in and around Kyoto. Raku is moulded (i.e. not thrown) earthenware, low-fired and with thick lead glaze usually black/dark coloured.

Reivers - historic border raiders of Northumberland

Salt-glaze: pottery: glaze with a rough, pitted surface applied to stoneware by throwing salt on the fire of the kiln.

Sgian - Scottish dagger also called sgian dhu/sgian dubh

Sgraffito: pottery: a 19th century English pseudo-Italian term for grafitto. A type of graffito decoration was used in the 1870s for Royal Doulton's so-called sgraffito ware.

Sinemay: banana leaf weave, traditionally used for hat-making

Skivers - leather - pared leather hides

Slab method: pottery - technique of building pottery by hand. A mass of wet clay is flattened to a slab with a rolling pin. The slab may be of various thicknesses and bent to any shape, joined to other slabs etc.

Slip: pottery - clay in a creamy mixture with water first used to render coarse clay more porous, and later for decoration; hence slipware

Slumped glass: glass put over a mould and fired in a kiln so that the glass 'slumps' to make a three-dimensional effect. Used for restoring antique window panes

Stoneware: pottery: very hard, dense, resonant grey/reddish non-porous non-translucent pottery.

Targe: armour - Scottish Highlander's traditional round shield, usually covered with leather and studded.

Terrarium - transparent glass globe containing growing plants

Tessera (pl. tesserae) - small, square block used in mosaics

Torque: jewellery - necklace of twisted metal especially as worn by ancient Britons

Trompe-l'oeil - a still-life painting, mural or object designed to give an illusion of reality (lit. translation 'deceives the eye')

Withy (pl.withies): basketry - shoot of willow or osier.

Wren, Christopher 1632-1723 - architect most famous today for the redesign and building of St. Paul's Cathedral, London. Also a professor of astronomy and Founding Fellow of the Royal Society. As principal architect amongst the commissioners appointed to rebuild London after the Fire of London (1666) Wren was responsible for the building of 51 churches.

Zeitgeist - literally, the spirit of the times i.e. a trend of thought/feeling in a particular period.

Index

Throughout *Hand Made in Britain* readers will find an abundance of exceptionally talented specialists producing the finest pottery, ceramics, metalwork, jewellery, glass, furniture, textiles, toys and other artefacts. They are all categorised in the regional sections of this book and are *not* included in this list.

The following index is to help readers locate unusual makers who are comparatively few in number and so may be difficult to find.

Vacation Work publish:

	Paperback	Hardback
Summer Jobs Abroad	£9.99	£15.95
Summer Jobs in Britain	£9.99	£15.95
Supplement to Summer Jobs in Britain and Abroad *published in May*	£6.00	–
Work Your Way Around the World	£12.95	–
Taking a Gap Year	£11.95	–
Taking a Career Break	£11.95	–
Working in Tourism – The UK, Europe & Beyond	£11.95	–
Kibbutz Volunteer	£10.99	–
Working on Cruise Ships	£10.99	–
Teaching English Abroad	£12.95	–
The Au Pair & Nanny's Guide to Working Abroad	£11.95	–
The Good Cook's Guide to Working Worldwide	£11.95	–
Working in Ski Resorts – Europe & North America	£10.99	–
Working with Animals – The UK, Europe & Worldwide	£11.95	–
Live & Work Abroad - a Guide for Modern Nomads	£11.95	–
Working with the Environment	£11.95	–
The Directory of Jobs & Careers Abroad	£12.95	–
The International Directory of Voluntary Work	£11.95	–
Live & Work in Australia & New Zealand	£10.99	–
Live & Work in Belgium, The Netherlands & Luxembourg	£10.99	–
Live & Work in France	£10.99	–
Live & Work in Germany	£10.99	–
Live & Work in Italy	£10.99	–
Live & Work in Japan	£10.99	–
Live & Work in Russia & Eastern Europe	£10.99	–
Live & Work in Saudi & the Gulf	£10.99	–
Live & Work in Scandinavia	£10.99	–
Live & Work in Scotland	£10.99	–
Live & Work in Spain & Portugal	£10.99	–
Live & Work in the USA & Canada	£10.99	–
Drive USA	£10.99	–
Hand Made in Britain - The Visitors Guide	£10.99	–
Scottish Islands Book 1 - The Western Isles	£10.99	–
Scottish Islands Book 2 - Orkney & Shetland	£10.99	–
The Panamericana: On the Road through Mexico and Central America	£12.95	–
Travellers Survival Kit: Australia & New Zealand	£11.95	–
Travellers Survival Kit: Cuba	£11.95	–
Travellers Survival Kit: India	£10.99	–
Travellers Survival Kit: Lebanon	£10.99	–
Travellers Survival Kit: Madagascar, Mayotte & Comoros	£10.99	–
Travellers Survival Kit: Mauritius, Seychelles & Réunion	£10.99	–
Travellers Survival Kit: Mozambique	£10.99	–
Travellers Survival Kit: Oman & the Arabian Gulf	£11.95	–
Travellers Survival Kit: South Africa	£10.99	–
Travellers Survival Kit: South America	£15.95	–
Travellers Survival Kit: Sri Lanka	£11.95	–
Travellers Survival Kit: USA & Canada	£10.99	–

Distributors of:

Summer Jobs USA	£12.95	–
Internships (On-the-Job Training Opportunities in the USA)	£18.95	–
How to Become a US Citizen	£11.95	–
World Volunteers	£10.99	–
Green Volunteers	£10.99	–

Plus 27 titles from Peterson's, the leading American academic publisher, on college education and careers in the USA. Separate catalogue available on request.

Vacation Work Publications, 9 Park End Street, Oxford OX1 1HJ Tel 01865–241978 Fax 01865–790885

Visit us online for more information on our unrivalled range of titles for work, travel and gap years, readers' feedback and regular updates:
www.vacationwork.co.uk